TEN GIRLS WHO MADE A DIFFERENCE

Irene Howat

CF4·K

TEN GIRLS WHO MADE A DIFFERENCE

LIGHT KEEPERS

Irene Howat

CF4•K

For Hilda

Reprinted 2003, 2004, 2005 twice, 2007,
2009, 2010, 2012, 2014, 2016, twice in 2017, 2019,
2020, 2022
Paperback ISBN: 978-1-85792-776-4
E-pub ISBN: 978-1-84550-852-4
Mobi ISBN: 978-1-84550-853-1

Published by Christian Focus Publications,
Geanies House, Fearn, Tain, Ross-shire,
IV20 1TW, Scotland, U.K.
www.christianfocus.com
email:info@christianfocus.com
Cover design by Alister MacInnes
Cover illustration by Elena Temporin
Milan Illustrations Agency
Printed and bound in China

All incidents retold in these stories are based on true situations. Where specific information about childhood incidents has been unobtainable the author has written these paragraphs using other information concerning family life, hobbies, home life, relationships freely available in other biographies.

Cover illustration depicts Maria Dyer (who became Maria Taylor, wife of Hudson Taylor but a missionary in her own right). She is leaving China to go to England with her sister. Both girls were being sent back to England to complete their education. However Maria returned to China some years later to start her own mission work and subsequently met Hudson Taylor and they fell in love.

Contents

Monica of Thagaste

Monica wiped her parched lips. 'I'm so thirsty,' she said. 'May I have some water?'

'You'll have water at dinner time,' the maid told her. 'Move into the shade and you'll not feel so dry.'

The girl licked her lips. There was no point in arguing. As she couldn't be bothered getting to her feet in the heat, she crawled the short distance to the shade of a wall.

'You'll get your clothes in a mess if you do that,' the maid told her. But before the woman could do anything else, Monica distracted her in the way she knew always worked. 'Tell me a story of when you were young,' she begged.

'I'll tell you something about the history of this town. A girl should know about the place she comes from.'

'What are you going to tell me?' Monica asked.

'Thagaste, as you know, has about 2,000 people living in it,' the maid began. 'When I was young, it wasn't nearly as big. But the Romans were still in charge. I loved watching the Roman soldiers marching. And I never heard one of them complain about needing a drink, no matter how hot it was in the sun,' she said, looking at the girl pointedly. 'There were all kinds of things to see and do. But one thing I didn't like was the slave market. I once saw a couple with three children for sale. The parents were sold to one man, and the children sold separately to three others. I've never forgotten that mother's cries as she was dragged away, or the look on her husband's face.'

'Where did the children go?' Monica asked.

'They were bought by traders on their way to the Mediterranean coast. They were probably sent to Italy.'

'Is that far away?' she asked.

'It's about two days' journey to the sea from here, then I don't know how far across the water,' said the maid. 'But you can be sure they would never see their parents again.'

'Slavery's cruel,' Monica said. The maid didn't comment as she wasn't a free woman. 'Go on,' the girl urged, wanting to hear more.

'Well,' said the maid, 'when I was twelve, I went to work for your grandmother. I'd heard strange stories about Christians, but she was the first one I really knew. You don't remember her, but she was one of the best people who ever lived. She loved the Lord Jesus with all her heart. At first I thought that was odd because Jesus had died about 250 years before that. I couldn't understand how anyone could worship a man who had died when we had all the Roman gods to worship. But your grandmother told me that Jesus died on the cross to take away my sins. It was through her I became a Christian. It was also because of what he learned from his mother that your father became a believer too.'

'It's time for dinner,' a voice called from the house.

'Thank goodness for that,' Monica said, 'I'm so thirsty I could drink the whole Mediterranean Sea!'

'I think you'd be even thirstier if you tried that!' laughed the maid.

The girl looked puzzled. 'Why?' she demanded.

'Because the seas are full of salty water,' her companion explained.

Monica looked at the old woman. 'Rubbish!' she said, and ran into the house for her dinner and a long drink. After her first glass of water she asked for another. 'You're thirsty today,' her father said. Monica started to giggle. 'Tell us all the joke,' he said. The girl repeated what her maid had said about salt water in the sea, though she could hardly do so for laughing.

'What did you say when she told you that?' her dad asked.

'I told her it was rubbish!' giggled the girl.

'Well, you were wrong and she was right. And as soon as you've eaten, you'll go and apologise.'

'But Father, she's just a maid!'

'Don't you ever say that again,' he demanded. 'She may be a maid but she's also a child of God.'

'Why don't you let me drink water between meals?' Monica asked the maid the following afternoon.

'If you drank on and off all day, you'd get into the habit of it. That's all very well now when all you drink is water and milk, but think what a state you'd get into when you're grown up and able to drink wine.'

'I promise I won't,' Monica pled.

The maid shook her head. 'I'm not taking any chances.'

'Could you bring some wine up from the cellar?' Monica's father asked, some months later. Monica ran to do what he asked.

Taking some wine from a cask, she poured it into a flagon.

'What does it taste like?' she wondered.

When the flagon was full she lifted it to her lips, sniffed, and took a tiny mouthful. 'It tastes funny,' she told the young maid who was with her, before coughing and spluttering as she swallowed. The maid wasn't at all pleased.

Monica couldn't wait for the next day when she could take another little drop. However, as the days passed, the little drops became bigger. It wasn't long before Monica was drinking quite a lot of her father's wine.

'Please don't drink any more,' the young maid said one day as they went into the cellar together.

'What's it got to do with you?' Monica demanded.

'It's not good for you,' the other girl explained. 'And, apart from that, when your father discovers his wine is going missing, he'll think I've been stealing it and drinking it myself.'

'It would serve you right!' spat Monica. 'Who do you think you are speaking to me like that? I could have you sold!'

The maid felt as though she'd been punched. But she couldn't stop herself replying. 'You're just an alcoholic,' she said. 'Every time you come down, you take a drink. You can't help yourself. You're just an alcoholic!'

Monica's anger rose. But instead of hitting the maid, what the maid had said hit out at her. A lesson was learned in the cellar that day.

'I've found a husband for you,' Monica's father told her some years later. 'Patricius is a decent man and he'll make a good husband.'

'But he's not a Christian,' the girl said, for by then she was a believer.

'Well it's up to you to be such a godly wife that he'll want to become one,' she was told.

That's exactly what Monica tried to do, though her mother-in-law didn't make things easy. Patricius was not the best of husbands, but Monica lived at peace with him and was a fine mother to their children.

'When I was a girl,' she told her son Augustine, 'we had a maid from whom I learned such a lot.'

'What did she teach you?' the boy asked, hoping she'd tell him once again the story of the salty seawater. That was one of his favourites.

'She told me the stories of Jesus,' Monica said, 'about him feeding great crowds of people, about him walking on the water and healing people who were sick and blind and deaf and those who had leprosy too.'

'Nonsense!' scoffed Patricius, who was just passing by. 'Your god can't heal lepers any more than the Roman gods can.' He laughed. 'Don't believe all your mother tells you,' he said, slapping the boy on the back. 'Half of what she says is fairy stories.'

Without saying anything to disagree, Monica rose and went into the house. When Augustine followed her, he found his mother on her knees praying for her husband and children.

'The boy's badly ill,' Patricius said, as he left their home with two chickens dangling from his hand.

'Where are you going?' Monica asked.

'I'm going to sacrifice these to the gods and ask them to make him better. Instead of just praying you should sacrifice something to your god too,' he snapped as he left.

Augustine moaned with the pain in his stomach. 'Will you make a sacrifice, Mum?' he asked.

'I don't need to, son,' she said. 'Jesus made all the sacrifice that will ever be needed when he died on the cross.' She knelt beside him, praying that he'd get better.

Augustine believed he was dying and thought about becoming a Christian. But he made an amazing recovery and decided not to bother. 'There will be plenty of time when I grow up,' he thought.

'Where is she?' yelled Patricius, as he came near his home.

'Mum's praying,' replied Augustine, who was now a boy in his teens.

'Poor woman!' the man laughed. 'For years she's been praying for you to become a Christian, but you've become just like your dad; you know a pretty girl when you meet one. No wonder your mother's at her prayers.'

Monica heard what was said. 'Lord Jesus,' she prayed. 'Please may the boy become a Christian. Do whatever you need to do to make him realise that he needs his sins forgiven.'

'Will you not trust in Jesus?' she asked Augustine, when she rose from her knees.

'One day,' he said, 'but not yet.'

It wasn't easy for Monica to watch the life her son led. He didn't pay much attention to anything she'd taught him. But this made her pray all the more for his conversion, especially after he went off to study in Carthage and then when he left Africa in

A.D 383 on his way to Italy. Not long after, Monica followed him there.

'How long will it be till he comes to faith?' she asked God, over and over and over again. 'Please make it soon. Please don't let him get into an even bigger mess than he's in just now.'

On the outside it seemed that Augustine was doing well because he was a very clever man, but he still led an immoral life that hurt his mum terribly. Every time they talked about Christianity, he said the same thing, 'One day, but not yet.'

When Augustine was thirty-two years old, he knew in himself he couldn't go on the way he was.

'When I was going along the street today,' he once told Monica, 'I saw a beggar laughing and I thought to myself he has nothing and I have everything, but he's happier than I am.'

Monica's heart filled with hope. Was Augustine finally thinking seriously about life? How delighted she was when he started going to church occasionally.

'Where are you two off to?' Monica asked Augustine and his friend one day.

'Just out to the garden,' they said. She noticed they had a book with them. It was some time before the men came in, and when they did, she saw her son's face. He was smiling as he'd not smiled for years. His eyes shone and he threw his arms around her.

'I was in the garden and I heard a child's voice saying, "Take it up and read it." At first I thought it was a nursery rhyme but then I realised it was God telling me to read the Bible. I opened this and read where it opened.' He held up the Bible book of Romans. 'It spoke right to me, telling me that I had to look to Jesus and leave my immoral life behind. And suddenly I knew it was true, that what you'd told me all these years was true!' Monica's heart was singing. 'I'm a Christian, Mum. Your prayers are answered.'

Augustine and Monica planned to leave Italy and go back to North Africa, but she died before they could leave. It didn't matter that she never knew her son became the most famous Christian of his day, one of the most famous Christians of all time. All that mattered to Monica was that her prayers had been answered - Augustine was a child of God, and she would see him again in the Kingdom of Heaven.

FACT FILE

The Romans: In the ancient world 'Roman' was the name given to the dominant people of the country we now call Italy. Many centuries before Christ's birth, these people settled in a village called Rome beside the River Tiber. They gradually came to rule the whole of Italy, and eventually the empire became one of the greatest the world has ever seen.

Keynote: Monica's life was very different to yours or mine. Not many people today have a maid, but Monica's family had several. Monica, however, had to learn respect for the people who worked for her family. Monica's father reminded her that her maid was also a child of God. Being a child of God means that you are part of the royal family of heaven - sons and daughters of the one true God. To be a child of God you must love and follow the Lord Jesus Christ.

Think: Monica had been warned that alcohol could have a bad effect on her life if she took too much of it. But she didn't listen to the warning and experimented anyway. It is easy to fall into bad and life-threatening habits such as drinking alcohol and taking drugs. Pray to God that he will protect you and that he will give you the strength to say no to sin.

Prayer: Lord Jesus, thank you for dying on the cross to save your people from their sins. Help me to lead a life that pleases you. Protect me from the danger of sin. If people try to persuade me to take drugs, drink or behave in a way that is against your law, help me to say no. Give me the strength to honour you with my life. Amen.

Katherine Luther

'Catch it if you can!' Katherine threw the wooden ball in the air. She was standing in a circle of girls, all with their eyes shut and their hands beating the air like windmills as they tried to catch the ball that might be coming in their direction. 'Missed!' Katherine yelled, delighted. If they all missed just twice more, she had won the game. And she really wanted to win because she really wanted the prize. The girls formed a circle again and waited. Katherine stood in the middle, twirled round and round then threw the ball. 'Catch it if you can!' Again twelve arms circled in the air, and once again no one caught it. 'Last time!' the delighted child said. 'And if nobody catches it, you've each got to go to Sister Mary's garden and bring me back a strawberry!'

Eyes were closed tight and hands held out all round the circle. The ten-year-old spun round and round then round again. 'Catch it if you can!' A dozen arms spun this way and that. 'Gotcha!' called out one. But the ball fell from her grasp and landed with a thud on the grass. Katherine von Bora clapped her hands with excitement. 'Now you've each got to get me a strawberry! But watch out that Sister Mary doesn't catch you.'

Katherine looked for a place where she could eat her strawberries in peace. There was no point in going to the schoolroom because the nun who taught them would still be tidying up. And the nun who milked the convent cow would be in the dairy. 'I know!' Katherine decided. 'I'll go to the orchard and climb an apple tree. The nuns won't see me there, and I can whisper down to the girls when they walk by.'

She chose a tree near the path that ran between the garden and the first convent building. Then she hitched her long dress up, tucking the hem into her belt, and climbed up into the shade of the leaves. 'Here they come!' she said to herself, as her guilty-looking friends appeared from behind the garden gate. 'Psst!' she whispered, when they passed underneath her. 'I'm up here.'

'Come down, you clown!' one girl said. 'No, you come up with my strawberries.' The girls checked that the coast was clear then one by one climbed up the tree beside Katherine. She was so pleased with herself that she shared the strawberries out between them.

'Where are those girls?' It was Sister Mary, and she was walking through the orchard!

'Shh,' Katherine warned. 'Don't even breathe!' The nun passed underneath the very tree they were in as she went to the garden in search of them. On the way back she looked from side to side between the trees. Then she stopped right under the apple tree. 'What's this?' she asked, picking up something from the grass. 'Since when did strawberry hulls fall from apple trees?' Without even looking up she said in a half cross, half-amused voice, 'Would the young ladies who are sitting on the branches above my head please descend to ground level?'

Katherine and her friends started to scramble down the tree, remembering just in time to untuck their dresses from their belts. Sister Mary would not have been pleased to see their underwear!

'Young ladies,' the nun said, 'each one of you comes from a good home, and your parents have placed you here to be cared for. It's not the acceptable thing for young convent school ladies to act like squirrels that steal fruit and scramble up trees. What would your mothers say? You'll do extra Latin homework this afternoon. And, to pay for the strawberries, you can help me in the garden for an hour tomorrow afternoon.'

The nun strode off leaving seven cross children behind her. But Katherine could never stay cross for long. 'Catch me if you can!' she called, as she ran in the opposite direction.

That afternoon, Sister Mary took Katherine aside. 'I'm disappointed in you,' she told her. 'How long were you in your last convent?'

'I think I went when I was five or younger,' the child answered.

'And seven years later you've not learned to behave!' the nun accused. 'Well, you'll soon learn. Marienthron is the best convent in Germany. And the sooner you learn the better. You're a bad influence on the other girls.' Katherine did learn to behave herself, at least when the nuns were looking!

'I've decided to become a nun,' she told one of her friends, when she was sixteen years old. 'I've grown to like this place and I do want to please God. In any case, I've lived in a convent since before I can remember and I wouldn't know how to live anywhere else.'

'We've also decided to be nuns,' two of her friends said. They were sisters. A little group of girls took their vows together, promising not to marry, not to have belongings of their own, and to stay in the convent for the rest of their lives.

'I need to talk to you,' Katherine said to her friend one day the following year. 'Meet me under the apple tree. And tell the others too.' After the day's work was done, the friends met together under the tree.

'What is it?' one of them asked.

'Listen,' Katherine von Bora said. 'Wait till I tell you this. A monk was visiting near here. His name's Martin Luther. Apparently he preached in German and not in Latin!'

'Wow!' said one of the young nuns. 'He'll be in trouble for that!'

'And he said that if we had faith in God, we would go to heaven, not if we did good works!'

'You're kidding!' another of the girls gasped. 'But wouldn't that be wonderful?'

'And,' went on Katherine, 'he said that we can pray to God instead of praying to the saints.'

'What are you doing?' Sister Mary asked. Nobody had seen her coming.

'Just talking,' Katherine explained. Somehow she knew that Sister Mary would not agree with the monk and that she'd better watch her step. But that didn't stop the young woman thinking.

Gossip came and went from the convent by the carriers who brought in supplies and who took the nuns' fruit, vegetables and honey to the nearby market.

'Luther says we don't need to be in a convent to serve God.' 'Luther says that the Pope isn't head of the church.' 'Luther says there's no such place as purgatory!'

That set the young women thinking. 'Does he mean that Christians go to heaven when they die rather than purgatory?'

'It must,' Katherine agreed. 'And he says that all his ideas come from the Bible!'

'Guess what else he says?' one of her friends giggled. The group waited to hear what was coming. 'He says that priests can get married!'

Every few days there seemed to be more news of the monk, Martin Luther. And each time, the news made the girls think about what they really believed.

Twelve young nuns, including Katherine von Bora, decided they would have to leave the convent.

'There's no way we can stay here when our hearts are telling us to get out and to follow the truth of the Bible rather than what the Roman Church is teaching.'

'It's exciting!' one of her friends said.

Her sister shivered. 'It's terrifying.'

'I think we should write to Martin Luther for advice,' the most sensible suggested. And his reply was to send a local merchant to help them escape. On 7th April, 1523, a student ran into Luther's town of Wittenberg and told his friends, 'A wagonload of young women have just come to town, all more excited at the thought of being married than they are about being alive!'

Indeed, the girls did marry, one after the other until only Katherine was left. 'I think you should marry her,' Luther's friend told him. 'She'd make a very good wife for you.'

'You say priests can marry,' another said, 'then why not monks? And you could lead the way.'

'I want you to marry,' Martin's father said. 'And when you have a son, he will carry the name Luther to another generation.'

It took him some time to make up his mind, but Martin did discuss marriage with Katherine.

'I believe that there is a great change, a reformation going on in Europe,' he said. 'The Roman Church has taught errors for so long that we now need to preach the Bible loud and clear, and we need to have it in our own language too. You know that I've made enemies by saying these things in public?' he asked.

'Yes,' replied the young woman.

'And do you realise that some people have been burned at the stake for preaching what I preach?'

'Yes,' she said.

'And you're still prepared to marry me?'

'Yes,' was her firm reply, 'I am.'

On 13th June, 1525, Katherine von Bora became Mrs Katherine Luther and she went to live in the monastery with her new husband.

Before long, Katherine made sure her husband was interested in more than church problems. He became a keen gardener, and they had hens, ducks, pigs and cows. Working in the garden and orchard helped him to relax.

'Martin needed a wife,' Katherine thought, 'and I'm so glad it's me.' And he did need a wife. Luther was so generous that he sometimes gave away things they needed. Once, when he was about to do that, his wife found out. 'I'm sending you a vase,' he wrote to someone in need, and then added, 'Katie's hidden it.' A year after they were married, Martin had good news to tell. 'My dear Katie presented me with a little Hans Luther yesterday at two o'clock, by God's grace.'

'Our first year of marriage was so happy,' Katie told a friend, 'but this year is hard going. The plague has hit several times, and little Hans has been terribly ill. Though Martin has not had the plague, he is suffering from depression. When he's very down, I read the Bible to him or get one of his friends to keep him company.

Music seems to help him too.' By the end of the year, Hans had a little sister called Elizabeth who would help cheer up their daddy. But little Elizabeth only lived for eight months.

'Katie, I'm needing your help today,' Martin often said. 'When I'm translating the Bible into German, I want to use the words that ordinary people would use. You're so good with words; will you come and help me?' 'Yes,' Katie would reply. 'I'll come.'

'What's the common word for making bread rise?' he asked. 'Not the long word that cooks use; the word that ordinary housewives would say.' His wife gave him the word he was looking for.

'What are you translating today?' she asked.

'It's Jesus' story about a little yeast making a whole loaf rise, just as a little sin makes a whole life bad.'

'Well, I think that's the word you want.'

'The more I preach the Bible, the more enemies I have,' Martin said to his wife one day. 'But there needs to be change in the church. Are you remembering this might cost me my life and you your husband?'

'God will care for us,' Katie said. 'Don't be frightened for us.' Her attitude allowed

Luther to preach freely and to risk even his life for the truth of the Bible.

But life in the Luther household was not always so serious. Martin could be great fun. He even had a bowling alley built in the monastery!

'How many children do you have now?' a visitor asked Katie, when their last one was born. 'We have eleven children which includes orphans and our own offspring. Some students of Martin's stay with us too.'

'My darling Katie keeps me young,' Martin told the visitor, 'and fit too,' he laughed. 'Without her I'd be totally lost. She puts up with my travels and she's always waiting for me when I come back. She nurses me through my depressions. She's patient with my tantrums. She helps with my work. And most of all she loves Jesus. Apart from God's gift of his Son, she's the best gift he has given me in all of my life.'

Katie squeezed his hand.

'All I've been is a wife and mother,' Katie commented, when they were alone. 'And I think I must have been one of the happiest wives and mothers in all of Germany.'

Martin held her close. 'Darling Katie,' he said, stroking her hair, 'I believe God has used me to help change the church for all time. And I couldn't have done it without you. If the history of this Reformation is ever written, I hope and pray that your name will be there with mine in the history books.' And it is.

FACT FILE

Latin: This was the original language of the Roman Empire, and, until about the 9th century, Latin was the only written language in Western Europe. Latin survived long after the collapse of the Roman Empire and was used throughout Western Europe by merchants, scholars and churchmen. Reformers such as Wycliffe and Luther, however, wanted the Bible to be read by everyone and not just educated people, and that's why they pushed to have the Bible translated into languages other than Latin.

Keynote: Katherine and her friends were delighted to hear that purgatory did not exist and that the Bible had nothing to say about it at all. One of the great things about following Jesus Christ and trusting in him is that when you die, you will immediately go to be with him in heaven.

Think: Katherine did not write books or preach sermons, but she was an invaluable help to Luther who did do these things. She was a great support to him. She looked after him and gave him advice. Katherine was hard-working and clever, and God used her abilities to bring his Word to the ordinary people. Ask God to use you to bring his Word to other people who do not know him yet.

Prayer: Thank you, God, for giving us your Word, the Bible. Thank you that I can read it in my own language. Thank you for schools and books that have taught me to read. Please help missionaries round the world who are translating your Word into other languages. When I read your Word, help me to understand it and obey it. Help me to tell it to others. Amen.

Susanna Wesley

Susanna counted, '... seventeen, eighteen, nineteen, twenty.'

'Well done!' her mother said. 'You're a clever girl. Now, what comes after twenty?'

The child thought. 'Twenty-one?' she asked.

'That's right. And then what?' But Susanna had reached the end of her numbers. 'Let's sing the number song to her,' Mrs Annesley told some of her other children.

'One, two, three ... twenty-one, twenty-two, twenty-three,' they sang to the tune of a nursery rhyme, 'twenty-four and twenty-five's Susanna.'

Then they all fell about in a fit of giggles. The youngest of them laughed too, though she didn't know what they were all laughing about.

'Why do you always sing "twenty-five's Susanna?" the five-year-old asked one of her brothers.

He grinned. 'It's because Dad and Mum had twenty-five children, and you're the youngest. That makes you the twenty-fifth!'

Susanna held up both hands and looked at all ten fingers. Then she made her hands into fists and opened them up again. 'That's twenty,' she told her brother. She made one fist and opened that hand again. 'And that comes to twenty-five. That's a lot of children,' the girl said. She made her little finger dance. 'And this one is twenty-five's Susanna!'

'I think we should be getting on with your school work,' Mrs Annesley told her youngest children. Three sat down on the floor at her knee to continue the lesson on counting. Four were on chairs round the table where they had reading to do. And four others were in Dr Annesley's study learning history with him. The rest were either out at work or away from home. When it was nearly lunchtime, their father came into the living room to ask them their daily questions. From a little book of questions and answers, which he called a catechism, he asked each a question.

'Who made you?' he smiled at Susanna.

'God made me,' she replied. Then it was the turn of the next one up.

'Why did God make you?'

'God made me to worship and adore him.'
'What else did God make?'

'God made all things.'

By the time Dr Annesley reached the oldest child, the questions were really quite difficult. But as he asked them every day, they all knew the answers.

'Where's Susanna? We want her to come out and play with us,' the little girl heard one of her sisters asking. But Susanna didn't answer. She was under the table in her father's study where he and his friends couldn't see her because of the heavy tablecloth that reached right down to the floor.

Although she didn't understand most of what the men talked about, she still loved to hear them speaking. Susanna pictured their faces. When her father said the name of Jesus, she knew his face would look warm and soft. And when sin was being discussed, she imagined his expression being sad. Whenever heaven was mentioned, she knew exactly how he would look, for her father couldn't speak about heaven without his eyes smiling. But the talk went on for a long, long time, and the child fell asleep.

'I think your pet is under the table again,' one of the visitors commented. A man who was new to the group thought there must be a dog in the room. But Dr Annesley knew better. He took a cushion from behind him and held it out to his friend. 'Put that under her head, please,' he said.

'I'd like to have a talk with you, Dad,' Susanna said, seven or eight years later.

'Come into my study,' her father smiled. 'There's nowhere else to talk quietly in this busy house.

'Now, what's worrying you?' he asked, when they were settled by the wood fire.

Susanna knew this could be difficult, but she had thought out what she wanted to say. 'I understand you felt strongly that you shouldn't join the Church of England when Parliament said all ministers had to. That's why you weren't able to preach in public until King Charles said you could do again. But I really believe that I should belong to the Church of England.'

Dr Annesley looked at his daughter. 'I've brought this on myself,' he thought. 'I've taught them all to use their brains and to think for themselves.'

'Tell me why you think so,' he asked Susanna.

The girl gave very clear reasons why she should leave the Dissenters and join the Church of England. And that's what she did shortly afterwards.

'Who's that young man?' Susanna asked her sister one day.

'That's Samuel Wesley, and you and he have something in common.' The girl looked at the stranger and wondered what that might be. 'We're about the same height,' she teased. 'Only he's stopped growing and I'll get taller than I am just now.'

Her sister laughed. 'It's not only your height you have in common; you're as strong-minded as each other.'

'How do you know that?' asked Susanna.

'Because he did exactly the same as you did. He left the Dissenters and went back to the Church of England.'

'Interesting ...' thought the young Susanna. 'We do have something in common after all.'

'November 1688,' wrote the nineteen-year-old bride in her diary, 'I married Samuel Wesley, minister of the Church of England. We're starting married life in London, where I'm going to have to be the best housewife in the whole city to make £28 a year to feed and clothe us.'

'I need two new shirts,' Samuel told Susanna, some months after they were married.

'I'm afraid you'll have to wait,' she explained. 'There's hardly enough money for food let alone new shirts. But I'll patch your old ones very carefully.'

Samuel held up an ancient shirt. 'You'll just be joining patches together,' he grumped. 'If you can't manage on what I earn here, I'll just have to find another job.'

Susanna wondered what expense she could cut back on, but she couldn't think of a single thing.

'I can have my new shirts now!' Wesley announced, as be burst into their little home some months later. 'I'm going to be a minister to the crew of a boat that works back and forward across the Irish Sea.'

Susanna looked horrified, thinking that she might have to live on board! She heaved a sigh of relief when he went on, 'You can stay in a boarding house while I'm away. And we'll be able to afford that because I'll be earning £70 a year.' But after just six months, Samuel was back on land and looking for yet another job. Being at sea didn't agree with him at all.

'You're a grandfather once again!' Mrs Annesley announced to her husband when, in 1690, little Samuel Wesley was born. She took her husband by the arm into the next-door bedroom where their daughter's baby had just been born. 'Hello Grandfather,'

Susanna said, as though the tiny infant in her arms was speaking. Samuel screwed up his eyes and looked at the world. He couldn't have thought much of it because he opened his mouth and yelled.

'I wonder if he'll be a preacher one day,' Dr Annesley said. 'He's certainly got the lungs for it.'

Susanna handed the baby to her mother and cuddled down to sleep, grateful that she had been able to come home for his birth. Her parents' home seemed so much more comfortable than any of the ones she and her husband had had in their first year and a half of marriage.

'Where's South Ormsby?' Susanna asked some months later, when Samuel told her they were moving there.

'It's in Lincolnshire,' he explained. 'It's a little village with a population of just over two hundred.'

'Lincolnshire!' wailed Susanna. 'That's worlds away from here.'

'Nonsense! It's only a hundred and fifty miles away. And you'll grow to like the countryside.'

Susanna picked up the baby, even though he was sound asleep. She needed someone to cuddle while she did some serious thinking.

'That means I won't see my parents. And I won't see my brothers and sisters either. What about my friends? They're not able to travel as far as that, and I can't afford to come back and see them.'

Tears started to roll down her face. She hugged baby Samuel close, wiping the tears away on his shawl so that her husband didn't see them.

'What's the house like?' she asked.

'It's simple,' her husband explained. 'Just a country house made of mud, with one room and a loft.'

Susanna thought of her parents' home. 'Do you know anything else about it?' she asked, dreading the answer.

'I understand that the village women are cleaning it out for us.'

She risked a smile. 'That's kind of them. Anything else?'

'Oh yes,' he said, turning away as he spoke. 'It seems that there's no glass in the windows, but there are shutters so it should be cosy enough.'

'No glass!' thought Susanna. 'And no natural light when the shutters are closed!' She sat down, rocking the baby to comfort herself, when a thought struck her. 'If that's where God wants us to be then it's the best place for us.'

The Wesleys spent seven years in South Ormsby before moving to Epworth, where they had a bigger home for their growing family.

'Will you run a school for us in Epworth?' one of the children asked, as they packed up their slates and chalk for the last time in their old home.

'I certainly will,' Susanna told her. 'I started the school as soon as my first little boy was old enough to begin learning, and I'll keep it going until the last of you girls is taught.'

'What's the most important lesson?' the girl asked. 'Is it reading or writing or counting?'

'They're all important,' her mother explained, 'but the most important lesson you can learn is that you need to trust in Jesus to be saved. There is nothing in the whole wide world more important than that.'

'Mrs Wesley has a little school in the rectory,' Samuel told some members of his new congregation. He was quite happy for more pupils to attend the classes his wife ran from nine to twelve each morning, and from two till five in the afternoons. He was especially happy if some parents gave a small gift towards the school, as he was forever running out of money.

'I hear Mr Wesley's wife is very strict,' the news went round the village after two of the local children joined the class.

'She is,' one of her new pupils admitted, when he was asked about his teacher. 'She's very, very strict. But she's fair with it.'

'Mrs Wesley's having Sunday meetings in the rectory,' was the local gossip one day. 'Her husband is away from home, and, although his assistant is taking services, she thinks there should be afternoon meetings too,' one of Susanna's neighbours told her friend. 'Will you come to the meeting with me?'

'Yes, I'll come along,' her friend agreed. And they went.

'Did you see how well the Wesley children listened to the sermon their mother read to us?' the neighbour commented as the two women walked home afterwards.

'I did indeed,' was the reply. 'No wonder she teaches our Tommy so well!'

'You must use your brains,' Susanna told her children and other pupils over and over again. 'Think everything through for yourselves. And the most important thing to think through is this: where will you go when you die? You may decide not to believe in God when you're alive, but do you think God will be taken in on the Judgment Day when you tell him he doesn't exist?' And when, in 1709, their home burned down, and their five-year-old son John was only just rescued from the flames, she reminded her family yet again that one day they would all have to meet their maker.

Samuel soon had a new house underway, and when they moved into it, Susanna wrote her thoughts down in her diary. 'Another new home, and a nice solid one too. I'm glad it's built of brick. It's so much safer than wood,' she added, thinking back to the fire. 'I suppose it's because the new house gives us a new beginning, that I'm thinking back over the years. They've not been easy, but I have so much to thank God for. Of our nineteen babies, we have ten still alive, though poor Mary is crippled. Some of them are now Christians, and that is the joy of my heart. I'll pray for the others to be converted, until the day I die. And every day, I pray that God will use my dear children to spread the good news that Jesus saves.'

As the years passed and the children moved away from home, Susanna wrote more in her diary, especially as her husband was difficult to live with. 'It seems that God is calling Charles and John to preach the gospel,' she wrote. 'My heart is singing!'

And they did become preachers, two of the most famous preachers England ever had. Like their mother, they had minds of their own. And also like Susanna, they left the church they'd been brought up in. But they didn't join another of the churches in England; they started the Methodist Church, which has since spread throughout England and to many other countries in the world.

FACT FILE

Brains: Sometimes we can be told to use our brains! This means to think something through. But here are some facts about brains you may not know. The brain of a grown-up weighs about 1.3 kilograms. It is made up of approximately 15, 000, 000, 000 cells. Your body is controlled by three different parts of your brain. The cerebrum controls body movement. It helps you to think and learn, as well as experience emotions. The cerebellum helps you to balance and it makes sure that your legs and arms work properly together. The medulla is very small and regulates your heartbeat and breathing. The brain is a wonderful thing. It didn't happen by accident. God designed it!

Keynote: Susanna thought for herself. She made decisions for herself, even when she was quite young. But more importantly, she prayed about these decisions. It is important to think for yourself, but it is more important to think about what God wants. Our thoughts and decisions can be wrong if we are not asking God to help and guide us.

Think: Susanna said that wherever God sent them, that would be the best place for them to be. Sometimes we have to move away to another town or city. It can be a difficult and exciting time. If you trust in God, you will realise that he always wants what is best for you. Ask God to show you how to be useful to him wherever you are.

Prayer: Lord, help me to obey you and trust you, whatever happens in my life. You are always with me, wherever I go. Help me to be obedient to your Word wherever I am. Amen

Ann Judson

Ann and her three sisters stood against the wall, each with a feather at her feet. 'Ready, steady, go!' their brother shouted from the other end of the room. All four girls scrambled down on to their hands and knees and began to blow their feathers along the floor.

'That's my one!' the oldest girl laughed, as she reached up to catch a feather that was in danger of blowing away.

'Come on!' their brother called. 'If you don't watch out, Ann will win again.'

Three of the girls blew with big breaths, and their feathers went everywhere. Ann, blowing with little breaths, kept her feather under control and in front of all the others. 'I've won!' she announced, when her feather hit the far wall of the room. 'Now, what's the next game?'

Mr and Mrs Hasseltine smiled from their seats by the fire. 'I just love to see them playing together,' Mrs Hasseltine said. 'I'd rather listen to the children's laughter than music.'

Her husband nodded. 'The new room will give them plenty of space to play just now, and we can use it for parties and dances when they're older.'

'Shall we tell them about it?' Mrs Hasseltine asked.

'What a good idea,' he agreed.

'Your mother and I have something to tell you,' Mr Hasseltine said, when the next game was over. The children sat down in front of the fire. Usually when their father said that, there was a treat in store. 'We've decided to build another room on to the house, a big room to use for parties. And when you're older, we'll hold balls in it too.'

Young John screwed up his face.

'By then there will be four young ladies looking for handsome husbands,' Mrs Hasseltine said, looking at her four daughters. 'Where better to meet young men than at a ball in your very own home.'

'That sounds wonderful!' Ann said.

'Balls sound boring,' teased her brother.

'Please be ready to leave for church in fifteen minutes,' Mrs Hasseltine told the girls one Sunday morning.

'I'll never be ready on time,' thought Ann. 'I can't decide which dress to wear.' There were four spread out on her bed, all with matching underwear. Along the pillow was a selection of hats, each with a variety of ribbons to choose from. 'If I wore my yellow dress, I could put on the hat with blue and yellow ribbons. Or if I wore my pink dress, I could choose between that hat and this one. But then I couldn't take my new yellow fan. She sat down in a heap of satin underskirt to make up her mind.

'Five minutes!' her father's voice called. Ann grabbed the yellow dress and slipped it on. She wrapped each of her ringlets round her finger, letting them fall loosely on her shoulders. Picking up her new fan, she peeked from behind it to see how she looked in the mirror. 'I must run,' she said, holding up the hems of her long dress to prevent herself tripping.

'Well! Well!' laughed Mr Hasseltine, as she ran down the stair. 'If I don't have the loveliest daughters in America, I don't know who has ... and the handsomest son too.'

Ann loved Sundays. After church, the family had a meal together and then went for a walk in the afternoon sun. The evening was spent reading or singing round the piano. Never a day passed, in the Hasseltine home, without a great deal of laughter and fun, and Sundays were no different. That night as she went to bed, Ann wrote in her diary,

'I think I am one of the happiest creatures on earth.'

'Don't forget to say your prayers,' Mrs Hasseltine said every night at bedtime. 'Remember to ask God to forgive you for all you've done wrong today.'

As it was so warm that Ann couldn't sleep, she lay thinking about what her mother had said. 'I wish I could stop doing wrong things,' she decided. 'I really do try, but I don't always manage.' Then she remembered a party she was invited to, and, before she could stop herself, she was working out what she would wear.

'Our new teacher is very serious,' Ann's older sister said. 'I think Bradford Academy won't be nearly such fun now he's come.'

'He says that if we don't trust in Jesus and have our sins forgiven, we'll go to hell when we die.'

Mr Hasseltine smiled at his children. 'This seems a very serious topic of conversation,' he commented. 'Perhaps too serious for dinner time.'

'But it would be very serious if we went to hell,' Ann said, 'so I'm going to try my very, very hardest to be good and go to heaven.'

Ann, who was by then fifteen years old, did try very hard. She read her Bible every day; she remembered to pray each morning and evening, and she tried to be much more serious.

'It's not enough just to try to be good,' her teacher told his class. 'You must repent and be forgiven.'

Ann listened to what he said, and it troubled her. She listened hard at church and she went to other Christian meetings as well. But it wasn't at church, or at a meeting, that Ann Hasseltine became a Christian. It was through a loving Christian aunt who explained to her that she had to confess her sins and believe in Jesus to be saved. 'Now I really am one of the happiest people on earth,' she decided. 'My sins are forgiven. Jesus is my Saviour and friend, and I know that when I die, I'll go home to heaven.'

'We're having a group of young people for lunch,' Mrs Hasseltine told the family. They were now grown-up, and Ann was a teacher. 'Make them all feel very welcome.'

'Would you like more soup?' Ann asked one of the young men, when he had finished what was in his plate.

'No, thank you,' he said, then changed his mind. 'It's worth a second plate of soup to have a closer look at Ann,' he thought. 'She's beautiful. Her skin is so smooth, and her eyes sparkle. Her black, curly hair is just perfect. Not only that, I can hear from what she says that she's a Christian!'

There was no doubt about it, their visitor, Adoniram Judson, had a very serious case of falling in love!

Not many months passed before Adoniram made an appointment to speak to Mr Hasseltine.

'I love Ann,' he told the older man, 'and I should like to make her my wife.'

'What kind of life will she have if she marries you?' the girl's father asked.

Judson looked him straight in the eye. This was not going to be easy. 'I believe God is calling me to be a missionary in India. If Ann marries me, she will have a life of service, but it will be a hard and sometimes dangerous one. As a small group of us hope to travel together, Ann would have company for the voyage. Beyond that, I really don't know. But God does,' he added.

'This isn't a decision I feel I should take,' Mr Hasseltine said. 'I will leave it up to Ann.'

When she replied to Adoniram's proposal of marriage, Ann wrote, 'I dare not decline an offer I believe to be God's will, even though many are ready to call it a wild, romantic undertaking.' They were married in 1811.

The journey to Burma took a very long time as they had to stay for a while in India. By the time they arrived, they had faced many dangers including a near shipwreck.

They had said sad farewells to the other young missionaries who sailed from America with them. And, most terrible of all, Adoniram and Ann's first baby was born dead and buried at sea. It was a broken-hearted Ann Judson who arrived in Burma.

She wrote home soon after their arrival, 'This country is full of beauty and ugliness. The women are dressed in the brightest silks. They look like butterflies, and the rustle of silk sounds like butterfly wings. But when you look at their faces, it's different. They chew something called betel that turns their mouths and teeth red; sometimes it even drips down their chins! The children often wear nothing at all, apart from bits of string tied around their wrists, ankles and middles. These strings are meant to protect them from evil spirits! And believe it or not, children as young as one smoke cigars! This is a very beautiful country, but such a strange one. What a difference it would make to the people if they were to believe in the Lord Jesus.'

'How will we ever learn to read this script?' Ann asked her husband, when they had settled down with a teacher. 'It looks just like a line of circles!'

Andoniram looked into Ann's lovely, dark eyes, 'We'll learn it,' he said, 'because we need to. There's no way of translating the Bible into Burmese without learning the language!'

Ann grinned. 'When you put it like that, it makes perfect sense!' she said.

Both the Judsons were good at languages, and before very long they were able to read and write some Burmese.

'Things are becoming dangerous,' Judson told Ann, after they had been missionaries in Burma for twelve years. 'With England and Burma at war, we're suspected of being spies. The Burmese can't tell the difference between the English and Americans.'

'It's not just us,' Ann said, looking at the two Burmese children in the room. 'We have these two little girls to look after now and whatever happens, we must keep the translation safe. It would be a tragedy if all these years of work were lost.' Ann looked round their little home. It was made of bamboo and built on stilts like all the other homes around them. She sat down to think.

'Are you tired?' Adoniram asked, full of concern for his pregnant wife.

'I'm weary,' she admitted, 'and if I don't keep praying, I feel fearful.'

Adoniram held her close. 'Maung Ing will look after you if anything happens to me,' he told her, knowing that their Burmese servant would do everything in his power to help them.

The door flew open the following evening, just as the family was about to eat. 'You're called by the King,' an official screamed, as he scrambled up the bamboo ladder and into the room. Two ferocious men climbed in behind him. 'Spotted Faces!' the little girls screamed. Ann threw her long, wide skirt around the children to prevent them seeing Adoniram being thrown to the floor before having his elbows tied behind his back. Maung Ing was horrified. The Spotted Faces were murderers and thugs the authorities used to do their dirty work. Ann pushed the girls in Maung Ing's direction and he hid them. 'Don't take my husband away!' she cried, but she could do nothing to stop him being thrown down the steps. Ann rushed to where she kept her money and raced after the men. They took what she paid them to slacken Adoniram's ropes, but they didn't do anything to make their prisoner more comfortable.

'Help me! Maung Ing,' Ann begged, as she climbed up the bamboo ladder. 'They'll be back to search the place.' She grabbed the New Testament translation. 'Get any old cloth you can find,' she urged. He scrabbled round and brought what she was looking for. 'Get string!' she told the wide-eyed girls.

'Find me string!' Kneeling on the floor, Maung Ing and Ann wrapped up the translation work and tied it tight. 'Wait here,' she said to the two little girls. 'You can watch from the door.' Turning to Maung Ing she said, 'We've got to bury this! We've got to keep it away from the Spotted Faces.' Ann and Maung Ing dug a hole near the house and buried the precious bundle. Then he stamped the earth to look like everywhere else. The pair of them climbed back up to the girls. 'We're just in time,' whispered Maung Ing. 'They're coming back!'

'Adoniram's in Death Prison,' was the news that Ann dreaded. It was an unspeakable place, where prisoners were hung up by their feet every night with only their necks and heads on the ground. Ann visited her husband, and watched him getting filthier and weaker and eventually unable to walk.

'Take this pillow to Adoniram,' she told Maung Ing two months later. The prisoner's eyes lit up. It was the bumpiest and most uncomfortable pillow ever, but Adoniram hugged it close. He had his precious translation work back in his arms!

'Tell Ann I love her and thank God for her,' he said to his faithful servant.

In all the terrible things that happened during that war, God kept the translation work safe. Adoniram and Ann's baby daughter, Maria, was born while he was still in prison. On the very last day of 1825, he was released from prison, having been held in desperate conditions for a year and a half.

However, by the end of the following year, both Ann and Maria had died. Sometime later Adoniram married again and continued with the work he and Ann had begun, and the Burmese people got God's Word in their own language.

But if it had not been for Ann Judson's quick thinking, the Burmese translation of the Bible might not have happened at all.

FACT FILE

Burma: The country of Burma is now known as Myanmar. You will find it in an atlas at the eastern side of the Bay of Bengal. It is surrounded by the countries of Bangladesh, India, China, Laos and Thailand. Over half of Myanmar is forest, and the city of Rangoon (now called Yangon) is situated on the coast and has 24.5 metres of rain each year. However, some mountainous regions of Myanmar have over 50 metres of rain every year.

Keynote: Ann thought that the country of Burma was very beautiful, but there were other things that frightened and disturbed her about it. However, Ann recognised that what the Burmese people needed was to believe in the Lord Jesus Christ. That is what you need - that is what your country needs wherever you live.

Think: Ann wanted to go to heaven, as she knew that hell was a real and awful place. She did not want to go there. However, she thought that in order to get to heaven she would have to earn salvation. Anne thought she had to become good before she would be allowed to go. But Jesus tells us that the only way to heaven and to God is through him. It is by believing and trusting in Jesus Christ that we are given eternal life. It is only Jesus who can make us ready for heaven.

Prayer: Lord Jesus, show me how sinful I am and show me how wonderful you are. Make me ready to go to heaven to be with you. Amen

Maria Taylor

Maria and Burella Dyer looked at each other, each wondering how her sister felt about what their stepfather had just told them.

'I've thought a lot about your future. I've prayed about it too,' he went on. 'And I really don't see any alternative to sending you both back to England. Your uncle and aunt have agreed to care for you.'

'But China is our home,' Maria said. 'We belong here.'

'We're almost Chinese,' added Burella. 'We won't know anyone at school in England. We'll always be the odd ones out.'

The kind man smiled at his stepdaughters. 'You will fit in after a while,' he assured them. 'But I have to confess that life in China won't be the same without you.'

Maria saw her chance. 'Then let us stay,' she pleaded.

He shook his head. 'I'm truly sorry. But that's just not possible.'

'Happy birthday to you!' Burella sang to her sister on 16th January, 1847. 'Imagine you being ten years old!'

Maria rubbed her sleepy eyes. 'It's not a happy birthday,' she moaned. 'It's the saddest birthday in my whole life because it's the last one I'll have in China. In less than a month we sail for England.'

Burella, who was eleven, hugged her sister tight. 'I know it is,' she said. 'But I have a plan.'

'What's that?' asked Maria.

Burella replied, 'When we go to England, we'll study very hard and become teachers. Then we can come back to China and be missionaries ourselves. Nobody could send us back to England then.'

The birthday girl cheered up. 'And we could run our own school,' she laughed. 'You could be the headmistress, and I could be the infant teacher.'

'Don't let's tell anyone,' Burella warned. 'Let's keep it a secret.'

'Goodbye!' the little group of missionaries yelled. 'Goodbye!' The Dyer girls waved from the boat as it eased away from the quay. They waved and waved, tears streaming down their faces so that they could hardly see their friends who had come to see them off.

Suddenly, the group on shore burst into song, 'God bless you and keep you, God care for you dear friends. God bless you and keep you now and till Jesus comes again.'

Burella wiped away her tears. 'They think we won't meet again until we're in heaven,' she told her little sister. 'But we'll be back one day. Dry your eyes,' she ordered. 'Or you'll miss your last sight of China.'

Maria did what she was told, and as the land faded into the distance, she imagined that ten years had passed, and that she and her sister were on their way back, catching their first sight of China, not their last.

'Why are you being sent back to England?' a boy travelling on the same boat asked.

'Our parents came from England,' Maria explained. 'They were missionaries in China. But Dad died when I was six. Two years after that Mum married again. Our stepfather is also a missionary.'

'Was he kind to you?' the boy asked.

'Oh yes,' said Maria. 'He's very kind.'

'So why is he sending you away?'

The girl took up her story again. 'A year after Mum married again, she became ill and died, leaving our stepfather to take care of us.'

The boy looked shocked. 'So you've not got a real dad or mum of your own now?' he asked.

'No,' Maria agreed. 'But we've still got our stepfather even though he can't care for us.'

'Who will look after you?'

'We're going back to England to stay with our uncle and aunt.'

'Are they nice?' she was asked.

'I think so,' the girl said. Her new friend was full of questions.

'Have you met them before?' was the next one.

Maria said she had, 'but I don't remember them very well. We lived in England from when I was two till I was four, but that was a long time ago.'

'I remember lots of things from when I was four!' the boy announced.

For the next five years, the Dyer sisters worked hard, first at school then at a college where they trained as teachers.

'Every day is a day nearer China,' Burella often said to her sister. And Maria would smile at the thought, though China sometimes seemed a long time ago and a very long way away.

'Do you think we will go back one day?' she asked.

'I don't think there's been a single day since we came home when I've not thought about going back,' her sister told her.

'All that's to be worked out is when and how.'

'There's a letter for you, Burella,' a teacher at the college said to her one day, when she was sixteen years old.

The girl tore it open. 'It's from Mum's friend Miss Aldersey!' she told Maria. 'Listen to this.

"Your uncle tells me that you've done well in your teacher training and that you would now be able to take a class. I am writing to ask you to come back to China, to teach at my school at Ningpo. You would be teaching Chinese girls. While some of your pupils will be your own age or older, from what your uncle says I think you could cope with that."'

Maria's face fell. She had a sudden vision of losing her sister, of being left in England alone.

Burella read on. '"And if you bring Maria with you, she, too, could help in the school!"' Their eyes met, sparkling with a mixture of excitement and tears.

'We're going back to China!' the older girl laughed and cried. 'We're going home!'

That night Maria lay in bed thinking. 'I can hardly believe it,' she smiled. 'In just a few months we'll be in China, not as daughters of missionaries, but as teachers ourselves. Dad and Mum would have been pleased to think we were missionaries.' Then she thought for a minute. 'I suppose what would have pleased them even more is that we're both Christians. That's what's most important of all. I remember when I was a little girl telling Mum that I wanted to be a princess, and she said it was more important to be a Christian. But then she said that when I was converted I'd become a daughter of the God who is King of Kings and I'd be a princess in the kingdom of heaven.' Maria went to sleep happy. In the next room, Burella was trying to remember all she could about Miss Aldersey. But all that came into her mind was that she was very strict.

In 1852, Maria and Burella Dyer sailed for China as teachers. The school at Ningpo was for Chinese girls,and Burella's memory of Miss Aldersey was quite right. She was a good teacher and a good headmistress, but she was strict, very strict.

'She's trying to be a mother to us,' Maria told her sister, when the headmistress seemed to be running their lives.

'I know that,' Burella tried to smile. 'But she forgets that we grew up in England, and that we're not little girls any longer.'

Three years after their arrival at Ningpo, there was an air of disapproval about the place.

'How dare an Englishman behave like that!' argued Miss Aldersey. 'He has no idea how to behave. The Chinese treat him like one of themselves! And he even has the cheek to treat people's diseases when he's not a fully qualified doctor!'

'He's certainly different,' Burella said to her sister, after they first met Hudson Taylor.

Maria smiled, thinking of the missionary they'd met. 'I think he suits his black pigtail,' she announced. 'And I think it's really quite brave of him to have his head shaved and grow a pigtail. Once he'd done that, he couldn't really go on wearing western clothes, could he?'

Her sister thought about it. 'I suppose not,' she said. 'A pigtail and black suit and tie would look ridiculous.'

Maria went on, 'It may be that one day we'll have to dress like the Chinese and become real friends with them, so that we can tell them about Jesus.' She caught a look on Burella's face. 'What are you grinning at?'

The older sister broke into a wide smile. 'I was trying to imagine Miss Aldersey in Chinese clothes!'

What happened after that was hard for both Maria and Hudson Taylor. They fell deeply in love, but Miss Aldersey disapproved of Hudson so very much that she refused to let them see each other. When that didn't put a stop to their love, the headmistress wrote to Maria's uncle, telling him what an awful fellow Hudson was and saying that there was no way the two young people should be allowed to marry. It took many months for that letter to reach England and for a reply to arrive. But when it came back, it was not as disapproving as Miss Aldersey hoped it would be. In any case, Maria was just coming up to her twenty-first birthday, when she would be able to make up her mind for herself whom she would marry. There was never any doubt who that would be. She married the Englishman who dressed as though he was Chinese and became Mrs Hudson Taylor on 20th January, 1858, four days after her twenty-first birthday.

Although Hudson and Maria loved each other, the beginning of married life was not altogether happy because the following year they lost their first baby, and just months later Burella became ill with cholera and died. She was just twenty-three years old. But in 1859, the young couple had a healthy little daughter whom they called Grace.

'There's so much work to do, I hardly see you,' Hudson whispered into Grace's little ear. 'But that doesn't stop me loving you.'

The baby cooed contentedly and reached out for her daddy's pigtail. 'And if it wasn't for friends back home in England sending gifts of money, there would be nothing to feed you on,' he thought aloud, as he stroked her neck.

'But God has never seen us hungry,' her husband said. Maria agreed, though both knew that there had been times when there was nothing at all in the cupboard and no money, yet food had always come from somewhere before hunger set in.

'Hudson, you're losing weight and you've no colour in your cheeks at all,' Maria said. 'If we don't go back to England for a while, you're not going to survive.'

Her husband started to say that there was too much work to do for him to leave.

'Listen to me,' Maria said gently but firmly. 'Of the two hundred couples that came out here in 1807, forty men died and fifty-one women. We don't want that to be repeated in our generation too.'

Hudson knew she was right. 'I'll make arrangements for the ship,' he agreed. 'We'll take Grace home to meet the English side of her family, and I can train as a doctor while we're there.'

The Taylors' trip home marked a new beginning. 'We can't depend on the CMS,' they said to each other from time to time. 'But we can depend on the Lord.'

One day, Hudson put that into practice. He opened a bank account in the name of the China Inland Mission and paid in £10. He and Maria prayed and planned.

'We'll ask God for men and women to be missionaries in the parts of China where nobody has ever heard about Jesus,' Hudson said. 'And we'll not ask anyone for money,' he continued. 'When we have needs, we'll pray for them to be met. Our missionaries will all do the same, working for no payment except from God.'

Maria's eyes shone. 'God has always cared for us and he'll do the same for the China Inland Missionaries,' she added.

When they returned to China in 1866, the Taylors, now with two sons, Herbert and Frederick, as well as Grace, took sixteen new missionaries with them. It was the beginning of the China Inland Mission.

Because she had been brought up in that country, Maria understood as nobody else could, what was involved in the work. She and her husband made up rules for the missionaries which would seem very strict now, but they set the China Inland Mission up in such a way that it's still running today, though it's now called Overseas Missionary

Fellowship (OMF). Through its work, countless people have come to know Jesus.

It was 22nd July, 1870, and Hudson thought that his wife was dying. 'The Mission will go on long after us,' she told him. 'The people of China need it.' Hudson held her hand to his lips. 'Yes, it will,' he said, 'and you'll be remembered as the mother of the mission, for all the love and wisdom and experience you've put into it.'

'It's not been easy,' Maria said weakly. Hudson thought of their children who had died, including Grace, and of the ones who were left, who were now losing their mother.

'No,' he said, 'it's not been easy. But God has given us everything we've needed.'

By the next day, it was clear that Maria would not live for more than a few hours. She and Hudson had a precious time together, sharing and talking about the children and about her going home to heaven. By the time evening came, that's where she was.

FACT FILE

China: China covers an area of 9,560,990 square kilometres. It has a population of 1,398,000,000 in 2019. It has two seasons - the wet summer and the dry winter. In South China you can find tigers, monkeys and salamanders. In the south- west you also find rare animals such as the panda. The Chinese people speak several different languages, but all their written script is the same.

Keynote: Maria realised that God was telling her to work for him in China. But she also realised that, before you became a missionary, you had to be a Christian. You can't work for God if you haven't asked him to forgive your sins.

Think: Maria's life was not easy. She was ill, her children fell ill and some of them died. She must have felt very sad at times. Think about what Maria suffered. She went through this because she realised the importance of telling the Chinese people about the Lord Jesus Christ. Jesus suffered too. He suffered more than anyone ever has or ever will, when he died for our sins on the cross. He did this because of God's love for us. Christ's death was the only way to ensure that those who followed him could have eternal life in heaven when they died.

Prayer: Lord Jesus, thank you for suffering so that I can have eternal life. Make me a worker for you in my home, at my school, with my friends. Help me to tell those I know the truth about you. Amen.

Susannah Spurgeon

Susannah sat in church between her parents and watched the pulpit, trying not even to blink.

'I'm going to see the minister coming in the door today,' she told herself, as she struggled to prevent herself blinking. Her eyes felt dry. 'Come quickly!' she whispered. Her eyelids quivered. 'Quickly!!' Then she blinked despite herself. And in the second her eyes were closed, the minister went into the pulpit. 'Now I've got to wait another week to see it,' she thought crossly.

There were no steps up to the pulpit in her church, and the minister came in through a door at the back. Every Sunday, Susannah tried to see him open the door, come in and close it again ... and nearly every Sunday she blinked. 'I wonder if he really does come in the door or if he just appears there,' she puzzled.

Turning her eyes from the preacher, Susannah looked at the man who led the singing. 'I think he looks like a gigantic robin!' she decided, as she took in his unusual appearance. 'I know the clothes he wears are right for an old-fashioned lawyer, but they do look odd. I wonder why old-fashioned lawyers wore black, long-tailed coats, knee breeches and silk stockings?' The girl found herself smiling. 'And he looks especially like a robin because he has such a round tummy!' She started to giggle softly.

'Are you all right?' Mrs Thompson asked.

'Yes, Mum,' her daughter answered, and tried to concentrate on the beginning of the service.

When she was a young teenager, Susannah became a Christian, but as the years passed, she lost her enthusiasm. Although she still went to church and often enjoyed it, services didn't mean the same to her as they had done when she was first converted.

'I don't think I'll go to the service,' she decided one day. 'What I hear of the young man who is preaching doesn't appeal to me at all. He sounds very rough and ready.'

'Please come,' her friends said that afternoon.

'All right,' she agreed eventually. 'I'll go this evening just to please you.'

The church was full, long before the service, and everyone watched for the little door in the back of the pulpit to open. Susannah didn't blink as it opened and she couldn't believe her eyes at what came in. Instead of a formal gentleman dressed in tailor-made clothes, the preacher was a very young man whose suit looked as though a village dressmaker had made it! Not only that, he had a big, black, satin collar and he carried a blue handkerchief covered in white spots! She had never in her life seen anything like it and she wasn't very pleased at all. That was Sunday, 18th December, 1853, a date Susannah wouldn't forget because the young man with the spotty handkerchief became her husband, Charles Spurgeon.

'Mr Spurgeon gave me a gift of *Pilgrim's Progress* by John Bunyan,' Susannah wrote in her diary sometime later. 'And it has helped me such a lot. Although I've been a Christian for years, I seemed to lose my love for the Lord. Thank goodness God never loses his love for his people. I feel as though I've fallen in love with Jesus all over again. Mr Spurgeon knew just the right book to give me. I can't imagine why I didn't like him when he first came to preach. I can understand why so many hundreds of people come to hear him.'

'It's 8th January, 1856,' Susannah said to herself as she wakened that morning. 'And it's our wedding day!' She spent most of the morning praying, before dressing to be married.

'What's wrong?' she asked her father, as their carriage neared the church in central London. 'What are all these crowds waiting for?'

'I think they want to see you both arriving at the church and leaving,' Mr Thompson suggested.

His daughter was horrified. 'But there are thousands of them! Look! There are even police out to keep them off the road!' Susannah looked up a side street as they passed. 'The traffic has all stopped!' she said, unable to take in that she was the cause of the hold-up.

Her father smiled. 'And it will all be on the move again when you and your popular young man are married.'

Charles Haddon Spurgeon was Susannah's favourite preacher by far, and he was London's favourite preacher too. But one group of people didn't seem to like him at all. They were the newspaper reporters. It wasn't long after the young couple were married that Susannah began to collect newspaper cuttings in a scrapbook. Some reported things accurately, but others told awful lies about her husband.

'Do the papers worry you?' Susannah asked him, after one particularly nasty article.

Charles smiled. 'When I look at my darling wifey I'm so happy that nothing worries me at all.'

And when twin boys were born, nothing the papers could have said would have taken away Charles' joy! He was over the moon!

'Susannah seems to be taking a long time to recover from the twins' birth,' Charles commented to a doctor friend.

'She's probably just tired,' the doctor said. 'One baby's tiring enough, two is plain exhausting!'

Months later, Spurgeon spoke to his friend again, but the reply was not as reassuring. 'You're right,' he said. 'Susannah is not looking well and she seems to have no energy at all. Let's hope it will pass.' But it never did.

Although Susannah had times when she was a little better, she also had times when she couldn't get out of her bed for weeks.

'It makes me sad to see her so poorly,' Charles thought. 'Yet she hardly ever complains.'

'Is there anything I can get for you?' Spurgeon asked one day when Susannah was really quite ill.

She thought for a moment then grinned. 'You could get me an opal ring and a bullfinch that will sing to me.'

Her husband smiled back, unsure if she was joking and knowing that he certainly couldn't afford an opal ring.

'This is for you,' Charles said, a short time afterwards. Susannah opened the little box and saw an opal ring. 'An old lady sent it to you as a present,' he explained.

A few months later, Charles brought another gift for his sick wife - a bullfinch that would sing to her. She laughed at the little bird as it puffed out its chest and twittered. Maybe the man who led the singing in church, when she was a girl, had been more like a bullfinch than a robin!

In 1875, Charles handed his wife a book. 'It's the proof copy of my first book *Lectures to my Students*,' he explained. 'I've got to give it one last check then it goes for printing.'

Susannah looked at the book. 'I just wish every minister in England could have a copy,' she said.

Spurgeon looked serious. 'How much will you give to make that happen?' he asked.

It was his wife's turn to look serious. Did he really mean what he'd said? Suddenly, Susannah remembered some money she had saved and kept in an upstairs drawer. When she added that to what was in her bank account, she discovered that she had enough to buy a hundred copies of the book. That was the beginning of Mrs Spurgeon's Book Fund.

'Ministers earning less than £150 a year are invited to apply to Mrs Spurgeon for a copy of her husband's book,' their church magazine said the following month.

'Listen to this!' Susannah exclaimed to her husband, when she opened her mail one day. 'This poor minister gets only £60 a year and he hasn't bought a book for ten years!' 'Listen to this!' she said, another day. 'The man who wrote this letter hasn't been able to buy his children winter coats, let alone buy himself books.' 'Listen to ...' she began, when the next day's mail came.

'You're going to read me another sad letter,' Charles said, 'but don't let all the sadness get you down because what you're doing is making these poor folk happy.'

'I just can't take in what's happening,' Susannah told her husband, who had come to sit on her bed and talk to her. 'We're getting gifts of money sent to the Book Fund that almost exactly equal the letters applying for books. Today a gift of £25 came, and letters came asking for £25 worth of books. Isn't God good!'

Charles nodded, then looked around the room. 'What on earth are they?' he asked, pointing to a pile of tatty books in a corner.

His wife shook her head wearily. 'Unfortunately, people also send us books they seem to think might be useful.'

Spurgeon rose from the bed and picked up the top few books. 'Advice to Mothers! Letters to a Son! Butterflies of Britain!' he laughed. 'Are these meant to help poor preachers write their sermons?'

Susannah, who was by then desperately tired, shook her head. 'I'm afraid some people think that anything in the shape of a book should be sent to your tired wifey.'

Charles looked down at her pale face and his heart ached. He kissed her goodnight and she was asleep before he put the useless books back on the pile.

'You're as busy as someone with a full-time job,' Charles told his wife some years later. 'And you manage it all from your couch.'

'If I couldn't manage it from here, I couldn't do it at all,' Susannah replied.

Spurgeon shook his head. 'How I wish you could be up and about. I wish you could get out to see the cherry blossom.'

'I can enjoy the memory of cherry blossom,' she said. 'And before you get any sadder, I want you to sit down and hear some good news.'

Charles drew up a chair beside his wife and waited. If Susannah said she had good news, it was worth paying close attention.

'Today a friend brought £100 for the Book Fund,' she began. 'I was so pleased because a lot of applications have arrived in the last few days. Then in the second post, a bill came in for books I've bought in the last three months. I'd forgotten the bill was due. If the £100 had not come today, the Book Fund would have been £60 in debt!'

'God knew what you needed even though you'd forgotten,' Charles said. 'How like him.'

'I know there are so many things I can't do,' Susannah said, taking her husband's hand, 'but he's so good in blessing the few things I can do.'

Spurgeon nodded. 'There are hundreds of ministers who would agree with you there.'

'How many books have you sent out altogether?' a visitor asked Susannah in 1888.

She picked up a huge notebook,that was always beside her, and opened it. 'In 1881,' she said, 'we distributed 7,298 books and

10,517 printed sermons that Charles had preached. Last year, that's seven years later, we distributed 10,311 books and 21,227 sermons.'

The visitor whistled. 'I suppose they go all over England,' he commented.

Mrs Spurgeon smiled. 'They do indeed, and to Africa, the West Indies and other countries as well.'

'How do you know where to send them?' the young man asked.

'Ministers write asking for books.'

Her visitor grinned. 'You must get a lot of letters!'

Susannah turned the pages of her book. 'This column shows how many letters come each month.'

The young man ran his finger down the column, hardly able to take in what he was reading. 'March 481, April 513, May 498, June 532, July 657, August 755!' He sat back, too amazed to speak.

'I wonder if Mrs Spurgeon will manage to keep the Book Fund going,' an elder at the church asked, after Charles died in January, 1892. 'They were more in love than any couple I've ever known. She'll miss him most terribly.'

Susannah did miss Charles more than she was ever able to put into words even to her twin sons, who visited their mother nearly every day. But the Book Fund continued.

'When I think of how many books my darling husband needed for his work, it makes me want to do even more for the poor men who can't afford to buy books,' she told a friend, not long before she died.

'Have you any idea how many ministers you've sent books to?' her companion asked.

Susannah smiled. 'Yes,' she said. 'I've always kept careful accounts and I can tell you that over 25,000 ministers have had books from the Book Fund, and all because Charles challenged me to make my wish come true.'

'What wish was that?' her friend asked.

'I wished that every minister could have a copy of his first book, and he asked me what I'd do to make it happen. Since then I've just done what I could.'

FACT FILE

Queen Victoria: During the life time of Charles and Susannah Spurgeon, Queen Victoria was the ruling monarch of the British Empire. This was from 1837 until 1901. She was crowned Queen when she was only eighteen years old. She married Prince Albert who, in 1851, organised the Great Exhibition. This was held in London and had more than 19,000 exhibits from all over the world. The venue was the Crystal Palace in Hyde Park - a building constructed from glass and iron. Many beautiful firework displays were held there until it burnt down in 1936.

Keynote: Susannah Spurgeon didn't let her illness stop her working for God. Even though she couldn't get out of bed to see the cherry blossom, the work she did for God went round the world. God can use anyone who loves and trusts in him to do great things for his Kingdom.

Think: Susannah was amazed to see how God provided for the Book Fund. When she needed money to buy books, the exact amount was sent. This proved to her that God was in charge of everything. Think about all the wonderful things God provides for you every day. Do you trust him to supply you with everything that you need? Is there a difference between what we want and what we need?

Prayer: Thank you, God, for everything you give me. Thank you for friends and family, food and drink, shelter and clothing. You care for all the things that my body needs. Thank you, God, for caring for my soul. Thank you so much for all the love you give to me and for saving me from my sin. Amen.

Bethan Lloyd-Jones

Bethan felt very grown-up. 'This is exciting!' she told her eight-year old brother, as they scrambled onto the train at Paddington Station in London. Dr Phillips climbed on behind them and put their luggage on the rack.

'Now you'll be good on the train,' Mrs Phillips said. 'Don't lean out of the window and don't go near the doors. When you reach Newcastle Emlyn, your grandparents will be there to meet you.'

'You look after your brother,' Bethan's father said. 'And look after your little sister,' he added, smiling at Ieuan. 'It's time we got off,' he told his wife, 'or we'll be heading for Wales with them.'

The children looked out of the train window at their parents. Both were excited but both had butterflies in their tummies. A whistle blew. Dr Phillips and his wife waved. There was a shudder. There was a judder.

Then the train began to pull away from the platform. 'Goodbye! Goodbye!' the children shouted as they left. And Mrs Phillips discovered she was still waving after the train was well out of sight.

'You're very young to be travelling alone,' another passenger said to the children.

'I'm eight,' Ieuan told her, thinking that was really quite old.

'And I'm six,' announced Bethan, pulling herself up to be as big as she could possibly be.

'Are you going far?' the lady asked.

'We're going to our grandparents in Wales,' Bethan explained. 'There's a revival there, and we're going to go to the meetings.'

'But it's not the school holidays,' commented the woman.

'My dad says we can go to school any day but we may never be able to go to a revival again,' Ieuan said.

'That may be true,' smiled the lady.

Ieuan went on, 'Dad says that this is a good year for the church in Wales and that a long time from now people will still talk about the Welsh Revival of 1904.'

The lady spoke to them again some time later. 'Do your parents always speak Welsh to you?' she asked, having heard them before they left London.

'We speak Welsh all the time at home,' Bethan said.

'How did you learn to speak such good English then?' was the next question.

Bethan explained that they had learned it at school.

'You're clever children,' smiled the lady.

The train chugged along, and Bethan thought about home. 'I'll miss my baby brother while I'm in Wales,' she thought. 'Mum says he'll soon be crawling. I wonder if he'll learn to crawl while we're away.' She watched as the train went through the countryside and into a town. 'What's a revival like?' she wondered, as they passed a crowd of people at a market. 'Dad says there will be crowds there. And he says the singing will be wonderful.' As the blue-eyed little girl watched the world passing, she twiddled her long, dark hair.

Bethan found out that her father was right. She wrote home to tell her parents about it. 'The church is full for the meetings, and people stand as well. Some even sit on windowsills and on the pulpit steps. A lot of people were crying last night. Grandad says that they were very sorry for the wrong things they had done.' Even when she was an old lady, Bethan never forgot the Revival where hundreds of people came to believe in Jesus. 'Father was right to take us out of school and send us there,' she often thought. 'I wouldn't have liked to miss it.'

'Mum,' the girl said, when she was a teenager. 'I think we should call our home "The House of None-go-by" because it's always so full of people.' Her mother smiled.

'Well, your dad does have a habit of bringing people home with him.'

'But where does he find them all?' Bethan asked.

Mrs Phillips sat down. 'The Bible tells us to be hospitable; that means to make people welcome in our homes. And that's what we try to do. When Dad sees people needing help, he brings them back here, and we try to help them.'

Bethan laughed, 'Especially if they're Welsh! We've had Welsh tramps and Welsh alcoholics and sick Welsh people and sad Welsh people as well.'

Her mother laughed. 'The Welsh are special!' she said.

Bethan went out into their beautiful garden and sat on the swing. A young man walked up to her. He was using crutches. 'The peace of this place does me good,' he told the girl. 'I don't know what I'd have done if your parents hadn't taken me in.' Swinging slowly backwards and forwards, she listened as he told his story. 'When I was injured in the war, I'd nowhere to go and nobody to look after me. Dr Phillips heard about me and came to the hospital and brought me back here. He says I can stay until I find a room of my own and a job.'

'But there's no hurry to do that,' Bethan said.

The ex-soldier looked at the girl. 'She's just like her parents,' he thought. 'She'll always want to help people too.'

When Bethan was fifteen years old, she met a boy called Martyn Lloyd-Jones at a church service. Fourteen years later, in January 1927, they were married. By then they had both trained to be doctors. But Bethan knew that she was not to be a doctor's wife. Martyn believed that God was calling him to preach. Soon after their marriage, the newly-weds set out for Wales where Martyn was to be a minister in a church called Sandfields in Aberavon. Although Bethan was brought up in a Christian home and had always gone to church, it was shortly after they moved to Wales that she really knew that she was a Christian.

'We enjoy the Women's Meetings so much,' a lady told Bethan one day. 'Could we have an evening Bible study as well?' Those standing around nodded their heads.

'I'll ask the Doctor,' Mrs Lloyd-Jones said.

'It's funny how she calls her husband the Doctor,' a new girl to the congregation commented.

Her friend smiled. 'Everyone does.'

'He's quite happy for us to have an evening Bible study, so long as it doesn't keep anyone away from the prayer meeting,' Bethan told the women, after she'd discussed it with her husband. That was the beginning of a meeting that came to mean a lot to the girls and women of Sandfields.

'Mrs Lloyd-Jones is so easy to talk to,' a girl in the church told her friend. 'I'd a problem that was really getting me down and I didn't know who to go to for help. Then I thought of the Doctor's wife, and she was great. Although she's so busy, she didn't make me feel I was keeping her back from other things. And she gave me such good advice.'

Her friend smiled. 'You're not the first to go to her for help. And nobody's ever turned away.'

But it wasn't only the women of Sandfields that Bethan was able to help. As she sat at the back of the church one day, a thin, grey-haired man with an amazing moustache appeared in church. 'Pray for him to be converted,' she was told. 'He's a wild man.

He'll do anything for a fight. If he has a few drinks there's no stopping him.'

Bethan prayed.

'He's so bad that he always takes two of his buddies when he goes looking for a fight,' she was informed later.

'Why does he do that?' the minister's wife asked.

'So they can haul him off his victim when he's knocked him unconscious. Even McCann knows that he's liable to kill someone.'

On just the second Sunday the man was in church, he became a Christian.

'It's a shame that McCann can't read,' a woman said to Bethan one evening, as they left a meeting in the church hall.

'Can he not read?' she asked.

'Not a word. And it's a pity because now that he's a Christian, he'd love to read the Bible.'

Mr McCann could hear what was being said, and Bethan noticed that he was hanging his head and shuffling his feet uncomfortably. 'Can you read anything at all?' she asked the new Christian gently.

'No,' he explained. 'I never learned. I didn't go to school much because I was always running away, so I didn't ever learn to read.'

Bethan thought about Mark McCann and she remembered her childhood home. 'It can't be too difficult to teach an adult to read,' she thought. 'Mother taught a man in his seventies, and they seemed to manage all right. And it's not all that difficult to learn; even small children do that!' These thoughts came and went in just a few seconds. 'I'm sure I can teach you to read, if you would like to try,' she told the amazed Mr McCann. He jumped at the offer, and they arranged a time for his first lesson.

'Let's start with this,' Bethan said, pointing to the words in her daughter's book, *The Little Red Hen.* But not a single word would go into the man's head. The next lesson was the same and the next. As they settled down the following week, Mark pushed *The Little Red Hen* away. 'I don't want to read about hens,' he said. 'I want to read the Bible.' Bethan reached for a Bible with good-sized print and opened it at John's gospel. Pointing with his finger, Mark started with Jesus' words, 'I am the good shepherd.'

'It looks as though he might learn after all,' Bethan told the Doctor that evening. 'Either that or he has a good memory for words and he's not reading it at all.'

'I think he needs spectacles,' Mrs Lloyd-Jones said after one evening service. 'Mark's eyesight doesn't seem very good.'

'Trust a doctor to notice that!' someone commented.

Spectacles helped Mr McCann a lot - or so it seemed.

'Let's try something from Mark's gospel,' Bethan suggested. But when they turned the pages back to Mark, the poor man couldn't read a single word!

'Funny, isn't it?' Mark McCann said. 'I can read John, but I can't read Mark, even though it's my own name!'

Bethan turned back to the book of John. 'Let's stick to this then,' she decided. And Mr McCann gradually learned to read his Bible.

'He's so excited about it,' people said. 'He just loves God's Word.'

Not long after her husband learned to read, Mrs McCann arrived at the Lloyd-Jones' door. Mark was very ill, and she wanted someone to visit him. As the Doctor was away, Bethan went herself. She discovered that he was dying. But, in the weeks that followed, Mark McCann spent many hours with his new spectacles on, tracing the words of John's gospel with his finger and sounding them out one by one.

'I love meeting Mrs Lloyd-Jones,' a lady in Aberavon told her neighbour. 'When she asks how I am, she really wants to know. It's not only my body; she wants to know how my soul is as well.'

The other woman nodded her head. 'So I've heard,' she said. 'But I doubt that she'd be interested in someone like me who doesn't go to the church at all.'

'She would if you needed her,' was the reply.

Suddenly the poor woman was in tears. 'If ever I needed help, I need it now,' she wept.

The two neighbours went to church together the next Sunday, and the woman was able to speak to Bethan. 'She was such a help,' sighed the relieved lady, as they walked home in the evening sun. But I hope she doesn't tell anyone what we talked about.'

Her neighbour shook her head. 'If you told Mrs Lloyd-Jones something private, wild horses won't tear it out of her.'

After twelve years in Wales, Martyn and Bethan Lloyd-Jones moved with their two daughters to London. He was to be minister of a church there for the next thirty years.

'I don't know how we get people to go home after the service,' one of the men in the London congregation said, following an evening service, not long after they moved. 'So many want to speak to the Doctor.'

His friend looked around the building and smiled.

'What's so funny?' he was asked. 'Just look at that,' his friend said. The two men turned round and looked at the queues of people. 'What do you see?'

'A whole line of people waiting to talk to the Doctor,' was the reply. Then the man broke into a wide smile. 'And an even longer queue waiting to talk to his wife!'

Just as he said those words, an elderly lady passed. 'I knew Mrs Lloyd-Jones' parents,' she told the two men. 'They always had time to speak to people and to try to help them. Bethan is exactly the same. What a difference people like her make, by opening their hearts and homes.'

The lady walked slowly on. 'What she said is right enough,' one man said to the other. 'But Bethan Lloyd-Jones has done more than that. I heard her say once that her job was to keep her husband in the pulpit. And she's done that too. If she hadn't been there to look after him, he'd have worn himself out years ago.'

FACT FILE

Welsh Language: The Welsh language is a Celtic language that has been spoken in Wales since about the time the Romans left Britain. Today, Welsh is taught in schools throughout Wales, even though English is used there more widely than in the past. Every year, there is a festival in Wales called the Eisteddfod. Prizes are awarded for Welsh songs and poetry.

Keynote: The revival that Bethan went to see happened in Wales in 1904-5. Revival is a time when Christians feel extra close to God and others come to believe in him. It is a special time. Revival can happen inside one person or inside many people at the same time. When God sends revival to Christians, they become more enthusiastic about obeying him and telling others about him. If you are a Christian, you should pray for a revival in your own life.

Think: Bethan's parents loved to look after people and invite them into their home. This is called being hospitable. Hospitality is when someone shows love and care to a visitor in their home. The Bible tells us to be hospitable. You may not own or have a home of your own, but you can always show love to someone new at school or in youth group and be hospitable in this way. When you are older and live in a home of your own, you can show God's love to others by using your home to look after them.

Pray: Thank you, God, for my home. Help me to be loving and caring to all who visit it. Help me to tell them about you. Amen

Edith Schaeffer

Edith looked at the scrambled egg and toast that was put on the table for her tea. 'I don't want eggs,' she said. 'I want what my amah's having' (amah means nanny).

Mrs Seville looked at her five-year-old daughter. 'Chinese food is far too rich for you to have all the time. You can have it one day a week just now, and perhaps when you're six, you can have it two days a week.'

The child thought about her mother's suggestion. 'That means I can have it every day by the time I'm twelve.'

Her mother smiled. 'Let's wait and see about that,' she said.

But although Edith ate her scrambled eggs, she had her Chinese food, too, because she often visited the Chinese families in the mission compound just as they were sitting down to eat.

'Funny how she knows just when to come,' the local people said to each other. 'And she has good taste,' one of them commented, 'because she told me that our food looks nicer as well as tastes nicer than what she has at home.'

'Let's play at houses,' Edith suggested to her friend one morning. 'I'll be the mum, and you can be the baby.'

For a while the game went well, then the baby grew fretful and started pretend crying.

'Shh, shh,' Edith said, patting her pal on the back. But the wailing grew louder and the patting harder. 'Shhh, shhhh,' roared the play mother. Her pretend daughter yelled at the top of her voice.

'Fichaw! Fichaw!' Edith screamed to make herself heard.

Mrs Seville, who had heard the racket, came running. Taking her daughter by the shoulders, she looked right into her eyes. 'Don't let me hear you say that again!' she said firmly. Edith looked puzzled. 'That's not a polite thing to say.'

'But that's what my friends say,' the girl cried, 'and they don't get a row.'

Her mother smiled. 'I know they do,' she said. 'But it means shut up, and I'm sure you were telling your baby to be quiet, not to shut up!'

Edith's eyes sparkled as she thought that with all the wailing her pretend baby had been doing, perhaps shut up was the right thing to say after all!

'There are disadvantages in being a working missionary mother,' Mrs Seville commented to her husband that evening. 'Although we dress as the Chinese do and you have your head shaved, apart from your pigtail, it's the girls who are most Chinese. It's just a pity that they pick up every slang expression they hear and don't seem interested in the polite ones!'

Her husband laughed. 'That's the price we pay for us both serving the Lord and relying on an amah to look after the girls.'

Mrs Seville smiled. 'It's a very small price. And it gives opportunities too. Even though Edith is just a little girl, I often hear her telling her friends about Jesus. She seems to have a real gift for sitting down beside other children and just talking to them about the Lord.'

'I hope that's a gift she'll continue to use as she grows up,' her husband concluded. 'Then all her slang language will have been worth it.'

'It's today Elsa comes home,' Edith said excitedly.

'You miss your sister when she's away at school,' her amah nodded. 'What are you looking forward most to doing with her?'

The child knew without thinking what the answer was. 'We'll play Pilgrim's Progress.'

Amah laughed. 'That's been your favourite game since the very first time you heard the story.'

And before the day was out, the game was well underway.

'You be Pilgrim,' Elsa told her little sister, as she handed her a pillowcase stuffed with things. Edith threw it over her shoulder. 'Now you climb up to the top of the hill on your hands and knees and leave your burden at the cross.'

Starting at the bottom of the stairs, Edith crawled up slowly, hauling her burden behind her. By the time she got to the top landing, she really was glad to dump it down. 'The burden of sin has rolled off!' she yelled down the stairs to her sister.

Elsa clapped her hands, 'Hallelujah!' she shouted.

'I hate China!' Edith Seville announced soon afterwards. 'It's a cruel place.'

'I've never heard you say such a thing before,' her father replied, looking surprised and worried. 'What happened when you were out?'

The little girl rubbed her eyes to stop herself crying, but didn't manage. 'I was going in a rickshaw to my friend's house.

The coolie was running along when a little boy toddled out from the side of the road. The coolie saw him but he kept on running. I screamed, but he just ran right over the little boy like he was rubbish on the street.'

'Was mother with you?' Mr Seville asked. 'Yes,' the girl wept, 'if she hadn't been there, I'd have fallen out of the rickshaw. I was leaning so far out to see if the boy was all right.'

'Was he?' the man asked gently. Edith wiped the tears from her eyes.

'I don't know.'

Mr Seville put his arm around his young daughter. 'This world is a wonderful place,' he said. 'God saw to that. But we human beings can be cruel and hurtful and do terrible things. Let's hope that someone came along to lift up the child and look after him.'

'I wish I could have done that,' said Edith. 'I would have cuddled him better.'

'Let's do something really nice for a while,' Mrs Seville suggested, because her daughter was so upset. 'What would you like to do?'

Edith looked out the window. 'Could we take out my kites?' she asked.

Her mother smiled. 'You always choose to do that when something's upsetting you.'

The pair of them took Edith's box kites to a little hill near the mission compound. Within minutes, the kites were dancing above them, weaving in and out of each other, sometimes soaring high into the sky then diving towards the ground only to rise again like birds.

'This will do her good,' Mrs Seville thought. 'It's hard to be sad when you're flying a kite.'

After a wonderful half hour the pair made their way home. Soon afterwards, the Seville family left China and returned to America. It was 1919.

'What do you remember about China?' a friend asked Edith years later, when they were both students.

'I often think about my time there,' the girl replied, and then told her companion about the little boy who was knocked over and about her kites. 'And although I didn't see it, I knew that girl babies were sometimes so unwanted that they were left out to die. That upset me because I was a girl. I used to wonder what would have happened to me if I'd been born into a Chinese home.'

'It sounds an awful place,' her friend commented.

Edith thought for a minute. 'Terrible things did happen there, but it was such a strange mixture. There was great beauty and awful hurt. Even though I was a child when we left, I still remember enjoying the beautiful things and wanting to cuddle everyone's hurts better.'

'And you've not changed a bit!' her friend said, thinking of the lovely little birthday present Edith had made for her, and of the times she'd been able to talk over her problems with her friend.

'Good morning, Mrs Schaeffer,' Francis said. 'How is my new wife this wonderful morning?' It was 1935, and Edith Seville and Francis Schaeffer had been married the previous day.

Edith grinned. 'Your wife is wonderfully well and wonderfully happy! Did we really get married yesterday, or is this just a dream and I'm about to wake up and discover that you're not real at all?'

As they drove off on their honeymoon, the young couple discussed their future.

'Remind me again how old you are,' Francis asked, although he knew already.

'I'm an old woman of twenty,' laughed Edith.

Her husband looked serious for a minute. 'I wonder what we'll be doing twenty years from now. Will you still love me?'

'Yes,' Edith answered. 'I promised you that at our wedding!'

'And will we have a houseful of children?' he went on.

Edith leant over and gave Francis a kiss. 'Let's just wait and see,' she said.

Twenty years later was a time of great change in the Schaeffers' life. They stood outside a large Swiss chalet, looking up at the mountains around them, breathing in the clean air, and dreaming their dreams.

'L'Abri is a good name for this place,' Edith said. 'It means shelter, and I hope it will be a shelter to those who come to stay with us here.'

'There's some work to be done before it's fit for anyone,' Francis laughed, 'apart from our own four children of course.'

'Let's go and see,' his wife suggested. They went from room to room.

'That ceiling will need repaired,' Francis said, looking at some cracks.

'And those pot-bellied stoves really must come out,' said Edith.

'We could drape curtains on that wall.' 'Those light shades look as though they've been chewed!' 'This floor is dangerously uneven.' 'Ugh! I couldn't live with that colour of paint!' There seemed to be no end of things to do.

'Do you hope to make L'Abri a conference centre?' one of their new neighbours asked.

Edith thought for a moment. 'No,' she replied. 'It's going to be a home – our home – and we'll share it with whoever comes.'

The neighbour looked up at the chalet and thought of all the work that was being done on it, mostly by the Schaeffers themselves. 'You must be expecting a lot of important people,' he said.

'Everyone who comes will be important,' Edith smiled. 'Even if nobody else thinks so.'

'What do you mean?' enquired the neighbour.

'Everyone is important to God,' Edith explained. 'We hope that this house will be a place where people can find quietness and healing and also the peace of God.'

'How do you do that?' her friend asked.

The heavy rucksack the man carried reminded Edith of her childhood game of Pilgrim's Progress. She told him that Jesus had died to take away the burden of sin, and that when she asked his forgiveness, God had given her his gift of peace.

'Are you sure I'll be welcome at L'Abri?' Sarah asked her university friend.

'I'm certain,' was the answer. 'Everybody's welcome at L'Abri.' And when the pair arrived, Sarah discovered how true that was. She wrote home to her sister, 'What a place this is! There are people everywhere. Francis Schaeffer answers questions all the time: by the fire, round the barbecue, even when we're out walking. And the questions! You have no idea the hard things that are discussed here. I had lots of questions myself when I came. I just didn't understand what the Bible was all about. But when I listen to Francis Schaeffer, I feel I'm beginning to understand. Perhaps by the time I leave, I'll believe in Jesus. The longer I stay, the more I want that to be true.'

'You wrote about Francis Schaeffer,' Sarah's sister said, after the girl had returned home. 'What about his wife? What's she like?'

A smile crossed Sarah's face. 'At first I couldn't work out what she did,' the girl explained. 'Then I realised what an amazing woman she is. While her husband answered difficult questions, she cared for people's problems. If my heart were breaking, Edith Schaeffer would be the person I'd go to. Not only that,' Sarah went on, 'but she spread beauty all around her. Every room had wild flowers and welcome notes in it. Even though there are so many people coming and going,

Edith Schaeffer makes L'Abri a home, not a conference centre.'

'She sounds like my kind of person,' her sister concluded.

The two girls walked along the road towards their home. 'Did the Schaeffers make you feel you had to become a Christian?' Sarah's sister asked.

'No,' was the reply. 'Absolutely not. We were able to ask all the questions that worried us, but that was all.'

'And did you become a Christian?'

'Yes,' Sarah stopped and smiled at her sister. 'Yes I did. But do you know something? It wasn't because Francis Schaeffer answered my questions - it was because Edith Schaeffer loved me. And I'm sure there are hundreds of people who have become Christians because God has used the pair of them.'

Her sister looked interested. 'I've got lots of questions myself,' she announced. 'Could we go to L'Abri together next summer?'

Sarah grinned from ear to ear. 'Try to stop us,' she said.

L'Abri has now spread beyond Switzerland, and although Francis and Edith Schaeffer have now gone to heaven, there are people in centres in several countries who continue the work they started.

FACT FILE

Kite-flying: Kite-flying is a very popular pastime in the Far East. In China, the ninth day of the ninth month is a kite-flying festival when grown-ups as well as children go out to fly kites. Sometimes there are kite-flying competitions where kite owners try to cut the cords of other kites. The winner is the first one to cut another kite's cord. When the kite falls to the ground the winner can keep it for himself.

Keynote: When Edith and Francis started 'L'Abri', they wanted everyone to feel welcome there. Anyone who wanted to come and stay with them could do just that. Everybody who came was important - no one was looked down on. It is good to treat people fairly. Jesus was friends with rich and poor people. We should be the same.

Think: Edith used to play a game when she was little in which she would pretend that a great big sack on her shoulder was the burden of sin. It was only Jesus who could get rid of the burden of sin. Sin can be a burden to us because it makes our lives miserable. We need to get rid of it, or it will be impossible for us to enter heaven. Jesus is the only one who can get rid of our sins for us. He can do this because he died on the cross instead of us.

Prayer: Thank you, God, for forgiveness of sins. I am sorry for disobeying you. Help me to love you and obey you more each day. Amen.

Sabina Wurmbrand

Sabina watched as her mother lit the candles one by one until all seven flickered into life. This was the time of the week the girl loved best. 'We're all here,' she told her mother.

Mrs Oster smiled. 'And in good time for the Sabbath meal.' The smell of chicken livers cooking wafted through from the kitchen, mingling with the warmth of new-baked bread.

'Come now,' Mr Oster said. 'The Sabbath meal is ready.' The large family sat down around the table, with the light of seven candles reflecting in all their eyes. Sabina's father prayed, and in the silence that followed she thought about all the other Jewish families in Romania who were gathering for their Sabbath meals.

The meal over, the seven-year-old curled in the corner of a couch where she could watch her father. He stood at the window, his skullcap on the back of his head and his prayer shawl draped over his shoulders. She watched as he fingered the fringes that hung from it, swaying backwards and forwards as he did so.

Mr Oster wasn't exactly singing, but from somewhere deep inside himself came the sound of a melody that reached back hundreds of years.

Sabina thought about her grandfather and great-grandfather who had said the same words. Sabina wondered if one day she would have sons who would say the same words in the same way?

'Are you praying, Papa?' the girl asked. Her words seemed to take time to come to her father's attention.

'Yes,' he said eventually, 'I'm praying.'

'Who are you praying for, Papa?' she went on.

Slowly, Mr Oster turned round to face his daughter and the other members of the family. 'I'm praying for our fathers and mothers, for our brothers and sisters, and for our children and our children's children.'

Sabina looked puzzled. 'But your children don't have any children,' she queried.

Her father's face took on a faraway look. 'Every Jew prays for his children's children,' he explained. 'It's part of the promise.'

As soon as she opened her eyes the next morning, Sabina knew it was the Sabbath by the heat in the room. 'That's nice,' she thought, snuggling her dressing gown around her. 'Imagine how cold it must be in Gentile houses this morning,' she said, looking out the window at the snow. 'They've got to wait until their fires are cleared out and lit before they have any heat. Because we don't work on the Sabbath, our fire is kept on all night, and our home is lovely and warm.'

'Papa,' the girl said, when her father came home from the synagogue, 'why do Jews not have a Christmas?'

Mr Oster's face coloured. 'Can a seven-year-old use that word and ask a question like that?'

It was Sabina's turn to blush. She knew that she couldn't say the word 'Christ', and she'd not realized that by saying 'Christmas' she'd broken that rule.

'This is the time of year when Gentiles celebrate the coming of the Messiah. But they're badly wrong. The Messiah has not yet come. We are still in the days of waiting for God's Promised One. The one they celebrate at this time of year is a man, and one who broke the Law at that.' Sabina looked shocked. 'Their so-called messiah was put to death for acting as though he was Jehovah himself.'

Mr Oster draped his prayer shawl round his shoulders and stood looking out the window. It was as though he could see to the farthest parts of the world. His fingers seemed to number the fringes, and then the low sound began inside him. It grew gradually louder until the room seemed full of the noise of it. As she listened, Sabina felt a very special connection to her people, the Jews, and for the first time she began to understand about children's children. The melody of her father's prayer flowed through her. What would the future bring for her and her children, she wondered, as her father's prayer drew to a close.

Sabina learned when to ask her father questions and when not to. 'Sometimes the look in his eyes hurts so much that I can't interrupt it,' she thought, wondering what the hurt was about. 'And other times, though not often nowadays, Papa's eyes look like sunshine, and then I can ask him anything.'

She watched and waited for his sunshine eyes. One day, when her father's eyes were shining, Sabrina asked the question. She was nearly sixteen and she knew she had to ask.

'Why are Jews such a sad people, Papa? We have the promise of the Messiah to look forward to, yet there is a deep sadness inside us.'

It was as though shutters slammed over her father's eyes, as though a brick had hit him, as though a great burden was bending his back. 'Sit down,' he said. And she did.

By the time Sabina stood up again, she was helping to carry the burden. She had learned the secret of Jewish sadness and felt that it would never let her go.

'I just can't take it in,' she thought, as she tossed and turned in bed all night. 'The man called Jesus broke Jehovah's Law; that's why they crucified him. How can it be that nearly two thousand years later people hate the Jews for putting him to death when it was his own fault? How can people hate me for what happened all that time ago? How can they hate my children's children?'

'We're living in a nightmare,' Sabina told her boyfriend, Richard. 'Jews are being persecuted throughout Eastern Europe.'

'Forget it,' he said. 'I want us to forget we're Jews and enjoy ourselves. What will we do tonight? The pictures? A walk? A drink?'

Sabina shook herself. 'Okay,' she said. 'Let's forget the world. Let's go for a drink, then find a film.'

Richard grinned. 'Anything for you!'

Perhaps it was a romantic film that made them think of wedding bells - for Richard

Wurmbrand and Sabina were married in 1936.

When Sabina married, she no doubt assumed that her family life would be much as hers had been. After all, she had married a Jew, a man from the same background as herself. But that was not to be. Before long, Richard became interested in the Christian faith. That was bad enough, but what followed was to his new young wife quite shocking.

'A Christian!' Sabina breathed, too shocked to say the word louder. 'But a Jew can't become a Christian,' she whispered, swallowing every time she used the word with Christ in it. 'If you do, that's the end of our marriage and our love.' It didn't matter what Richard tried to say, or how tender and loving he was, it was as though their marriage had died. He tried every way he could think of to interest Sabina in his newly found faith, but he hit a stone wall every time. Then he had an idea.

'Would you like to go to the pictures?' he asked brightly one night. Sabina looked surprised, then agreed. Richard took her to the most disgusting film that was on, and stayed until Sabina was sick of it.

'Want to party?' he asked. His wife thought that would be an improvement on the film they'd seen. But she was wrong. Very cunningly, Richard had done his homework and he took her to a party where people were horribly drunk and awful things were happening.

'Let's go home,' Sabina begged.

'Not at all,' he laughed.

'Please!' she hissed. 'Let's get out of here.' These outings brought the young woman to her senses. She realised that what she'd seen had been life without God, and she knew from the change in her husband, that the God who made a difference was the Lord Jesus Christ. Sabina Wurmbrand became a Christian. It's hard to imagine how her family and friends must have felt when she told them that she believed that Jesus was the Messiah.

It was 1943, the Second World War was raging, and Romanian Jews were being deported to Nazi concentration camps.

'You're so thin,' Richard said sadly, looking at what seemed like just a shadow of the girl he'd married. He put his arm around Sabina and steered her to a chair.

'How much more can happen?' she asked. 'How much more?' She shuddered. 'My parents, my sisters and my brother all dead, all dead in the camps,' she said weakly. 'Why did the Nazis kill them? Why?'

'May God forgive them,' prayed Richard. Sabina looked at him and nodded.

'May God forgive them,' she repeated. 'And I'll pray that prayer over and over again until I mean it with all my heart.' And that's exactly what Sabina Wurmbrand did.

'Let me introduce you,' the editor of the most popular newspaper in Romania said to the men on either side of him, the following year. 'Richard, this is Stephen; Stephen, meet Richard.'

Stephen held out his hand. 'Well, am I pleased to meet you!' he said. 'I've heard so much about you and your wife.'

Wurmbrand smiled. 'She's quite a woman,' he said.

'Our friend here has told me about the work you do,' Stephen commented. 'But I'd really like to hear about your wife's work.'

'How long have you got?' laughed Richard, having had a nod from the newspaper editor assuring him that it was safe to talk. They sat down together in the soundproof newspaper office.

'Sabina has had a busy war,' Richard began. 'She's smuggled many Jewish children out of the ghettos. Every day she preaches to the people gathered in bomb shelters. She and I have helped start the Jewish-Christian Church. And she's one of the Romanian underground's most enthusiastic workers. If this war is won,' he concluded, 'it will be won by the likes of my wife. My job is to preach the gospel; her job is very much more hands-on helping.'

'How have the pair of you kept out of prison?' Stephen asked. Richard nodded in the direction of the editor. 'Thanks to my good friend here,' he explained. 'Although we've been arrested several times, he's managed to say a word for us where it matters.'

Communism settled its grey cloud on Europe after the Second World War, and Sabina did what she could to help those who were caught in the poverty that followed.

'What's the programme for this week?' Richard asked most Mondays. 'Helping in the soup kitchen,' she replied sometimes. 'Smuggling food to refugees.' 'Trying to get salt to Budapest.' 'I must get on with planning the camp for religious leaders.'

Each time he asked the question, the answer seemed to be different. 'Life's not boring,' he commented from time to time.

Sabina looked up. 'Boredom? What does that feel like?' she grinned.

'It's 1948,' Sabina wrote in her diary, 'and everybody outside Europe thinks the War is over and peace has broken out. But the only thing that's broken today is my heart. Richard has disappeared! Little Mihai is crying for his daddy. How can a boy understand that his daddy has disappeared? Someone told me that he was lifted off the street and driven away. But where? And for how long?' The waiting time had begun.

'Your husband has gone and left you!' two members of the secret police told Sabina, some months later. 'Divorce him and forget he ever existed.' She looked at Mihai. 'Can I forget my husband?' she asked. 'Should I forget my son's father?' 'Think about it,' one of the men said, trying to sound kind. 'We'll give you time to think about it.'

Clocks all over Romania ticked the minutes away; days full of minutes, months full of minutes, and years full of thousands of minutes.

'Divorce him!' the secret policeman hissed. 'He doesn't exist any longer. Divorce him and give your child a new father.'

Sabina and Mihai's eyes met. 'Richard will hardly recognise him. Mihai has grown such a lot in the last three years,' she thought, then said aloud, 'I will never divorce my husband.'

The man turned on his heels and stomped towards the door. 'You're running out of time!' he growled as he left.

'I thank God for that,' Sabina told her son. 'Every day that passes, we are nearer seeing your father again on earth or in heaven.' But Sabina Wurmbrand didn't spend her time idly waiting, even though the authorities refused to allow her to work. She was as busy as ever helping Jews and spreading the gospel and encouraging Christian people to keep on believing, whatever happened to them.

'You'll take me away from my son?' Sabina asked, horrified.

'You've brought it on yourself,' she was told. 'Now you'll pay for your stubbornness.'

She did, with three years' hard labour. 'They can do what they like to me,' she often thought, as she worked on building a canal, 'but they can't stop me praying.' And as she loaded boxcars with stones, she prayed, 'Father, forgive them. And be with Richard and Mihai; hold them close to yourself.'

In the fifteen years following her release, Sabina worked to help both Jews and Gentiles, and Mihai grew to be a young man. From time to time they heard news of Richard, but the last they heard was that he was dead. For the first time in all their years apart, Sabina believed it.

'Mum! What's wrong?' Mihai yelled, as Sabina slumped to the floor sometime later. She had collapsed as she answered the phone. The shock of hearing Richard's voice was too much for her. Completely out of the blue, he had been released from hospital prison. And a little time later, looking just like skin and bone, he arrived on their doorstep. That was the beginning of the end of Sabina's lonely journey and the start of their work together to tell the West about the reality of Communism as well as helping the persecuted church worldwide.

FACT FILE

Ghetto: This word is used today to describe an area in a city where one group of people or a nationality live. The word was originally used hundreds of years ago to describe an area of a city where Jewish people lived. During the Second World War, Jewish people were once again forced to live in ghettos. The Nazi government under Adolf Hitler would not allow Jewish people to live with other nationalities. These ghettos were not safe, as the Nazis would often raid them in order to capture Jews and take them off to concentration camps. Men and women like Richard and Sabina Wurmbrand did all they could to help these people escape.

Keynote: Sabina realised that her husband Richard had changed for the better because of Jesus Christ. Jesus Christ has the power to cleanse you from all your sin and change your life for the better too.

Think: Sabina forgave her enemies - even those who had killed her family. Jesus tells us to love our enemies. Would you love your enemies? Do you find it hard to forgive? If you do, ask Jesus to help you.

Prayer: Lord Jesus, thank you for being my friend. Help me to love other people and treat them in a way that I would want to be treated. Give me the strength to love those who hate me. Forgive me for my sin and help me to forgive others. Amen.

Ruth Bell Graham

Wang Nai Nai called to the little girl to wave goodbye to her dad, who was going off to work in the hospital. The child came running, waved till there was no longer any sight of her dad, then gave her amah a hug. These two, a Chinese woman and an American child, loved each other. Ruth, when she looked at her amah, saw a face so lined with laughter that it was beautiful. Others also saw lines caused by the hardship of many generations of poverty and things that the child was far too young to understand. There were no lines on Ruth's face apart from when she screwed up her eyes in the sunlight, and when she looked into Wang Nai Nai's twinkling eyes, there was nothing at all to trouble her.

A second girl ran into the room and was caught in her amah's arms.

'Where were you?' Wang Nai Nai asked. 'You didn't come when I called you to wave to your dad.'

'I'm sorry,' Rosa said. 'I didn't hear you.'

The woman nodded. 'Let me guess,' she said. 'You were reading a book.'

Rosa grinned and nodded. 'It's a good book too.'

'I've never met a family like the Bells for reading books. And when you read, you seem to leave the world behind and go into the world of your storybook.'

'That's an idea!' Rosa said, clapping her hands in excitement. 'Let's play at Alice in Wonderland.'

Ruth's eyes shone. 'You be Alice, Rosa, and Amah, you can be the Mad Hatter.'

There was no response from Wang Nai Nai, and when the girls eventually tracked her down to her bedroom, they knew they would have to do without the Mad Hatter, because their amah was sitting on a low stool singing from a book of Chinese hymns that had been carefully bound together by hand.

'She can be the Queen of Hearts,' Rosa whispered, as they went downstairs, 'because she doesn't come into the story for a while.'

'Mummy,' both girls said together. 'Can we please have clothes from the barrel to play with?'

Mrs Bell looked at her daughters. 'You are both growing so quickly, I was thinking we'd have to look in the barrel anyway.'

Rosa and Ruth had a happy morning going through a barrelful of clothes, deciding what could be used for Alice in Wonderland and what the girls had grown into.

It was only after the barrel was repacked that Mrs Bell realised Ruth was looking sad. 'What's the matter?' she asked the seven-year-old.

Ruth tried to explain. 'All the Chinese people wear pretty colours and shiny material, and our clothes are never as nice.'

Mrs Bell pulled Ruth on to her knee with one arm and put her other arm round Rosa. 'People back home in America are very kind to missionaries such as ourselves,' she said. 'They give money for doctors, like Dad, and they pay for all the things in the hospital too. Not only that, but they keep their children's best clothes after they have outgrown them and send them halfway round the world so that you can have good, warm clothes to wear in the cold climate of China. It's really very kind of them.'

'I know that,' Ruth told her mum. 'But sometimes I'd like a new dress of my own.'

Wang Nai Nai came into the room. 'I'm ready to be the Queen of Hearts,' she announced. Ruth, forgetting all about new dresses, set her mind on being the Mad Hatter.

Saying goodbye was something Ruth got used to doing. Each day she waved to her father as he left the mission house to go to work in the hospital. Other missionaries came and went over the years and each had to be welcomed and waved goodbye.

There was a time when the Bells waved to their Chinese friends, especially Wang Nai Nai, as they left for a trip to America. But even saying goodbye to her amah was not as hard as what was to come.

When Ruth was twelve years old, Rosa was sent away to the Pyeng Yang Foreign School in North Korea. For a whole year, Ruth tried to push out of her mind the thought that she would soon be going to join her sister. But it wouldn't go away. She begged her parents to allow her to stay at home with them in China. Many nights she cried herself to sleep. And the night before she left for school, she prayed that she would die before morning. She didn't.

On 2nd September 1933, thirteen-year-old Ruth was one of five missionary children who climbed on board the Nagasake Maru that was berthed in the Whangpoo River. She felt as though her heart would break as the gangway was dragged on board the boat, then the ropes were loosened on the quayside. And when the vessel creaked into motion and edged into the muddy midstream, she knew that childhood was behind her, and happiness too. Ruth Bell didn't believe that away from her parents, apart from her amah, and outside of China she could find any happiness at all.

'There's the Yangtze!' one of the children shouted, as they came to where the muddy Whangpoo joined the even muddier, great Yangtze River. There were excited runnings and shoutings, but nothing stirred in Ruth. It was the same when the Yangtze flowed into the East China Sea. Each landmark made Ruth more miserable, and she thought her misery was complete when she eventually arrived at the Pyeng Yang School.

For a time, she was so utterly homesick it was as though she was split in two, her heart in China and her body in North Korea. It was only when she became ill and had to spend some time in the school infirmary, that Ruth found any comfort at all, and that was because she spent her time there reading the Psalms in the Bible. Although she was just thirteen years old, she read all one hundred and fifty psalms.

At first it surprised Ruth to read that King David, who wrote most of the Psalms, had sometimes felt miserable too. As she read on, she was comforted to discover that God had been with King David in his miserable times and he was with her too.

Four years later, Ruth, having finished school, was again being bundled off on a journey. It was 1937. Japan had attacked China near Beijing, and Japanese forces were beginning to overrun the northern part of the country.

Dr Bell, convinced that there was going to be war, was doing what he could in the hospital to prepare for it. Mrs Bell was busy too, packing and repacking Ruth's belongings for her to sail to America where she was to attend Wheaton College. And Ruth? She was sure of two things: that she would never marry and that God wanted her to be a missionary. 'So why,' she asked her mother as they folded her clothes, 'do I need to go all the way to college in America?'

The Bells were delighted with what their daughter wanted to do with her life, but they still put her on a ship for America, knowing that she had a lot to learn and that college would do her good.

The kind of freedom Ruth had at college was completely new to her, and she made such good use of it, that she was nearly asked to leave just a few weeks after she arrived! The authorities didn't appreciate her coming in so late that the doors were locked. And they liked it even less that she climbed in her bedroom window rather than knock and wait for the door to be opened! Ruth was given the choice of being expelled or grounded. She chose to be grounded. Had she been expelled, she would never have met William (Billy) Franklin Graham, a young Baptist minister who arrived to study at the same college.

'Billy's six foot two at least,' one of Ruth's friends told her.

'And he's twenty-one years old,' said another.

'He's from North Carolina,' Ruth added, 'and he's already a minister.'

One girl smiled dreamily. 'Have you seen his eyes?' she asked. 'They are the clearest, bluest eyes I've ever seen.'

It was no wonder he had plenty of girlfriends!

But before long, there was one special girl in Billy's life. He and Ruth Bell made a wonderful pair. Although Ruth had thought she would never be married, as soon as she knew Billy Graham, she was sure he was the young man God meant for her. And on 13th August 1943, William Franklin Graham and Ruth Bell became man and wife.

After all the goodbyes Ruth had said in her life, it was a relief to her to feel the time had come to settle down with the man she loved, to build up a home, to have children. She could picture in her mind what her future might be like. They would have a comfortable home and a friendly church. As Ruth felt that Billy was a gifted preacher, she pictured him taking meetings all around the area. But he'd be at home in his study each morning, she thought. That would be lovely if God gave us children, though they would have to be quiet outside his study and not disturb him. He would be there for the children; he'd be there for her. As Ruth sewed curtains for their first home, it was as though she was stitching dreams together.

'It's a wonderful opportunity,' Billy told his wife, two years later. 'Evangelism is what's in my heart, and this would let me do it full-time.'

'We could move near Dad and Mum,' Ruth said. 'It would be so good to be nearer them now that they've retired back to America.'

They prayed about it, talked about it, worked out all the details, and decided that Billy should give up being a regular minister and become a full-time evangelist. What Ruth had perhaps not realised was that she was signing away her dream of an at-home husband and father. As time passed, Billy's preaching trips took him further and further away, more and more often. Ruth, who had thought she had said goodbye to goodbyes, now regularly found herself waving to her husband as he left, yet again, with his suitcase in one hand and his coat trailing from the other.

Billy and Ruth Graham had five children: three daughters and two sons. Gigi, Anne, Bunny, Franklin and Ned grew up with a dad who became better known every year. He was on radio and television and had books written about him too. But to his sons and daughters he wasn't Billy Graham, the world famous preacher; he was Dad.

They loved it when he was home, enjoying the rough and tumble, the stories he told of faraway places and interesting people, of strange food eaten in strange places. And when he went away, they knew that Mum would be quiet for a day then go into busy mode to keep her mind off the goodbye.

'Why don't you travel with Dad?' the children asked her often, after they had grown up a bit.

'It's not for me,' she explained, 'though you know I've gone some places with Dad. My job is to keep the nest warm here for all of you and for him when he comes back home.'

'This is a bit like a nest,' one of the girls told Ruth. It was a bright, sunny day, and they were sitting outside their cabin home, surrounded by trees in Little Piney Cove.

'The cabin kind of nestles here, and, because so much of it is wooden, I can almost imagine it's on the branch of a great tree,' the teenager went on.

Ruth thought about what she was hearing. 'I'm glad you feel like that,' she said. 'Because that's what I set out to do here, to make a nest for the Grahams, to make a nest for your Dad.'

'You've never got used to Dad being away so much, have you?' the girl asked.

Ruth thought before answering. 'It's our way of life,' she said carefully, 'and God has given us both the strength to be often apart but still to love each other so much. But no, I've never really got used to partings.'

'Mum,' her daughter said, feeling somehow that Ruth was in a sharing mood, 'you once said that you thought God wanted you to be a missionary. But you're not, are you?'

Ruth smiled at the teenager and thought how she was growing up. 'I am,' she said, 'because the Lord has allowed me to talk to many people about Jesus. But I think my missionary service has been to agree to your Dad's preaching trips. I often had to say goodbye as a girl, and it was always hard. Now I realise that was part of my training for being Billy Graham's wife.'

'I suppose that's right,' the girl agreed. 'Because if you'd insisted that Dad settled down to work in one church, he'd not have told millions of people about the Lord.'

Ruth's eyes were closed against the glare of the sun. 'It's amazing really,' she said softly, as if to herself. 'He has preached in over sixty countries, even in Communist Russia, and he's told millions and millions of people the good news that Jesus is the Saviour.'

'So it's been worth it?' her daughter asked.

Ruth was instantly upright and wide awake. 'Worth it?' she said. 'Of course it's been worth it. Not easy ... but worth every single painful goodbye.'

The girl got up and poked the charcoal on the barbecue. 'Just nine more days till Dad comes home now,' she said.

Ruth laughed. 'Now where's my list?' she asked. 'I'll have to remember to get his favourite hot chocolate and popcorn and ...'

'It's okay Mum!' her daughter said, grinning, 'you've got a whole nine days to get all his favourites ready before you welcome him back to the nest, and you've started to flutter already!'

FACT FILE

Yangtze River: The Yangtze River is China's greatest river and third longest river in the world. It flows for 6,300 kilometres from its source in Tibet to the point it enters the East China Sea. The Explorer, Marco Polo, once mentioned how impressed he was with the number of boats using the river. But nowadays heavy rains in summer sometimes cause disastrous flooding.

Keynote: Ruth was upset when she had to leave her parents in order to go to school. She was depressed and very homesick. However, she read the Book of Psalms and found that other people understood what she was going through. It also made her realise that God was with her. When you feel down and depressed, pray to God, ask him to give you comfort in his Word, the Bible.

Think: Ruth and Billy were both involved in evangelism. Evangelism is telling others about Jesus Christ. You can evangelise anywhere you go. You can evangelise in other countries, in other cities and you can also evangelise in your own home. Telling the people you know and love, that Jesus wants to save them from sin, is very important. But we are also told by Jesus to go into all the world to preach the gospel.

Prayer: Lord, you are amazing and wonderful. You are the God of love. You are the only true God. Help me to tell others about you and to do my bit to spread the good news around the whole world. Amen.

Author Information: Irene Howat

Irene Howat is an award-winning author and poet who lives in Scotland. She has published many biographical books for all ages and is particularly well-known for her biographical material. She has written many books about the lives of different Christians from around the world. She has also written an autobiographical work entitled: *Pain My Companion.*

Quiz

How much can you remember about these ten girls who made a difference? Try answering these questions to find out.

Monica of Thagaste

1. Monica grew up in a town in North Africa. What was its name?

2. What was the name of Monica's son?

3. Which country did Monica move to when she left Africa?

Katherine Luther

4. What was Katherine's last name before she married Martin Luther?

5. What did Katherine become when she was sixteen years old?

6. How many children at one point were living in Katherine and Martin's home?

Susanna Wesley

7. How many older brothers and sisters did Susanna have?

8. Who did Susanna eventually marry?

9. What happened to Susanna's home in 1709?

Ann Judson

10. What country did Ann travel to?
11. What was the name of Ann's husband?
12. What did Ann hide inside a pillow and smuggle into a prison?

Maria Taylor

13. Which country did Maria have to travel to when she was a child?
14. What hairdo did Hudson wear?
15. What was the name of Maria and Hudson's little girl?

Susannah Spurgeon

16. Which book did Charles give Susannah before they were married?
17. What presents did Susannah ask Charles to get her one day?
18. What did Susannah send to ministers who earned less than £150 a year?

Bethan Lloyd-Jones

19. What did Bethan and her brother go to see when Bethan was only six years old?

20. Which two languages did Bethan speak when she was a little girl?

21. What job did Bethan's husband Martyn do?

Edith Schaeffer

22. Which country did Edith live in as a young girl?

23. What did Edith like to do most when she was feeling sad?

24. Which country did Edith and Francis move to when they set up their new home, 'L'Abri'?

Sabina Wurmbrand

25. Which name was Sabina not allowed to say when she was a child?
26. Which country did Sabina live in?
27. What did the communists do to Sabina's husband Richard?

Ruth Bell Graham

28. Where did Ruth and Rosa get their clothes from?
29. What part of the Bible did Ruth read when she felt very homesick?
30. What did Ruth's husband, Billy Graham become after he was a pastor?

How well did you do?
Turn over to find out.

Answers:

1. Thagaste.
2. Augustine.
3. Italy.
4. von Bora.
5. A nun.
6. 11.
7. 24.
8. Samuel Wesley.
9. It burnt down.
10. Burma.
11. Adoniram.
12. The Burmese translation of the Bible.
13. England.
14. A Chinese pigtail.
15. Grace.
16. The Pilgrim's Progress.
17. An opal ring and a bullfinch.
18. Books.
19. The Welsh revivals of 1904-05.
20. Welsh and English.
21. A Preacher.
22. China.
23. Fly kites.
24. Switzerland.
25. Jesus Christ.
26. Romania.

27. They put him in prison.
28. A missionary barrel.
29. The Psalms.
30. An evangelist.

Start collecting this series now!

Ten Boys who used their Talents:
ISBN 978-1-84550-146-4
Paul Brand, Ghillean Prance, C.S.Lewis, C.T. Studd, Wilfred Grenfell, J.S. Bach, James Clerk Maxwell, Samuel Morse, George Washington Carver, John Bunyan.

Ten Girls who used their Talents:
ISBN 978-1-84550-147-1
Helen Roseveare, Maureen McKenna, Anne Lawson, Harriet Beecher Stowe, Sarah Edwards, Selina Countess of Huntingdon, Mildred Cable, Katie Ann MacKinnon, Patricia St. John, Mary Verghese.

Ten Boys who Changed the World:
ISBN 978-1-85792-579-1
David Livingstone, Billy Graham, Brother Andrew, John Newton, William Carey, George Müller, Nicky Cruz, Eric Liddell, Luis Palau, Adoniram Judson.

Ten Girls who Changed the World:
ISBN 978-1-85792-649-1
Corrie Ten Boom, Mary Slessor, Joni Eareckson Tada, Isobel Kuhn, Amy Carmichael, Elizabeth Fry, Evelyn Brand, Gladys Aylward, Catherine Booth, Jackie Pullinger.

Ten Boys who Made a Difference:
ISBN 978-1-85792-775-7
Augustine of Hippo, Jan Hus, Martin Luther, Ulrich Zwingli, William Tyndale, Hugh Latimer, John Calvin, John Knox, Lord Shaftesbury, Thomas Chalmers.

Ten Girls who Made a Difference:
ISBN 978-1-85792-776-4
Monica of Thagaste, Catherine Luther,
Susanna Wesley, Ann Judson, Maria Taylor,
Susannah Spurgeon, Bethan Lloyd-Jones,
Edith Schaeffer, Sabina Wurmbrand,
Ruth Bell Graham.

Ten Boys who Made History:
ISBN 978-1-85792-836-5
Charles Spurgeon, Jonathan Edwards,
Samuel Rutherford, D L Moody,
Martin Lloyd Jones, A W Tozer, John Owen,
Robert Murray McCheyne, Billy Sunday,
George Whitfield.

Ten Girls who Made History:
ISBN 978-1-85792-837-2
Ida Scudder, Betty Green, Jeanette Li,
Mary Jane Kinnaird, Bessie Adams,
Emma Dryer, Lottie Moon, Florence Nightingale,
Henrietta Mears, Elisabeth Elliot.

Ten Boys who Didn't Give In:
ISBN 978-1-84550-035-1
Polycarp, Alban, Sir John Oldcastle
Thomas Cramer, George Wishart,
James Chalmers, Dietrich Bonhoeffer
Nate Saint, Ivan Moiseyev
Graham Staines

Ten Girls who Didn't Give In:
ISBN 978-1-84550-036-8
Blandina, Perpetua, Lady Jane Grey,
Anne Askew, Lysken Dirks, Marion Harvey,
Margaret Wilson, Judith Weinberg,
Betty Stam, Esther John

CHRISTIAN FOCUS PUBLICATIONS

Christian Focus
Christian Heritage
CF4K
Mentor

Christian Focus Publications publishes books for adults and children under its four main imprints: Christian Focus, CF4K, Mentor and Christian Heritage. Our books reflect our conviction that God's Word is reliable and Jesus is the way to know him, and live for ever with him.

Our children's publication list covers pre-school to early teens. We also publish personal and family devotional titles, biographies and inspirational stories that children will love.

From pre-school board books to teenage apologetics, we have it covered!

Christian Focus Publications Ltd,
Geanies House, Fearn, Ross-shire,
IV20 1TW, Scotland,
United Kingdom.
www.christianfocus.com

CF4•K
Because you're never too young to know Jesus

TEN GIRLS WHO USED THEIR TALENTS

LIGHT KEEPERS

Irene Howat

CF4•K

Reprinted 2007, 2008, 2010, 2012, 2014, 2015, 2016, 2019, 2020, 2022

Paperback ISBN: 978-1-84550-147-1
Epub ISBN: 978-1-84550-856-2
Mobi ISBN: 978-1-84550-857-9

Published by Christian Focus Publications,
Geanies House, Fearn, Tain, Ross-shire,
IV20 1TW, Scotland, Great Britain.
Tel: +44 (0)1862 871011
Fax: +44 (0)1862 871699
www.christianfocus.com
email: info@christianfocus.com
Cover design by Daniel van Straaten
Cover illustration by Elena Temporin,
Milan Illustrations Agency
Printed and bound in China

All incidents retold in these stories are based on true situations. Where specific information about childhood incidents has been unobtainable the author has written these paragraphs using other information concerning family life, hobbies, home life, relationships freely available in other biographies as well as appropriate historical source material.

Cover illustration: This depicts Helen Roseveare waiting for the train on her way to boarding school. Helen came to love the Lord Jesus and then went on to do medical work in the Belgian Congo. Today she travels, writes, teaches, speaks, runs youth groups....

Dedication
for Gemma and Carol

Contents

Anne Lawson

Anne Lawson sat on the top bar of the gate and swung her legs. Pip, her corgi dog, lay in the sun beside her. The eight-year-old looked around. East Mains Farm had been her home for as long as she could remember, though she had been born a short distance away in the splendidly named Mains of Machermore. She even knew the colour of the bedroom in which she'd been born. It was pink. But Anne was not a particularly 'pink' girl. Pink made her think of dresses and fluffy things. She was more at home in jeans, and the fluffy things she liked best of all were young animals.

'What do you want to do when you grow up?' visitors to her home asked from time to time.

'Why do people always want to know that?' Anne wondered. 'It's almost as though what you do as a child isn't important, that you've got to be at least fifteen to do anything that matters.'

But Anne knew that wasn't the case. There were always things to be done around the farm, and she knew that she did lots of things that were important in their own way. She especially liked helping her dad, both with his work with the animals, and with any technical things he had to do. If there were loose screws to be tightened, she was there among her dad's tools. If there were rusted nuts and bolts needing oiled to loosen them, she knew fine how to do that too. It was far from unusual for Mr Lawson and Anne to have their heads together under the hood of their Massie Ferguson tractor examining its engine parts.

As she and Pip walked over the field towards the farmhouse, Anne heard a noise that made her legs break into a run. It was the sound of voices. Pip heard them too. Anne had four cousins who stayed on a nearby farm. In fact, the land from one farm led right on to the land of the other. From the fever pitch of laughter that came from the farmyard, Anne knew that all four were in the mood for some fun.

'Just give me a minute to feed the cats,' she yelled to her cousins.

Within two minutes Wee Harry and Arthur had been fed and the fun began.

But when Anne was alone there were two things she especially enjoyed doing. One was reading, and the other was watching the wild creatures that lived in and around the farmyard. Even the books she liked reading were about animals – but prehistoric ones.

'It's Scripture Union day,' Anne thought one morning, as she left for school.

She didn't know why she liked going but she did. It was as though something drew her there.

'You all know about the two Margarets,' the teacher who took S.U. said, 'but it's good to remember their story, especially as they lived so near here.'

Anne listened as her S.U. leader told the story she knew so well, of a teenage girl and an old woman, both called Margaret. They lived at a time in Scottish history when it was not easy to be Christian. If they believed that the Bible said something, and it was different from what the king believed, they could even be killed. The two Margarets were Christians who were tied to stakes in the sands near Wigtown and left there to drown as the tide came in over them. The monument to the two brave Margarets was so well known to young Anne Lawson that she hardly ever noticed it. Nor did she notice the people who visited her part of south-west Scotland. They came to see where the two Margarets and other Christian martyrs had died in the 17th Century because of their faith in Jesus.

When Anne was ten years old, life changed for her. Dad and Mum Lawson sold their farm and moved into a cottage for six months before buying a house in Wigtown. That would have been a big enough change for any girl but, at nearly the same time, Anne went off to boarding school in the Lake District of England.

'I'm going to a group a bit like Scripture Union,' she wrote in a letter some time later. 'Miss Gunning takes it, and it's very good.'

But although she liked and respected Miss Gunning, after a time Anne stopped attending. There seemed to be so much to do as the years passed that there was little time to think about God.

'What do you do at boarding school?' one of her friends from Wigtown Primary School days asked her.

'Work, most of the time,' Anne laughed. 'But you're right, we do loads of other things too.'

'Like what?' the girl asked.

Anne thought about the lunch hours she and her friends spent singing around the school piano, and of her own cello practice, but decided that wasn't what her friend wanted to hear about.

'We go fell-walking,' she said, 'and canoeing and sailing. In fact, we built a canoe last term.'

'It's a shame,' her friend moaned. 'We don't do that kind of thing at school here.'

Anne looked her in the eye. 'Would it really be a good idea?' she asked.

The girl's face creased into a grin. 'Guess not,' she admitted. 'Living in a part of Scotland famous for its treacherous sinking sands would probably not make canoeing the most sensible sport to take up.'

'What are you going to do when you leave school?' her friend asked, as they walked through Wigtown.

It was that question again, but it really was time to think about it seriously now.

'I'm thinking about becoming a vet,' Anne said. 'I've always loved working with animals.'

When Anne did go to university, she went to study zoology. Much of the teaching in her course was based on the theory of evolution, and before long she came to the conclusion that evolution answered all her questions and that God didn't even exist. And that was what she believed when she went for her first job. Anne started work along with four others, two Christians and two who were not. The two Christians, Nash and Kenny, made such an impression on her that she started to read the Bible.

Having done a degree in zoology, Anne discovered that working with dead animals was just what she didn't want to do. She retrained as a metallurgist - someone who understands about metals. After qualifying she looked for a job on an oil rig, but there were no jobs and she found work on land instead.

For eight years Anne searched for the answers to her many questions and she eventually found the answer at a wedding.

'Tell me how you became a Christian,' she was asked, years later. Anne smiled at the memory.

'On 8th July 1989,' she said, 'I went to Kenny's wedding in London. It was the first truly Christian wedding I'd ever been at. Kenny asked me if I was a Christian yet. When I said I was still sitting on the fence, he and his new wife took me into a side room during their own wedding reception, and spoke to me about the Lord Jesus. When I left the room I was a Christian, and I had peace in my heart for the very first time.'

'Would you like to come to a missionary meeting with me?' a member of her church asked Anne, not long afterwards.

Anne Lawson smiled. Her friend seemed to spend her life at missionary meetings.

'Sure, I'll come,' she replied.

'You'll be a missionary one day,' said a lady to the young Christian.

'Yes, I will,' Anne agreed, even though she wasn't quite sure what missionaries really did.

But as she thought back over the years of her life, especially over the last eight years, she realised just how much Jesus had done for her, and told the Lord that she was prepared to be a missionary - or anything else, for that matter - if that's what he wanted.

'Lord, I wish you would show me what you want me to do with my life,' Anne said, as she tidied her writing desk in 1990.

As she spoke aloud to God, she took some leaflets and letters out of the desk. One was a booklet about Mission Aviation Fellowship, and it was appealing for people to serve as aircraft engineers in Tanzania. Anne knew that God had answered her prayer. This was the way forward but what did she have to do first? The following three years were spent training to be both a missionary and an aircraft engineer. And then ... Tanzania!

'We begin the day in the aircraft hangar at Dodoma with worship,' Anne wrote to a friend. 'There is no way I'm going to try to keep aircraft in the air without God's help!'

Then she smiled and settled down to writing a newsy letter.

'You asked what I do, so here we go. Monday was the first day of the Cessna 210

OPS 1 check - and I'll explain that to you. OPS (operational) checks are carried out in stages on every aircraft to spread the maintenance. Doing it this way means that aircraft are out of service for short bursts of time on a regular basis rather than being grounded for long periods when they might be needed, and needed urgently.

'Remember,' she went on, 'some of our flights are life saving. The other day a young boy, who had been hurt in an accident, was flown to hospital. The doctor said he would have died before he arrived if he'd gone by road.

'But, back to the maintenance ... the Cessna 206s and 210s have four inspections for every 200 hours of flying. The first one involves a detailed inspection of the fuselage, cabin and landing gear, and a routine inspection of the engine, propeller, wings and tail.'

Anne read over what she'd written and grinned.

'She did ask about my work,' she laughed aloud.

Taking up her pen again, she continued writing.

'The rudder pedals in the cockpit need to be removed for the inspection. And if you think there's no room in a canoe, you've never removed rudder pedals from a Cessna 210. There is space to do it, and space to breath ... lightly. Seriously, getting spanners into some of the spaces is really hard and can take ages. But it needs to be done.'

'I walk miles each day in this hangar,' said Anne to a visitor, after she'd been working there for five years. 'And I'm not just checking aircraft.'

'What else do you do?' the man asked.

'The metal parts of aircraft are not the only things with strengths and weaknesses,' Anne explained. 'All the members of the engineering team have their strengths and weaknesses too. It's up to me as Hangar Foreman to look out for them. Keeping aircraft in the air is a serious business, and everyone involved needs to do their part well.'

'So your job is about people rather than aircraft?' he commented.

'No, it's about both. And it's about housework too.'

The visitor looked puzzled.

'Do you see the size of this huge hangar?' Anne asked. 'Well, it's part of my job to make sure it's kept tidy.'

As they were talking, someone came with a message for Anne.

'Have all the ground checks been done on the Cessna 210?' she was asked.

'Yes,' said Anne, 'and the test flight too.'

'So the aircraft is operational?'

'Yes. Is there an urgent call?'

'A mother giving birth is having problems. Both her life and the baby's life are in danger.'

That was all Anne needed to know. The Cessna 210 was rolled out of the hangar ... and the mother was airlifted to hospital where her baby was born safe and well.

The visitor was still there when, several days later, the aircraft flew to the hospital to pick up the mother and take her home with her new baby.

'That must make all your hard work worthwhile,' he commented to Anne.

'Yes,' she agreed. 'But it's not all about emergency flights. Many of our flights are routine: taking missionaries to remote areas, medical teams to villages, equipment and supplies to hospitals and mission stations and food to areas affected by drought. It's amazing what a day brings.'

Just occasionally, when Anne came back to the UK and spoke about her work, people assumed that she was just an engineer rather than being a missionary herself. They soon learned that things were very different.

'From time to time,' she told them, 'I organize a team of about ten people to go out to villages to encourage the Christians there. After breakfast each morning we have a time of worship. Then we break up and do different things. Some teach new Christians or church leaders, others - and I love doing this - talk to the villagers about the Lord Jesus. Following lunch we have a big outdoor meeting and afterwards we pray for those who are sick. In the evenings we show films in nearby villages using a portable projector and a huge screen. It's exhausting, but great.'

As Anne Lawson sat outside her little home in Dodoma in Tanzania, she looked around and thought of God's care for her. From those distant days at East Mains Farm with Pip at her feet, to Tanzania with Bracken, her Rhodesian Ridgeback dog, God had been with her. Anne returned to Scotland in 2010. She died and went home to heaven six years later.

FACT FILE

Female Aviator

Amy Johnson was one of the world's first female aviators and she flew a Gipsy Moth. She learnt to fly in 1928 at Stag Lane Aerodrome, near Edgware, in the U.K. where de Havilland Moths were built. Unusually she also gained a ground engineer's licence - the first woman in Britain to do this. It was in a Gypsy Moth that Amy made the first solo flight from England to Australia by a woman, in May 1930. She wrote of her 16,000 kilometre (10, 000 mile) flight: 'The prospect did not frighten me because I was so appallingly ignorant that I never realised in the least what I had taken on'.

Keynote: Do you think missionary work is glamorous and exciting? Anne maintained planes that saved people's lives. She worked in a different country and met interesting people. However, it is a hard job too. Even missionaries can find some things tedious and tiring. But Anne started the day at the aircraft hangar with worship. Each and every day that we have - be it a good day or a bad day - we should start it off with God. Bring every day to him and ask him to take charge of it.

Think: Anne Lawson prayed one day for God to show her what to do with her life. It is important to pray to God about what he wants us to do. We should ask his opinion about what decisions need to be made. Think about the plans you have for the future – bring them to God first of all. Remember that in the Bible, in Proverbs 16:9, it says that you can make plans in your heart but it is God that is in charge of what actually happens. You may be planning university or college, you may want to get a good job – all these things are fine if that is what God wants you to do. Pray to God to guide you and then do your best at whatever you choose. If you are trusting in God and looking to him for guidance then he will guide your heart and mind to choose the right thing.

Prayer: Lord God, I have plans for my life but I want these plans to please you. Help me to look to you for guidance. Show me the kind of person you want me to be through your Word. Give me friends who love and trust in you and who will give me good advice. Help me to listen to your Word and to obey it.

Selina, Countess of Huntingdon

'Tell me about Grandfather Shirley,' said Selina. 'It's strange having a grandfather you don't know.'

Sir Robert Shirley looked at his nine-year-old daughter and wondered how much to tell her. Had the time come when she should know more about her family? He decided, with a heavy heart, that it had.

'I think we should go for a walk together,' suggested Sir Robert.

Selina was delighted. She loved her father very much and enjoyed his company.

'Let's go back two generations,' Sir Robert said, as they walked through their land. 'Great-grandfather died a prisoner in the Tower of London. His son, Grandfather Shirley, was born just after he was imprisoned. He married my mother when he was twenty and she was just fifteen. I was the second oldest of eleven children. My older brother died.'

Selina, a very serious-minded girl, listened carefully, remembering every detail.

'My mother died young, and my father married again and more children were born, six of whom are still alive.'

They walked on in silence for a long time. Sir Robert was deep in thought and Selina was trying to work out all she had learned.

'Father,' she said, after a while. 'That still doesn't explain why we don't see Grandfather Shirley. Is it because he's very busy with all his other children?'

Sir Robert shook his head. 'No, I'm afraid not. In fact, your grandfather has fallen out with nearly all the children my mother had. I really don't know how he gets on with the children from his second marriage.'

A weight of sadness seemed to pass from father to daughter as Selina realised exactly why she didn't know her grandfather.

'Father,' said the girl quietly. 'Now that I know these things, will you tell me why Mother left us when I was six years old?'

Sir Robert sighed. 'I can't tell you that, my dear,' he said, 'because I honestly don't know. I suppose your mother expected to be rich and didn't like it that we were not. But after your sister Mary was born she just decided to take the baby and go. They've lived between France and Spain ever since.'

'It's strange not knowing my grandfather,' said Selina, 'but it's even stranger not really knowing my mother and little sister.'

Sir Robert took her hand and they walked together.

'Your mother does keep in touch with you by letter though.'

'Yes, occasionally,' Selina hesitated. 'But they don't really feel as though they come from my mother. They feel as though they've been written by a stranger.'

A few months later Selina saw a very sad thing. A girl about her own age died and she saw the child's body on its way to be buried. She followed the procession and watched all that happened. It made a terrible impression on Selina's young mind and she very often visited the little girl's grave.

'What a serious child Selina is,' a visitor told Sir Robert.

'Yes, I'm afraid that's true. I've done my best for her and her older sister Elizabeth, but they haven't had a normal home life.'

In 1717, when Selina was ten years old, Sir Robert discovered how little he meant to his father. The old man died and, although Sir Robert was the oldest surviving son who should have inherited the family's estates, he was left just £20. Several of his half-brothers and half-sisters were left £5,000.

'I'll fight this through every court in the land,' raged Sir Robert, when he heard the terms of his father's will. How dare he leave an insulting £20 to me, and 250 times that to some of the others. It's a bad business, and the courts can sort it out!'

So began legal battle after legal battle that lasted until after Sir Robert's own death. Selina's father inherited very little from Grandfather Shirley, but she inherited something she would rather not have had - she inherited his very quick temper.

'Everyone is always talking about money,' Selina complained to her sister Elizabeth. 'And it's always about how little they have.'

'But we need money to live on,' said Elizabeth.

'I know that,' agreed Selina, 'but I'm sure there don't need to be all these arguments and court cases. I'm sure we were happier when we lived in Ireland and Father was just a Coldstream Guardsman.'

'Before Mother left home with Mary?'

'That's right,' agreed Selina.

'Look,' said Elizabeth. 'I'm older than you and I can remember things from when you were little, and I can tell you that it wasn't very happy then either.'

Selina then went to her special place to be alone. Tucked away in her special place, she had space to think and pray.

'Please, Lord,' she prayed, 'if you want me to be married one day, please may it be into a serious family.'

Sometimes in her secret place Selina would write letters. Her writing and spelling were awful. Although she grew into a very clever woman, her writing and spelling didn't improve at all.

When Selina married Theophilus, 9th Earl of Huntingdon, in June 1728, she became part of a family with as many problems as her own.But her husband and his half-sisters were different. They were the best of friends. They welcomed Selina into their hearts and she discovered for the very first time what it was like to live in a relaxed and happy home.

Their home, Donnington Park, was welcoming. Many visitors came and went. As Theophilus was not good at business matters, Selina soon knew the estate workers and farmers by name, and all about their families.

'Please make me up a basket of food for the Archer family,' she instructed her cook. 'Mr Archer is ill and his children are hungry.'

'I'll pray for you,' she told people in trouble. And she meant it.

Selina's life was suddenly busy with people she could help and support, and it became busier still when her son was born just a year after she was married.

'Father is hoping to come to Francis's baptism,' she wrote to her sister. 'I'm so looking forward to seeing him.'

But that was not to be. Sir Robert was busy with yet another legal claim involving his wife, then he died quite suddenly just two days before the baptism.

'I'd like to buy Bibles and Prayer Books to distribute when I'm visiting,' Selina told her husband one day.

'What a good idea,' he said. 'You do that.'

Money was no problem now, and Selina was very generous with her wealth. In 1729 she sent £10 to the Society for the Propagation of Christian Knowledge. That was quite a large sum of money then.

Although Selina tried to please the Lord by doing good work, she was not a Christian lady. She had never truly confessed her sins nor asked Jesus to be her Saviour. It was in the late 1730s that she first heard the Bible really being preached, and it wasn't until 1739, when her sister-in-law was converted, that she saw the difference Jesus could make.

'Since I've known and believed in the Lord Jesus Christ for life and salvation, I've been happier than I've ever been,' Lady Margaret enthused.

'Explain to me what you mean,' said Selina.

Lady Margaret did just that, and not long afterwards Selina became a Christian, then Theophilus too.

'This is an exciting time to live,' Selina told her husband. 'Charles and John Wesley, George Whitefield and others are teaching the Bible in a way that's not been done before. No wonder the Church of England won't allow them in their pulpits. We really must do something to help these fine men.'

'What do you suggest?' asked Theophilus. 'Should we help them set up a church?'

'I don't think that's what they want or need,' she replied. 'I think they hope that people's hearts will be changed and that they'll stay in the national church and change it.'

At that time the Church of England was going through difficulties, and the Bible was not being preached as it should have been.

'I think we should help them with money as they don't have a church to provide them with what they need.'

And that's what Theophilus and his wife did. They also attended services held by these keen young men, who were becoming known as Methodists.

'Have you heard about Theophilus and Selina?' one very grand lady said to another. 'They've gone all religious.'

'Really?' questioned her friend. 'They've not joined the Methodists, have they?'

Another woman laughed behind her fan. 'They'll be at prayer meetings next. Talking about religion in public too.'

'It's so unpleasant when people embarrass you by talking about their religion. Some things should be kept strictly private,' complained a sour-faced woman.

'I agree,' said her friend. 'Religion, politics and money should never be discussed in good company.'

A young woman giggled. 'Unless it's someone else's money that's being talked about.'

The woman with the sour face looked so sour that milk might have curdled!

Selina's young sister Mary returned to England and was shocked at her sister's Christian faith. She wrote to Lady Margaret about it. It seems that her writing and spelling were no better than Selina's!

'That sect (Methodism) Is so Generally exploded that It's become a Joke of all Compagnys, and Indeed I Can goe no whare but I hear of the uncommon piety of the Donnington family.'

What people thought, didn't stop Selina from doing what she believed to be right. Having been brought up comparatively poor, she might have become a mean woman when she became rich. But she did not. She was generous with her money and gave many Bible preachers enough to live on. Even after Theophilus died in 1746 her generosity continued.

'I've been thinking,' she told Lady Margaret. 'Buildings have to be licensed in order to hold official church services in them. The Church of England won't licence buildings for these good men who are preaching today. I wonder if we can do anything about that.'

Lady Margaret shook her head. 'I don't think that even you will manage to change the law, I'm afraid.'

'Perhaps not,' agreed Selina. 'But private chapels are allowed. I think I'll establish private chapels in a number of towns and the Bible can be preached in them.'

'Really, Selina,' laughed Lady Margaret. 'You are full of bright ideas.'

Selina's chapels were built. They were within the law of the land, just. She chose the sites very carefully. All were in towns where the grand people of England went on holiday. She knew that people, who would only go to the Church of England when at home, might try something new on holiday.

'I'm not starting a new church,' she insisted. 'I want people to trust in the Lord Jesus, then go back to the Church of England to spread the good news.'

But that was not how it worked out and Selina was in a way involved in the split.

'What are we going to do?' she asked. 'The students we support are no longer to be accepted for training at Oxford.'

'We could open our own college,' someone suggested.

Immediately Selina was on the case.

'Of course,' she said. 'That's just what we should do.'

That was how Trevecca College in South Wales was started and much of it was paid for by Selina, Countess of Huntingdon.

'The students trained there will be missionaries throughout England,' Selina told her friends. 'Even throughout the world.'

But she was so impatient to see things happen that the young men at Trevecca were sent out preaching so often that for a while they had very little time to study at all. Only as a result of some wise advice in Selina's ear were they given time and peace to get on with their studies.

Trevecca College caused a real problem in the Church of England. Eventually the two groups split and the Countess of Huntingdon's Connexion was formed. There are still some Huntingdon Connexion churches in England today. Just as Selina longed for people to come to the Lord Jesus Christ, those churches today that bear her name still have a strong missionary spirit.

Selina died in 1791.

'What an amazing woman she was,' someone said at her funeral.

'Indeed,' a friend agreed. 'She had such a sad start in life with all her family's rows and ructions. I suppose that's what made her so strong that she was able to do all she did.'

'I'm not as enthusiastic about my religion as Selina was about hers,' said a bystander, 'but I know God changed her life.'

'How do you know that?' he was asked.

The man smiled. 'I knew Selina, Countess of Huntingdon for a very long time. She inherited from her grandfather nothing but his fiery temper. But, after she became a Christian, that temper was tamed. And, if you knew her family, you'd know that only God could tame a Shirley temper.'

FACT FILE
John Wesley
John was born on 17 June 1703 in Epworth, Lincolnshire. He was a renowned preacher and spiritual leader of the 'Methodist revival'. From the 1730s until his death, John Wesley travelled many thousands of miles around Britain on horseback and by carriage, preaching several times each day. He also wrote or edited 400 publications.

Keynote: Selina's family life was very difficult. She barely knew her mother and younger sister. Her grandfather had fallen out with her father too. Family life can indeed be difficult. Selina's family was not happy. Her grandfather was rich but wasn't happy. Her father got married - but he wasn't happy either. His wife left him. Selina was from what we would call a noble family - but without her mother and sister and grandfather her childhood was troubled. Some time later she discovered another family - the family of God. Selina learned that all people are welcome into that family - rich and poor alike. Slaves and noble people are treated the same by our just and merciful God.

Think: Selina's family was famous for having bad tempers. It was said that a bad temper was all that Selina inherited from her grandfather. Think about different things that you have inherited? Perhaps you look or sound like someone in your family? Maybe you have the same name or character? There are lots of things we can 'inherit' from other people. If you have been taught about the Lord Jesus Christ - that is a wonderful inheritance. People have given you the truth from God's word. Ask yourself - 'Do I believe this truth for myself?' You cannot inherit salvation from parents, teachers or anyone else. You must believe in Jesus Christ for yourself. He is the only way to heaven - you can't get there by hitching a ride with another person.

Prayer: Thank you, Lord, for those people in the past who believed and trusted in you. Thank you for the example they left. Thank you for how your Word was taught and how it is still spread around the world today. Help me to trust in you for myself. May I believe in you, and may my family believe in you too.

Mildred Cable

'Where is that girl?' demanded Mrs Cable. 'She moves faster than greased lightening.'

Although she was only seven years old, Mildred Cable was an adventurer. Had the slopes of Mount Everest begun outside her home in Surrey, England, she would have set off to climb it.

'There she is,' her husband laughed. 'Up that tree on the other side of the lane.'

'Which one?' asked Mrs Cable.

'The highest one, of course,' was the answer she expected and the answer she received.

It was Sunday afternoon and the family was out for a walk. But Mildred wasn't looking for a walk - she wanted adventure!

'What would you like to do on the first day of the school holiday?' the child was asked as the end of term drew near. It was 1886.

Mildred grinned. 'I'd like to skate on the frozen River Thames, sledge down the highest hill in England and sail across the Atlantic.'

Mr Cable laughed. 'You need to learn to live in the real world, young lady.'

'What's that?' asked Mildred, a little puzzled. The world that was real to her had no limits because she had such an active imagination.

The reality of Mildred Cable's life was just a little different from what went on in her mind. Her father had a draper's business and, rather than skating on the frozen Thames, sledging down hills and sailing the Atlantic, when she was old enough she found herself sometimes helping her dad at work.

'Could you unpack that box of ribbons?' Mr Cable said, 'and put them in the second drawer from the top.'

Pulling the ribbons between her fingers was lovely. They were pure silk and soft as could be.

'Where do these come from?' she asked.

'That's Chinese silk,' her father replied. 'We sell a lot of Chinese silk ribbon. It's all the fashion just now for threading through white cotton lace.'

But Mildred wasn't listening. The very word Chinese sent her imagination halfway round the world. She was no longer behind the counter of a draper's shop. Instead, she was in a crowded Chinese market, among men with long black pigtails and women dressed in bright-coloured silks.

'For goodness sake, Mildred, you're in a dream.'

Grinning mischievously Mildred proceeded to unpack the ribbons.

'They're just starting to build a Trans-Siberian railway,' she said, 'so you'll maybe be able to buy things from Vladivostok before long.'

Mr Cable shook his head.

'When I was your age I didn't even know Vladivostok existed.'

'It sounds an exciting place, doesn't it?' asked his daughter.

'Mildred,' her mother said in a very serious voice not long afterwards. 'You're a big girl now and you're going to have to start behaving like one. Even your teachers say that you're more interested in adventure than schoolwork. There are plenty of jobs for hard-working young women, but have you ever heard of anyone looking for a female explorer?'

'But I do work at school,' objected Mildred. 'Especially in subjects I like.'

Mr Cable, who was listening to the conversation, realised that geography was one subject his daughter liked. How else would she have known where Vladivostok was? But he decided that he'd best not mention that for fear Mildred told her mother it sounded an exciting place.

'May I go to the mission meeting?' Mildred asked her parents one afternoon.

Her father thought for a moment. 'I don't see why not.'

The meeting in Guildford made a great impression on the girl.

'There's another mission meeting tonight,' she told them the following afternoon. 'May I go to it?'

Mr Cable wasn't quite so keen second time round.

'I don't think so,' he said. 'Anything can happen at meetings like that.'

Mildred couldn't imagine what might happen that her father would worry about. When she didn't appear at the next few mission meetings, her minister decided to speak to Mr Cable.

'I'm just not sure about her going,' the draper said firmly.

'Why not let her come to the closing meeting on Sunday afternoon then?' suggested the minister. 'She can't go to any after that because there aren't any more to go to.'

Mr Cable gave in and Mildred, full of excitement, went to the Sunday afternoon mission meeting. And it turned out to be the beginning of a life-long adventure because she trusted the Lord Jesus that day and came home a Christian. From then on Mildred was a changed girl, even her parents had to admit that.

'There's a missionary from the China Inland Mission speaking tonight,' she told her friends in 1893. 'I'm really looking forward to hearing her.'

Mildred listened to what the young woman had to say with great interest, but something kept catching her eye.

'What is she wearing?' she wondered.

Afterwards, she had an opportunity to speak to the missionary.

'Why do you have a Bible text embroidered on to your collar?' asked the astonished teenager.

'I always do that in China,' the woman explained, 'and I don't see any reason not to do it here.'

Mildred took a deep breath. 'It's not exactly fashionable,' she said, rather too honestly. 'In fact, I think it's embarrassing.'

It says a lot for the missionary that the two of them went on talking on good terms.

'I think the Lord wants you in China,' the woman told Mildred, as they left the hall together.

'If I do become a missionary it will be in India,' the girl announced.

The woman stopped and looked at her young companion.

'You must go where the Lord sends you,' she said. 'If you are Christ's, you must be his entirely.'

Within a year of that conversation Mildred felt sure that God was calling her to be a missionary in China. But she still had no intention of having a Bible verse embroidered on to her collar. From school she went to C.I.M.'s Candidate's Department in North London for six months. C.I.M. stands for China Inland Mission. After that she did a course especially tailored to her needs - a mixture of human sciences, medicine and pharmacy. She did not do the long training required to become a doctor. On 25th September 1901, Mildred sailed for China. Her first year was spent learning the language.

'We have decided to send you to Hwochow in Shansi province,' the young woman was told, when she met with her C.I.M. superior. 'You'll travel there with Evangeline French, an experienced missionary.'

When that decision was made, no one could possibly have guessed that Mildred and Evangeline (Eva), along with Eva's young sister Francesca, would become known worldwide as adventuring missionaries. But to start with there was just Mildred and Eva.

'What beautiful flowers,' said Mildred, as they drew near Hwochow. 'The whole valley is covered in them.'

'Yes, and more's the pity,' Eva replied. 'These poppies are grown for the opium trade. And there's more opium[1] in the air of Hwochow than oxygen!'

'Now, these two rooms are for a girls' school,' they were told, as they were shown round their new home. 'You'll have to work hard here in Hwochow. We all do. Our motto is "When the pressure of work is too heavy, then extend the pressure of work."'

Before long Eva and Mildred knew what was meant by 'the pressure of work.' The two rooms were soon crowded with girls eager to learn, and married women also came for month-long courses in the Christian faith.

Very soon it was known that Mildred had some medical training.

'Send the white woman to cure my ladies' toothache,' the Mandarin of Hwochow ordered.

The young missionary had already discovered that whenever she produced her forceps people clamped their mouths shut. So she carried them where they could not be seen and waited until each patient laughed before thrusting them into the open mouth and extracting the offending tooth.

'The mission starts next week,' Eva told the Hwochow women. 'Bring your friends.'

These missions were a sight to be seen. Women arrived by foot, on donkeys and in mule carts.

1. Opium: a highly addictive, narcotic drug.

'Look at them,' said some men who were standing on a street corner. 'There must be 300 women there!'

'I've heard that the men in the church are doing the cooking during their conference,' another commented. 'And look,' he said, pointing in the direction of the church. 'They've laid out books for sale.'

'Let's go and see if there are any interesting books we can buy,' his friend suggested.

Each mission lasted for six days, and nearly every hour of each day was full.

For just over twenty years Mildred and Eva worked in Hwochow.

'Do you think we'll be here for the rest of our lives?' asked Eva, who was beginning to feel that might not be the case.

'No,' replied Mildred. 'I think the time may be coming when we should leave Hwochow, though we love it here.'

'That's how I feel,' Eva agreed. 'But we won't make rash decisions. We'll pray until we're quite sure what we're meant to do.'

Only after a whole year of prayer did the two women agree to leave Hwochow. Both felt that the Lord was leading them to North West China. They were led by God to travel the Gobi Desert gossiping the good news about the Lord Jesus Christ as they went, and distributing Bibles and Christian leaflets along the way.

'You mean you're going to settle in a desert village and start a church there?' someone asked.

'No,' said Mildred. 'We mean that our home will be by the side of the road and that our mission station will be the Silk Road through the great Gobi Desert.'

It was at this point that Eva's sister Francesca joined them. The three women became known as The Trio. The Silk Road was given its name because it was the ancient trade route along which silk and other goods were taken from the East to the West.

From Hwochow the Trio set out with their cart and all their belongings in June 1923, and it took them till March the following year to reach where their long trek was to begin, perhaps because they travelled at about three miles an hour.

'The Gobi Desert is the most amazing place,' said Mildred, two years and many miles later, 'quite apart from being a splendid mission field.'

'It's not much of a field really,' laughed Francesca. 'There is sand everywhere.'

Mildred nodded. 'True,' she said. 'At over 1,100 miles across it's a fair sized sandy mission field.'

'It's interesting, people think of deserts as being flat,' added Eva. 'They don't realise that they are mountainous places, and that hundreds of miles upon hundreds of miles look just the same.'

'Which is probably why people are happy to stop and talk to us about the Lord Jesus, and to come to the meetings we arrange. If you were travelling for many miles you'd be glad to stop and speak to someone.'

'And,' said Mildred, 'if you were on a mule cart, you'd be willing to buy a Bible. You could read right through it in the time it takes to travel the Silk Road.'

'What amazes me,' Eva added, 'is how soon people discover that you have a medical training. You seem to attract those who need your help.'

'It's God who leads us to people, and who leads the right people to us,' concluded Francesca.

That was certainly true about a little girl who arrived at their door in 1925 to beg for money. The poor mite could neither hear nor speak, and she had a dog bite on her leg.

'Why did your dog bite my little girl?' a woman yelled the following day, before demanding money from the missionaries.

'Go away,' said the missionaries' cook very firmly. 'You're a wicked woman.'

When Mildred, Eva and Francesca discovered the girl's story, they heartily agreed.

'The child was seven or eight years old, the daughter of a Mongol chief and a peasant girl. She was sold to that woman when she was just weeks old,' Mildred told a friend, some years later. 'But when she discovered the little girl was deaf and unable to speak, she kept her as a slave rather than a daughter, and sent her out begging every day. That's why we adopted Topsy and brought her up as our own.'

'She's like a daughter to you,' her friend said. 'And a very loving one too.'

In 1936 the three women left their work in the Gobi Desert and returned to the United Kingdom. Topsy went with them, of course.

'Have you retired now?' someone asked Mildred, when the four of them had settled in a little house near Shaftesbury in Dorset.

'It doesn't feel like it,' she replied. 'The Bible Society supported us while we were working abroad. Now we're working for the Bible Society as long as we're able. We continue to write our books. Having travelled to so many interesting places, the least we can do is write about it for others.'

Mildred Cable died in 1952. Eva and Francesca French both died eight years later. And Topsy, who led a happy and interesting life, lived on until 1998. The four women who spent their lives together on earth are now together in heaven with their Lord.

FACT FILE
The Gobi Desert
This is a large desert region in Northern China bounded by the Altay Mountains and the steppes of Mongolia on the north, the Tibetan Plateau to the south-west, and the North China Plain to the south-east. The word Gobi means 'very large and dry' in Mongolian. It was part of the great Mongol Empire.

Keynote: Francesca French mentions in the story that 'It's God who leads us to people, and who leads the right people to us.' Think about the people that you know. God might be leading you to someone for a very special reason. Perhaps he wants you to learn about his love for you and he is bringing someone into your life to teach you. Perhaps he wants to use you to bring someone else to trust in Jesus. Think about the people in your life - and pray about them. Show respect to those Christians who are older than you. If you have older people in your life, they are also gifts from God.

Think: The missionary lady with the Bible verse sewn into her collar said something to Mildred which is very important. 'You must go where the Lord sends you,' she said. 'If you are Christ's, you must be his entirely.' Remember this as you go about your day. Everything that you do should be done for the glory of God and you can't hold back any part of your life from the Lord Jesus. The way you act with family and friends should show them that you love Jesus. The things you do at school and outside school should be obedient to God. Don't just follow God at home and at church and then forget about his Word during a sports match.

Prayer: Lord, help me to see that you are my Creator and the only Saviour. May I realise that every good gift comes from you. You have given me so much, including your Son, the Lord Jesus Christ. Touch my heart so that I will want to belong to you entirely.

Katie Ann Mackinnon

Katie sat on the doorstep and pulled off her wellington boot. Her sock followed, then the eight-year-old had a good look at her heel.

'I knew it,' she said. 'I've got a blister. That's a pest!'

But it wasn't so much of a pest that it would stop her doing what she wanted to do. For when Katie put her mind to it, a little blister wouldn't prevent her having her own way. In fact, when Katie Ann Mackinnon put her mind to something, very little would stop her. With her wellington boot pulled on, she went right back to skipping with her sister. That night she had a really sore heel to show for it.

'Why didn't you come in and take off your boots?' Mum asked.

Katie frowned. 'Imagine being in the house on a nice day in winter. It's bad enough being stuck in when the rain comes and thinks we want it to stay. Why is Scotland so wet?'

'Just because it is,' was the only answer her mother could think of.

That night the girl thought about her blister as she lay in bed. She couldn't help herself, because every time she curled up her heel rubbed against the sheet and reminded her.

'I'm not going to let a stupid blister stop me sleeping,' she told herself. And she didn't!

A day or two later, one of Katie's school friends annoyed her.

'You're a ... You're just a ...'

Katie couldn't think what to call the boy who was being such a pest. Finally, in exasperation, she found the perfect word. 'You're a blister!'

The classroom was suddenly silent as everyone waited for the roof to fall down. But the teacher didn't give Katie a row, for she was struggling not to laugh.

'I've known some real blisters in my life,' she thought, 'Katie Ann Mackinnon among them.'

Katie recognised a close shave when she saw one, and it was probably relief that made her more boisterous than usual when she arrived back home. She was hardly in the door when her mother had to speak sharply to her.

'I'm sorry, Mum,' she said. And she meant it, for Katie's heart was soft and she really didn't like getting into trouble.

One of her sisters let the cat out the bag at teatime, telling Dad that she'd been cheeky in the classroom. As Dad was from the 'punish now and ask questions later' generation, Katie had her telling-off before he heard the whole story.

'You're a real wee blister yourself,' he said, when she explained that she'd not sworn at the teacher. But as he went down to the cowshed, Mr Mackinnon smiled to himself. 'That's a good word for a pest. Trust Katie to think of it.'

'It's not fair,' the girl decided in bed that night. 'I get punished whether I try to be good or not. I can't seem to please anyone at all ... ever.'

Most of all, Katie felt she could never please God. She hated listening to the long sermons preached in her church, and she could never keep her mind on the prayers that seemed to last till the week after next.

One day in 1948, in the town of Oban, Katie discovered someone she could please. And the good feeling it gave her made her decide what she wanted to do with her life. She was in hospital having her appendix out. Normally being stuck in hospital would have bored Katie into mischief – for she was just ten years old – but there was a baby in a cot next to her. Katie watched the nurse working with the baby, and did what she could to help Nurse Mackenzie to care for the little boy.

The nurse was the nicest and kindest person Katie could imagine.

'I'll be a nurse one day,' she decided that night, as she struggled to find a comfortable way to lie to stop her stitches hurting. 'And I'll nurse babies.'

Being away from home and in hospital wasn't easy for a little girl, especially when home was on an island and her family couldn't visit her every day. But Nurse Mackenzie made everything all right.

'I'll be just like her,' thought Katie. 'And everyone will like me for a change.'

Lying in her hospital bed, the girl could imagine what life would be like. She'd spend her days in a sparkling white uniform, gliding from bed to bed fixing a pillow here, changing a bandage there. Just her presence in a ward would make her patients feel better. 'Nurse Mackinnon,' she said softly. 'Sister Mackinnon,' she whispered. 'Yes,' she decided. 'That sounds just right.'

It was eight years later when Katie Ann Mackinnon spent her first day on the wards. She'd been at college for two years, then spent six weeks in nursing school. Now, here she was, ready for whatever was waiting for her on the ward. By the end of day one she had decided that the Ward Sister was the biggest blister she had ever encountered, apart from those on her poor tired feet.

'Have you had a good day?' another student nurse asked her.

'If you'd clapped eyes on my Sister you wouldn't ask that question!' snapped Katie. 'I've danced attention on her all day and she thinks I don't deserve the air I breathe.'

The truth was that Katie had loved it. She was a nurse at last. Well, not exactly a nurse ... not for another three years yet.

Katie's life seemed blighted by blisters. If they weren't on her feet and hands from working so hard, they were telling her what to do. She had many good points, did Nurse Mackinnon, but coping with people in authority wasn't one of them.

'Matron wants to see you in her office,' the young woman was told, some time into her training.

Wondering what she'd done this time kept her busy as she walked briskly along the hospital corridor to her interview. When she left the Matron's office her walk was very different. It was more of slow crawl.

'So,' she gasped, as she headed in the direction of her ward, 'I'll get the sack if I don't improve.'

She could hardly believe what was happening to her. Had she not always wanted to be a nurse? Did she not put everything into caring for patients? What was wrong with her? It didn't take Katie long to answer her own questions. It always boiled down to the same thing. She didn't like doing what she was told if she didn't see the point of it. And she especially didn't like doing what she was told if she didn't respect the person who was doing the telling.

There was one student nurse in the Royal Northern Infirmary in Inverness whom Katie respected very much. Her name was Jean. In her heart Katie knew that she wanted to be friends with Jean, but her fellow student was a Christian and that put her off in a big way. To Katie Christianity meant everlasting sermons and endless long prayers. In one word, Christianity was, in her opinion, B-o-r-i-n-g with a capital B. But after a very serious heart-to-heart talk with Jean and her boyfriend, George, who was a doctor in the hospital, Katie discovered that the opposite was the truth. To her total and utter amazement Katie Mackinnon suddenly realised that what the Bible taught was true, Jesus does change lives. That night he changed her. Katie became a Christian.

Life didn't suddenly become easy for Katie but it was certainly different. She didn't get the sack. In fact, she passed her final exams well and went to work as a staff nurse in Greenock, near Glasgow. After a time there she left to train to be a midwife.

'I said I wanted to nurse children,' she thought. 'Now I know that it was God who put it in my heart. But I wonder what he wants me to do with my life.'

There was a time when Katie Mackinnon was only interested in what she wanted to do. As a Christian it was now her heart's desire to please God.

'Serving God is like being a piece in an enormous jigsaw puzzle,' a missionary told her. 'God has planned for each of us a place of our own and nobody else can fill it.'

In May 1971 Katie Ann Mackinnon discovered where she fitted. Accepted by Africa Inland Mission, she flew to Kenya to work as a missionary nurse among the Kipsigis people. Her work was based in Litein Dispensary, a little hospital with nearly fifty beds ... and no resident doctor.

'I have a pain here,' a man said, after standing in the long queue waiting for treatment.

Katie looked where the man pointed, decided what she thought was wrong with him, and gave him medicine to take for a week. Next in the queue was another man ... and another ... and another. The women were right at the end of the queue.

Katie smiled as each new patient smiled at her. Even without much language, the people knew their missionary cared for them. But they knew she cared for their babies best of all. Katie's face lit up each time she held a tiny baby or a squirming toddler. She had no children of her own but she had space in her heart for every child she met.

'This one won't live,' a helper in the dispensary said, looking at the newborn baby whose mother had died.

When Katie first saw Chepkirui she thought of all that could have been done in Scotland for such a small, ill baby. But neither the equipment nor the medicines were available in Litein.

'Give her a tiny amount of warm milk every three hours and keep her warm. Cuddle her to let her know she's wanted,' she told the teenage hospital carer.

On returning after a clinic, she found Chepkirui abandoned and ignored. When she demanded an explanation, Katie discovered that people thought that babies whose mother died should be left to die too. There was no way that the staff could be persuaded to nurse Chepkirui in a way that would save her life.

'I'll take her home and look after her myself,' decided Katie, much to the astonishment of the hospital staff.

Closing her house door behind her, the missionary felt a surge of joy at the prospect of nursing this scrap of a baby to health and wholeness. And that's just what happened. Chepkirui took her feeds, grew, smiled, giggled and loved Katie with all her tiny heart.

After Chepkirui came Kipngeno, a little boy cursed by a witch doctor.

'She won't risk taking him,' the local people said.

They didn't know Katie. Kipngeno joined Chepkirui, and the pair of them gave her many sleepless nights that were followed by busy days working in the dispensary.

'She'll never keep it up,' some said. 'You're being very silly,' added others. 'You're here to be a missionary, not a mother.' Some people even tried to make life more difficult for Katie than it already was, what with juggling her job and the care of her babies.

'They're real blisters,' she thought, ignoring them when she could, and struggling to work with them when they couldn't be ignored.

It wasn't long before tiny premature Kipkoech joined Chepkirui and Kipngeno. 'She's running a baby home,' some folk said, amazed at Katie's love for these children. That's exactly what God led her to do. Missionary Katie Mackinnon, who had objected to authority as a young person, wanted more than anything to do God's will. Bit-by-bit, the Lord showed her that he wanted her to organise care for needy little children in Kenya.

'How many children are you caring for now?' she was asked, when there were more than twenty.

'Enough to appreciate all the help I can get,' she said. 'Are you offering?'

A couple did offer to help. Matthew and Priscilla, themselves Kenyans, took much of the burden of the children's home - which, by then, was recognised as an official centre for the care of needy children.

'Leave Litein!' Katie gasped. Africa Inland Mission had told her to move to Mulango Dispensary, which was more of a slum than a clinic. Katie was not happy. But at that point she didn't know about Philip, John, Mutuo and Musembe, the first four Mulango babies whom she would love as her own, nor about the others who would follow them. She didn't know about the baby home that would one day be built at Kitui. God had still to show Katie what her part was in his Mulango jigsaw.

'Never in my wildest dreams could I have imagined that we'd have eighty children in the Kitui home during a famine, and that 700 people would come here for food to keep them alive till God sent rain again,' she thought in amazement, after a particularly difficult time in Kenya.

Some years in the future, God had another jigsaw into which Katie was to fit. In 1998,

Matthew, Katie, an architect and a quantity surveyor met in her office. They were drawing up plans for a third home for Kenyan children. This time in Mogogosiek.

'How much money do you have?' the architect asked.

'None,' was Katie's reply.

The two visitors could not have been more surprised if she'd handed them all the money they needed with an ice cream on top!

'God will give us the money as we need it,' explained Katie.

The look on the faces of the architect and quantity surveyor said it all.

But God did just that. Money came in as it was required, and the baby home in Mogogosiek was opened in 1999, not one penny in debt! When Katie Ann Mackinnon retired to her native Scotland, she left three children's homes in the care of Matthew and Priscilla. They were part of God's jigsaw too.

FACT FILE
Africa Inland Mission
AIM was founded over 100 years ago when Peter Cameron Scott gathered around him a group of fellow workers. Cameron Scott records that he '... seemed to see a line of mission stations stretching from the coast, on into the mysteries of the Sahara Desert.' The small group that arrived in Mombasa in 1895 made their way inland. It was not long before disease overtook them and before two years had passed, all but one of them had died. Scott himself died of blackwater fever. But all was not lost. The survivor stayed on and before long others joined him. Over the years the work has spread, initially from Kenya out to Tanzania, Congo, Uganda and Central Africa Republic.

Keynote: As a Christian, it was Katie's desire to please God. Pleasing God does not mean that we are rewarded with forgiveness of sins. Jesus loved us while we were still sinners. He loved us so much he died for us. Forgiveness is given to those who ask for it. It's a gift - not a reward.

Think: Katie was asked by AIM to leave Litein. She had been very happy there and didn't really want to go at first. But in the end she discovered that it had been in God's plan for her to leave as God had seen the needs of the people in Mulango. Sometimes we have to do things that we don't really want to do – like move away from home, go somewhere we hadn't planned or do a job we don't really want to do. God has things to teach us during difficult days as well as during good ones. He can send us in directions we don't want to go and, like Jonah in the Bible, we may want to run in the opposite direction. Instead, we should be obedient and trust in God to help us.

Prayer: Thank you, Lord, for providing for all our needs and for providing for the orphans and children in Katie's orphanages. Thank you that there are people around the world like Katie who have followed your example by loving the people that nobody else wanted to love. Thank you, Lord Jesus, for showing your love to sinners by dying for them on the cross.

Sarah Edwards

Sarah sat on the floor in front of her mother for the nightly ritual of hair brushing. As it was Saturday the hairdressing routine was interesting. The child's long hair was separated into eight or ten bunches then each bunch was wrapped in a strip of damp cloth that was tied at the end. The following morning the cloths - which had dried overnight - were unwrapped and Sarah's fine hair fell into long ringlets around her shoulders. The seven-year-old did a twirl. She liked the feel of her ringlets swinging around her head.

'You look like your grandmother,' her mother said.

'Why?' the child asked. 'Does she twirl to make her hair dance?'

Mrs Pierrepont laughed at the thought.

'I suspect that it's a very long time since Grandma did a twirl,' she said. 'But when she was your age, I'm quite sure she did.'

'Tell me about when my grandmothers were young,' Sarah said.

Her mother thought for a moment.

'Both your grandmothers came from important families. One of your great-grandfathers was the first mayor of New York and another was a founder of Connecticut.'

'How did he found Connecticut?' Sarah asked. 'Was it lost?'

For a minute her mother wasn't sure if the child was being serious, but then she saw the twinkle in her eye.

'Our friends at church will think we're lost if we don't get a move on. The service starts in an hour and you're still not properly dressed.'

Getting dressed in 1717 was a long job. First of all Sarah put on her shift. It was made from rectangles of white linen sewn together and it slipped over her head. Next she put on her stays. This amazing garment was made of heavy linen with wooden splints sewn into it to make her sit and stand properly.

'Don't pull my stays so tight that they pinch,' Sarah told her mother.

'Of course not,' Mrs Pierrepont said. 'Though some women wear their stays so tight I just don't know how they can breathe!'

Having pulled the crisscross laces until they were just comfortable, Mother Pierrepont tied the laces together and tucked them into her daughter's stays.

'I like my Sunday gown,' laughed Sarah, as the material tickled her on its way over her head. 'It's blue like cornflowers.'

Before they left for church the girl wrapped herself in her dark blue cloak and put on her wide-brimmed bonnet, tying its ribbons into a bow to the left of her face. That was the fashion of the day.

'Your father would have loved seeing you looking so fine,' Mrs Pierrepont said, as they walked together to the congregational church in New Haven, on the Atlantic Ocean coast of New England.

'Father died half my life ago,' Sarah said sadly. 'I was four when he died, and I'm nearly eight now. But I remember him very well,' she added.

'What do you remember best?' her mother asked.

'I remember him preaching in church and you sitting at the front facing the congregation – just where you sit now. I could see you both together, and I liked that.'

'It's a strange custom in our church that the minister's wife sits at the front during the service rather than looking at the minister.'

'Did your mother and her mother sit in the same kind of high seats?' the child asked, knowing that her grandfather and great-grandfather had also been ministers.

'Yes, I'm sure they did,' was the reply, as they reached the door of the church.

'Now, Sarah, remember to be quiet and pray before the service. We need to prepare our hearts before we can worship God.'

That was no problem for the seven-year-old. Sarah was often very aware that God was near her, even nearer than people in the same room. There were few times in the week she enjoyed more than the minutes before the church service began. She loved to sit quietly thinking about the Lord. When the service began, she joined the congregation singing praise to God, Sarah was as happy as could be.

'Sarah is a most unusual girl,' a friend told Mrs Pierrepont, as they sat side by side sewing. They always sewed in the window seat, for that's where the light was best.

'I know that,' was the quiet answer. 'Even when she was a little child toddling around at our feet, she seemed to have a sense that the Lord was with her. My husband often said he had never known such a child. But perhaps he was biased,' Mrs Pierrepont smiled. 'After all, she was his own little girl and he was well past the normal age of having a baby daughter to admire.'

The friend thought of the Sarah she knew and loved, and agreed with the late Mr Pierrepont. She was indeed a very special little girl.

In 1723, when Sarah was thirteen years old, a minister and college teacher named Jonathan Edwards met her for the first time. Although he was twenty, he was very taken with the girl.

'She is of a wonderful sweetness, calmness, and universal benevolence of mind,' he wrote. 'She will sometimes go about from place to place, singing sweetly, and seems always to be full of joy and pleasure and no one knows for what. She loves to be alone, walking in the fields and groves, and seems to have someone invisible always conversing with her.'

It was quite true. Sarah did like walking alone, and the 'someone invisible' who kept her company was the Lord.

Just four years later Sarah and Jonathan were married. She was seventeen and he was twenty-four. That was on 28th July 1727.

'Tell me all about your family,' said Jonathan. 'I just love to hear you talking.'

Sarah relaxed beside him. 'We're like your family,' she said. 'Both our families came over from England in order to have freedom to worship God as they wished. And my family has done very well. We have kept to our faith and the Lord has blessed us.'

Jonathan thought of the family into which he had married, and agreed.

'That is true,' he said. 'You're the daughter of a minister, who was the son of a minister, who was the son of yet another minister. And now you've gone and married a minister yourself.'

'And where are you going to be minister?' Sarah teased her new husband.

He laughed heartily. 'In Northampton, with my grandfather, who's a minister. And my father's a minister too. What a pedigree!'

'What a privilege,' said Sarah. 'All those generations of our family have served the Lord. May we also serve him with all our hearts.'

Sarah's first Sunday in Northampton followed the local tradition. She attended church wearing her wedding dress, and sat right at the front, facing the congregation, as she had seen her mother do. It was an honour to sit there, but a problem too.

'What would people think if I yawned?' Sarah asked herself. 'Would they decide that I was finding the sermon boring?'

For the first few months the young couple lived with Jonathan's Grandfather Stoddard. Then they moved to their own home, a homestead with land around it and more land some distance away.

Marriage to Jonathan Edwards was interesting, not least because Sarah saw the back of her husband's head more often than she saw his face.

'How many hours a day does he spend in his study?' a visitor asked one day.

'Thirteen or fourteen,' Sarah replied. 'That's why he's up at five o'clock each morning.'

Her friend smiled. 'I expect you snuggle down to sleep for another hour or two.'

'Not at all,' said her hostess. 'We are all up at five a.m. There's so much to do.'

And Sarah's life was certainly busy. Jonathan had worked out a regime of exercise, diet and sleep that allowed him to concentrate during the long hours in his study. Although she had servants to help her, Sarah made it her business to ensure that his routine went as smoothly as possible. She was a wise woman, for God blessed Jonathan's time in his study. He wrote Christian books that are so important that they have never since been out of print, and can still be bought in shops today.

'What's happening in Northampton?' Sarah asked her husband, soon after their daughter Mary's birth in 1734. She was their fourth daughter. 'The people I meet in the town want to talk about Jesus rather than about their children. I've been asked to more women's prayer meetings recently than ever before.'

Jonathan smiled. 'It's an extraordinary time,' he agreed. 'People are becoming

Christians every week. God is pouring out blessings throughout Connecticut.'

Early the following year he was able to say that thirty people were being converted each week. Sometimes those wanting to talk about Jesus actually queued at the Edwards' door. This wonderful time became known as the 'Great Awakening,' and it continued for eight amazing years. But not everyone was pleased, and Jonathan faced opposition that was hard to bear.

In 1742, just as the Great Awakening was drawing to an end, Sarah had an experience she was never to forget.

'Oh, Mr Edwards,' their servant said, when he came back from preaching away from home. 'Mrs Edwards has been taken really poorly. We've even feared for her life.'

Rushing to his wife, Jonathan discovered that it was not quite as the servant had described, though his poor wife was utterly exhausted.

'Tell me all about it,' he said gently.

Sarah described the experience she had gone through. For seventeen days and nights she had been totally overwhelmed by a sense of God's presence. 'And,' she concluded her story, 'I've handed everything over to God – our lives, our deaths, our everything. It's all in his hands.'

Sarah's trust in God was soon tested. By 1744, when their latest daughter was two and baby Jonathan had just been born, a stranger visited them.

'What's happening?' the man asked Jonathan, seeing soldiers in a watchtower in the Edwards' garden.

'As you know France and England are at war and, amazingly, that puts New Englanders in the thick of it. Some French Canadians are paying Indians to attack our English settlements. A number of locals have been scalped.'

Throughout it all, Sarah was able to put her trust in God.

War was not their only problem. In 1747, having nursed a young missionary who then died of tuberculosis, the Edwards' daughter Jerusha died. She was just seventeen years old. Although Jonathan and Sarah grieved for their daughter, still they were able to trust in the God who does all things well. And they continued to do that when baby Elizabeth was born, even though she was a sickly little girl.

There were even difficulties in the church at Northampton. An issue arose that resulted in Jonathan being asked to leave in 1750. Having been brought up in a wealthy family, for the first time Sarah found herself with no income just weeks after their eleventh, and last, baby was born. He was called Pierrepont, his mother's name before she married.

'It seems that our life is to take on a new direction,' Jonathan said, not long afterwards. And it certainly did, as he became a missionary to the native Indians who lived in Stockbridge, about sixty miles West of Northampton, in October 1751.

'What are you doing?' little Elizabeth asked.

Sarah smiled. 'We used to be able to buy paper for Papa to write on, but we don't have enough money now,' she explained. 'So I'm sewing together all the scraps of paper I can find for him to use.'

'But how can they ever become books?' asked Elizabeth.

Sarah smiled. 'They will if that's what God wants,' she said, pulling Elizabeth on to her knee beside her baby brother.

'Why do you think God brought us here?' asked her son Jonathan, who was thirteen years old.

His mother looked at the tall lad. Many of the Edwards family were tall for their age.

'We don't know what God's plans are,' Sarah said. 'But we do know they are good.'

And God's good plan was that he should learn two American Indian languages and become a missionary to the people whose languages he spoke.

Esther Edwards fell in love with Aaron Burr, and they were married in 1752.

'Your father is a remarkable man,' someone said to her, at the wedding.

The bride agreed.

'And my mother is a most remarkable woman,' she added.

'In what way?' Esther was asked.

'God gave Mother the gift of accepting what happens without grumbling, knowing that the Lord always does what is good, even when we can't see what good will come out of it.'

Five years later, Sarah Edwards' gift of accepting God's will was put to the test yet again. The President of New Jersey College died. Jonathan Edwards accepted an invitation to become President and moved to Princeton in advance of Sarah. Smallpox was a problem and Jonathan was inoculated against the disease. The injection caused him to develop smallpox from which he died. Just before he went to heaven, he was heard to thank God for his married life. But Jonathan and Sarah were not to be separated for long. Shortly after her husband's death, Sarah became unwell and died after just five days' illness. Knowing that God always does what is best, she died in peace.

FACT FILE

Connecticut

This is one of the states of the United States of America. Connecticut is New England's second smallest and southernmost state. It is bordered by New York State on the west, Rhode Island on the east, Massachusetts on the north and by Long Island Sound on the south.

Keynote: Sarah Edwards recognized that being brought up in a Christian home was a privilege. Many of her family were Christians, and many of those family members from her past had been believers in Jesus too. She said, 'May we also serve him with all our hearts.' If you belong to a family who love God, ask yourself, 'have I given my life and heart to Jesus?' If your family doesn't love God, ask yourself the same question. We all need to be saved. If you love Jesus and your family doesn't, you can pray to God to save them too. In the future you may have a family of your own and you can teach your own children to worship God and follow Jesus.

Think: Marriage and careers and work are things that people often think about while growing up. They wonder whom they will marry or what job they will do. If you live your life under God's guidance, reading his Word and obeying his instructions, he will guide you in the right path. The choices you make will be right ones and you will honour God with your life. This is the right thing to do. 'In all your ways acknowledge him and he will direct your paths.' Proverbs 3:6

Prayer: Lord and Heavenly Father, help me to teach others about you, even members of my own family. Teach me from your Word so that I may teach the children of the future to obey your Word and trust in you.

Patricia St John

'Please tell me again about when I was born,' said Patricia. It was one of her favourite stories.

Mrs St John laughed. 'You know it so well you could write a book about it.'

The six-year-old grinned.

'Please ....'

'All right then,' her mother agreed. 'Dad and I were missionaries in Brazil. We loved it there, despite our home being aptly nicknamed 'The House of a Thousand Fleas.' However, Dad was asked to set up Bible schools in remote villages, which would have meant a life of travelling. That was why he went back alone and I stayed here in England with your sister and brother.'

'But you've missed out me being born!'

'Oops. Right, in 1919, not long before Dad returned to Brazil alone, he borrowed a pram big enough to take both your sister and brother. He wasn't used to pushing a pram. It ran out of control and Hazel and Farnham were thrown out. They weren't hurt, but I got such a fright that you were born a few hours later.'

Patricia grinned. 'What a start!'

'Write a story about home,' the teacher said. 'Just a few sentences.'

Patricia St John picked up her pencil.

'Home is called Homesdale and it's in Malvern. Great Granny lives there, and Granny and Mum. Then there's my big sister Hazel and my big brother Farnham, and me. Dad is a missionary in Brazil and only lives with us when he comes to England. We laugh a lot in our home.'

Mrs St John laughed very heartily one day when Patricia's younger brother Oliver was about four. Oliver had made a pretend train with three chairs, one in front of the other. When she came home, the train had Oliver on the front chair driving and Great Granny in her nightgown on the second. Both were bumping up and down saying, 'Puff puff, puff puff'.

'Why are there no other children in our church?' Patricia asked. 'Apart from the Stayputs?'

Granny shook her head. 'You mustn't call those dears the Stayputs. They're so good when they come to church when they're here on holiday.'

The girl nodded. 'That's why we call them the Stayputs. Their hats are always straight on and they never move during the service.'

'Unlike you?' suggested Granny.

'I love church, but I need to move sometimes. And I love Sunday afternoons.'

Smiling, Granny agreed that Sunday afternoons were special.

'Mind you, I don't know how your mother finds time to make these wonderful missionary scrapbooks for you to look at on Sundays.'

'I like our Sunday biscuits,' Patricia said. 'I'm sure there's not another family in England that has Sunday biscuits made in the shape of the letters of the alphabet so that the children can make them into Bible verses.'

After a Sunday story about a little Chinese girl who learned the verse 'Fear not, I have redeemed you; I have called you by name; you are mine' (Isaiah 43:2), Patricia prayed a special prayer. Kneeling down beside her bed, she told God, 'My name is Patricia, and if you are really calling me I want to come and be yours.'

'Look!' she shouted in delight the following morning. 'What beautiful flowers!'

Having become God's child the little girl saw, even more clearly than before, what a beautiful world her Lord had made.

In 1926 Mrs St John took her young family to Switzerland for a year.

'I won't understand what anyone says,' said Patricia, as she set off on her first day at school.

'You'll learn French quickly,' her mother assured her. 'And you'll make friends too.'

She was right. All her life Patricia was a noticing person. She noticed little details and was able to remember them. So, many years later when she wrote *Treasures of the Snow*, she was able to remember details from that year in Switzerland.

Although Patricia had asked the Lord to be her Saviour when she was six, and despite being brought up in a loving Christian home, she was not always a happy teenager. Much of the reason was that her love for the Lord had grown cold. One day, after an angry outburst, Patricia stormed to her room. She was in her mid-teens at the time. Picking up an old Bible that she'd rarely read for some years, she opened it.

'Behold, I stand at the door and knock,' she read from Revelation 3:20, 'if any man hear my voice and open the door, I will come in.'

'It was wonderful,' she told her best friend the next day. 'I seemed to see Jesus standing in a storm saying, "If you will ask me in, I will take you where you want to go."'

Patricia wasn't immediately a happy, carefree teenager, but things began to get better as she read her Bible and prayed to her Lord. But there were always some things that could make her smile.

'What's that noise?' a visitor asked one day.

Patricia's mother was on her feet immediately and on her way to the door.

The girl giggled. 'I think we have unwelcome visitors,' she explained. 'We have ducks down at the end of the orchard. If they see our front door open they march up in single file and come in.'

'What do they do then?' she was asked.

'Well, either Mum chases them out again or they march right through the house and go out the back door.' She laughed at the sounds from the hall, 'It's a Mum chasing them day!'

After school Patricia had hoped to study medicine like her older brother. Unfortunately there was a mix-up with her application form that prevented her from going.

'You can work for me,' her aunt, who ran a school, suggested.

'Helping to teach primary children is not exactly what I want to do,' the girl thought. However, she discovered she enjoyed it very much indeed, thought that job was only a stopgap.

'I've been accepted for nursing training,' she told her aunt in 1942. 'I'm starting at St Thomas's Hospital in London next January.

'What a battle-axe,' Patricia thought, after only two days on the ward. 'I'll never be able to please that Sister.'

'Do this quickly! Do that immediately! Do the other thing yesterday!' barked the Sister, all day, every day.

'Oh my poor fingers,' moaned the young nurse. 'One of them's gone septic.'

Not long afterwards some of her toes became septic too.

'What happening to me?' she asked herself. 'I'm falling apart!'

After a spell off work, Matron suggested she might not be cut out for nursing.

In a fit of despair Patricia went for a walk, eventually arriving at the railway station. There at the entrance, in huge black letters, she read the words, 'Jesus said, "Do you not believe that I am able to do this?"'

Standing in front of the large poster for a long time, the young woman thought hard.

'Yes,' she decided. 'I believe you are able.'

Walking back to the hospital she continued her nursing and did well. When she completed her training, Patricia went home and worked for a local doctor before becoming housemother at her aunt's school.

'You know,' she told her friend. 'So many of these children have missionary parents and they don't see them for years at a time.'

'Do you mother them then?'

Patricia smiled. 'Over the winter months I light a fire in the evenings and the children come down in dressing gowns, clutching their teddy bears, and I tell them a story while they're having their cocoa and biscuits.'

That was the beginning of her storytelling. It was then that she wrote *The Tanglewoods' Secret*. She wrote it, first and foremost, for the children at Clarendon School.

In 1949 Patricia packed her cases and went to be with her brother, a doctor in Tangier, Morocco. For the next year she kept house for him and helped in the hospital. Then the time came when the Lord led her to work in a mountain town above Tangier.

'My little house has a wonderful view,' she wrote home. 'I look down on the market place, then over layers of many roofs to the mountains. Mind you, it does have some disadvantages. Yesterday my room flooded again and I came home to find my saucepan bobbing along like a boat in full sail. Time to go – must get on with my language study.'

And that's what kept Patricia busy for her first few months there, that and completing *Treasures of the Snow*.

'Hello,' she said when she opened her door one day.

'I'm hungry. Can I have some bread?'

Patricia looked at the thin little lad on her doorstep.

'Of course, come in and have some.'

The following night he arrived with five or six of his friends. They'd never tasted bread and treacle before, and they loved it.

'Would you like me to tell you a story?' Patricia asked, as they licked their fingers.

They grinned and said they would. She told them about Jesus, the Good Shepherd. Bread and treacle with a story was a recipe that kept the boys coming back. Wherever she went, Patricia reached right to the heart of children, usually through her stories.

'Goodness me,' laughed Patricia, as she unpacked a parcel one day. 'A clockwork mouse!'

It had come from someone who had heard about the children. The boys and girls loved it, and they were not the only ones.

'Thank you for coming,' the missionary said to the ladies who had attended her meeting.

Nobody moved and more women started to appear. Patricia gave another talk and again thanked the women for coming. No one moved. Puzzled, she waited for an explanation.

'We've come to see the mouse,' admitted one of the ladies.

Greatly amused Patricia took out the clockwork mouse, wound it up, and watched as her visitors screamed at its antics.

'That's one way to encourage women to come to meetings,' she thought, when they did eventually go. 'And they heard two talks about Jesus.'

When winter drew on, and children kept coming to her home for stories, Patricia started to write *Star of Light*, based on what she saw around her at that time.

'Would you come and visit the sick people in our village?' she was asked after a while.

'Yes,' replied Patricia, delighted to have the opportunity to help and to talk about the Lord Jesus Christ.

'Now then,' she said to her helper. 'What do we need?"

Patricia went through a list, 'Iron tablets, malt for mums-to-be, eye ointment and worm medicines, sulphur tablets for babies who have sickness and diarrhoea. What else?'

'Do you have the gentian violet for sores?'

'What would I do without you?' Patricia smiled, popping the gentian violet into her bag.

When she was asked to stay overnight in villages there was more storytelling.

Five years after moving to town, the missionary work began to be opposed.

'There have been complaints about your activities,' she was told. 'And I'm afraid we're cancelling your helper's visa.'

Patricia St John was not the only one who was broken-hearted at the thought of leaving the town. She left many sad friends behind, adults as well as children, but they still remembered her stories. However, as she travelled to England for Christmas she thought over her work in Morocco and smiled. As well as teaching and nursing she'd written *Three Go Searching, The Fourth Candle* and *Star of Light.*

When Patricia returned to Morocco, it was to Tangier where Farnham was a doctor.

'You attract young people,' her brother said, when she set up home with seven teenage girls, all of them student nurses.

'What do I do?' she wrote home in answer to a letter. 'I teach the girls, help look after them, and child-mind for Farnham and Janet's six children when I can. As well as that I help at the baby milk clinic, do what I can in the hospital - and tell stories to anyone who will listen. It's a busy life!'

Patricia's life certainly was busy. In 1966 she left Morocco to go to Rwanda in order to research a book on the history of a period of church growth known as the Rwanda Revival. For some years God blessed Rwanda in an amazing way and Patricia was asked to write a book about it. Of course, her time in Rwanda made her long for revival in her beloved Morocco, that Muslim land in which teaching about Jesus was often far from welcome.

'I've always been fascinated by the story of Onesimus in the Bible,' Patricia told a friend.

'Why don't you write about him then?' was the reply.

'I can't,' explained the storyteller. 'I can only write about places I've been to.'

'Then go!'

That was the start of a trip round Bible sites that enabled her to write *Twice Freed*, the story of Onesimus, the runaway slave.

'I can hardly believe that it's ten years since I wrote about Onesimus,' said Patricia to her sister Hazel in 1976. 'Or that I'm back in the Middle East. What a busy city Beirut is.'

She had gone to help Hazel for a few weeks after she'd fractured her hip in a fall.

'You're doing well on those crutches,' Patricia laughed. 'In fact, you're hopping around like a kangaroo. It won't be long until you'll be well enough to wave me goodbye and send me back to England.'

'No doubt you'll put this visit to good use and write a book based on what you've seen.'

Her younger sister laughed. 'You never know.'

She did. It's called *Nothing Else Matters.*

From then until her death in November 1993, Patricia St John was based in England, though she continued to travel from time to time. When she died and went to heaven she met Jesus, whose stories she had known and loved since before she could remember.

FACT FILE
Morocco
Also known as the Kingdom of Morocco it is bordered by the Mediterranean Sea, the Atlantic Ocean, the Western Sahara, and Algeria. Rabat is the capital and Casablanca the most populous city. Central Morocco consists largely of the Atlas Mountains which rise to 4,167 metres. In the south lie the sandy wastes of the Sahara Desert. The vast majority of Moroccans are Muslims of Arab-Berber ancestry. Arabic is the official language, but French, several Berber dialects, and Spanish are also spoken. On the Atlantic coast, where there are extensive plains, olives, citrus fruits, and wine grapes are grown.

Keynote: Patricia read the words of Jesus Christ, 'Do you not believe that I am able to do this?' When you have problems do you bring them to God and ask him for help? Or do you try and muddle through on your own? Jesus tells us not to worry. He reminds us that God loves us and will look after us. God looks after the sparrows and he will look after you and help you with problems big and small.

Think: 'Behold, I stand at the door and knock, if any man hear my voice and open the door, I will come in,' Revelation 3:20. This is the verse that Patricia read and which brought her back to a stronger relationship with Jesus. She imagined that she could see Jesus standing in a storm saying, 'If you will ask me in, I will take you where you want to go.' Have you asked Jesus into your heart? Are you willing to let him take control of your life and to take you not just where you want to go but to where he wants you to go?

Prayer: Lord Jesus, thank you for all the wonderful stories you told in the Bible. Thank you for the teaching and the truth that we read. Your Word is truth. We can trust it completely. Help me to realise that nothing else matters but you, and that you are the only one who can truly save me from sin.

Helen Roseveare

'You have a new baby sister,' the nurse told Helen, when she was nine years old.

Helen knew all about younger sisters as she already had two. She smiled, 'That means Bob is outnumbered by four to one.'

Numbers played a big part in Helen's home because everyone was so good at doing things with them. Mr Roseveare was a mathematician. Bob, her older brother, could do sums in his head that most people could not do on a sheet of paper. Helen was always top of the class in Maths, and in nearly everything else. In fact, if she was not top of the class, she felt empty inside, as though she had let everyone down. Of course, that made her very popular with her teachers, but it didn't make her popular with the other girls in her school in Preston, Lancashire.

Mr Roseveare, who had started his working life teaching mathematics, was by then a school inspector.

'That's why we move house every three years,' he explained to Helen one day. 'It is very hard to be fair about the work done by people you know and like. And it's even harder to be fair about the work done by people you know and dislike.'

'I dislike moving school so often,' Helen replied.

'It's not for much longer,' smiled her father. 'By next year you'll be ready to go to boarding school.'

In 1937, when she was twelve years old, Helen went to a boarding school in the north of Wales.

'It's different from the other schools Father and Mother took me to see,' she thought, looking round her fellow pupils.

One thing made it especially different and really very modern for its day, and that was the summer uniform. Instead of wearing school dresses and hats, the girls wore culottes and different coloured short-sleeved shirts that opened with three or four buttons at the neck. Of course, they didn't call them culottes in those days; they were known as divided skirts.

Helen felt strange, and very much the new girl. However, before very long she had the beginnings of a friendship - with a Maths teacher. Because she loved Maths and did it so well, her teacher remembered her name very quickly. And as she was an excellent teacher the woman enjoyed her excellent pupil. But not everyone did.

'Teacher's pet,' she heard girls whisper from time to time, though she couldn't always pick out who had said it.

'Helen's a natural hockey player,' the gym mistress said, one lunchtime in the staff-room.

'And a natural mathematician,' said the maths teacher.

'But she's a loner,' another teacher pointed out. 'We'll have to keep an eye on her. Girls who are good at too many things sometimes have problems making friends.'

In a way Helen did have a problem. It wasn't that she felt she had been sent away to boarding school out of her parents' way. Not at all. It was just that she didn't feel loved or special. That made her work hard and play hard because winning prizes and winning games made her feel good.

'The First Form prize this year goes to Helen Roseveare,' the Headmistress said, at her first speech day.

'The Second Form prize this year goes to Helen Roseveare,' she announced, at her next speech day.

'The Third Form prize this year goes to Helen Roseveare,' said the Headmistress, the following year.

'Congratulations!' Her father smiled, pleased with her success.

'Well done!' agreed her mother. 'You're a credit to us.'

Helen felt good. She had pleased her parents by working hard and gaining prizes.

The Second World War broke out in 1939. For a couple of years war had seemed a possibility, then a probability. It was still a shock when Neville Chamberlain, the Prime Minister, made his famous radio broadcast announcing that Britain was at war with Germany. It was hoped that war would be over in a few months. But it wasn't.

Just as she went off to boarding school Helen's family moved to Kent, south-east of London. Wartime visits home could be dramatic.

'Come and count the planes,' her youngest sister called one evening, when the British bombers flew overhead on their nightly mission to drop bombs on Germany.

'One, two, three, four .... Twenty-seven, twenty-eight,' they counted them out.

'Hurry! Hurry! Here they come!' yelled her sister, when the first of the planes could be heard in the distance as they returned. 'Twenty-six, twenty-seven, twenty-eight. They're all back safely!' There was a real sense of relief.

But there were nights when a shadow fell over the household. Sometimes a plane didn't come back from the bombing raid. Helen was old enough to know what that meant to a family somewhere in the United Kingdom.

Of course, bombing raids were made in the other direction too, and they also counted German bombers in and out. There were plenty of them to count, for the bombing was fierce and furious at times. Occasionally a plane was shot down nearby. With her sleeves rolled up, Mrs Roseveare set about cleaning up injuries and comforting the young German pilots.

'I don't know how you can do that,' Helen said. 'They're our enemies!'

Mrs Roseveare looked at her oldest daughter and realised that, although she would soon be going off to university, she still had some growing up to do.

'Why have I come here?' Helen asked herself fearfully, as she looked round Room 12a in Clough Hall on her first day at Cambridge University. 'I'll never fit in. I don't know anyone at all.'

Helen looked in the mirror at her strained face and saw a card tucked under the frame.

'If you don't know anyone, and have nowhere to go after supper, come and have coffee in Room no. 8, at 8 pm. Dorothy.'

Relief, fear, excitement and homesickness hit Helen one at a time, and sometimes all together. But a least someone called Dorothy cared.

As the clock struck eight, Helen made her way to Room 8. She knocked, wondering what kind of reception awaited her.

'Can you make a fire?' a kneeling Dorothy asked, from amidst a swirl of smoke.

What a relief! She could make a fire. And no, Dorothy wasn't perfect, didn't know everyone and everything ... at least she didn't know how to make a fire. Dorothy's welcome and friendship helped Helen settle down at university. But what Helen didn't know then was that Dorothy loved the Lord Jesus Christ and longed for her new friend to love him too. Many prayers were prayed for Helen Roseveare.

'I can't go home at Christmas,' Helen told her friends. 'My young sister has mumps.'

'Why don't you come to the house party at Mount Hermon Bible College?' she was asked.

That's just what she did, and that house party changed her life.

'I'm a failure,' Helen wept, at the end of her last full day there. Tears poured on to her pillow as she lay, face down, on her bed. In desperation she prayed for God to show himself to her. Raising her eyes, she saw a Bible verse on the wall. 'Be still, and know that I am God,' she read. Suddenly her heart filled with peace and joy. She was still, and for the very first time Helen knew God.

'Look at Helen,' a fellow student whispered, when she eventually went downstairs again. 'Her face is absolutely shining!'

From that day on Helen's aim was to discover what the Lord wanted her to do with her life, and to do it as best she could.

'I don't need to struggle to please people now,' she realised one day. 'My life's work is to please my Heavenly Father.'

After graduating from university as a doctor, Helen set off for the Belgian Congo (known today as Democratic Republic of Congo) to serve as a medical missionary with World Evangelisation for Christ (W.E.C.).

On Friday 13th February 1953, in London's Liverpool Street Station, a crowd of friends gathered round her. As the time drew near for Helen's train to leave, an accordion played the first line of a well-known song, and those who had come to see her off joined in the words, 'God be with you till we meet again.' The whistle sounded, the railway guard waved his green flag, and Helen watched as her friends faded into the distance, arms still waving until they could no longer be seen at all.

Helen's journey ended as it had begun, with a crowd around her. 'Welcome to Ibambi,' said a red banner strung across trees decorated for the occasion.

Africans and Europeans sang and smiled and laughed all around her.

'Welcome home, dear,' said Jessie Scholes, a senior missionary.

Then Pastor Ngugu spoke on behalf of them all. 'We, the church of Jesus Christ in Congo, and we, her elders, welcome you, our child, into our midst.'

Helen's heart filled with joy. 'Yes, this is my home,' she realised. 'And I'm loved here.'

All her life Helen had struggled to make people love her. Now, in the Belgian Congo, she was welcomed with love before anyone knew her at all.

From her heart of love Helen served the people who lived in Nebobongo in the rain forest. She delivered babies, performed operations (though she'd never done that before she left England!), and cared for all the needs of a needy people. She even helped build a hospital where Congolese people were trained. There didn't seem to be enough hours in the day to do all that needed to be done. Helen's African friends began to call her Mama Luka, and the more people Mama Luka treated the more people wanted to see her. But Helen never forgot that she was there to share the good news that Jesus is Lord.

It was during a prayer time with some orphan children that a very special thing happened. Helen told the boys and girls about a mother who had died leaving a tiny new baby and a two-year-old daughter. 'The baby needs to be kept warm,' she explained, 'and our very last hot water bottle has burst.'

Ruth, a ten-year-old orphan, prayed for God to send a hot-water bottle today, and a dolly for the baby's sister.

'Help,' thought Helen. Not a single parcel had arrived in all the four years she'd been there.

But a parcel did arrive - that very afternoon. The orphans watched it being unpacked - and there was a hot-water bottle. Ruth rushed forward, knowing what else was inside. She was right. At the very bottom of the parcel was a doll for the baby's big sister.

Twelve years after Helen arrived in Congo there was a rebellion in the country (the Simba Rebellion). White people were no longer welcome and some were cruelly treated. Dear Mama Luka was attacked most terribly. But, even as it was happening, she knew God was with her in a very special way. What happened was so awful that many people reading about it in the newspapers back in the United Kingdom thought Helen would come home, find a job as a village doctor, and try to take life easy. God's plans were different.

'As children we moved home nearly every three years,' Helen remembered, when talking to a new friend in 2006, over forty years later. 'I didn't know that he was preparing me to move from place to place and job to job for the rest of my life.'

'I know you were a missionary doctor till the troubles in the Congo,' her friend said. 'But what else have you done?'

Helen sat upright - she always did - and remembered back over the years since the Simba Rebellion.

'After a time at home I went back to the Congo in 1966, to serve the small town of Nyankunde and a rural area the size of France. An American, Dr Becker, took charge of the hospital in Nyankunde, and my job was to build up a training school. Literally.'

'What do you mean?'

Helen smiled. 'All I had was a hillside and a dream. God gave me a dream of a training school: dormitories, classrooms ... everything. We sent a message out by talking drums asking for students - who were more than surprised to discover they had to build their own dormitories and classrooms. But they did. And in 1973, just before I came home, the school at Nyankunde received official Government recognition.'

'You must have felt that was just the right time to retire.'

Helen Roseveare looked at her new friend and smiled. 'I may be eighty, but I've still not retired. Let me tell you a little bit of how I've spent the last thirty and more years. The Lord allowed me to look after my mother, then to spend some time speaking on behalf of my Mission. After that I spent a year going around the country working with the Girl Crusaders' Union. Amazingly, I have found myself speaking to student groups numbering thousands. God has taken me to Europe, America, Australia and the Far East, even to one country I can't name for fear of Christians there being persecuted. And between all of these things I've written a number of books.'

'I'm speechless,' the other woman said.

'And I was nearly speechless just two years ago when, in 2004, I had the opportunity to go back home to my beloved Nebobongo and Nyankunde, and to see those of my friends there who are still alive. One day I'll see the others again, when we're all home in heaven with Jesus.' Dr Helen Roseveare died and went home to Jesus in 2016.

FACT FILE

W.E.C. International

A man with a burning passion to share the Gospel of Jesus Christ with the un-churched founded W.E.C. International. At fifty-two years of age, Charles T. Studd sailed for Africa in January, 1913. He was called a fool and a fanatic, but a great work was established for the Lord around the world. By the year 2005 W.E.C. had more than 1,719 active workers from forty-nine nations serving in seventy-six different countries, among eighty-three unreached people groups. By 2020 the number of workers has now increased to 1800.

Keynote: After Helen was attacked in the rebellion many people thought she would come home for good, but God's plans were different. The Bible tells us that God's plans are different to our plans. Isaiah 55:8 says, '"For my thoughts are not your thoughts, neither are your ways my ways," declares the Lord.'

Think: Helen said, 'All I had was a hillside and a dream. God gave me a dream.' Think about the dreams and hopes you have for the future. Some of these may be just normal dreams that we all have for the future like marriage or college or some such thing. Other dreams may be ones that God doesn't want for us. But there are still other dreams that have been placed in our heart by God. God will accomplish his plans and, if you are trusting in him, your dreams may be his plans. God will never grow tired or weary. Isaiah 40:28 says, 'The Lord is the everlasting God.'

Prayer: Heavenly Father, you are what a father should be. You are loving and gentle and strong. You are just and fair and right. Thank you for your protection. Change my heart from wanting to please myself to longing to please you.

Harriet Beecher Stowe

It was 14th June 1811, and the cries of a new baby were heard throughout the house. Mr Lyman Beecher looked up from his books and smiled.

'It sounds like a fine strong baby,' he thought, as he rose from the chair and went to meet the newest family member.

'God's given you another healthy little girl,' the nurse told him.

'I wish it had been a boy,' grumbled Mr Beecher, before he went in to see his wife and daughter.

There was no shortage of boys in the Beecher family. By the time all the children had been born, Baby Harriet had two sisters and five brothers.

'Now, remember to say your prayers,' Harriet's older brother told her one night, when she was four years old. 'Ma's ill and can't come to say them with you.'

Harriet knelt, as she always did, at the side of her bed. 'God bless Pa and Ma,' she prayed, 'and all my family. Please forgive me for all I've done wrong, for Jesus' sake, Amen.'

'What have you done wrong?' her brother demanded to know. 'I think you should tell God all about the things you've done wrong.'

'No,' said the little girl. 'Ma says God knows what's in our hearts.'

'But Ma's ill and I'm seeing to your prayers. Pa says I'm old enough to do that.'

Harriet was by then curled up between her sheets and pretending to be asleep.

'Please make Ma better,' she prayed, as she tucked her hand under her cheek and nodded off.

The following morning Harriet knew that her Ma wasn't better even before she opened her eyes. Mrs Beecher suffered from tuberculosis, and the little girl could hear her harsh cough right from the other end of the house. She shivered with fear because, even though she was so young, she knew that people sometimes died of tuberculosis.

'Do you think God will make Ma better?' she asked the cat that had slept all night on her bed. 'Or do you think he'll take her to heaven? He took Mrs Baker to heaven, and she coughed just like Ma.'

'Miew,' the cat said, stretching one leg straight up in the air and washing behind it.

'This house is so quiet since my wife died,' thought Mr Beecher, just two weeks later. 'I never thought I'd miss the noise of my wife's terrible cough. But I do. And the children creep around and hardly make a sound.'

There was a knock at his study door.

'Pa,' said Harriet. 'I've written a story.'

Although she was so young, she had learned to read and write by watching the older children being taught.

'Bring it here and read it to me,' said the minister.

Harriet climbed up on the chair beside her father and began to read.

'There was once a mother who loved her children very much,' she read, following the writing with her finger. 'But Jesus loved her too and wanted to take her home to heaven. When she went away all her children were very sad.'

Mr Beecher blew his nose hard.

'Thank you, Harriet,' he said. 'I'll keep that story in a safe place.'

As she closed the study door behind her, he shook his head.

'To think that I wanted a boy rather than that little girl,' he thought. 'Shame on me.'

Two years later Lyman Beecher was away for a while. Harriet, who slept in the nursery with her two little brothers, knew he was due to come home. The noise of a carriage arriving woke them up.

'Why, here's Pa!' she shouted, as she ran into his arms.

From the shadow behind her father a woman's figure appeared. 'And here's Ma!' a cheery voice called out. Then, bending down to speak to each one of them, the new Mrs Beecher said, 'I'm your new mother. And I love little children.'

'Off to bed now,' Mr Beecher insisted.

'But we want to talk to our new Ma,' the children said together.

Mr Beecher looked stern - and he could look very stern. 'Off to bed.'

Without a word the children left the room. Their new stepmother had spoken the truth. She did love children and she made them very happy.

'What a hustle and bustle,' said Harriet in 1826, when she was fourteen years old. 'There's so much stuff to pack.'

The family was moving from Litchfield in Connecticut north-west to Boston, where her father was to be minister in a larger church.

While Mr Beecher could seem stern and was a very serious preacher, there was another side to him only a few people knew.

'Where's Pa?' asked Charles, Harriet's young brother.

'He's down in the cellar playing in his sandpit,' she replied and giggled. 'Who would ever think a grown man would keep a load of sand in his cellar to shovel from one side to the other just to get rid of excess energy.'

Charles laughed. 'And who would think that a man like our father would have parallel bars, rope ladders, and other such things in the back yard to play on.'

'To keep himself fit on,' corrected Harriet. 'We mustn't laugh at Pa.'

As a teenager Harriet had times of sadness and depression. Her sister Catherine once wrote to Mr Beecher showing how concerned she was.

'I have received some letters from Harriet which made me feel uneasy. She says, "I don't know as I am fit for anything, and I have thought that I could wish to die young. You don't know how perfectly wretched I often feel: so useless, so weak. I tried to appear cheerful, and succeeded so well that Papa reproved me for laughing so much."'

By 1830, Harriet wrote an altogether happier letter to her brother Edward.

'I have never been so happy as this summer. I began it with more suffering that I ever before have felt. But there is One whom I daily thank for all that suffering, since I hope that it has brought me at last to rest entirely in him.'

Harriet had come to realise that it was the Lord Jesus Christ that gave real and lasting joy. That same year there was great excitement in the Beecher household.

'Pa says it's all because of the evil of whisky,' one of his younger children said. 'It wouldn't have happened if that silly man hadn't been storing whisky in the basement of the church.'

'But Pa didn't know when the man rented the room that he was going to use it as a whisky store. He certainly never imagined that what was kept in the basement of the church would explode and burn half the building down.'

As Mr Beecher was furious at what had happened, the children dropped the subject like a hot potato when he entered the room.

'Let that be a lesson to you!' he said firmly. 'You've heard me preaching on the dangers of drink. Now you can see yourself how dangerous it is. When that whisky ignited our church was burned. Those who give themselves over to drunkenness will come to a bad end too!'

There was nothing else to be said on the matter.

Two years after the fire the Beecher family was on the move again, this time to Cincinnati, where Harriet's father was appointed President of Lane Theological Seminary. Cincinnati was just over the river from where slaves were still traded. One day, when Harriet arrived home, she was shaking with emotion.

'It was the most ... the most awful thing I've ever seen,' she said quietly, with tears in her eyes. 'I'll never forget the screams of that poor woman who was sold to a different owner from her husband.' She swallowed hard. 'I caught her husband's eye for a moment. He looked as though his heart had been ripped right out.' Harriet wept at the memory of the terrible scene she had witnessed. 'How can human beings buy and sell other human beings?' she asked. 'How can anyone separate a husband and his wife just for money? I will never forget what I saw today.'

And she never did.

Catherine and Harriet were natural teachers; even as little girls they had loved being taught and teaching. It was not a surprise when they decided to teach and to open a school for girls, the Western Female Institute in Cincinnati.

'We need a geography book for the girls and I can't find one I like,' said Catherine. 'We'll just have to write notes ourselves.'

The sisters could be found late at night in their room listing the rivers of America and the goods that were bought and sold in the major ports. Eventually their work turned into a book that was used in many other schools as well.

'You're good at writing,' people told her. 'God's given you a gift.'

Harriet's gift of writing was confirmed shortly afterwards when she won a writing competition in *The Western Monthly Magazine.*

'I can hardly take in that by this time tomorrow I'll be a married woman,' Harriet told her sister in 1836. She was twenty-five years old and about to marry Calvin Ellis Stowe, a professor at her father's seminary.

'You'll be happy, I'm sure,' her sister said. 'But I'm afraid you'll never be wealthy.'

'I don't care,' laughed Harriet, 'so long as we have enough to live on.'

Calvin and Harriet had seven children in the next fourteen years. Harriet wrote stories and essays to earn money because they really were very poor.

'This is a terrible law!' Harriet raged. It was 1850, and her last child had just been born. 'The Fugitive Slave Law says that anyone giving help or shelter to an escaped slave can be sent to prison. Not only that, but those slaves who have already escaped to freedom in the north are to be sent back to the south to slavery again.'

She sat with her head in her hands. Playing in her mind, like a film repeating itself over and over again, she could see the slave couple of long ago being sold to separate owners. She could still hear the screams of the woman as she watched her husband being shackled. And she could still see the wounded eyes of the poor man as his wife was dragged away.

'I'd do anything to get rid of slavery,' she said aloud. 'Anything at all.'

Harriet's heart was tender. All the talk of slavery kept the subject in her mind. Then the poor woman's heart was broken when her baby son, little Samuel, died of cholera.

'The Lord gave and the Lord took away, blessed be the name of the Lord,' the minister said at Samuel's funeral.

Quietly Harriet said her 'Amen.' Amen means 'so let it be,' and Harriet was handing her baby to her Heavenly Father, knowing that everything he does is right.

The time that followed was busy for Harriet, because she had an idea for a serial story.

'I'll pay you $400 for it,' said the Editor of *The National Era*. 'I'll publish it in forty instalments.'

The National Era was an anti-slavery weekly paper and Harriet's story was very anti-slavery.

'Tell me what it's about,' a friend asked Harriet.

'Wait and see,' she said, 'I've not worked out the end yet. But it's about a gentle giant of a slave called Uncle Tom who is sold by his owner and sent away from his wife and family. Uncle Tom's a Christian and I've just reached a point where the Lord uses him to help the daughter of his new owner to accept Jesus as Saviour.'

Harriet sat writing for hours at a time. Sometimes she was so caught up in the story that tears flowed as she wrote. One such day was when she was writing about how Uncle Tom felt when he was sold.

'O, mas'r, when I was sold away from my old woman and the children, I was just a'most broke up. I felt as if there warn't nothin' left; and then the good Lord, he stood by me, and he says, "Fear not, Tom," and he brings light and joy into a poor feller's soul - makes all peace.'

Months later Harriet's friend called again. 'Do you know how the story ends yet?' she asked. 'I read it every week in the paper and I'm just longing to know how it finishes.'

Harriet, who had just completed the story, nodded. 'Yes,' she said. 'Would you like me to read it to you.'

'I would indeed.'

Harriet sighed. 'Uncle Tom never did get back to his wife and children,' she said. 'He died and, when the message reached the man who had sold him apart from his wife, this is how it was told.' She picked up the final page. *'So, when you rejoice in your freedom, think that you owe it to that good old soul, and pay it back in kindness to his wife and children. Think of your freedom every time you see Uncle Tom's Cabin, and let it be a memorial to put you all in mind to follow in his steps, and be as honest and faithful a Christian as he was.'*

Having been serialised in *The National Era*, *Uncle Tom's Cabin* was published as a book. Slavery was an issue that divided America, an issue that divided families and friends. *Uncle Tom's Cabin* caused a sensation and helped many people to decide that buying and selling people was a terrible thing to do.

Some time later Harriet Beecher Stowe met President Abraham Lincoln. 'So, you're the little woman who wrote the book that started this great war,' said the President, when he realised who she was.

And that war, the American Civil War, was to bring about the end of slavery in America.

Harriet Beecher Stowe died in 1896, having written many other books. But only one of them, *Uncle Tom's Cabin*, helped change the world.

FACT FILE

Uncle Tom's Cabin

Published in March 1852, this book sold three thousand copies on its first day. By the end of its first year it had sold three hundred thousand copies. Harriet Stowe was an ardent abolitionist. It was when her family moved to Cincinnati that she gained first-hand knowledge of slavery and The Underground Railroad. The Underground Railroad was a network of clandestine routes by which African slaves in the 19th century United States attempted to escape to free states, or Canada, with the aid of abolitionists. Other routes led to Mexico or overseas. At its height between 30,000 and 100,000 people escaped enslavement via The Underground Railroad.

Keynote: The fictional character Uncle Tom says the words, 'The good Lord, he stood by me.' Many people who suffered under slavery could testify to the fact that God was with them in their troubles, comforting and helping them. God stood by people in the Bible, like Joseph and Daniel. He stands by us today in the same way. We can rely on our faithful God.

Think: Slavery still exists in many countries today. Even though it has been banished from Western nations, slaves are still smuggled into many countries to work illegally. Many people stood up against slavery and injustice in the past. Christians were strong in taking this stand. Those people believed God's Word and obeyed it. God's Word is true and we must stand up for the truth. We must stand up for those people who are suffering injustice. In Isaiah 7:9 it says if you do not stand firm in your faith you will not stand at all. Christians must stand up for the widows and the fatherless, for the poor and the sick and the suffering. It is one thing to say we believe God's Word, but we must show that we believe it by acting on it.

Prayer: Thank you, God, for the freedom that Christ brings. Thank you that you are our defender and protector. Lord, help Christians to stand up against injustice and to be the hands that help those who suffer.

Mary Verghese

'I think this is the best place in the whole wild world,' said Mary to Muthi, her ayah[2].

The young woman looked round about her.

'You would think that, Mary, because the Verghese compound is very beautiful. But you don't have to go far down the road to see some very ugly things indeed.'

'But I don't want to think about ugly things today,' argued nine-year-old Mary. 'I want you to play games with me among the trees where it's shady. It's so hot in the sun.'

As they walked together through the beautiful acre-and-a-half compound, Mary struggled to think about nice things. She knew that many people around her home were poor. But she wasn't poor, and today was sunny and she didn't want to be reminded about anything sad.

'I planted that mango tree and the chamba tree over there,' the girl told Muthi. 'My father helped me plant it but I watered it all by myself.'

---

2. Ayah - Indian name for nurse or nanny.

'Did he really help you plant these trees?' Muthi asked in surprise. 'I thought he would have one of his servants do that.'

Mary smiled. 'No, he helped me himself. You see, my brothers had already planted trees and mine is in competition with their ones. Father helped me to dig a hole and prepare the soil in order that the trees would root well and catch up with the boys' ones.'

'You have a good father,' Muthi commented. 'Not every little girl in India has such a good father.'

Mary stood under the shade of a plantain tree and looked around.

'Will you play "I spy" with me?' she asked her ayah.

The nursemaid nodded. 'I spy with my little eye something beginning with T.'

It only took Mary one guess to know it was a tamarind tree.

'Again!' she demanded.

'I spy with my little eye something beginning with J.'

'That's the jackfruit,' guessed Mary correctly. 'But it's going to be boring if you only spy trees.'

'OK then,' said Muthi, who was bored with the game anyway. 'I spy with my little eye something beginning with J.'

'We've done the jackfruit,' Mary sulked.

'It's another J.'

Mary looked around with interest, but couldn't see a single thing beginning with J.

'I give up. What is it?'

The ayah was pleased with her success. 'It's Joseph. He's at the gate.'

A shudder went up Mary's back.

'I'm going to play with my doll. That was bad of you to make me guess Joseph.'

Sitting in the veranda of her home, Mary looked as though she was playing with her doll, but she was not. In fact, she was watching and listening, because a very interesting thing was happening at the garden gate.

'Pakavum,' said one of the maids, warning the others of danger.

'Why do they think Joseph is dangerous?' Mary asked her doll.

Then there was her mother's voice. 'Adukkallai!'

'It's all right, Mum,' the girl called. 'I'm not going to go near.'

Mary hugged her doll.

'It's strange,' she said. 'One is shouting "dangerous" and another is shouting "don't go near," while Joseph at the gate is shouting "Praise the Lord!" I wonder why I'm not allowed to go near Joseph. Can it be just because he's so ugly. Perhaps they think I'd be frightened if I saw him close up. But I'm not frightened of ugly things, I just don't like to see them on sunny days.'

The next time she heard Joseph's voice further along the road, Mary hid behind a pile of coconut palm leaves near the gate and waited until someone in the house heard him shouting, 'Praise the Lord.' She did not have very long to wait.

'Here comes Muthi,' she whispered to her doll. 'And the cook has given her a basket of food for Joseph.'

She watched as Muthi came down the path to the gate, walking more slowly as she drew near Joseph, even though there was a wall and a gate between them. Fascinated, Mary stayed out of sight.

'Look,' she whispered. 'Muthi has opened the gate, laid the basket down, and rushed away. Surely Joseph can't be so ugly that my ayah's frightened?'

Suddenly the girl felt as though she had turned to stone. She didn't see much of the beggar's face and hands but she saw enough. Joseph had leprosy! Scared out of her wits, she scrambled right through the scratchy coconut palm leaves and ran into the house.

'Mum! Mum!' she called. 'Don't let Muthi give Joseph any more food. He has leprosy!'

Mrs Verghese settled in a shady part of the veranda and pulled her daughter on to her knee.

'Yes,' she said. 'I know Joseph has leprosy. And now that you are a big girl, I have to explain to you about leprosy because you will soon be old enough to leave the compound without your ayah, and you need to know what to do if you meet someone with leprosy.'

'I'd run away,' said Mary. 'Fast!'

'I want you to listen very carefully to what I have to say,' Mrs Verghese said. 'These poor sad people have a disease that damages them terribly. It eats away at their fingers and toes, sometimes even at parts of their faces.'

Mary turned away from her mother. 'I don't want to know,' she said. 'It's sunny and I don't want to think about ugly things.'

Hugging her daughter close, Mrs Verghese refused to be put off. 'There are many ugly things in life, Mary, and they are there whether the sun shines or not. It's time you realised that.'

The girl knew from her mother's tone of voice that she had lost the battle. She was just going to have to sit and listen to whatever was to be said.

'If you meet someone with leprosy you do not turn and run away. Think how you would feel if you had that terrible disease and everyone ran away from you,' said Mrs Verghese.

'But I could never touch one of them,' the girl whispered.

'Of course not,' her mother said, horrified at the thought. 'But you smile at them then walk on quickly, being very careful not to go near them, and certainly never to touch them.'

Mary Verghese came from a family in South India that was wealthy enough to educate daughters as well as sons. When the time came for her to decide what she wanted to do with her life, Mary chose to study medicine.

'I don't know how you can do that,' one of her school friends said. 'You have to clean dirty wounds, and you might even have to work with people with leprosy.'

'I certainly won't be doing that,' insisted Mary. 'But there are lots of other kinds of medicine.'

'Where do you want to study?' asked her companion.

'I want to go to Vellore, to the Christian hospital there that was founded in 1918 by a woman called Dr Ida Scudder.'

It was in 1946, when she was twenty-one years old, that Mary was accepted to train as a doctor at Vellore. She was thrilled ... and very scared. Dr Ida was, by then, an elderly lady. But the students saw her nearly every day and she prayed for them all individually. Mary loved listening to Dr Ida praying, for she seemed to be speaking to her very best friend.

1947 was a momentous year for India. That was when the land gained its freedom from Britain and began to govern itself. It was like a birth for the people of India and the rejoicing was tremendous. And there was another kind of birth too, for when Mary Verghese was a student she was born again, just as Jesus said we need to be to go to heaven. Mary Verghese became a Christian. Her family saw a difference when she went home to visit them.

'Pakavum! Adukkallai!' she heard the old cries once again. She strode to the gate and opened it.

'Joseph,' she said kindly. 'Someone will bring you food. But let me see your hands.'

The man held out his leprous hands in amazement.

'You need to go to the hospital,' Mary told him. 'The doctors there could help you.'

The following January it looked as though doctors would not be able to help Mary Verghese.

'Poor Mary,' her friend said. 'She went out on a drive with a crowd of students and the station wagon went off the road. Mary's terribly injured.'

'How terribly?'

'She may never walk again ... and her face has been slashed from her cheekbone to her chin.'

The two students stood in silence. There were no word to express the grief they felt.

The months that followed were awful for Mary. It was summer and the temperature soared. Her injuries were so serious that she was strapped into a plastic brace and perspex jacket. She felt as though she was cooking.

'Can you feel that?' nurses and doctors asked over and over again as they pricked her legs.

'Feel what?' Mary replied, not realising what they were doing.

'Am I ever going to walk?' she asked one day. That question took every ounce of her courage, for she already knew the answer. Her worst fears were true.

'I'm praying for you,' Dr Ida assured her. 'God hears and answers your prayers too.'

'But I'm never going to walk,' wept Mary. 'I'm never going to be a doctor.'

Dr Ida's eyes filled with compassion. 'You may not walk, my child. But don't rule out being a doctor.'

On black days Mary ruled it out totally. Her life was finished! But over the long months God helped her to begin to see just a tiny chink of light at the end of the tunnel.

'Mary,' said Dr Brand, when he called into her room one day. 'I think it's time you began thinking about your future.'

'I think about it all the time,' said Mary wearily.

'I mean your career as a doctor.'

'You must be joking,' the young woman snapped. 'That's over!'

'Why? Another few months and you'll be in a wheelchair. You have good arms and splendid surgeon's fingers. Your mind is the same as it was before.'

When Dr Brand left the room, Mary had to pinch herself to make sure she was awake.

Dr Paul Brand was a famous surgeon, and his speciality was operating on patients who were deformed because of leprosy. His encouragement and help led Mary to have hope for the future. Eventually she began seeing patients in the leprosy clinic. A month later Dr Brand had a surprising suggestion to make.

'Your best subject was surgery, Mary. What about it?'

His friend looked astounded. 'I'm a paraplegic.' (Paraplegic means Mary was unable to use her legs.)

'You don't operate with your feet,' Dr Brand said. 'Now, tomorrow I'm going to perform a hand operation and I want you to help me. Will you do that?'

It's hard to imagine all the feelings and thoughts that must have gone through that young woman's heart and mind before she smiled and said, rather shakily, 'I would like to very much.'

Dr Mary Verghese proved to be a splendid surgeon. It was not at all easy operating when sitting in a wheelchair, but she found new ways of doing things. She discovered that God's word is true, that with him all things are possible.

'Good afternoon, Mr Achamma,' she said, as her patient came in on crutches. 'Please sit down.'

The man sat down grumpily.

'Now, let me see your hands.'

Mary examined his damaged hands, and thought of the long ago time when she would have been terrified to touch someone with leprosy. 'I think we can help you. You may even be able to work again.'

'It's all right for you,' Mr Achamma complained. 'You don't know what it's like to have people looking at you and pointing at you all the time. It's horrible.'

Wheeling her chair round from behind her desk, Mary pulled it to a stop beside the man.

'I do,' she said. 'Yes, I do.'

'What a difference it makes having Mary in the department,' Dr Brand told a visitor. 'The patients can see how she copes with her difficulties and that inspires them to cope with their problems too.'

It was not always easy and there were times when it was terribly hard. Mary suffered a great deal of pain, especially in hot weather. But she knew God was with her, even in the hardest times. She met each new challenge head on. It took years, but Mary eventually learned to walk with braces on her legs, though she still often used a wheelchair. Towards the end of her life she was bed-ridden, but even then she inspired people.

'You went to America!' an amazed visitor exclaimed, looking at the elderly lady propped against her pillows.

'Yes,' smiled Mary. 'I studied at the Institute of Physical Medicine and Rehabilitation in New York. In fact, rehabilitation – helping people to make the most of what they are able to do – became my life's work. That's why I helped set up the Rehabilitation Department here at Vellore twenty years ago, in 1966. There was a day when I never thought I would be able to work, but I've had a wonderful life as a doctor. I've seen so many patients who thought their useful lives had ended – people damaged by, for example, accidents, tuberculosis, cancer, cerebral palsy – and I've seen them go on to do very worthwhile things.'

'And I hear you won the World Vision Award,' said the visitor.

'My work, and the work of many others, gained that award,' Mary said. 'And the money is being used to add to the rehabilitation block.'

Dr Mary Verghese did not see the building work completed. She died and went home to heaven in December 1986. Six years later her family donated money to build a little chapel on to the department. They knew that Mary's strength came from the Lord Jesus and they wanted to encourage others who were disabled to look to him for their help and their strength.

FACT FILE

Dr. Ida Scudder

Dr Ida Scudder was a medical missionary to India and the founder of the Vellore Christian Medical Centre. After graduating, she received a grant of $10,000 and opened a medical dispensary and hospital in Vellore. In 1918 she opened a medical school for women. Then in 1945 the college was opened to men as well as women. In 2003 the Vellore Christian Medical Centre hospital was the largest Christian hospital in the world, with 2000 beds. Its medical school was one of the premier medical colleges in India.

Keynote: Mary Verghese discovered that God's Word is true, that with him all things are possible. It is amazing that she managed to do all that she did from a wheelchair. But it is good to know that God can use us despite our problems and failures. Patients saw how Mary coped and it inspired them.

Think: As a child Mary didn't like to see ugly things. However, her mother told her that horrible things happen and that we have to face up to them. Think about this: when bad things happen we don't have to face up to them alone. God not only gives us the gift of other Christians to befriend us, God is with us himself. Jesus has promised that he will never leave us or forsake us. Sometimes human friends do leave us and we cannot always rely on people but we can always rely on God.

Prayer: Thank you, God, for the strengths and abilities that you have given me. Thank you for the strength and inspiration that Mary Verghese was to her patients. Even as she struggled she showed people your strength. Help me to show you to others in the way I live my life.

Maureen McKenna

Nine-year-old Maureen pushed the toes of her wellington boots into the shallow cracks in the stone wall and pulled herself up until she could just see over the top without being seen from the other side.

'Come on, Jean,' she whispered. 'There's nobody there.'

Jean and her friend scrambled on to the top of the wall and slid down the other side. They were as agile as cats and just as quick. Dodging between the shrubs, they crept into their favourite place in the doctor's garden. The sun shone down on them and the oak tree screened them from the back windows of the house. A rope swing hung from a branch on the tree, but the girls knew from past experience that it was best to wait a while in case anyone was at home who might come out into the garden and catch them.

Closing her eyes against the sun, Maureen wondered what it would be like to live in a fine house like this rather than in Glasgow's McAslin Street.

'When I grow up, I'll have a great big house with a garden,' she told Jean. 'I'm going to have clothes like the American film stars. I'll have my hair long enough that I can sit on it, and I'll have a refrigerator in the kitchen and a carpet on the kitchen floor.'

Jean giggled. 'Who do you think you are? Elvis Presley or Marilyn Monroe? I don't think they'll even have carpets on their kitchen floors. Imagine the mess it would get into when you were scrubbing your clothes on the washing board.'

Maureen thought of her mother up to her elbows in soapsuds, rubbing the dirty clothes up and down the corrugated washing board to clean them.

'Actually,' she said, in her very grandest voice, 'I'll have a maid to do my washing.'

'And I'll have wings and fly,' giggled Jean.

Dreams cost nothing, and Maureen could dream as much as she liked. Anything that cost money was different, for there wasn't much money around McAslin Street. At least, much of what there was found its way into the local public houses rather than the women's purses.

'Look,' Maureen said to her brother, half-way through a Friday evening. 'There's Mr Kelly staggering up the street again as usual. You'll never catch me drunk like that. Imagine him drinking his wages away when his two girls don't have shoes to wear.'

'You don't have shoes either,' her brother pointed out.

Maureen looked at him fiercely. 'But at least I've got wellington boots to keep my feet dry.'

Maureen had the marks on her legs to prove it. Because she wore wellington boots all winter, she had red raw rings around her legs where they rubbed when she walked.

'When I'm grown up,' she laughed aloud, 'I'll walk through puddles wearing such high heeled shoes that my feet won't get the least bit wet.'

Maureen's mother looked at her and smiled.

'What a dreamer you are,' she said. 'I hope your dreams come true.'

Before many years had passed, one of Maureen's dreams looked as if it might come true. She dreamed of swimming for Scotland and she was heading in the right direction.

'How did you get the money for the swimming pool?' Jean asked her friend, as Maureen went to the Townhead Baths for the second time in a week.

'I got a penny from Mrs Murphy for scrubbing her kitchen floor, and three pence for a lemonade bottle at the shop.'

'Where did you find the lemonade bottle?' demanded Jean, who would have liked three pence herself.

'That's my secret,' Maureen said, winking at her friend. 'Let's just say that there's a certain man who is sometimes so drunk that he puts glass bottles in the bin rather than getting three pence back on them. And I know which is his dustbin.'

'I'd like you to go for trials with a view to swimming for the South West of Scotland team,' Miss Wolfe, her gym teacher, said.

Maureen ran home as though her feet had wings. But it wasn't all good news, for it meant a new swimming costume. Although Mr McKenna thought his daughter was wasting her time swimming, his wife scrimped and saved for a swimming costume. Maureen could not have been happier if she'd been given a golden silk ball-gown.

'Remember to go to the doctor,' Mrs McKenna said, as Maureen left for school.

'I'll remember,' called the girl. 'But he's useless. I can't hear very well, and he doesn't help. It's a waste of time going.'

But that afternoon, when she was at the Ear, Nose and Throat Clinic, Maureen McKenna's world fell apart.

'I know you're keen on swimming,' the doctor said. 'But the pressure under the water is making your hearing worse. You'll have to choose between swimming and hearing.'

Whatever he said after that was completely lost on Maureen for she was screaming inside herself. And each silent scream yelled out that life isn't fair. 'It just isn't fair!'

It was not that Maureen's father was unkind, it was just that he didn't know what to say when he heard the news.

'No, it's not fair,' he agreed. 'But so what? That's life.'

Because Maureen was a clever girl, she was selected to go to a different school from her friends in McAslin Street. That meant she was different from her friends, and she felt different from her new school friends too. Some of them had refrigerators in their kitchens and a number of her new friends had piano lessons after school. Others did country dancing. Maureen was different. Her after-school activity was scrubbing the communal staircases in several of the closes in McAslin Street.

'Walking back to happiness,' she sang, as she scrubbed.

Some of the women on the stair joined in the pop song, for Maureen had a fine voice and could be heard in the flats.

'How can you sing when you're scrubbing stairs?' Jean asked. 'I'd grump my way up every step.'

Maureen grinned. 'I love the job,' she said. 'I start at the bottom and scrub my way up dozens of steps till I reach the light of the roof window at the top. I feel as though I'm climbing a ladder to heaven. And I get paid for the pleasure.'

'Fine chance you have of going to heaven,' Jean laughed.

Not long afterwards the McKennas had a visitor.

'God bless you,' he said, as he left. 'God is good.'

'I don't believe that any more,' Maureen snapped. 'Because every time something good happens to me, it's just snatched away.'

'A bus driver?' thought Maureen, when she saw the advertisement some years later. 'I'd like to be a bus driver. That would turn a few heads, for I don't think I've ever seen a woman at the wheel of a double-decker bus.'

Maureen went through the training and, much to her passengers' amazement, began driving a bus.

'Look! It's a woman at the wheel!' children shouted, as she drove past.

'I don't like the look of that,' said an elderly man, as he took his life in his hands and climbed on the bus.

'You're just old fashioned,' his wife told him. 'A woman will be as good as a man if she gets us home with the shopping.'

Sadly Maureen's life did not go 'happily ever after'. Having started to drink in the early 1960s, when she was in her mid-teens, she took up with a man who also drank, and who was bad to her. They moved from place to place and job to job, but their situation went from bad to desperate. Maureen often went back to her mum, bruised and broken-hearted. Each time she used alcohol to drown her sorrows. After a particularly bad spell, she went to a meeting of Alcoholics Anonymous, hoping to find help. There she met a recovering alcoholic named Hugh McKenna though they were both McKennas they were not related. Hugh was a Christian, and the Lord had helped him to come off drink and stay clear of it. He told Maureen that he had a friend who could help her, and his name was Jesus. After more troubled times Maureen became a Christian, and some years later she and Hugh were married. They loved each other very much indeed, and they both loved the Lord Jesus Christ.

'Tell me about Hugh's job,' someone asked Maureen, soon after they were married. 'He seems to work very strange hours.'

'He works the hours he's needed,' Maureen answered. 'You see, Hugh's job is to go down into the city centre late at night to help people in need.'

'What kind of people?'

'Many are drug addicts,' Maureen explained, 'some of them just young teenagers. Then there are the homeless people, and other poor sad souls out on the streets at all hours.'

'And what does Hugh do?'

Maureen thought about her husband's work as she replied. 'He takes them soup, tea and sandwiches. And he listens to their problems and worries.'

'He must hear some terrible things.'

'Yes,' said Maureen. 'And so do I.'

'What do you mean? Are you out at night with Hugh?'

'Some nights,' said Maureen. 'You see, sometimes he meets young women on the streets, and it's better if I'm there.'

'But what about Paul?'

Maureen smiled at the thought of her little boy.

'Mum looks after him while I'm out with Hugh. He's asleep in his bed anyway.'

'I don't know how you can do that,' her friend commented, shaking her head.

'We do it because we believe that's what God wants us to do,' Maureen said. 'And you'd be surprised at how often we're able to tell the people we meet about the Lord Jesus.'

Maureen became more and more involved in the work in the centre of Glasgow. She and Hugh were well known by some of the most needy people in the city, from young children being brought up in poverty and teenagers addicted to drink and drugs, through to mothers struggling to made ends meet, and old men and women who had nowhere to call their home. Eventually, in 1998, they founded Open Door Trust Glasgow, a charity dedicated to the work they were doing.

Jackie Ross, who lived in the North of Scotland, knew about the work Hugh and Maureen were doing. For years Mr Ross had been involved in work with Blythswood Trust, which also helped poor and needy people, both in the UK and abroad. Blythswood helped supply Open Door Trust with clothes and other things that they needed for the people they met. Mr Ross invited the McKennas and a friend to travel north to visit Blythswood's depot.

'Could you make use of an old double-decker bus?' Mr Ross asked his visitors.

'Look at this!' exclaimed Hugh, as they climbed the stair of the bus. 'The downstairs is equipped with a cooker, fridge, sink, tables and chairs. There's even a children's playroom there. And the upstairs would be ideal for talking to people in private.'

'Could we use it?' whistled Maureen. 'We most certainly could! We could go out in it for our city centre night patrol. It would be ideal for serving our snacks, for sheltering the mothers and children we sometimes meet, when they've been thrown out of their homes. Then there's people who just want to talk. They could meet with us upstairs.'

'The only problem is that you'd need someone with a Public Service Vehicle Licence to drive it,' admitted Mr Ross. 'And it would take time for that person to do his training.'

Maureen grinned from ear to ear.

'That person would be a her rather than a him, and it would be me,' Maureen laughed. 'I used to be a bus driver.'

Hugh just loved the expression on Mr Ross's face.

The Big White Bus was serviced, cleaned and had its name painted on the side, before being delivered to Glasgow. With Maureen in the driver's seat, Open Door Trust Glasgow reached out and helped those the Lord took them to. People came on board for soup and friendship, for sandwiches and advice, for tea and shelter, for support and safety. And some, who came on board looking for a friend, discovered that the best friend of all is Jesus.

'We'll never run out of work,' Maureen said, early in 2000. 'Last year there were 104 drug-related deaths in and around Glasgow.'

'That was last year's bad news,' said Hugh. 'But remember the good news. Remember the day we took twenty-five city children to visit a farm and gave them the day of their lives.'

'And remember buying them each a pair of shoes on the way home,' added Maureen. 'They were so pleased with them.'

Maureen smiled, and thought back to the days when her only footwear was wellington boots that rubbed a red ring round her legs.

'And wasn't Christmas wonderful?' Hugh remembered. 'God used Open Door Trust Glasgow to make so many children happy, children for whom Christmas would not have been special otherwise.'

'Think what we can do in the future,' said Maureen.

Even though she was in her mid-fifties she still had dreams, just as she had had as a child.

But God had other plans. At Easter 2002 Maureen McKenna died after a short illness. Having worked with many people who were distressed, who were hurting, who were dying, God took her home to heaven where there is no sadness, no pain and no death. The work of Open Door Trust, Glasgow, still continues today with the help of many others who have the same love for Jesus and humanity that Maureen had.

FACT FILE
Glasgow
Glasgow has a population of around 600,000. It is Scotland's largest city and commercial capital. It is the U.K.'s largest retail centre after London. The motto of Glasgow used to be, 'Let Glasgow Flourish through the preaching of his Word and the praising of his name.' This reflects Glasgow's strong Christian past.

Keynote: Maureen McKenna had quite a struggle with alcoholism. She made mistakes but in the end she sought help. She met Hugh but more importantly she came to love Jesus Christ. God used her to reach out to others who struggled with life, drug abuse and homelessness. We all make mistakes and failure is difficult to come to terms with. In Psalm 77 David realised something amazing about God. 'You are the God who performs miracles; you display your power among the peoples.' God can display his power in your life by taking your mistakes and disasters and making something good out of them. He can change you. Jesus Christ can be your Saviour. People will see your life and realise how great God is.

Think: Maureen's life saw hardship, disappointment, mistakes, failure and success. We should realise that all these things are part of life. We need to face up to disappointment and success and there can be problems with both. If you have disappointment in life, don't dwell on it and get bitter. Take your trouble to God. If you have success, don't dwell on that either. Thank God for giving you strengths and abilities to be successful.

Prayer: Dear Lord, thank you for my life and help me to make the most of it. When things go wrong or when things go well you are with me. Help me to work for you and to study your Word so that I will know the truth and be able to teach the truth to others. Help me to pray to you regularly so that I can know you and bring others to you.

Quiz

How much can you remember about the ten girls who used their talents? Try answering these questions to find out.

Anne Lawson

1. What was the name of the girl martyred in Wigton?
2. What did Anne study at university?
3. What mission did Anne work for?

Selina, Countess of Huntingdon

1. How much money did Selina's father inherit?
2. What did Selina inherit from her grandfather?
3. What were the names of the three preachers Selina heard during the 1700s?

Mildred Cable

1. What did the missionary have on her collar?
2. What desert did Mildred travel through?
3. What is the name of the trade route through that desert?

Katie Ann Mackinnon

1. What did Katie Ann decide to be when she was ten years old?
2. What country did Katie Ann go to in 1971?
3. How many children's homes did Katie Ann leave when she retired to Scotland?

Sarah Edwards

1. How old was Sarah when her father died?
2. Who did Sarah marry?
3. To what people did Sarah's husband go as a missionary in 1751?

Patricia St John

1. What country did Patricia's father work in?
2. What country in Africa did Patricia go to?
3. What was the name of the book Patricia wrote about Onesimus?

Helen Roseveare

1. What did Helen and her sister see in the skies above Kent during the 2nd World War?
2. What happened to Helen when she went to a house party instead of going home at Christmas?
3. What was Helen's nickname in the Congo?

Harriet Beecher Stowe

1. What awful sight did Harriet witness in Cincinnati?
2. What was the name of the weekly paper that published Harriet's anti-slavery story?
3. What was the name of the book when it was published?

Mary Verghese

1. What disease did Joseph suffer from in the story?
2. What happened to Mary which meant that she had to use a wheel-chair?
3. What award did Mary win for her work?

Maureen McKenna

1. What sport did Maureen enjoy as a young girl?
2. What city did she work in?
3. What surprising skill did Maureen learn which helped her help the homeless?

How well did you do?

Go to the opposite page to find out.

Quiz Answers

1. Margaret.
2. Zoology.
3. M.A.F. (Mission Aviation Fellowship).
4. £20.
5. His temper.
6. John Wesley, Charles Wesley, George Whitefield.
7. An embroidered Bible verse.
8. Gobi Desert.
9. The Silk Road.
10. A nurse.
11. Kenya.
12. Three.
13. Four years old.
14. Jonathan Edwards.
15. Native American Indians.
16. Brazil.
17. Morocco.
18. *Twice Freed.*
19. British and German bombers.
20. She became a Christian.
21. Mama Luka.
22. A slave auction where a husband and wife were separated.
23. *The National Era.*
24. *Uncle Tom's Cabin.*
25. Leprosy.
26. A car accident.
27. The World Vision Award.
28. Swimming.
29. Glasgow.
30. She learnt to be a bus driver.

Author Information: Irene Howat

Irene Howat is an award-winning author and poet who lives in Scotland. She has published many biographical books for all ages and is particularly well-known for her biographical material. She has written many books about the lives of different Christians from around the world. She has also written an autobiographical work entitled: *Pain My Companion.*

Ten Girls who Made a Difference:
ISBN 978-1-85792-776-4
Monica of Thagaste, Catherine Luther,
Susanna Wesley, Ann Judson, Maria Taylor,
Susannah Spurgeon, Bethan Lloyd-Jones,
Edith Schaeffer, Sabina Wurmbrand,
Ruth Bell Graham.

Ten Boys who Made History:
ISBN 978-1-85792-836-5
Charles Spurgeon, Jonathan Edwards,
Samuel Rutherford, D L Moody,
Martin Lloyd Jones, A W Tozer, John Owen, Robert Murray
McCheyne, Billy Sunday,
George Whitfield.

Ten Girls who Made History:
ISBN 978-1-85792-837-2
Ida Scudder, Betty Green, Jeanette Li,
Mary Jane Kinnaird, Bessie Adams,
Emma Dryer, Lottie Moon, Florence Nightingale, Henrietta
Mears, Elisabeth Elliot.

Ten Boys who Didn't Give In:
ISBN 978-1-84550-035-1
Polycarp, Alban, Sir John Oldcastle
Thomas Cramer, George Wishart,
James Chalmers, Dietrich Bonhoeffer
Nate Saint, Ivan Moiseyev
Graham Staines

Ten Girls who Didn't Give In:
ISBN 978-1-84550-036-8
Blandina, Perpetua, Lady Jane Grey,
Anne Askew, Lysken Dirks, Marion Harvey,
Margaret Wilson, Judith Weinberg,
Betty Stam, Esther John

CHRISTIAN FOCUS PUBLICATIONS

Christian Focus Christian Heritage CF4K Mentor

Christian Focus Publications publishes books for adults and children under its four main imprints: Christian Focus, CF4K, Mentor and Christian Heritage. Our books reflect our conviction that God's Word is reliable and Jesus is the way to know him, and live for ever with him.

Our children's publication list covers pre-school to early teens. We also publish personal and family devotional titles, biographies and inspirational stories that children will love.

From pre-school board books to teenage apologetics, we have it covered!

Christian Focus Publications Ltd,
Geanies House, Fearn, Ross-shire,
IV20 1TW, Scotland,
United Kingdom.
www.christianfocus.com

CF4•K
Because you're never too young to know Jesus

TEN GIRLS WHO DIDN'T GIVE IN

TEN GIRLS WHO DIDN'T GIVE IN

LIGHT KEEPERS

Irene Howat

CF4·K

Dedication
for Dionne and Katherine Ann

Reprinted 2005, 2006, 2007, 2009, 2011, 2014, 2015, 2016, 2017, 2018, 2019, 2020, 2022
Paperback ISBN: 978-1-84550-036-8
Epub ISBN: 978-1-84550-850-0
Mobi ISBN: 978-1-84550-851-7
Published by Christian Focus Publications,
Geanies House, Fearn, Tain, Ross-shire,
IV20 1TW, Scotland, Great Britain.
www.christianfocus.com; Email:info@christianfocus.com
Cover design by Alister MacInnes
Cover illustration by Elena Temporin
Milan Illustrations Agency
Printed and bound in China

All incidents retold in these stories are based on true situations. Where specific information about childhood incidents has been unobtainable the author has written these paragraphs using other information concerning family life, hobbies, home life, relationships freely available in other biographies.

The cover illustration depicts Anne Askew who lived in the 1500's at a time when the Reformers were beginning to challenge official church practice. Anne decided to follow the Scriptures rather than tradition and lost her home, husband and life as a result.

Contents

Blandina

Two girls stood together at the well with their mother. She was waiting to draw water for her mistress, and the children were there because they were still too small to work.

'Run and play while I draw the water,' the woman said, 'because we'll have to get home quickly as soon as I've had my turn at the well.'

Blandina touched her friend on the arm.

'Tag!' she said, and then ran off.

The other child recognised the game immediately, though she wasn't best pleased that Blandina wanted to play tag.

'It's no fun chasing someone who can't run nearly as fast as you,' she thought. 'I could catch her every time, and sometimes I need to slow down and pretend I can't run any faster.'

But, having grumped to herself, the girl immediately perked up and played the game. After all, it wasn't every day that the children of slaves were free to have a runabout.

'It's my turn next!' Blandina's mother shouted to the girls. 'Watch to see when I've drawn the water and be ready to come right away.'

The woman in front of her filled two wooden pails with water, then staggered off under the weight of them. Blandina's mother, who was a strong and healthy young woman, filled her pails in no time, and when she lowered the second one to the ground, the girls were right there beside it.

'You are good, the pair of you,' said the slave woman. 'One of the other mothers had to go and look for her son then drag him back home! Now, off we go.'

It was quite a long walk from the well, and the sun was beating down on them.

'I wish it wasn't so hot,' said Blandina. 'I'm going to melt into a little grease spot on the ground.'

Her mother smiled and thought of something interesting to tell the children to stop them slowing down.

'Did you know that there are parts of the Roman Empire that are much hotter than it is here in Lyon? Gaul (that's modern day France) is in-between the hot Roman Empire and the cold Roman Empire.'

'Where is it coolest?' Blandina asked.

'Well,' said her mother, 'your father was talking to some soldiers who were passing through Lyon on their way home to Rome. They had been serving the Emperor in the north of England, and they said it was cold there and that it rained nearly all the time!'

'Why does the Emperor put his soldiers as far away as that?' queried the child.

'Apparently, he had them building a wall right across England to show the people who was in charge!'

'And where's the hottest part of the Empire?' the other girl asked.

They were nearly home now, and almost running in case they were seen and thought to be slacking.

'I think that will be Rome itself,' said the slave woman. 'I've heard it's a fearfully hot place in the summer.'

As soon as they went into the courtyard, the children disappeared as though they had indeed melted into grease spots on the ground. Slave children learned to do disappearing acts. It was the best way to keep out of trouble.

'I'm worried about Blandina,' her mother said that night, when the girl was sound asleep. 'Do you think she's a healthy child?'

Her husband looked concerned.

'She seems healthy enough. But she's not what I'd call strong. Although she tries hard, she does run out of energy before other girls her age. But that's probably because she's smaller than they are.'

'I'm worried that she won't grow,' said the woman. 'There's no place in this hard world for a slave girl who can't pull her weight when there's work to be done.'

'You're worrying too soon,' her husband decided. 'She'll put on height, and then she'll strengthen up. You wait and see.'

'She's not even what you'd call a pretty girl,' said the woman, who was in a mood for sharing her troubles.

But as her husband was not in a mood for listening, that was as far as the conversation went.

Blandina's mother did wait, but she did not see very much of a difference. True, her daughter grew, but she grew into a spindly sort of a girl. She was very willing to work, and so far her owner didn't seem to have noticed that she hadn't much muscle about her. That was a comfort to her mother, but it didn't stop her worrying.

'Now listen to me,' she told Blandina, when she was beginning to grow up. 'When the mistress is around, always, always be busy. Don't ever be seen standing doing nothing. I know you sometimes feel worn out and need a rest, but just be sure you take your rests out of sight of the mistress. She won't want to buy food for a slave that's not earning her keep.'

Advice like that was necessary in those days, but it had the effect of making Blandina feel nervous and on edge. She kept watching to the side and behind her, just to make sure that she was working hard enough when she was within sight of anyone who mattered.

By the time Blandina was almost an adult, she was a servant-cum-slave to a Christian woman. We don't know how that came about, but could it have been that the woman felt sorry for the girl?

'She's a timid girl and not strong,' the Christian lady told her sister, 'but have you looked at her face? It's not a handsome face, but she has character.' Then, as an afterthought, she added, 'She has a kind of strength of character that you don't see in many girls her age.'

Was it through working for a Christian that Blandina was converted? We don't know. But we do know that, while she was still in her teens, she learned about the Lord Jesus Christ and became one of his followers. When she was able to meet with the other Christians in Lyon, her mistress was also one of the congregation!

It was during one of these meetings that Blandina caught her mistress's eye, and a smile went between them that the girl thought she would always remember.

'One of the men was reading God's Word,' she told another slave girl as they settled down to sleep that night. 'He read wonderful words that I'd never heard before. He said that those who are followers of Jesus are all alike in his eyes, that God doesn't see Jews different from Greeks, or men different from women ...'

Her friend's eyes were closing with exhaustion, and Blandina nudged her to hear the best bit of all. But the girl was shocked into total wakefulness by what Blandina said next.

'... and he said that God doesn't see slaves any different from people who are free!'

'Do you believe that?' her friend asked.

'I do!' said Blandina. 'And I'm sure the mistress believes it too, for when the preacher said it, she looked round at me and smiled!'

'Tell Blandina to come and help me,' the mistress told one of her slaves. 'She does things how I want them done.'

As time passed, this happened more and more often, until the two women were in each other's company quite a lot of the time. Sometimes the older woman even read from the Bible to her slave! Yet more surprising, there were times when her mistress asked Blandina to pray for her. The first time that happened, the girl almost jumped in surprise

... and perhaps in fear. Things that were out of the ordinary could still make the young woman feel nervous.

'These are troubled times,' the preacher told his congregation one Sunday. 'The Emperor Marcus Aurelius has no time for Christians. Since he became Emperor (in A.D. 161), vicious things have happened to believers. And I have news for you, brothers and sisters; the noose is tightening around Lyon. I believe that the persecutions are coming here, and that some of you might even have to die for the Lord.'

On hearing what he said, Blandina's first reaction was to enjoy the warm feeling that she always experienced when the preacher called the congregation 'brothers and sisters'. She was a slave, away from her family, but the little church in Lyon was her family in a very real way. Then the rest of the message sank into her head.

'Some of you might even have to die for the Lord ...'

Looking round the congregation, she saw fine, tall, strong young men - most of them slaves like herself - and she wondered if they would be first to be rounded up and tried.

'But why should they be?' she asked herself, as she walked home alone. 'The Roman soldiers could arrest me as easily as them.'

Then she stopped in her tracks. 'My mistress! Surely they'll not arrest my mistress! Surely they'll only take slaves ...'

When the whole force of Marcus Aurelius's anger was unleashed, he didn't care whether Christians were slaves or free, he just wanted them killed in the most horrible and public ways possible.

'We must pray for each other, you and I,' her mistress told Blandina, when news of terrible happenings reached them. 'We're sisters in Jesus, and we must help each other as best we can.'

Blandina looked at her mistress. 'How strong you are,' she thought admiringly, 'and how brave. If the soldiers arrested you, you would walk to the prison with your head held high.'

And looking at her servant, the woman thought just the opposite. 'What a frail young woman you are. And I wonder how you'll cope when we're arrested, as I'm sure we will be. I'll do everything I can for you.'

The Emperor's anger raged hot and centred itself on Lyon. Roman soldiers did a great sweep of Christians, and many, including Blandina and her mistress, were thrown into prison. In her cell the young woman looked even more frail and more nervous than she did at home.

'Pray for Blandina,' her mistress whispered to the other Christians one at a time. 'Pray that God will give her the courage to bear what's going to happen. Pray that she'll not deny the Lord Jesus just to be set free.'

The next morning the prison guard barged in and went to drag Blandina out to trial. But she didn't need to be dragged. She went willingly, with her head held high. All day the prisoners wondered what was happening to her, and they were amazed when they heard the news. Blandina had endured so much torture that her torturers had given up in exhaustion!

'My dear child,' her mistress said, when the young woman's broken body was returned to the cell overnight. 'My dearest child.'

Her loving words were like cool water to Blandina, who fell asleep in her arms.

The following day the same thing happened. The slave girl was taken from the cell and accused of terrible things.

'I'm a Christian,' she said over and over again. 'And we've done nothing evil.'

Her torture went on all day. Once again she was returned to her cell where her mistress waited to soothe her wounds and pray with her. The following day Blandina was taken to the amphitheatre with three other Christians to be fed to wild beasts.

Those left in the cells prayed as they'd never prayed before. At first the beasts didn't go in Blandina's direction, but eventually her tormentors were satisfied she was dead. What they didn't know was that the one they had just killed was alive in heaven, and happier at that very moment than she'd ever been on earth!

The number of Christians meeting to worship God the following Sunday was much smaller than it had been the previous week.

'Brothers and sisters,' the preacher said. 'This has been a terrible and a wonderful week for us. We have seen many of our members pass from death to glory, and that is both terrible and wonderful. Not only that, but we have seen an example of such Christian courage as will be remembered a thousand years from now. Our little sister, the timid and weak Blandina, showed herself to have courage and strength that could only have come from the Lord. In her death, she was an example to us that one day we may need to follow. If we should be called on to be martyrs for Jesus, may we be just like our sister Blandina.'

'Amen and Amen,' said every single person there.

It is over 1800 years since Blandina died rather than deny her Saviour. Her name is to be found in just a few pages of some very old books. But it is good to begin a new book with her story, and to keep her name alive into the 21st century. This book tells the stories of ten girls who gave up their lives for Jesus. May they be shining examples to us to live our lives for the Lord.

FACT FILE

Gaul: The natives of the area where Blandina lived would not have called it Gaul. That was the name given to it by the Romans who conquered it in stages from 222 - 51 B.C. The part that Blandina lived in was conquered in the last stage (between 58 and 51 B.C.) by Julius Caesar. He wrote a famous book about his conquests called 'The Gallic Wars'. The people who originally lived in Gaul were Celts, who spoke a language related to modern-day Welsh or Gaelic. As the Roman Empire began to collapse in the west, they gradually lost control of Gaul. But it was conquered again by tribes such as the Franks that came in from east of Gaul.

Keynote: Blandina might not have been as strong or as fast as other girls, but that did not mean that God didn't want her. Even though she was weak physically, God gave her great strength so she could bear torture and not deny her Lord. This is still true. God doesn't always choose to use big, strong, people. The Bible tells us that his strength is made perfect in our weakness (Phil. 4:13).

Think: It was not the custom for a slave's mistress to say anything to her except for instructions. However, Blandina's mistress did not behave that way because she knew that God did not see slaves and free people differently. The Bible tells us that we should not behave differently to rich and poor people either (James 2:1-10). Think about how you can make sure that you do not show favouritism towards the people you meet.

Prayer: Lord Jesus, thank you for accepting sinners like me, whether or not we are big, strong or popular. Help me to love you as I should, and not to show favouritism. Amen

Perpetua

It was a warm, sunny day in the city of Carthage in North Africa. And it was just the time of day when people rested from the sun. Perpetua was glad to rest.

'My head is going to burst,' she told her friend. 'One day my teacher spends hours doing Latin, and the next we spend hours doing Greek. Sometime I'm going to open my mouth and not know which language to speak!'

'It's mathematics that I find difficult,' her friend complained. 'All those shapes and lines and angles.'

Perpetua laughed. 'If I help you with your mathematics, you could help me with my language work.'

The other girl giggled. 'That sounds a good idea.'

Just then a slave arrived with freshly squeezed orange juice for the girls. As they relaxed in the shade, enjoying their drinks, Perpetua noticed that the slave girl was working in the full glare of the sun. Having squeezed fruit to make drinks for all the family, she was now back at her job of milling wheat for bread.

'She doesn't have to bother about either mathematics or Latin or Greek,' said the visiting teenager.

But when Perpetua looked at the sweating child, who was only about ten years old, she knew that, however hard schoolwork was, it was easier than being a slave.

'I'd rather be me,' she told her friend. 'Or perhaps I'd rather have lived in earlier days, or in another country, where only boys are educated. It's jolly hard work being a girl in Carthage today.'

'The sun's going down now,' Perpetua said. 'Let's get my young brother and play a game.'

Summoning her slave, the teenager explained what she wanted. 'Bring my brother, and bring cloth so that we can dress up and pretend to be goddesses.'

The slave ran as fast as she could to the house and was back in no time at all. One arm was full of fabric, and the other was full of protesting boy.

'I didn't want to come outside to play,' the eight-year-old complained. 'I can't be bothered.'

The two girls were not really interested in whether he could be bothered or not, even though they knew his lack of energy was because he was ill. In fact, it suited the game quite well, that after the lad was dressed in white, he lounged around under a tree.

'Imagine he's one of the gods watching us pretty girls playing,' said Perpetua. 'Let's dance to please him. Dad says we should always be finding ways to please the gods, or they'll turn nasty on us.'

'Let's dress up as priestesses of the god Ceres,' suggested Perpetua, 'and pretend that my brother is Saturn. That'll be fun.'

Gathering the cloth around them, they prepared for their roles. And the dance the two priestesses of Ceres danced for Saturn was very elegant indeed. But the little boy hardly bothered with their dancing at all. He lay on the grass under the tree and watched the sunlight through the leaves. And by the next time her friend came to visit, Perpetua's little brother had died of the disease that had weakened him for so long.

Did her little brother's death make Perpetua wonder what good all the gods did, or did it make her wonder if the Christian God was real after all? Nobody knows, for the next few years of her life have been lost from the pages of history. The next time she is heard of, Perpetua is a young, married woman with a tiny baby boy of her own. And she's a Christian! We have to guess how that happened, but our guesses join up with facts when she was twenty-two years old. We know the girl wasn't brought up in a Christian home, so she must have heard about the Lord Jesus elsewhere. Some of the Christians in Carthage at the time (it was just under 200 years after Jesus was born) were slaves. It may be that her father bought a slave who told her about the Lord. Or she might have heard the gospel spoken about in the city. Jesus really was the talk of the town because of what happened to some of those who believed in him.

Fast-forwarding Perpetua's life takes us to her twenty-third year and a diary she kept of what happened to her. A friend who finished her story completed the diary. At that time, Christians in Carthage had relative freedom, and only very occasionally did the Romans feel a need to make martyrs of them. The Roman Emperor, Septimius Severus, decided that one such time had come, and his Proconsul in Carthage carried out his orders.

'The Christians are disloyal to our gods,' he told his advisors. 'And if they anger the gods, there's no saying what they'll do to us. Angry gods don't make good friends.'

'But do we need to kill the Christians?' one of the men asked.

The Proconsul stamped his foot. 'Of course we don't! All they need to do is offer incense to our gods to keep them in a good mood, then we can set them free ... till the next time. Take that young Perpetua,' the Proconsul went on. 'Why anyone from her background wants to get involved with slaves, who make up most of the Christians here, I really don't know. Bring her in, and we'll sort her out. And bring her friends with her.'

So it was that a small group of young Christians were arrested: several youths, along with Perpetua and another girl about her own age. She was called Felicitas, and she was a slave. They knew each other from church.

'You're summoned to appear before the Proconsul's court!' the Christians were told.

The young people prayed then followed the guard without looking back. Their trial came to an end when the prisoners refused to sacrifice to the Roman gods.

'If you don't make sacrifices to them,' the Proconsul warned, 'you will be sacrificed to them.'

There was no misunderstanding what the man meant, but none of the young folk as much as flinched. In fact, they thought that giving up their lives for Jesus was the best thing in the world they could do.

The prospect of dying didn't seem to trouble Perpetua much at all, but two things did upset her: the thought of giving up her baby son before the day of her death, and the horrible state of the prison. Having been brought up in a wealthy home, she found the filthy prison hard to endure. But that night her mind was far from her prison, as God gave her a vision of heaven, a vision that showed her that she would soon be martyred for her faith.

'After a few days, there was a report that we were to have a court hearing,' Perpetua wrote in a diary that was found many years later. 'My father came to the hearing, bringing my baby son with him. "Have pity on me, my daughter!" he cried. "Have pity on your father. I brought you up to become what you are. You are my favourite. Think of me, or your brothers, your mother and aunt. And think of your son! Just tell them you're not a Christian, and they'll set you free." As he spoke, my father kissed my hands then threw himself at my feet, begging me to do what I needed to do to be set free.'

'I looked at my father,' she wrote on, then pointed to a jug that was close by him. '"What would you call that?" I asked him. "It's a jug," he replied. "Would you not call it by another name?" I asked. "No," Father said. "I can't call it anything other than what it is. And it's a jug." So I said to my father, "I am a Christian. I can't call myself anything else because that is what I am."'

Perpetua and her friends were returned to prison. But they didn't go alone as she was allowed to take her infant son with her.

'It's a strange thing,' Felicitas said, as they sat together in prison, 'but we are brothers and sisters together in the Lord, even though I'm a slave and you were born free.'

'That's what the Bible means when it says that we are all one in Christ Jesus,' agreed Perpetua. 'And now it looks as though we are going to end our lives together.'

Felicitas looked worried.

'Are you afraid, little sister?' asked Perpetua.

'I'm afraid of only one thing,' Felicitas explained. 'My baby is due in about a month from now, and you know what the law says: a woman who is going to have a baby should not be put in the arena. So I'm afraid that you'll all go in the arena and be taken home to heaven, and I'll be left here in prison until I have my baby. Then I'll be thrown to the wild animals along with criminals rather than Christians.'

Perpetua could understand how her friend felt, and the two of them prayed about it. Their prayers were answered when Felicitas had her baby early. A member of the Christian church in Carthage took the child home to bring her up as her own.

'Let's tell each other Bible stories,' one of the young men suggested.

'Who'll start?' asked Perpetua; then she nodded to Felicitas. 'You go first.'

The slave had no doubt what she would share with her friends.

'I love the Revelation of John,' she said. 'His vision of heaven makes me want to go there.'

The others looked at her, knowing that they would indeed soon be in heaven if things didn't change dramatically for them.

'What part do you like especially?' Perpetua enquired.

Felicitas smiled as she quoted the words: God 'will wipe every tear from their eyes. There will be no more death or mourning or crying or pain, for the old order of things has passed away.'

'Amen,' said the others together.

And the word 'amen' means 'so let it be'.

The day soon came when the young people were to die. The men were scheduled to be killed by wild beasts in the arena, all for the enjoyment of those people of Carthage who had paid to watch the spectacle. But the boar turned on its keeper, and the bear refused to leave its cage. The captive leopard, which was hungry and desperate for food, pounced on one of the young men and fatally injured him.

Then it was the turn of Perpetua and Felicitas.

'Put these on,' the guard ordered, handing them clothes such as were worn by the priestesses of Ceres, robes like the ones Perpetua had dressed up in as a child.

'We cannot wear these,' Felicitas said quietly. 'We do not worship Ceres; we worship the Lord God.'

Angered by their refusal, the guards were about to take the women's robes off and send them into the arena wearing only thin underskirts. Although the crowds thought there was nothing wrong with watching Christians fed to ferocious beasts, they wouldn't have approved of them being seen in public in underskirts! So the two young women were dressed decently when they were led in to meet a fierce and hungry wild bull. Perpetua was led to the front.

'Keep on believing,' she said to her friend, and then faced the beast that was racing towards her.

The bull, foaming at the mouth from the teasing it had endured to make it angry, charged at the young woman, catching her just below the waist, and threw her to the ground. Perpetua, seeing her tunic torn, covered herself to be decent. Again the bull charged, and again she was thrown. As she struggled to her feet, she saw her friend was also wounded. Raising her hand to encourage Felicitas, Perpetua slumped to the ground

The crowd decided it was time for a break, and the beast was caught and led away. But the break was only to give a little variety to the onlookers; it was not for the good of the prisoners. Rather than bore the paying public with too many animal displays, the guards brought out their Christian prisoners, stood them where they could best be seen by the audience and prepared to put them to death by the sword.

'Slay them!' the guard yelled to the young executioner.

Raising his sword, he ran it through Felicitas and the young men, but he bungled killing Perpetua. Looking him straight in the eye, she grasped the point of the sword and held it to her throat.

'Kill her!' the crowd screamed in excitement. 'Kill her!'

And he did.

Around 200 years after Perpetua, Felicitas and their friends had given their lives, rather than deny their Lord, one of the most famous teachers in all of Christian history became a bishop in North Africa. His name was Augustine, and he wrote books that are still being read today, 1,600 years later! He knew the story of the two women very well, and he pointed out to his students how well-named Perpetua and Felicitas were. 'If you put their names together, Perpetua Felicitas, and translate the words, they mean Everlasting Happiness, which is what they are now enjoying in heaven.'

FACT FILE

The Roman Arena: Violent spectacles were a big part of Roman entertainment. The Colosseum in Rome was used to host many gladiatorial contests where participants were forced to fight each other as well as wild beasts. The fights were usually to the death, although the crowd could cry for mercy on a gladiator they approved of. Occasionally, important people chose to fight as gladiators, most famously the Emperor Commodus. Those convicted of crimes could be forced to fight in the arena, or they were simply thrown to the lions in public, as many Christians were. While the Colosseum was the centre for such activity, most Roman cities had an amphitheatre for the purpose.

Keynote: Perpetua had a very privileged upbringing, and many around her would have thought that Christianity was beneath her, because most Christians at the time were slaves. She loved Jesus so much that she was willing to associate, and even die, with other Christians. She realised that her social status was helpful in this life, but that it would not impress God when it came to dealing with her sin.

Think: Perpetua and her friends encouraged themselves by remembering bits from the Bible when they were facing execution. The Bible contains many passages and stories which can help us when we are afraid. Can you think of any of them? Which would you remember in a situation like Perpetua's?

Prayer: Lord Jesus, please help me to remember that I will never be above needing your forgiveness, and give me the strength not to deny you under pressure. Amen

Lady Jane Grey

Jane looked at her baby sister and felt sad. Mary was just two, and Jane loved her dearly. But now she wasn't going to see her again for ages.

'Why do you have to go away?' Catherine, the middle sister, asked. 'I want you to stay here at Bradgate. Don't you like it here?'

Nine-year-old Jane looked out of the window at Charnwood Forest.

'Yes, I like it here,' she said. 'It's one of the loveliest places in England. But Father and Mother say that I've to live with the Dowager Queen Katherine Parr.'

'What is a dowager queen?' asked Catherine.

Jane, who thought she understood, still had problems explaining it. 'She was married to King Henry VIII until he died. After that her step-son Edward VI became king, and as she doesn't really have a title of her own, she's called the Dowager Queen.'

'If she is a widow and is finished being a queen, does that mean that Katherine Parr is very old? '

Jane ruffled her little sister's hair.

'No, she's not very old at all. She was much younger than King Henry VIII.'

Noticing a tear beginning to run down Catherine's cheek, Jane gave her a hug.

'I don't want you to go,' the seven-year-old said. 'I want you to stay here with us.'

Later that afternoon, Jane stood at the nursery window and watched the hunt come home. Her parents had been hunting with friends, and they made a great deal of noise when they returned. Taking a seat at the window, where she couldn't be seen from outside, she listened to what the adults were saying.

'Come and see my hawks,' her father said.

'This is the best hunter I've ridden,' commented her mother, and Jane could picture the elegant Lady Frances patting her horse's rump.

'We'll meet in the games room after dinner,' suggested another voice.

'Cards it is!' laughed Lady Frances. 'A good hand of cards and a fine flagon of wine. What could be better!'

Having listened to the returning adults, Jane's mind was in a spin.

'I won't be sorry to leave Father and Mother,' she thought. 'They are so loud, and they don't like me anyway. But I'll miss Catherine and Mary a lot.'

So it was, that in 1547, Jane, aged just nine, left her family and moved into the home of the 'retired queen'. Her father took her to her new home in a fine carriage drawn by two of his best horses.

'Are we very rich?' Jane asked her father, when they passed poor people walking.

Henry Grey looked down at his daughter and thought she was a foolish thing.

'Of course we're rich!' he said. 'Do you think the Dowager Queen would want a poor child in her household?'

'Why does she want me there?' enquired Jane.

The Marquis of Dorset (that was her father) growled into his beard. 'Because you've got to learn to be queen just in case.'

Jane thought she'd misheard, but didn't have the courage to ask him to repeat himself.

'Are you missing home?' Queen Katherine asked Jane, a month after she arrived.

The child frowned as she thought, then she grinned.

'No, ma'am,' she said. 'I miss my little sisters, but I don't miss home at all.'

'And are you happy here?'

Jane's freckled face broke into a wide grin.

'I'm happier than I've ever been in my life before!' she said.

'Why is that?' she was asked.

'This is a happy place,' the child said. 'And you don't mind children taking part in things.'

Queen Katherine was puzzled. 'What do you mean?' she enquired.

'At home we weren't allowed to talk with adults,' Jane explained. 'And they didn't want to know what we thought.'

'Well, I do like to know what you think,' the handsome lady said. 'And I also like to know what you believe.'

Jane's face lit up. 'Ma'am, I believe what you do. I've heard you speaking, and I believe that the Lord Jesus Christ is my Saviour.'

Delighted with the child, Queen Katherine sat down beside her and asked about her faith.

'Tell me, Jane, what exactly you believe.'

Without any hesitation, the child began. 'I believe that our Lord came to save us from our sins, and that we have to put our faith in him. I pray to the Lord and confess my sins every day, Ma'am.'

'And don't you need a priest to do that?' asked Queen Katherine.

'Oh no, Ma'am,' Jane said seriously, 'I can speak to God through the Lord Jesus.'

'And what about the Mass,' the older woman asked quietly. 'What do you think about the Mass?'

Jane knew the answer. She certainly did know what she believed. 'I don't believe in the Mass,' she said. 'I don't believe that the bread and wine actually become the body and blood of Jesus. They are just pictures to help us understand that the Lord Jesus died for us on the cross.'

Queen Katherine put her arm round her young friend. 'Jane Grey,' she said, 'you are a fine little Protestant. Where did you learn it all?'

'Ma'am,' said the girl shyly, 'I listened to what you and the others were saying, and learned how much you loved Christ. That made me want to know more, so I kept listening until I knew enough to believe for myself.'

'God bless you, my child,' said Queen Katherine, rising to go, 'and I'll pray for you.'

In September 1548, a terrible thing happened. Queen Katherine, who had married again, died a few days after her baby daughter was born. Jane was sent home to her parents, and she went with a broken heart. Although it was good to see her sisters again, the months that followed were very unhappy. Jane wrote about them in her journal.

'When I am in the presence of Father or Mother, whether I speak, keep silent, sit, stand or go, eat, drink, be merry or sad, be sewing, playing, dancing, or doing anything else, I must do it as it were in such weight, measure and number, even so perfectly as God made the world; or I am sharply taunted and cruelly treated, sometimes with pinches, nips, and bobs and in other ways.' The only real happiness Jane found was when she was with her tutor, Mr Aylmer. 'He teaches me so gently, so pleasantly ... and when I am called from him, I fall on weeping because whatsoever else I do but learning is full of grief, trouble and fear.'

Jane was not a happy girl.

To understand what happened to Jane a few years later needs 100 words of history. When King Henry VIII died, he wanted Jane to be queen if his children had no children. His son Edward VI and his younger daughter, Elizabeth, were Protestants. His older daughter, Mary, was a Catholic. The most powerful man in England, Dudley, married his son Guildford to Jane, who didn't love him. Edward died young and childless, and Dudley took Jane to the Tower of London and pronounced her queen. Dudley gave her the crown and said he'd have one made for his son. Jane realised what he was up to and announced his son would never be king. Phew! That was exactly 100 words!

'Lord, if it's your will that I am to be queen,' Jane prayed, 'then I will trust you to help me govern England for your glory.'

Jane knew she needed all the help she could get, for she was only sixteen years old!

'Look at the Queen!' a boy shouted, as she journeyed down the river Thames on a barge on 10th July, 1553.

'She's very tiny and thin,' someone said. 'And what red hair she has!'

'She's even shorter than she looks,' a girl pointed out, 'for she's wearing cork-soled shoes to make her look taller!'

But although some people did stop to look at the new young queen, most didn't think she was queen at all! They thought that Edward VI's sister, Mary, should be queen, not her cousin Jane Grey.

Jane, having an interest in fashion, prepared to dress like a queen.

'Call the Master of the Wardrobe,' she told her maid.

When he arrived, he discovered that the Queen had a shopping list.

'I'll need twenty yards of velvet for dresses,' she told him, 'and plenty of fine linen cloth from Holland. Remember to order lining material for my dresses too.'

And when he went away, she began to think about the royal jewels. Having discovered what had belonged to Henry VIII, she arranged to have a strange collection of things delivered to her: some royal jewels, a collection of fish-shaped toothpicks, and the late king's shaving materials!

While Jane was busy about these things, her father-in-law had war on his mind.

'Mary is going to put up a fight for the throne,' he told Jane's father. 'I'm appointing you in charge of an army to fight against her.'

'There is no way Father is marching against Mary's army!' Jane told Dudley, when she heard the news. She knew very well what he was up to. If her father was killed, she would be completely under her father-in-law's control, and she certainly didn't want that to happen.

'You leave me no choice but to march with the army myself,' Dudley told Jane, still hoping she would change her mind.

She did not.

Dudley set out at the head of his army, but as they marched, he heard of one town after another siding with Mary. Even his own army couldn't agree who should be queen. England was in a mess, and it could easily have exploded into a bloodbath. But just nine days after Jane was proclaimed queen, she found herself a prisoner under the new Queen Mary of England. Her father, who broke the news to Jane, left London and promptly became a Catholic in order to keep in with the new queen, in order to keep his head firmly attached to his shoulders.

'Your Majesty, you must do something about the traitors who tried to prevent you becoming queen,' the royal advisors told Mary.

'If you mean Jane Grey, I think all she is guilty of is being young and being manipulated by powerful politicians like Dudley,' the Queen replied.

'And what will you do with Dudley?' they insisted.

Queen Mary was unwilling to have Jane beheaded, but Dudley was a different matter altogether. He was sentenced to death and executed, even though he became a Catholic at the very last minute.

Jane Grey, who was still imprisoned in the Tower of London, had a staff of four.

'I don't know what I'd do without you,' she told them, 'especially you, Ellen.'

Ellen had been her nurse and lifelong companion.

'I'm glad Queen Mary is prepared to pay you to look after me until she decides on my future.'

She did not have to wait long. In mid-September Mary gave in to pressure and ordered that Jane, her husband and his three brothers, all of them Protestants, should stand trial.

Two months later, that's just what happened.

'Look at that!' a child said, who was passing the Tower of London as Jane was led out to her trial. 'What's happening?'

His mother explained. 'Lady Jane Grey is being taken to court. The man in front with the axe is the executioner, and if she is found guilty, she'll be marched back with the blade of the axe facing her.'

'She looks dressed for her own funeral,' the woman standing next to her said. 'She's all in black, and she's carrying her prayer book.'

'Let's wait to see what happens,' the boy said.

They waited, and when she arrived back at the Tower, the blade of the axe faced Jane.

'Does that mean she's going to have her head chopped off?' asked the child.

'It does,' his mother explained. 'And she's no more than a child herself.'

Over and again, Queen Mary sent priests to the Tower of London to try to persuade her cousin Jane to become a Catholic.

'I'll spare her life if she gives up the Protestant religion,' she said. 'She doesn't need to die.'

'I can't give up the Lord I love, the Lord Jesus who died for me. If I need to, I'll die for him,' Jane told Ellen.

Wiping a tear from her eye, Ellen realised that's exactly what was going to happen.

'I've come to give you one last chance to change your mind,' the Queen's priest said, as he entered Jane's sitting-room on a cold winter morning in February 1554.

'I will not deny my Lord,' Jane said firmly. 'But I thank you for your kindness.'

Before he left, Jane asked the priest to accompany her to her execution, and prayed that God would show him the truths of the Protestant faith.

'Help me to prepare,' the teenaged Jane asked Ellen.

'I'll do everything I can for you,' her old nursemaid assured her.

Between them, they chose what dress Jane would wear to her death, what she would say before she was beheaded, and where she would be buried. Ellen watched as she wrote her last letters, one to her sister and one to her father. Because Jane was a member of the royal family, a small number of people were invited to see her beheaded. Among her last words, she thanked the Queen's priest for his kindness. Then she knelt, in the faith that within minutes she would meet the King of Kings.

FACT FILE

The Tower of London: Jane was not the first important person to be imprisoned in the Tower of London. It was used as a prison for Sir Thomas More, who did not think that Henry VIII should be the head of the Church of England, and for Anne Boleyn and Catherine Howard, two of Henry's wives. Later, it was used to imprison Sir Walter Raleigh. The Tower wasn't always a prison though. William the Conqueror built the first part as a fortress to frighten the inhabitants of London and secure his control of the city. The word 'Jane' is inscribed on the wall of one of the rooms in the Tower.

Keynote: Many people in the past have sought to use religion to gain political power, but Jane took a very different attitude. She was willing to become Queen if that was what God wanted for her, but she did not grasp power. Far from giving up what she believed to secure power, she even refused to deny Jesus to save her own life. In doing this, she showed that she realised that what was really important was a right relationship with God, not any power or authority in this world.

Think: Jane learned what she needed to know to believe in Jesus, by listening carefully to the Dowager Queen and her friends when they talked of their love for the Saviour. Think about the chances that you have to listen to people talking about Jesus. Do you always make the most of them? How do you think that you could?

Prayer: Lord Jesus, you are the King of Kings and you are far more important than anyone in this world. Please help me to remember that, and not to let the things of this world distract me from following you as I should. Help me to do whatever you want me to do in this life. Amen.

Anne Askew

The two young teenagers sat on either side of the window seat and looked out over the green fields of Lincolnshire.

'This is the best place to sit when you're sewing,' Anne said. 'These tiny stitches make my head ache if I sew by candlelight.'

Her older sister smiled. 'So it's nothing to do with the view from the window?' she teased. 'And nothing at all to do with Father's groom, the young, fair-haired one, who looks up to the window every time he passes.'

Anne's blush began in the lower half of her neck, then it climbed slowly upwards. She willed her face not to turn red, but nothing she could do stopped the most delightful blush covering her entire face. Knowing how she looked, the girl didn't raise her eyes from her sewing, and certainly didn't look at her sister. And remembering what it was like to be thirteen, her sister didn't mention it either. Both girls continued with their embroidery in silence until well after Anne's face had returned to normal.

The morning passed pleasantly with the sisters chatting together as they sewed. And when lunchtime came, they packed away their material and threads in preparation for lessons in the afternoon.

'I think we're very fortunate,' Anne said, as they climbed the stairs to the schoolroom. 'Not many girls around here are educated.'

Her sister agreed. 'Of course, it's only because Father can afford to pay for a tutor.'

Anne thought of her father and laughed. 'If Sir William Askew, Knight of Lincolnshire, can't educate his daughters, who can?'

Their tutor heard the tail end of the conversation and suggested that they make the most of the time and study one of the gospels.

Delighted with the suggestion, Anne sat down in the happy anticipation of a fascinating story about Jesus. If there was one thing their tutor could do well, it was tell a story. And the ones he told best of all, were from the gospels.

'I want you to imagine the River Witham,' the tutor said.

That wasn't a problem as it ran near the girls' home.

'Now,' the man went on, 'I want you to imagine many rivers joined together side by side to make a sea.'

Anne smiled. Her tutor always described the sea in the same way. Even though Anne had never seen the sea, she felt it must be much more dramatic than several times the river Witham.

'Now, the story I'm going to tell you today happened on the Sea of Galilee, when the Lord Jesus and his friends went out in a boat. It was lovely when they set out, but a sudden storm blew up, and the boat was in danger of sinking.'

'Sometimes boats sink in the Witham,' Anne said, 'especially in the spring floods.'

'Quite so,' agreed the tutor. 'Jesus' friends were terrified, especially as the Lord was sound asleep in the stern of the boat and making no effort to help them at all.'

Anne, who knew the story well, could picture it all.

'Eventually, the men woke the Lord and accused him of not caring if they drowned! Can you remember what happened then?'

Smiling, the older girl completed the story.

'Jesus stood up and told the wind to stop. It did, and the waves became calm too.'

'And why did that happen?' their tutor asked.

Both girls, having been very well taught, answered at once, 'It happened because

Jesus, who made the wind and the sea, has the power to make them do what he wants them to do.'

Pleased with his pupils, the man told them they could have another gospel story if they liked. And, seeing their smiling faces, he embarked on the story of Jesus calling the fishermen to be his disciples.

'I want you to imagine many rivers joined together side by side to make a ...' he began, then caught sight of the girls' grinning faces and laughed.

Within a few years, everything changed in the Askew household. Anne's sister was thought to be old enough for marriage, and that seemed to be the most common topic of conversation in their home.

'Will you marry someone tall, dark and handsome?' Anne asked, as they sat in their favourite window seat sewing. 'Or will your husband be someone like the groom out there, stocky and fair-haired?'

'I've no idea,' the older girl replied, 'and there's not much point in me even thinking about it. Father will choose my husband, and I'll not have any say in the matter.'

'I know that,' agreed Anne. 'But that doesn't stop you dreaming, does it?'

Her sister admitted that she did have her dreams. And putting down her sewing, she dreamt aloud.

'What I'd really like is a kind and considerate husband. It doesn't matter whether he's dark or fair, but he would have soft, kind eyes. He'd be a good horseman, and he'd have to like children too because I want to have a big, happy family.'

'Do you think I'll make a good aunt?' asked Anne.

Looking at the clever and good-natured teenager, her sister assured her that she would.

Sir William Askew did have thoughts on who would be a suitable husband for his elder daughter, and as soon as he felt she was old enough, he introduced Mr Thomas Kyme to the household.

'Kyme's a very suitable match,' Sir William told his wife. 'He's wealthy enough, has land of his own, and seems to be strong and in good health.'

'Will he be a loving husband?' Mrs Askew asked.

'Loving!' spat Sir William. 'You women are all the same. Loving! Would you like her loved and poor? I tell you this,' he went on. 'If she doesn't love Kyme when she marries him, then she'd better learn to love him afterwards, because my mind's made up.'

Mrs Askew knew better than make any comment, but she did want her older daughter to have a happy marriage.

Sir William's plans were finalised and arrangements made. But before the wedding could take place, the young bride-to-be fell ill and did not recover. Instead of celebrating her older sister's marriage, Anne attended her funeral, heartbroken.

'I'm determined to have Thomas Kyme as a son-in-law,' Sir William announced to his wife, not long afterwards. 'And that being the case, I've offered him Anne.'

'Anne?' his wife said. 'But she's not ready to be married.'

'She had better be,' her husband said firmly, 'because Kyme is, and he's agreed to take her as his wife.'

As soon as she possibly could, Mrs Askew rushed to Anne's room to tell her what was proposed. But she was not quick enough, as she knew from the sobbing she heard when she opened her door. Without a word, she put her arms round her daughter, and they wept together.

'I don't want to marry Mr Kyme,' Anne said, when she had pulled herself together. 'I don't love him. Why won't Father listen to me?'

Knowing that she could never change Sir William's mind, Mrs Askew told Anne what she hoped would be true.

'You'll grow to love him,' she said. 'Give yourself time, and you'll grow to love him.'

As soon as her mother left the room, Anne knelt beside her bed and prayed to the One she loved more than anyone else at all.

'Heavenly Father, if I have to marry Mr Thomas Kyme,' she prayed, 'please help me to be a good wife.'

Anne took over the Kyme household, but in fact she spent much of her time reading the Bible. And the more she studied, the more perplexed she became.

'I can't find anywhere that teaches that the bread and wine become the body and blood of the Lord at the Mass,' she told one of the priests who visited her home. 'And I've read right through the whole Bible and can't find a word about Purgatory in it anywhere. Where does the Catholic Church find its teaching on these things?'

'You should leave these things to bishops and priests,' the man told her. 'Don't worry your head about them. The Church will tell you what to believe.'

But Anne's tutor had done a good job. He had trained her enquiring mind to ask questions and seek answers; and that was what she did.

'I'm more than confused,' the young woman told the priest one day. 'It seems to me that the Catholic Church believes more in human tradition than in the Word of God.'

'But what's wrong with that?' the man asked. 'Church traditions are just as important as the Bible. In fact, my advice to you is to stop reading the Bible and just listen to what I tell you.'

But that was one piece of advice that Anne's faith and conscience would not allow her to take.

'Your wife is a heretic!' the priest told Thomas Kyme, when he lost patience with the young woman. 'I've reasoned with her. I've told her what to believe. I've even threatened her, but nothing will make her change her mind.'

'What are you saying?' Kyme demanded. 'Speak clearly man!'

The priest took a deep breath. 'I'm saying that your wife is a Protestant!'

Kyme sat down heavily.

'Are you sure?' he asked.

'I know,' the priest said. 'I know she is.'

As far as Kyme was concerned, that was unforgivable, and before Anne had time to make plans for her future, she was put out of her home with no money to support her, and left to fend for herself. Knowing that her husband had overstepped the mark, she headed for London to try to sort things out through the authorities there. But her reputation as a Protestant went before her.

'You are arrested on the charge of being a Protestant,' Anne was told in March 1545, not long after she arrived in London. 'And you will stand trial at the Saddlers' Hall.'

'Do you have anything to say?' she was asked.

'No, sir,' Anne replied. 'I will keep all I have to say until my trial. That way it cannot be twisted into what I've never said at all.'

When the day of her trial arrived, questions were thrown at her thick and fast.

'Do you admit that you said you'd rather read five lines in the Bible than hear five Masses said?' the prosecutor asked.

'I did say that,' Anne agreed. 'Five verses of the Bible do my soul good where five Masses do not.'

The faces of those in the Saddlers' Hall lost their sympathetic look. Anne might be a woman, but she still seemed to be a heretic.

'The prisoner certainly knows what she believes,' a man said to the person sitting next to him. 'Even if it's a lot of anti-Catholic propaganda.'

It was a long trial, but Anne was eventually discharged into the safekeeping of some friends, provided she remained with them in case she was recalled to the court.

Less than a year passed, when she was again summoned to appear before the Council.

'The charge,' announced the prosecutor, 'is that the prisoner refuses to believe that the bread and wine of the Mass are the actual body and blood of the Lord.'

For five hours Anne was questioned, and for five hours she stood firm in her belief that the Bible is the Word of God, and the basis for faith rather than the teaching and traditions of the Catholic Church.

'Remand the prisoner until tomorrow when the case against her will be continued,' ruled the exhausted judge, at the end of two days of questioning.

The following day, although Anne Askew was very unwell, she was taken before Sir Richard Rich, who did all he could to make her give up her Protestant faith. When he totally failed to do that, he had her sent to the Tower of London to be racked. Anne was laid on the rack, and her arms and legs were stretched until they were almost out of their sockets. In fact, her legs may have been pulled out of their sockets, as she was unable to walk again. Anne held true to her faith despite all that was done to her.

'If you become a Catholic, you'll be safe and well looked after,' the Lord Chancellor told her. 'But if you don't, you'll be sent out and burned.'

Anne held firm.

On 16th July, 1546, an enormous crowd gathered at Smithfield in London to watch the burning at the stake of four heretics, one of them a woman. The three men walked to the unlit fire that was prepared for them. Anne, who was crippled after being on the rack, was carried there in a chair.

'What are they doing to her?' a woman asked her husband.

'They're chaining her chair to the stake,' he explained.

After all four Christians were secured to their stakes, a priest preached a terrible sermon to them. When he'd finished speaking, the four prayed together.

'Take it to them,' said the Lord Chancellor, after the prayer.

His servant walked over to the four Protestants with a piece of paper saying that, if they agreed to give up their Bible beliefs, the King would pardon them.

Anne refused even to look at the paper, and the three men were equally courageous.

'Let justice be done!' the Lord Mayor shouted.

Raising a blazing torch in the air, the executioner walked towards the prisoners and set light to the fire, so making them martyrs. Anne Askew and her three companions gave up their lives rather than deny the Lord Jesus, and the fires were still burning when they were welcomed home to heaven.

FACT FILE

Lincolnshire: The county where Anne lived is on the east coast of England, and, although she had never seen the sea, part of the county where she lived was once under water. A large area was drained and reclaimed by a Dutch engineer, called Cornelius Vermuyden, in the 17th century, so Lincolnshire is larger now than it was in Anne's day. The Witham is one of three rivers in Lincolnshire, and, while it may flood at the spring tide, the Trent can have a wave over one metre high on it at the same tide.

Keynote: Anne did not want to marry Mr Thomas Kyme, but she had no option because of the social conditions of her day. In that situation, she humbly submitted to God and asked that he would help her to be a good wife. We may find ourselves in situations that we would have preferred to avoid, but even there we must seek to glorify God and do our job as well as we can.

Think: Anne was able to see that the things the priest was telling her were wrong, because she had learned to look at the Bible for herself and to think about what it said. If she had not done so, she would not have known any better, than to believe the wrong things that she was being told. What can you do to learn to read the Bible for yourself, so that you can do the same thing?

Prayer: Lord Jesus, thank you for giving us the Bible so that we can understand the difference between truth and lies. Please help me to be faithful to your Word in every situation. Amen.

Lysken Dirks

Lysken slipped her feet into her new clogs and clopped across the stone floor of her home. Then she did a little tap dance that made her father smile.

'Are they the right size?' Mr Dirks asked.

'Yes, Papa,' the child grinned. 'They're the right size, the right shape and just the right sound. I love the clopping of new clogs.'

Tap-dancing to her mother, who was sitting on a low seat by the fire feeding the newest member of the family, the child clipped to a standstill in front of her, then did a twirl that made the baby smile.

'May I go with you to the market tomorrow?' she asked.

Mrs Dirks laughed. 'Would this sudden interest in going to the market have anything to do with clip-clopping along the street like a newly shod pony?'

The eight-year-old smiled. 'I'll not be sure that they're quite right for walking in the town, unless I try,' she said. 'And tomorrow is your vegetable day, and I could help you to carry them home.'

'Indeed you could,' her father said. 'And I think that's a very good idea too. You're growing into a big girl, and Mama could certainly use your help.'

To get to the market, Mrs Dirks and Lysken had to walk quite a long distance. But it was a sunny, January day, just right for trying out new clogs, and Grandmother Dirks was looking after the baby.

'Let's go by the Vlaeykensgang,' suggested Mrs Dirks. 'You'd like that.'

Forgetting all about her new clogs, Lysken ran at her mother's side. 'Is that where the bell-ringers play, and where all the shoemakers work?'

'Yes,' the woman agreed. 'It's one of the shortest streets in Antwerp, but one of the most interesting.'

'Tell me about it,' said Lysken, as they wove through the narrow town streets.

'In the evenings, amateur musicians gather in the Vlaeykensgang, great numbers of bell-ringers among them. Then, when the bell in the cathedral tower begins to ring, they all join in and make wonderful tunes together. It fills the whole night sky with sound.'

'We only hear them at home when the wind's in the right direction,' the girl pointed out. 'May I come to hear them one night?'

Mrs Dirks smiled. 'When you're older you can,' she said.

'Older seems such a long time away,' Lysken said. 'But I suppose it will come one day.'

Just then, they reached the right corner and turned into the Vlaeykensgang. The tap-tapping of hammers drowned out the clopping of Lysken's clogs.

'That's like music too,' the girl said.

'So it is,' laughed Mrs Dirks. 'But that's the music of shoemakers hammering soles on leather shoes.'

The pair wandered the length of the Vlaeykensgang, looking at one shoemaker after another. Some worked on clogs, but others made shoes out of fine leather.

'Will I ever have leather shoes like those ones?' asked the child.

'You would have to marry a very rich man to wear leather shoes,' Mrs Dirks pointed out. 'And I think you'd rather marry a good and a happy man than a rich one.'

The girl agreed ... though wearing shoes made of leather dyed red seemed a lovely idea.

From the Vlaaykensgang, the pair walked to the vegetable market where they filled a sack with food for the family.

'I'll carry it,' Lysken said.

Taking the heavy sack from her mother, she swung it over her back, and they set off for home. The sun was setting, and the bright, winter light shone in their eyes as they walked.

'It's hard to see!' laughed the girl. 'The sun is so low in the sky that it almost joins up with its reflection in the water.'

'And there's a lot of water in Antwerp!' laughed her mother. 'There are waterways all through the city, and then there is all the rain that falls.'

'Don't let's talk about the rain,' Lysken teased. 'This is the best day we've had for weeks, so let's enjoy it.'

That's just what they did as they walked along the towpath of one waterway, then along the side of another, before reaching the little street where their home was.

Although older felt a long time away when she was eight, the years seemed to pass quickly, and in a shorter time than she had imagined, Lysken was eighteen.

'Would you like to walk along the waterside?' asked Jeronimus Segerson. 'It's a lovely evening, and we have so much to talk about.'

It's probably safer to talk as we walk,' the young woman agreed. 'It seems sometimes as though the house walls of Antwerp have ears, and we have to be so careful these days.'

Although the young couple were in love, their conversation that night was not about happy things.

'Being a Christian here is very dangerous just now,' Jeronimus said. 'And being a Baptist is even more so.'

Lysken agreed.

'Do you know what the King did in Brussels some time ago?' she asked, though she didn't wait for an answer. 'They hung pictures of the reformers at the gates of the city and paid people to give them in to the authorities. The rewards were so great that many people reported their friends and neighbours for being Protestants!'

'And I don't think any of them survived,' said Jeronimus sadly, 'for a law was passed before that, saying that death by fire was the punishment for Baptists who would not deny their faith. If they did deny their faith, they were killed by the sword. But that wasn't a choice for them, for no true believer in Jesus Christ would deny their faith just to be run through with a sword.'

A shudder went up Lysken's back.

'Are you all right?' Jeronimus asked.

Nodding, the young woman straightened her back and walked briskly along the towpath. 'Yes,' she said. 'I'm all right. But I wonder if I would be as courageous if the same were to happen to me.'

'God grant that it won't,' he said. 'I pray that it won't.'

All marriages in Holland and Flanders had to be conducted by the Catholic Church. That caused a problem for Jeronimus and Lysken when they decided to get married.

'We can't go to a priest to marry us,' she said.

'No,' Jeronimus agreed. 'But we could be married in our own congregation and by our own minister. The state wouldn't recognise us as man and wife, but God would.'

So it was that the young couple were married in the presence of their Christian friends. Having found a humble home in Antwerp, they settled down to a quiet life, knowing that the less they were seen in public, the safer they were. Sunday after Sunday they met with their friends for worship, changing the venue regularly in order not to make neighbours suspicious. Their Baptist friends were a great support to them.

In 1551, King Charles V, in a fit of rage against Protestants (especially Baptists), clamped down on those living in Antwerp and other large towns. Soon his men were seen pounding the streets on Sunday mornings searching for gatherings that might be Christians worshipping. Sometimes they rammed doors down just to discover gamblers playing cards or groups of men gathered for cockfights and dogfights. Underhand tactics were what the soldiers were best at. 'We'll help get your son out of trouble, if you tell us which of your neighbours are Baptists.' 'We'll give you protection if you give us information.' And sometimes their methods were more brutal. Young people were beaten up and questioned to try to make them give information about their parents and their friends.

It was inevitable that Jeronimus and Lysken would come to the notice of the King's men eventually, especially as none of their neighbours could remember them being married in the Catholic Church.

'They're not married at all,' the gossip next door said. 'They're just living together.'

'You don't say!' whispered her neighbour, rushing off to pass on the news to all her friends.

'Maybe they are brother and sister,' suggested a kindly lady down the road. 'Perhaps their parents are dead, and they look after each other.'

But the gossip soon scotched that suggestion. 'Have you not noticed?' she said. 'That young woman who calls herself Mrs Segerson looks to me as if she's going to have a baby.'

Tongues wagged their way right along the street, and down all the side streets too. Whether or not that's how the King's men found out they were Christians doesn't really matter; what matters is that the young couple were arrested within a year of being married, and before their baby was born. They were thrown into separate cells in the prison and never saw each other again.

Lysken and Jeronimus were not able to speak to each other, but they were able to write. For some reason, they were allowed pens, ink and paper in their cells. Perhaps the soldiers expected them to write things that would incriminate them, or perhaps they hoped they would mention the names of other Christians in their letters, so allowing them to be arrested too. If that's why the prison guards allowed the young couple to write to each other, they must have been very disappointed.

'Let's see what he's written this time!' growled the guard on duty to the one who was just going off.

Unfolding the sheet of paper, the man looked at it and spat.

'Poetry!' he gasped. 'You would think, when they were going to be killed, they'd write something more interesting than poetry!'

The other guard took the page and read it aloud.

Fear God always,
In loathsome cell,
guarded and strong, I lie
Bound in Christ's love,
his truth to testify.

Though wall be thick,
no hand the doors unclose,
God is my strength,
my solace, and repose.

Then the two men burst out laughing, truly horrible laughs.

'So he thinks his cell is loathsome, does he?' one said. 'Let's see how much worse we can make it for him.'

The other rubbed his hands at the thought. 'I wonder if he'll feel bound in Christ's love after we've done our worst!'

But whatever was done to them, the two young people held fast to their faith and trusted in Jesus to care for them.

After their trial, at which Lysken was judged to be 'the greatest heretic in town', Jeronimus wrote a letter to encourage his young wife.

'My most beloved wife, submit yourself to all that is happening to you; be patient in all your troubles; keep praying, and focus your mind on the precious promises God has made to those who trust in him to the end.'

Lysken's reply was equally moving. 'My most dearly beloved husband in the Lord, ... If we suffer for Jesus, we shall also reign with him. I leave you in God's hands ... The grace of the Lord be with us.'

When offered the opportunity to deny his faith and avoid being burned at the stake, Jeronimus stood firm. Lysken had an even harder time than he did, because the court tried to tempt her to abandon her faith in Jesus for the sake of her unborn baby. At the time she stood upright and brave, but on returning to her prison cell, the young woman wept in anguish.

'Don't worry about our baby,' Jeronimus wrote, when he heard how she was. 'Our friends will care for it. The Lord will watch over it.'

With the love of her husband, whom she could not see, and the prayer support of her Christian friends, Lysken struggled through that terrible time and once again found peace in her Lord.

In September 1551, Jeronimus was burnt at the stake, one of over 400 Protestants who lost their lives in Holland and Flanders because they believed that the truths of the Bible were worth dying for. Lysken's case was longer coming to its conclusion, though, in the end, the authorities rushed events to prevent a scene.

'On Saturday morning we rose early, some time before day,' wrote someone who was in Antwerp at the time,' but the crafty murderers were quicker than we were. While we slept, they finished their murderous work between 3 a.m. and 4 a.m. Taking Lysken from her prison cell, they put her in a sack and drowned her before we arrived. A few people were there and told us that she went to her death courageously. Her last words, on behalf of her baby and herself were, "Father, into your hands I commend my spirit."'

Secretly, and in just ones and twos, her friends visited the place over the next few days.

'We often walked along the waterways of Antwerp,' one said. 'And as we walked, we talked of Jesus and all he had done for us. Sometimes we spoke of heaven, and now Jeronimus and Lysken are there with the Lord.'

'Why do I feel so sad, when I know they are now so happy?' her friend asked.

They stood in silence for a minute or two, watching the reflection of the setting sun on the water where Lysken had drowned.

'We're sad because we'll miss them. But Jesus remembers what it's like to lose a friend, and he understands.'

Turning from the terrible scene, they set out for home with the warmth of God's sun shining down on them.

FACT FILE

The Low Countries: Britain was not the only place where there were arguments between the Protestants and the Catholic Church. The Low Countries were under the influence of Spain at the time. When the teaching of the Reformers began to take hold in the Low Countries, they were put down very forcefully as part of the Spanish Inquisition, during which the Catholic Church and Spanish government tried to stamp out all that they regarded as heresy.

Keynote: Lysken's neighbours gossiped about her living with someone that she was not married to, because she had not gone through a Catholic marriage service. People were misinterpreting her actions and using them to spread gossip about her. But Lysken was prepared to put up with that for the sake of what she knew was right. We cannot control what other people say about us, but we know that God knows the truth, and it is his opinion that matters.

Think: Lysken and her husband loved each other very much, and it must have made both of them sad to think of the other suffering. But neither of them advised the other to give up. It can be tempting to do the wrong thing, or to suggest that someone else does the wrong thing to stop people getting hurt. In the end, however, God is in control, and he wants us to do what is right.

Prayer: Lord Jesus, thank you for the people who encourage me to follow you. Please help me to encourage others to do the same, and keep me from pulling them down with gossip. Amen.

Marion Harvey

Marion and her mother walked along the shore. Because Marion was just ten years old, it wasn't so far for her to bend down to the sand, at her feet, to gather the smaller pieces of driftwood which the last tide had brought in. But for her mother it was backbreaking work, and work she did every day of the year, except Sundays. And this was Saturday.

'I hate doing this,' the girl complained. 'I want to go and play.'

'It needs done, my child,' said Mrs Harvey. 'If there's no wood for the fire, there's no food for the table. It's as simple as that.'

Rebuked, but only slightly, Marion changed tack.

'I hate gathering wood on Saturdays because we need to carry so much. Why can't we just come tomorrow and get Sunday's wood instead of doing twice as much today.'

The woman sighed deeply but quietly, so that Marion didn't see how much her complaints hurt.

'Tomorrow's the Sabbath, my child,' Mrs Harvey explained yet again – because this conversation was carried on most Saturday mornings – 'and the Good Book tells us that we shouldn't work on the Sabbath. It's the day on which God rested after his work of creation, and he's given it to us as a day of rest too.'

'But it's not really a rest if it just means we've got to do twice as much the day before,' the ten-year-old insisted.

Mrs Harvey had had enough. 'It does you no credit to argue with God's Word, my child.'

Knowing that was the end of the conversation, Marion separated from her mother and gathered the driftwood more and more slowly, not feeling in the least guilty that it meant her mother would have to carry even more.

Although Marion thought she was worked hard as a child, she discovered what hard work was really like just a few years later. She became a servant girl to a wealthy family in her home village of Borrowstounness, on the shores of Scotland's Firth of Forth. (Borrowstounness is now called Bo'ness.)

'I can't wait to get home for a break,' she told the other servant in the household. 'This work is killing me.'

'The mistress will kill you before the work does, if you don't get on with it,' her friend replied.

Marion was sitting on the kitchen floor putting black polish on the stones round the open fire where all the cooking was done. She rubbed so hard for a minute, that it seemed she was trying to rub the whole world into the ground. Which, if the truth be told, was exactly what Marion Harvey often felt like doing.

'I spend all week slaving here and looking forward to going home for a break. Then most Saturday evenings, I'm allowed home for a whole twenty-four hours, and what happens there? Dad spends all his time reading the Bible and going to conventicles, and I've got to sit and listen to all his readings and long prayers. When I'm here, I wish I was at home, then when I get home, I remember what it's like and wish I was here. What a life!'

The other maid seemed to know what her friend was thinking.

'Looking forward to Saturday?' she asked cheekily.

And she was one very lucky girl, because if the mistress of the house had not come into the kitchen at just that moment, she might have had a smear of black lead applied to her face! Marion contained her irritation with her friend and her mischievous prank until the kitchen door was safely shut with her mistress on the other side.

'It's so annoying,' she said. 'The truth is that I really respect Dad for what he believes. He's dead against the King trying to make the church in Scotland like the church in England, with bishops and all that. He says that's halfway to becoming Catholics again. That's why he signed the Solemn League and Covenant, and why he's forever out on the hillsides listening to illegal preachers.'

'Have you ever gone with him?' asked the other servant girl.

'Once or twice,' moaned Marion. 'These things are so important to Dad and Mum that we were taken along if they thought we'd be safe enough.'

'And was it all fire and brimstone?' giggled her friend. 'Were the preachers all old men with bad tempers and long beards full of crumbs?'

Marion sat back on her knees and laid the polish down at her side. Her face took on a dreamy kind of a look.

'Actually, it wasn't like that,' she said. 'Much of the time the men preached about the love of God. And they weren't old men, at least not all of them. There were some really nice young men among the field preachers.'

'Oh yes!' teased her friend. 'Good-looking, were they?'

Marion, whose mind was up on a hillside near Linlithgow, didn't realise she was being made a fool of.

'Some of them were,' she agreed. 'Some of them were very good-looking.'

Just then the mistress barged into the kitchen, obviously having listened from outside the door.

'Marion Harvey!' she said. 'This is neither the time nor the place to be discussing young men, good looking or not. And if you don't get on with the work, you'll be discussing them elsewhere, for you'll be no servant of mine!'

Picking up the black lead, Marion rubbed like she'd never rubbed polish before.

When the door slammed shut, she found herself worrying that the mistress might have overheard about the conventicles, but decided from the row that only the discussion about good looks had been overheard.

The next Sunday set the pattern for many others to follow. Marion made it clear that, although she would sit through the family Bible reading and worship, she was doing it out of politeness rather than because she was really interested. And even though it made both her parents very sad, she went out with her friends on Sundays.

'That's not how the Lord's Day should be spent,' Mr Harvey said sadly. 'It should be spent in worship and meditation on God's Word.'

'I'll leave the rest of you to do that, Father. But I'm going out with my friends.'

What Marion would have known, had she thought about it at all, was that, as soon as she left the house, her father knelt down and poured out his sad heart to the Lord, pleading that his rebellious daughter would soon know the truth.

Marion and her friends decided to go for a walk, and set out from Borrowstouness east along the Firth of Forth to Blackness and back. As they walked, they discussed all the things girls discuss. They were louder than well-brought-up girls of the day, and even Marion was a little taken aback by the language some of them used. It was so foreign to all she'd been brought up to accept as right. Some of her friends even used the Lord's name as a swear word! The first time Marion did that, she thought the heavens might open and swallow her up, but they didn't. And somehow it became easier to do the more she did it. By the time they were halfway home from Blackness, Marion was beginning to feel quite at home with how she was speaking.

'Watch it!' she said to herself, as she entered the door of her parents' house. 'If I do that here, Dad will die of heart failure.'

Not many years passed till, one day, Marion Harvey decided to go along to a conventicle. Perhaps one of the good-looking young men was to be the preacher, or perhaps curiosity just got the better of her. She told the other maid in the household what she was going to do.

'Don't be a fool!' her friend said. 'You know what'll happen if you're caught.'

'I'll not be caught,' said Marion. 'Most of the meetings are in hollows between the hills, and the worshippers post lookouts on all the hills round about. Any sign of the King's troops and there's a warning whistle that sends everyone heading off in all directions. The most the soldiers would find, when they reached the meeting place, would be some downtrodden grass.'

Marion did go to the field meeting, and she went back again and again. Perhaps her friend noticed the change in her first, when she stopped swearing and began talking about people in a much kinder and gentler way. Or it may be that her parents were first to see the beginnings of answered prayer when their daughter came home on Saturday evenings and didn't look irritated when her father took the Bible down from the shelf, or sigh with boredom several times during his prayer. Whoever noticed it first doesn't matter because before long, her family and friends knew for sure that Marion had changed. Her eyes shone, her language was pure, and she seemed to love the family times of worship. Not only that, she was first to have her shawl round her shoulders when her father was getting ready to go to the field meetings on Sundays.

'Where are you heading tomorrow to hear your blood-and-thunder preaching?' her fellow servant asked one day in 1680. 'Is it off to hear that fanatic Mr Donald Cargill?'

Marion refused to let her friend annoy her.

'It is,' she replied. 'And a man less given to preaching blood and thunder would be hard to find. Mr Cargill preaches about the love of God so beautifully that I not only know I love the Saviour, I feel IN love with him. And there's nothing more beautiful than that.'

Seeing the scorn on her friend's face, Marion tightened her jute brat (apron) around her waist and went back to work.

It was near Edinburgh that Marion was caught, along with others, walking to a conventicle some months later. Edinburgh, which is over twenty miles from Borrowstouness, didn't seem too far to go to the meeting, as they wanted so much to be there. Marion, who was used to the wide open spaces of the Firth of Forth, who loved the air blowing in her hair and the taste of sea salt on her lips, found herself locked up in prison. Although her body was incarcerated, her mind could roam free. She imagined herself as one of a great crowd listening to Donald Cargill, and she could almost hear the psalm-singing echoing round a hollow in the hills. With great concentration Marion remembered what she'd heard preached and thought over the points in her mind. It was better, she thought, to think about such things than to think about the future. Although the not-so-far future was a joyous thought, and she took comfort in thinking of heaven.

The King's court had little sympathy with Covenanters like Marion, and when she was tried, she found herself surrounded by clever men who aimed to confuse her. She answered as best and as truthfully as she could.

'What age are you?' she was asked.

And even that question was hard for her.

'I'm not sure.' Marion replied. Age was not much of an issue with servant girls in the 17th century.

'Put down that she's twenty,' the clerk said.

'How long is it since you saw Mr Donald Cargill?' asked the prosecutor.

'I don't know exactly,' Marion said truthfully.

'Was it within the last three months?'

'It might have been.'

'Do you hold to the Covenants that would see a Scottish Presbyterian church, even though it's against the law and the wishes of the King?' the questioning went on.

'Yes,' said Marion, 'because they agree with the Bible.'

'And do you hold to the authority of the King?'

Marion answered as best she could. 'Yes, so long as the King holds to the truth of God. But when he broke his oath and robbed Christ of his kingly rights, we were bound to disown him.'

The questioning might as well have stopped there, though it did not, for Marion's words had condemned her.

Some months later, in January 1681, Marion went through another trial before the Lords Justiciary; she was pronounced guilty of treason, and the sentence was given.

'Marion Harvey, you will be taken to the Grassmarket of Edinburgh on Wednesday next, between two and four o'clock in the afternoon, and there be hanged on a gibbet till you be dead, and all your possessions are to be forfeited to His Majesty's use.'

Marion's possessions would not have been much good to the King, for she was only a poor servant girl.

Marion, and another Covenanter called Isabel Alison, were to be hung together with five women guilty of child murder. And if the two Christian women were concerned about being hanged along with criminals, they most likely remembered that Jesus was hung on the cross between thieves. Edinburgh's Grassmarket nestles at the foot of the great Castle Hill, and the people who came to watch the spectacle no doubt sat on the steep hillside to get a good view. They saw two young women walking meekly to be hanged, and heard them singing a psalm before the ropes were put round their necks. What the other five women did or said is not recorded.

'That's the end of the troublemakers,' said one of the lawyers who came to watch.

'And the King's better off without them,' replied the other.

What they neither knew nor cared about, was that Marion Harvey and Isabel Alison had gone from their presence to be with the King of Kings.

FACT FILE

Going into service: Many years ago there were very few jobs available to young girls. Universities were very slow to allow girls to go there to study, and poor people could not afford to go in any case. One of the few options was going to stay with a rich family and work as a servant. This often meant living a long way from home and working very hard for long hours. The government did very little to prevent employers from mistreating their servants.

Keynote: When Marion was young, all of the things that her father did seemed very boring. But later, she was willing to die for doing the same things. In between, she learned that they had a value which she could not see until she came to love Jesus herself. In the end, Jesus was worth far more than anything else she could ever have. When God teaches you to love Bible reading and prayer, you will realise that they provide you with greater riches than the rest of the world can give.

Think: When Marion first began to use the Lord's name as a swear word, it really frightened her. But, little by little, it got easier and easier, until she had to take special care not to do it in front of her father. This is the case with a lot of sins. The more we do them, the more hardened we become to them. Can you think of occasions when this has happened to you? What can you do about it?

Prayer: Lord Jesus, please help me not to be scared when people in authority try to make me disown you. Help me to remember your great promises and the blessings you have given to your people over the years. Amen.

Margaret Wilson

It had rained all day, every single minute of it. Now, just before sunset, the rain stopped, and Mrs Wilson suggested that a walk would be a good idea. 'You'll not sleep tonight if you don't get a breath of fresh air into your lungs.'

Margaret was delighted with the suggestion. She'd had a really hard day looking after her sister and brother, while their mother worked on the farm. Not only that, but she'd had to make butter as well.

'Can we help make the butter?' Agnes and Thomas had asked, over and over again.

Patiently, Margaret had given them each a shot at turning the handle on the butter churn, all the time knowing that their young arms made no difference at all to the production of butter, other than making the job last longer. And when the butter was almost on the turn, she made sure that the youngsters were there to turn the handle, so that they felt they'd done the job.

'We made the butter for Margaret!' the boy and girl had said excitedly, when their mother came in from feeding the hens.

Mrs Wilson knew that entertaining her younger children was no easy job, and she was sure Margaret would enjoy a walk in the evening sun. As soon as they left Glenvernock (their father's farm), the younger children ran on in front like dogs let off a leash.

'You're good with the wee ones,' said Mrs Wilson. 'I hope you know I appreciate your help, especially on a day like this when they couldn't get out to let off steam.'

'They can be menaces,' the girl laughed. 'But they're great company really.'

And just as she said that, the 'great company' arrived back in a flurry of arms, legs and loud shouts.

'We saw someone up on the hill!' Thomas said. 'Do you think it was a thief or a robber?'

'More likely to be a shepherd,' Mrs Wilson laughed. But there was an edge to her laugh that only Margaret noticed. 'In any case,' the woman said, 'the sun's nearly down, and it's time we turned for home.'

'Can't I go and see if the shepherd needs help?' pleaded Thomas, sensing an adventure in the making.

'You certainly cannot,' his mother said firmly. 'Ten-year-olds need their sleep.'

'What about seven-year-olds?' Agnes asked.

Mrs Wilson laughed. 'They need it even more!'

Margaret, who was twelve, knew she wouldn't be put to bed as soon as they arrived home. She was glad about that, as there was something she wanted to ask her mother.

'That man on the hillside,' she said, as soon as the younger two were tucked up, 'do you think he was a shepherd?'

Looking at her daughter curiously, Mrs Wilson wondered what was behind the question. 'How much does the girl know?' she considered.

And the answer came back immediately.

'I thought he might have been a Covenanter,' said Margaret. 'I've heard they're often in the hills around here.'

Her mother looked anxious.

'I'm sure they are,' she said. 'And I hope tonight's little encounter was as near as you'll get to meeting any of them.'

'But what's wrong with them?' Margaret asked. 'I thought they just held church services out on the hills, and that sounds great!'

'Don't let your father hear you say that,' her mother warned. 'They may only be holding services, but they're also breaking the law. And some of them don't live to come home and tell their wives about it.'

'Why not?' the girl asked, confused by her mother's answer.

'Ask your father when he comes in if he's not too tired,' Mrs Wilson said, and Margaret knew that was her last word on the subject.

Margaret did ask her father that night, and the story he told her made the girl sad.

'Over a hundred years ago, in 1560, the church in Scotland was changed from Catholic to Protestant,' he began.

'Was that a good thing?' Margaret asked.

Her father smiled. 'Yes,' he said, 'it was. The Catholic Church was in a mess at the time. But don't interrupt me, because you put me off my story. Where was I? Yes, that change was called the Reformation. Mary Stuart was Queen of Scotland then. But when James became king, he wanted the Scottish church to be the same as the English church, and that became law. The men in the hills want the Scottish church to be restored, and they argue that it's more in line with what the Bible teaches. But they're breaking the law holding their meetings - they call them conventicles - and when they're caught, they're punished.'

'Are they called Covenanters because they hold conventicles?' enquired the girl.

Her father screwed up his face in thought. 'No,' he said. 'It's because they signed a covenant to show what they believe.

'Do you think they're wrong?' the teenager asked.

'Yes,' he said. 'Your mother and I are more than happy to worship the way the King wants. And you will be too.'

Over the years that followed, Margaret discovered more about the Covenanters, and she read her Bible too.

'They're right,' she decided. 'They are good, brave men and women who are standing up for what Jesus teaches.'

Several times she tried to ask her father more about the subject, but she met with a stone wall. The King was right, and that was all there was to say. But by the time she was sixteen, Margaret was quite sure in her heart that the King was wrong. Not only that, she discussed it with her brother and sister and they agreed with her.

'Should we head for the hills to join the Covenanters?' Thomas asked.

Margaret's heart said a loud 'yes', but she was in a terrible quandary. She could make that decision for herself, but could she make it for her brother and sister? Even Agnes had decided she would go, if Margaret did. But in the end no decision was taken.

One day, when the Wilson children were out in the fields, a soldier barged into the farmhouse and addressed their mother,

'We've heard that your children are sympathetic to the Covenanters.'

'But they're not here,' Mrs Wilson gasped.

'Very well then,' barked the officer. 'We'll be back, and then they will have to take the Abjuration Oath.'

The colour drained from Mrs Wilson's face.

'Tell me what the Abjuration Oath is,' she whispered.

The soldier cleared his throat. 'Taking the Oath shows you support the King, and that you agree with him that the church should be run by the state.'

Turning on his heel, the soldier left.

'We'll be back!' he said, as he slammed the door behind him. 'Soon!'

Although it broke their parents' hearts, the young people had no choice but to head for the hills.

'Where'll we go?' Agnes asked.

Margaret had already thought through her plan. 'We'll go inland from Wigtown. And if we keep going to the headwaters of the Malzie, we should get some shelter. There are trees there, and there will be plenty of fresh water.'

It was a brave trio of teenagers who tramped up the riverside, taking wide detours when they passed the house at Newmilns and the Torhouse Mill.

'There aren't any more houses are there?' Agnes asked.

'Not for a while,' Margaret assured her. 'But we've got to keep to the Malzie or we'll be lost. One hill looks just like another, and the streams look the same too.

'There are the trees!' Thomas said. 'Is that where we're heading?'

'Not quite,' said Margaret. 'That's Corsemalzie, and we'll have to detour round it, before we turn south along another stream that will take us up to Airriequhillart. We should have cover and safety there, and we might meet up with the Covenanters.'

That was just the beginning of their adventures; for Margaret, Thomas and Agnes knew that they could never return home again. They were outlaws, and their lives were in grave danger from the King's men. They moved from place to place, eating whatever they could find and sheltering in caves, under bushes and even up trees when they thought they heard soldiers. Whenever they could, the young folk attended conventicles where they heard the Bible preached faithfully. And when they could not, they talked about sermons they'd heard, and prayed together.

'It's the soldiers again!' Mrs Wilson told her husband. 'They're coming back.'

Mr Wilson shook his head. 'And they'll keep coming back till they find the children, wherever they are. They probably think we're leaving out food and clothes for them.'

His wife sobbed. 'I only wish we could.'

'We'd be shot if we tried,' Mr Wilson said, 'and we might be shot anyway.'

Few homes were more closely watched by the King's men than Glenvernock. The young folk knew they could never go back there, so they steered well clear of the place. However, sometimes they managed to get news to their parents that they were safe and well.

The winter was worst.

'There are no berries left,' Agnes said, 'and no nuts.'

'God won't see us starve,' Margaret told her young sister. 'There are still fish in the rivers, and I've almost gathered enough wild things to make us some soup.'

'Do you remember our mother's broth?' asked Thomas, and then wished he had not. He could almost smell the stuff, and it made his heart ache as well as his tummy.

But that afternoon, when they arrived at the conventicle, a woman they knew gave them a wooden bowl of broth - cold, but broth. And it tasted just as good as their mother's.

'Now that you're fed, you can be lookout,' Thomas was told.

He climbed the hill nearest the gathering, and then lay down behind a gorse bush to watch for soldiers. No sooner had the psalm singing begun, than Thomas saw movement in the valley below. Watching for a minute or two, he decided he was right. The boy slithered down the hillside to the meeting and gave the warning. Amazingly, the forty people, who were present, were able to melt into the hillside, and by the time the soldiers arrived, there was nobody there to be caught.

'Someone must have tipped the soldiers off,' said Agnes. 'We're going to have to be even more careful.'

In February 1685, Margaret and Agnes decided to risk a secret visit to friends in the small town of Wigtown. Thomas stayed up on the snowy hillside and awaited their return.

'Let's drink the King's health!' suggested someone in the company they were visiting.

Agnes looked at her sister, and then looked quickly away.

They didn't raise their cups to toast the King. Had anyone noticed?

Someone got up from the table and went out of the door. Margaret and Agnes realised they were going to be betrayed to the authorities.

'You're the Wilson girls!' a man they didn't recognise said. 'We've been waiting for you to come!'

There was nowhere to run. Margaret and Agnes were trapped, and they couldn't even get news to their brother.

'Where are you taking us?' Margaret asked the soldier who was called to drag them away.

'You're going in the Thieves' Hole,' spat the man, who was sick to death of Covenanters, and just wanted to get home to his wife.

'But we're not thieves,' Agnes protested.

'Maybe not!' the soldier sneered. 'Maybe the Thieves' Hole is too good for the King's traitors.'

But that's where they landed, and they suffered there for seven long weeks.

Two months later, on 13th April, Margaret and Agnes stood trial, along with an old widow woman and a servant girl. All were Covenanters; all trusted in the Lord Jesus with all their hearts.

'Guilty!' the verdict was pronounced.

Margaret Wilson was sentenced to death along with the old woman, whose name was Margaret McLachlan. Mr Wilson paid a large amount of money to have young Agnes released into his custody, and she went home to pray.

It was four weeks later, on 11th May, 1685, that the sentence was carried out. Agnes knew exactly what would happen, and she prayed that the two Margarets would be brave, and that the end would come soon.

At low water, the tide at Wigtown goes out a very long distance, leaving acres of wet sand. When the tide comes in, it rushes up, what used to be the path of a river, so quickly that many people have been drowned there as they tried to reach dry land. Margaret Wilson, aged 18, and Margaret McLachlan, aged 63, could not run to safety for they were tied to stakes securely hammered into the sand. The older woman was put further out in order that she drowned first, in full view of young Margaret. And a crowd gathered to watch it all happen.

'If they shout out that they'll take an oath to the King, run in and cut them free before it's too late,' the soldiers were told.

They waited. They listened for a scream, but none came. Margaret spoke only of the Lord. And as the waters began to lap about her feet, she sang a verse from one of the psalms.

My sins and faults of youth
Do thou, O Lord, forget;
After thy mercy think on me,
And for thy goodness great.

Someone ran from the crowd when the girl was almost drowning. Grabbing Margaret, and holding her up above the water, he told her to say, 'God save the King.'

'God save him, if he will, for it is his salvation that I desire.'

A woman on the shore gasped out, 'There, she has said it; now let her go!'

But one man with a vicious temper snarled, 'We don't want that wench's prayers. Make her sign the Oath.'

Margaret was asked to sign the Oath, and she refused.

'I will not,' she said. 'I am one of Christ's children; let me go.'

They did, and the water flowed over her head. That was when a new day began for Margaret in heaven.

FACT FILE

The Killing Times: The two Margarets were killed in 1685, during a period known as the Killing Times, when there was widespread persecution of Covenanters and a great many killed, often without any trial at all. Magistrates were ordered to get everyone in their district to take the Abjuration Oath, and to kill anyone who refused. The Oath was there to get people to renounce the Covenants, which had been signed in protest at the king interfering with the church. They were forceful in their terms, however, and the government regarded them as statements of open rebellion.

Keynote: Margaret's refusal to take the Oath made her an outlaw. Normally, we think that we can always rely on the government and the law to keep us safe, but in God we have a help even more sure than that. God was with Margaret, even when the forces of the law were against her, or the waves were rushing around her. God is still our refuge in time of need.

Think: The soldiers wanted Margaret to take the Abjuration Oath, but she could not do that because it meant she would be putting loyalty to the king above loyalty to God. God cannot accept anything less than being first in our hearts. Think about the things that you might be tempted to love more than God, and why he is far better than them.

Prayer: Lord Jesus, thank you for your continual protection and encouragement. Please sustain me in times of difficulty. Teach me to trust you more than anything or anyone else. Amen.

Judith Weinberg

It was the early summer of 1910, and Judith and her two younger sisters were as excited as could be.

'How many days till we go to visit Grandfather and Grandmother?' Judith asked her youngest sister, who was learning to count.

Holding up both hands the dark-haired six-year-old struggled to separate her fingers, and was eventually satisfied with the result. Judith might have laughed, but she did not. One small hand had two-and-a-half fingers up, and the other had three-and-a-half. Though the little girl didn't exactly mean to do that, the result was the same.

'That's right,' smiled Judith. 'Six days from now we'll be leaving the town and heading into the forest for the summer. Grandmother will have begun baking already. She knows how much you like her sugar ginger biscuits.'

Much though Mr Weinberg loved his three daughters, especially Judith, he was not sorry that they were going off on holiday. Summer was a busy time for his business, and, in any case, Judith was going through a tiresome stage. She asked question after question after question ... after question, so much so that sometimes his head was in a spin trying to keep up with her.

'How am I meant to know all the answers?' he asked his wife. 'I study the Talmud, but I'm not a Rabbi. What Judith needs is her own personal Rabbi who can take time to answer all her questions.'

'She'll have one soon,' Mrs Weinberg grinned. 'And I'm sure Grandfather Weinberg will give her the answers she's looking for.'

'I hope so,' Judith's father said, smiling, 'though he didn't always have the answers to my questions when I was growing up.'

The six days passed in a bustle of packing and repacking, as the three Weinberg girls organised themselves for several weeks in the forest. Judith was more concerned about what books to take with her, and her sisters couldn't agree on which of their wooden dolls were absolutely necessary. Eventually, the great day came, and Judith, with her two young sisters and their mother, climbed into the horse-drawn carriage, settled themselves down, and watched as the coachman whipped the horse into action.

'We're on our way,' Judith thought silently, winging her thoughts to her grandfather. Her sisters chattered nearly every minute of the journey, and from time to time Mrs Weinberg looked at her oldest daughter and smiled.

'What a lovely girl she's growing into,' the woman thought. 'Her dark hair shines. Her brown eyes sparkle like stars. And what a nice olive complexion she has.'

Suddenly, as though Judith read her mother's thoughts, her olive skin turned pink with embarrassment. At thirteen years of age, Judith was discovering what it meant to be self-conscious.

Grandfather Weinberg was all that Judith needed him to be for most of that holiday. Although he was a Rabbi, he was also a busy timber merchant. But he still made time for his grand-daughter, and he answered her questions as best he could.

'You want to know so many things!' he laughed often. 'It's as though you're training to be a woman Rabbi - and we can't have that, can we?'

Judith chose her questions carefully, and, without her grandfather knowing it, they were all leading to the biggest question of all. Partly out of fear of old Mr Weinberg's reaction, and partly because she was working the answer out for herself, she kept it right to the end.

'Tell me about Jesus,' the teenager asked, when she thought the right time had come. 'Who was he? And why don't we talk about him?'

There was no way that the girl could have guessed what her question would do to the grandfather she loved. The man changed colour, his face went from angry to sad to … something she could not quite work out. And it seemed a long time before he began to answer her question at all.

When she went to bed that night, Judith was more confused that ever. Rather than going straight to sleep, she turned over in her mind all she knew about Jesus. He had lived about 1,900 years ago. Jesus was a Jew like herself. Some people thought he was the Messiah that Jews were waiting for, but he couldn't have been because he was crucified. And Grandfather Weinberg pointed out that the Scripture said that anyone who died on a tree was cursed, and the Messiah could not be cursed. Yet, reasoned Judith, Christians believed that Jesus was the Messiah. Could Christians be right about him being the Jewish Messiah, and Jews be wrong? It seemed very unlikely. But the thought wouldn't leave Judith alone, though she decided it was best not to broach the subject with Grandfather again.

On arriving back home after the summer, Judith used her eyes and her mind to try to answer her questions without bombarding her father with them.

'What a relief!' Mr Weinberg said, when the family had been home a week. 'Dad seems to have answered all Judith's questions after all; either that or she's run out of things to ask.'

His wife smiled. 'So it seems.'

But Judith's questions still came into her mind thick and fast. 'Why do Christians hate Jews?' she asked herself, then decided it was because Jews were involved in the trial of Jesus Christ, even though it was the Roman authorities that put him to death. But that didn't fit the facts either, because there were Christians at her school who really went out of their way to be kind to Jews. 'Why do Christians fight with each other if they all think the Messiah has come?' was another question that bothered her. Yet she could see that there were Christians in her town who really loved each other.

Four years later, in 1914, Judith and her family had to move from their home town, and they had to move quickly. Fighting had been raging in Russia for years, but now the possibility of a European war was beginning to cause a great deal of fear among those who lived, as the Weinbergs did, near the Russian-German border. Jews were especially fearful of what would happen to them. Then, on 1st August, the worst happened. War was declared. The First World War had begun. Judith's family, like thousands of others, fled from the area near the German border. The Weinbergs, carrying all that they could of their possessions, walked for four days before boarding a crowded freight train that they hoped would take them to safety. And it seemed that was just what happened. Settling in what was thought to be a safe town, they picked up the pieces of their lives, and Mr Weinberg once again established himself in business.

Judith left many things behind in her old home, but she took her thoughts and her questions with her. It was some years before they became a real problem again.

'Solomon,' she said to the young man she loved and to whom she was engaged to be married, 'are you very interested in religion?'

The handsome young man shrugged his shoulders. 'Not really,' he admitted, 'but I'll always be a Jew.'

'Wouldn't you like to know what Christians believe?' asked Judith.

'Not particularly,' Solomon said.

'Will you come to church with me?' she went on. 'I'd like to see what goes on there.'

That caught Solomon off guard. He thought he was very sophisticated and didn't really believe anything, but he was Jewish enough to baulk at the thought of going to a Christian meeting .... But he loved Judith and would do anything for her.

'All right, why not?' he asked. 'I'll come with you.'

Had Solomon known what would happen, he would have run a hundred miles in the opposite direction!

As a result of what she heard at the Christian meeting, Judith attended with Solomon, she became a Christian. Understanding her parents' reaction is difficult. When some Jewish people look back over history, they see hundreds of years when those who claimed to be Christians were their enemies. Over the centuries, Jewish people have grown to fear 'Christians', though no Jew has anything to fear from someone who truly loves the Lord Jesus, who himself was Jewish.

Because the Weinbergs loved Judith deeply, they tried to persuade her to change her mind. Her father talked to her, argued with her, pleaded with her. Judith's mother wept over her and tried to love her back into her Jewish faith. Even her young sisters did what they could to persuade her to give up her new beliefs. But it wasn't that easy. As a young Jewess, Judith had believed in her head what she was taught, but as a Christian she knew in her heart that what the Bible said was true: Jesus was her Messiah, her Saviour. And when she thought of what he had done on the cross to save her from her sin, there was no way she could give up her new-found faith just to please her family. Eventually she left home knowing that her parents would have nothing more to do with her, and that they would not allow her young sisters to keep in touch.

'Where do I go?' Judith asked, as the door of her home slammed shut behind her. And that was one question that didn't take long to answer. 'I'll go to my Christian friends.'

When she knocked on the door of her pastor's home, she was welcomed in like one of the family. And that's what she was. Before long, plans were made for her to move to a different town where she could build a new life within the Christian community.

'Are you going to the meeting tonight?' a friend asked, not long after she had settled in her new home.

'Yes, I am,' Judith replied. 'I've heard about the speaker, and I'm really looking forward to hearing more about the work he's doing.'

That night, Judith listened with her heart as well as her mind, as the speaker described the work he did.

'We travel from town to town, from village to village, telling people about Jesus.'

Judith could picture herself doing just that; after all, she already visited people in her spare time to talk about her faith.

'The work isn't easy,' the man continued. 'Sometimes we have to walk miles in the cold Russian weather. And I remember times when I've not been in dry clothes for days at a time.'

Looking at her warm dry clothes, Judith knew that she wouldn't even mind being cold and wet if the people she spoke to trusted the Lord.

'There are days when we eat very little, and occasionally nothing at all,' said the man. 'But for all the hardships, I wonder if there is anyone here who will join us in the work.'

Silence filled the church for an uncomfortably long time, before a quiet and steady voice said, 'I am willing to answer the call of the Lord.'

It was Judith.

The work she began soon afterwards, was just as it had been described. With the little groups of missionaries, she travelled in all kinds of weather. The speaker had told the truth. Her clothes often didn't dry out by morning, and there were times when her empty, rumbling tummy tried to keep her awake at night. But Judith loved it! The rain didn't matter, and the mud didn't bother her. She even thought it was a privilege to be hungry in order to serve Jesus.

One day, Judith knocked at the door of the last house in a poor little village. When there was no reply, she pushed the door open and could hardly take in what she saw. Several orphaned children were lying unconscious from typhus fever. Rolling up her sleeves, she nursed the children, cleaned their filthy home, and did all she could. So it was no surprise when she caught typhus herself. The only surprise was that she recovered from it after being very near to death. Just as soon as she was well enough, Judith was back at work once again. She never tired of talking of Jesus.

'Why does the name Jesus make the soldiers so full of rage?' she asked the mission leader, when she was spat on.

'They hate the name of Jesus,' the old man explained. 'They think that religion is just a way of deceiving people.'

'Don't they know that Jesus is the Truth, that he won't deceive anyone?'

'No, my child,' was the reply. 'That's what we're here to tell them.'

It was autumn, and the evenings were short. On her way home from visiting, Judith just loved kicking the dry autumn leaves, and feeling them crunch under her feet. It reminded her of times in the forest with Grandfather. As she walked, she prayed for her family whom she still loved, even though they would have nothing to do with her.

The mood of a group of soldiers in the village grew uglier and uglier every time they heard the missionaries telling people about Jesus. And for some reason, their rage overflowed when they thought of Judith.

One day, she was arranging a meeting in another village nearby, when the soldiers lost control of themselves. Barging into the meeting she was leading, they grabbed the young woman, accusing her of terrible things. Having seen murders before, the villagers left the meeting and slid into the relative safety of their own homes. The last they saw of Judith was when she was marched - surrounded by soldiers with their swords held high - to a barn near the end of the village. Her body was found the next day with her Bible right beside her. News of Judith's murder spread through the village like wildfire.

'She loved us with Jesus' love,' an old woman told her husband.

Tears prevented an answer. The man just nodded his head in agreement.

And as they grieved together, Judith enjoyed the wonderful love of Jesus to the full.

FACT FILE

Jewish Diaspora: In Jesus' day, most Jews lived in Israel, although some had moved away (like the Apostle Paul's family). By Judith's time, however, very few of the people living in Israel were Jewish. Around A.D. 70, the Jewish people tried to overthrow their Roman rulers, but they were unsuccessful. The Romans were not pleased about this, and their army destroyed the Temple and scattered a great many Jews throughout the known world. Many of them suffered a lot of prejudice and persecution for years. They were sometimes forced to wear special badges, marking them as Jews, and to live in areas called ghettos. This scattering of Jews is sometimes called the 'Jewish Diaspora'.

Keynote: When Judith decided to become a Christian, her family expelled her. Things like this can be very difficult and painful, but Jesus warned us that such things would happen (Matthew 10:34-39). Jesus understands what it feels like because his own family thought he was mad (Mark 3:21). He also promises to look after us. We find a new family amongst his people because we become part of God's family.

Think: Judith was keen to tell other people about Jesus, but that did not stop her from giving practical help when that was what was needed. Judith knew that people had a body as well as a soul. In fact, her practical help probably made people more willing to listen to what she had to say. Can you think of any ways in which you could help people practically?

Prayer: Lord Jesus, thank you for the good news that is available for everyone, whatever their background. Help me to love and help people because they need it, rather than because of any benefit I hope to get myself. Amen.

Betty Stam

It was winter and very, very cold. In fact, it was as cold as it could be at the beginning of winter in China. Betty Scott could hardly move. She was dressed in full Chinese winter clothes. All you could see was padded, and what you couldn't see was padded too.

'I can hardly bend at the knees,' she laughed. 'And my elbows won't bend either.'

Her mother smiled.

'I'm sure if I gave you some nuts, you'd manage to get them into your mouth!'

Betty grinned. 'I guess I would.'

'Chinese winter clothes always feel so bulky when you first put them on, but you'll soon get used to them.'

'I remember that from last year,' eight-year-old Betty said. 'Then in the spring, when I went back to ordinary clothes, I felt like a butterfly coming out of a chrysalis!'

Dr Charles Scott, Betty's father, smiled at the thought of his heavily padded, eldest child becoming a butterfly.

'You say the most extraordinary things,' he commented. 'In fact, you're really quite a poet.'

Betty grinned. She loved writing poems, and she knew her parents liked the ones she showed them.

Looking at her well-padded sisters and little brother, Betty wondered what life was like for her cousins far away in America. Were they waddling around in padded clothes?

Dr Scott smiled at the thought.

'I guess it's very different for them,' he said. 'And you'll discover that for yourself when you go back to America for college.'

Betty shook her head. 'I left America when I was six months old,' she laughed. 'China's my home, and I'll go to college here then marry and have my own children right here.'

Then she laughed. 'And I'll pad them all up each winter and pack them in a drawer until the summer comes again! They'll not feel the cold that way.'

'I think it's time we were leaving for church,' Dr Scott said. 'And we'll delay discussion on your adult life until you're at least ten years old!'

That seemed a good idea to Betty, who waddled down the street towards the church where she knew her Chinese friends would be waiting for her. A girl and boy came along the road to meet her, and she immediately changed from speaking English to her dad, to speaking in a Chinese dialect to her friends. It happened without Betty realising what she was doing, as she was perfectly at home using both languages.

Although Betty wanted to stay in China all her life, she didn't quite know where. Her earliest memories were of Tsingtao in the province of Shantung. But when she finished primary school in Tsingtao and went to boarding school in Tungchow, her family moved to Tsinan. The first time she went home on holiday to Tsinan was very strange.

'I know it's home,' she told her family, 'because you are all here. But it's very odd going into the street and not seeing any faces I recognise. I really miss seeing my old friends.'

Mrs Scott understood Betty's sadness and made a point of introducing her to some girls her age that attended church. Because Betty found it easy to write down her feelings, several times that holiday her parents discovered her curled up in a sunny corner with her notebook of poems. Before her first holiday in Tsinan was over, Betty was beginning to feel that it was really becoming home.

'Would you like to read us some of your poems?' Dr Scott asked one evening, after they had eaten and before the last of the sunlight faded.

Betty flicked back through the pages.

'Here's one I wrote when I was ten,' she said, and then settled down to read it.

I cannot live like Jesus
Example though he be
For he was strong and selfless
And I am tied to me.

I cannot live like Jesus
My soul is never free
My will is strong and stubborn
My love is weak and wee.
But I have asked my Jesus
To live his life in me.

I cannot look like Jesus
More beautiful is he
In soul and eye and stature
Than sunrise on the sea.

And before she was able to read the last few lines, a cloud went over the setting sun, and it was too dark to continue reading her tiny handwriting.

An hour later it was completely dark. Betty's two little sisters and two little brothers were sound asleep in bed, and she was still wide awake. Instead of tossing and turning, she rose and felt her way through to the living-room where her parents were reading by the light of a Chinese lantern.

'In you come and join us,' Dr Scott said. 'We don't often have you all to ourselves.'

Betty curled up beside her mother and felt loved.

'That was a beautiful poem you read to us,' Dr Scott said softly. 'Can you remember how it finishes?'

Screwing up her eyes, Betty tried to remember but couldn't.

'No,' she said. 'It's ages since I've read that one. But it ends with a couple of lines about how those who believe in Jesus, will be just like him when they go home to heaven.'

'That will be a wonderful day,' said Mrs Scott.

The three of them talked for a long time that night. But when Betty went back to bed, it was that great day, when she would go to heaven and be like Jesus, that came into her mind. Although she didn't sleep for quite a while, her thoughts were so full of the wonder of being like the Lord, that being awake in the middle of the night didn't seem to matter at all.

When Betty was seventeen years old, in 1923, her parents were due to go back to America on home leave. Betty had been back before, but this time was different for she was going to remain in America to attend

Wilson College in Pennsylvania. Although she'd been away in boarding school for several years, the thought of being on the opposite side of the world from her parents, was a very odd one. Sometimes the thought of it ate at her heart.

'We've decided to travel home to America by the scenic route,' Dr Scott told Betty, as they planned to leave China for their time of home leave. 'In fact, we're going to have really quite an exciting journey!'

Betty thought that the route of one long sea voyage would be much the same as the route of another. After all, what difference would it make which sea they passed through; they were all wet, wavy and some shade of blue.

Dr Scott continued what he was saying. 'We're going to America by way of Palestine, Egypt, Greece, Italy, France and England.'

Now, Betty was a very ladylike seventeen-year-old, so it was more than a little unusual to see her with her mouth wide open as though she were catching flies!

'Is that a surprise?' her father asked.

Realising that her mouth was open, Betty closed it ... then opened it again to say just one word. 'Wow!'

The journey back home to America was all Betty imagined it would be. When she wasn't answering the younger children's questions about the places they travelled through, she was asking her parents questions or looking up things in the guidebooks they carried with them. By the time they arrived in America, Betty felt more able to cope with being left there. After all, she had travelled the world ... or a very large part of it!

China was never far from Betty Scott's mind. Every single day she pictured what her parents would be doing, imagining her sisters at boarding school and her two young brothers still at home. Before falling asleep, she often imagined herself back in China, and sometimes, if she woke in the night, she was almost surprised to find herself in her room at Wilson College.

Having become a Christian as a child, Betty was very involved in Christian activities at college right from the start. Her letters home encouraged her parents because she wrote of the Christian friends she made and the meetings she attended. One letter in particular, written in 1925, gave them special joy.

'I've just returned from a conference in New Jersey,' she wrote. 'I've had such a wonderful time, and I've rededicated my life to the Lord. He seemed to speak to me very directly, telling me that after college I should prepare to be a missionary – that he wants me back home in China!'

Betty knew what she should do with her life, but how was she to do it? First, she knew she had to work hard at college and get a good degree. And while she was doing that, she found out about missionary training colleges and decided that the right place for her to go was the famous Moody Bible Institute in Chicago. Thousands of missionaries had done their training there, and the thought of joining them was very exciting. She might have been even more excited had she known that God was sending a young man to Moody who would become very special to her.

John Stam had intended to go into business, but God had another plan for his life. He found himself, just seven years after he was converted, heading for Moody Bible Institute. Betty and John met and became fond of each other. It's hard to imagine how they felt, in the summer of 1931, when Betty graduated and prepared to sail for China to serve the Lord with China Inland Mission.

'I'll follow you next summer,' John promised, thinking how long his last year at Moody would seem without the girl he loved.

'And if we still feel the same about each other after we've worked in China for a while, we'll get married,' Betty reminded him.

As her ship nudged away from the docks, John's mind was in a spin. China seemed so far away. When would they meet again? After all,

China was a big place, and they could be at opposite sides of the country. Would Betty still love him in a few years' time?

Having watched her ship until it was just a blur on the ocean, John spun round and walked away. He didn't know the answers to his questions, but he knew someone who did. As he walked, he talked to God, and Betty was talking to him too. The one thing they were both sure of, was that the Lord understood what they were feeling.

In October 1932, Betty had to go to Shanghai for medical treatment and to visit her parents. She was still there on the day that John's ship arrived. Scanning the crowds for a face that might belong to a fellow missionary, he had the nicest surprise of his life when the one missionary he knew in China grinned back at him. It was Betty!

And did they still feel the same way about each other? Nobody who saw them meeting that day would have needed to ask that question! Very soon, they became engaged, then after a year of language study and working in different places, John and Betty were married.

Were they the happiest people in the whole wide world? They certainly felt it. And their happiness was complete, the following autumn, when their little daughter was born. They called her Helen Priscilla.

'My sister Helen will like that,' Betty said, stroking her baby's soft cheek and looking deep into her baby-blue eyes.

Just a few weeks after Helen's birth, her parents took her to Tsingteh.

'Haven't missionaries been evacuated from there in the past?' a friend asked, when she heard where they were going.

'Yes,' Betty admitted. 'But it seems to be safe from the Communists just now. In any case, the local magistrate has guaranteed our safety from Communist attack.'

Her friend still looked worried. 'Look,' Betty said, 'Communists are everywhere, and if we think about them, we'll be frightened out of our wits. But if we remember that we are safe in the hands of Almighty God, we'll cope whatever happens.' She believed with all her heart that was true.

On 6th December, 1934, Tsingteh suffered a sudden and totally unexpected attack from Communist forces, and the city fell. It was early morning when Betty heard what all the noise was about, while she was in the middle of bathing little Helen. John and Betty knelt with their Chinese friends and prayed for God's will to be done.

'Would you like tea?' Betty asked the Communists, much to their surprise, when they arrived to interrogate John.

But the tea and the kindness did nothing to soften their hard hearts. John was tied to a chair and taken away. Before Betty had time to think what was happening to her husband, his captors came back and took her and Helen too.

'Don't follow us,' Betty urged the servants. 'They'll shoot you if you do.' Then in a whisper, she added, 'If they kill us, please look out for Helen.'

Later that day, John was allowed back to collect some things, and he too comforted their broken-hearted friends.

The following day, John, Betty and Helen were taken twelve miles over the mountains to Miaosheo. It is hard to write about what happened next, but only a few words will tell the story. On 8th December, Betty and John were beheaded, and the instant that happened they met Jesus face-to-face in heaven. Three-month-old Helen was left alone in a house to die. And it was there that she was found, thirty hours later, by a Christian friend. Snug in her Chinese padded sleeping bag, and none the worse for her lack of food, little Helen Stam was unharmed. The Lord, who had taken her parents home to heaven, took care of the little girl they left behind. As a child, Betty thought it would be a long time till she saw Jesus. But it wasn't very long after all.

FACT FILE

China: By the time Betty was born, China had been a country for longer than any other state that was still in existence. Recorded history in China reaches back to around 1736 B.C. When European travellers first went there, they were astonished to discover paper money, which was not known in Europe at the time. The Chinese are also credited with inventing gunpowder and building the only man-made structure visible from the moon - the Great Wall of China.

Keynote: Even when Betty realised that she would not be able to look after her baby, she knew that God would. And God did. It is amazing to think that such a young baby could survive without any care or food for so long. God is able to care for all of his children, even when they cannot care for themselves.

Think: John must have been worried when he arrived in Shanghai for the first time. It was a huge country, and he had never been there before in his life. God sent the one person he most wanted to see, to meet him. God is very kind to us in his providence, running the whole universe very smoothly and sometimes giving us happy surprises that we don't expect. Can you think of some of the ways in which God has been kind to you?

Prayer: Lord Jesus, you are a great God who is in charge of the whole world. Thank you for caring for people like me. Please help me to care for those around me every day. Amen.

Esther John

Qamar Zea was eight years old and busy at work. Crouched on the ground outside her home in South India, she was picking her way through the fruit that had been gathered the previous day.

'Take out the bruised fruits, and we'll use them right away,' her mother said. 'And don't leave any bruised ones in the basket, or all of them will rot.'

The child did as she was told, but she cast longing eyes at her brothers who were heading off to play.

Noticing where her daughter was looking, Qamar Zea's mother shook her head.

'Girls are never children,' she thought. 'Indian boys have a childhood when they can run and play with their friends, but the girls work from as soon as they're able.'

'There is so much fruit to go through,' the child moaned, looking at the flat basket piled high.

'Just you be grateful that we live in a part of India where there is enough rain to make the fruit grow,' the woman said, impatient to get back to her cooking. 'Further north there's nothing but dryness and dust.'

Looking at the greenness of the area in which she lived, Qamar Zea sighed then set about the job she had to do, knowing that when she was finished, another one would be waiting for her.

Before many more years had passed, the girl often helped her mother with the cooking. She enjoyed that, as it gave them time to talk together.

'I don't understand,' Qamar Zea said one day. It was a Friday. 'Why is it that on Fridays, when the men in our family go to the mosque to worship Allah, most of the other men in the village spend the day working?'

'That's life in India,' said her mother. 'It is a land of three peoples. Most are Hindu. They worship many gods; so many gods I don't know how they know who to worship on what day of the week.'

The girl looked shocked. 'But God the Lord is one God,' she said, having been taught the Koran, even though, as a Muslim girl, she was rarely inside a mosque. 'And who are the other two peoples?' she asked, fascinated.

'There are Christians in South India,' her mother explained. 'And there have been for hundreds of years. It's said that one of the Prophet Jesus' disciples came to Kerala and told the people about his Master.'

'And there are Muslims like us,' said Qamar Zea, 'who know that God the Lord is one God and that he is Allah, and that Jesus is one of his prophets.'

The woman smiled.

'Shh, girl, and stir the stew. You're training to be a cook, not a Muslim teacher.'

Qamar Zea was privileged because she attended school. Not all girls in her village went, although most boys did. During her eighth class in the government school, her father became seriously ill, and she had to stop school for a time. When he recovered, she went to a Christian school, which was more convenient for her home.

'I've never known anyone like our teacher before,' she told one of her new friends. 'She speaks to us in such a gentle way, and she's so kind to all her pupils.'

Watching this woman carefully made a great impression on Qamar Zea.

'How can a person be like her?' she asked herself. 'She does her work so well and lives a better life than anyone else I know. I wonder what makes her so different.'

This was particularly surprising to the Muslim teenager, as she had been brought up to believe that Christians were blasphemers who spoke against Allah, and not good people at all.

'Don't let your teachers tell you lies about Allah,' the girl was warned by the men in her family.

Qamar Zea held her peace. None of her family knew that, two days each week she studied Old Testament in school, two days she studied New Testament, and on the fifth day she learned Bible verses by memory.

'Christians believe that there is only one God,' she thought, as she studied. 'But they believe that Jesus is God rather than just one of the prophets. I'm confused.'

Not long afterwards, on one of the days for memorising Bible verses, the girls in her class were given part of Isaiah 53 to learn. Qamar Zea read the verses over and over again as she tried to remember them. 'We all, like sheep, have gone astray, each one of us has turned to his own way; and the Lord has laid on him the iniquity of us all.'

Later, she explained what happened that day.

'We were memorising some parts of Isaiah 53, which was very hard for me. Then I began to realise that Jesus is alive for ever. Thus God put faith in my heart, and I believed in Jesus as my Saviour and the forgiver of my sins. Only he could save me from everlasting death. That was when I began to realise how great a sinner I was, whereas before, I thought my good life could save me.'

Now for a sixty word history lesson. The landmass that is now India, Bangladesh and Pakistan used to be all part of India. In 1947, it split into three parts: India, East Pakistan and West Pakistan. East Pakistan eventually changed its name to Bangladesh. The main reason for this split was religious. The new India was mainly Hindu, and Pakistan was set up as a Muslim state. That was exactly sixty words; check it if you like!

When the Muslim state of Pakistan was founded, Qamar Zea's family moved north-west to live there. They settled in the city of Karachi. She was eighteen years old.

'Are you Qamar Zea?' a stranger asked the young woman one day.

'Yes,' she answered. 'But who are you?'

'I'm a Christian friend,' the woman explained. 'My name is Miss Laugesen, and some Christians in India have asked me to do anything I can to help you.'

Qamar Zea smiled.

'Is there anything you need?' the woman asked.

'Just one thing,' said Qamar Zea. 'Would it be possible for you to get me a New Testament?'

The Christian worker brought her a New Testament under cover of darkness, because it would have caused terrible trouble in Qamar Zea's family if she had been found out.

It was seven years before she would meet Miss Laugesen again, and it was at a time of deep trouble for Qamar Zea.

'My family have planned a Muslim marriage for me,' the young Christian explained, when she arrived at Miss Laugesen's home. 'That's why I've come to you.'

The Christian worker welcomed the girl, and they set up home together.

It wasn't long before Qamar Zea's brothers found out where she was and followed her.

'Come home with us,' they demanded. 'Your father has a good marriage partner for you.'

'No,' their sister said quietly. 'I cannot come.'

But her brothers persuaded her to return to see her mother. She did, but was soon back in the safety of Miss Laugesen's home. From there, she went north to Sahiwal in the Punjab where she worked in a Christian hospital. During her time in Sahiwal, she was baptised as a Christian believer and took a new name, Esther John.

'I feel God wants me to be a teacher of the Bible,' she explained at her baptism. 'This book has great power. I want to see it do for others what it has done for me.'

In 1956, the brave young woman began a completely new stage of her life. She left Sahiwal and went to the city of Gujranwala, to attend the United Bible Training Centre in order to train as a Bible teacher. For a Muslim family like hers, it was a disgrace that she had become a Christian, but even more so when she went to train as a Bible teacher. Esther John's brothers were enraged at what she had done, and no doubt her mother wept many tears.

The United Bible Training Centre was a residential centre then run by missionaries from America and Britain. Within the compound, there was a building with a central courtyard where Esther John lived with other women who were training to be Bible teachers. Each day began with worship in the small chapel. Then they had classes in which they studied the Bible, but they also learned practical things like cooking and ordering food. For recreation, they went out on the lawn where they played games, skipped and did things Esther John and the other students hadn't had the opportunity to do as children at home. One of the fun activities was done for a serious reason, and that was learning to ride a bicycle. This was very unusual for Pakistani girls.

As part of her training, each girl cycled to local villages with a missionary. There, they gathered the women for Bible reading, prayer and singing, and on other occasions they taught Bible stories to the children. Saturdays and Sundays were different. Saturdays were busy with cleaning, laundry, hair-washing and preparation for the next day. Then on Sundays they went to the local church and often returned home to the United Bible Training Centre for some hymn-singing and reading. After her busy week, Esther John enjoyed her quiet Sundays.

Following three years of training, Esther John left Gujranwala and moved to the little town of Chichawatni.

'I would like you to live in our home with us,' a Christian worker, called Mrs Dale White, told her.

And that's what Esther John did.

'Chichawatni is my lovely home,' she said, smiling, as she looked around the shady well-watered compound, with its brightly coloured flowering trees. Then she laughed, 'And as Chichawatni is now my home, I'm going to dress as the women do here.'

Until then, Esther John had continued wearing her Indian sari. Getting dressed each day was very different from then on, as she put on her shalwar kameez (baggy trousers and long tunic top). Finally she had always to wear the dupatta that covered her head and shoulders. The outfit was not complete without the dupatta, as in a Muslim country it was not proper for a woman to show bare skin.

Not only did the new Bible teacher surprise her friends by wearing Pakistani clothes, she amazed the people of Chichawatni by riding her bicycle!

'Look at her!' people said, pointing in Esther John's direction. 'What next?'

And there was a next .... that was the Punjabi language. If ever a young woman was determined to do all she could to spread the good news that Jesus Christ is the one and only Saviour, Esther John was that young woman. With Mrs White, she travelled from village to village and town to town to speak to any women who would listen. And many did. Muslim women were often restricted to their own homes or compounds, but somehow God opened the way for these two intrepid missionaries to meet them there.

'You still have the light of the holy Prophet Muhammad in your face!' one Muslim woman told Esther John.

'It's the light of Jesus,' the Bible woman explained. 'It is he who is my Saviour, and it is he who makes my face shine.'

'But how could you leave your Muslim background?' she was asked, over and over again.

'God's grace was upon me,' was her often repeated reply.

Then with a smiling face and a great deal of enthusiasm, she shared the story of Jesus in word, picture and song.

'Let's prepare a special play for Christmas,' she said to the children in Chichawatni.

From then on, every spare minute was spent doing just that, amid much fun and laughter.

But there was a shadow over Esther John's life, as her family had begun sending her frequent letters asking her to return home. The thought disturbed her, but eventually she agreed to go at the end of the year on two conditions.

'I must be allowed to live as a Christian,' she wrote home, 'and I must not be forced into a Muslim marriage.'

'I sent that letter by registered mail,' she told Mrs White, some time later, 'but I've had no reply.'

Because of that, Esther John was unwilling to go home to her family, so she arranged to go off on mission with the Whites for a month before returning to her much-loved Chichawatni.

On the evening of her return, Esther John sang happily as she polished her pots and pans. Having a slight cold, she went off to bed early. The house was full of guests, which is perhaps why the intruder was not heard. But there was an intruder, and he only did one thing. Nothing was stolen, nothing was disturbed, but Esther John was attacked and murdered. She was not the first Muslim convert to die because she had dared to become a Christian, and she will not be the last. Muslims in Chichawatni joined Christians at Esther John's funeral. Of course the police were called in, and they investigated the murder. The result of their investigations was a wonderful tribute to a lovely lady. 'Sir,' they told Mr White, 'we have found no clue. This girl was in love only with your Christ.'

Although the Whites grieved for their friend, they knew she was in heaven with Jesus whom she loved best of all.

FACT FILE

Names: We don't normally think about names very much, but in the past they were seen as very important. In the Bible, we are often given the reason for someone's name when they are born. Many people changed their names, when they became Christians, because their old names sometimes referred to heathen gods. This practice was so common in Britain in the past, that we often call a person's first name their Christian name.

Keynote: Qamar Zea had been brought up to think that she could please God by being good, but as she learned the verses from Isaiah, she learned she was a great sinner in God's eyes and only Jesus could save her from her sins. When we look around us, we might think that we are doing not too badly, but we have to look to the Bible to find God's standard and God's solution.

Think: Qamar Zea was very impressed by the gentleness of her teacher in the Christian school. She was so impressed, that she wanted to know how she could live like her teacher. Her teacher was following Jesus' command to be a light in the world and to love her neighbour. It had a great effect! How do you think you could show the same gentleness and kindness?

Prayer: Lord Jesus, I know that I am a sinner, and that I can't save myself with lots of good deeds. Thank you for offering salvation through your free grace and forgiveness. Please help me to show something of the gentleness and kindness that you command us to show. Amen.

Author Information: Irene Howat

Irene Howat is an award-winning author and poet who lives in Scotland. She has published many biographical books for all ages and is particularly well-known for her biographical material. She has written many books about the lives of different Christians from around the world. She has also written an autobiographical work entitled: *Pain My Companion.*

Quiz

How much can you remember about the ten girls who didn't give in? Try answering these questions to find out.

Blandina

1. What was Blandina's mum doing when she was playing tig with her friend?

2. Which city in Gaul did Blandina live in?

3. Which words from the preacher always gave Blandina a warm feeling?

Perpetua

4. Where is Carthage?

5. Which book of the Bible did Felicitas refer to when she was waiting to go into the arena?

6. What do the names Perpetua and Felicitas mean when you put them together?

Lady Jane Grey

7. Which king of England had the Dowager Queen been married to?

8. What relation was Jane to Queen Mary?

9. Who tried to make Jane queen and his son king?

Anne Askew

10. How did Anne's tutor describe the sea?

11. Why did she, and not her sister, have to marry Thomas Kyme?

12. How was Anne tortured to try and make her change her mind?

Lysken Dirks

13. Which town did Lysken live in when she married?

14. What did the guards find that Jeronimus had written?

15. Why did the authorities kill Lysken early?

Marion Harvey

16. Which Firth is Bo'ness on?

17. Which preacher was Marion arrested for going to hear?

18. What did her friend think that he preached about and what did he really preach about?

Margaret Wilson

19. What was Margaret's father's job?

20. How did the people at the meal notice Margaret and her sister?

21. Which town is near the place where they drowned?

Judith Weinberg

22. What position did Judith's grandfather hold, apart from being a timber merchant?

23. Which war began in 1914?

24. What was wrong with the children that Judith nursed?

Betty Stam

25. What did Betty say she felt like when she got into her summer clothes?

26. Where did Betty go to train to be a missionary?

27. What did Betty offer the Communists when they arrived?

Esther John

28. Which part of India did Qamar Zea's mother tell her that the Christians lived in?

29. What did the name of East Pakistan eventually change to?

30. What did Esther give up wearing when she moved to Chichawatni?

How well did you do?

Turn over to find out...

Answers

1. Drawing water from a well
2. Lyon
3. 'Brothers and sisters'
4. North Africa
5. Revelation
6. Everlasting Happiness
7. Henry VIII
8. Her cousin
9. Dudley
10. Like the River Witham over and over again
11. Her sister died before the wedding
12. She was stretched on the rack
13. Antwerp
14. A poem
15. To prevent a scene
16. The Firth of Forth

17. Donald Cargill

18. She thought that he preached about fire and brimstone but he really preached about the love of God.

19. He was a farmer

20. They didn't drink to the King's health

21. Wigtown

22. He was a Rabbi

23. The First World War

24. They had typhus fever

25. A butterfly

26. Moody Bible Institute

27. Tea

28. The South

29. Bangladesh

30. The Indian Sari

Start collecting this series now!

Ten Boys who used their Talents:
ISBN 978-1-84550-146-4
Paul Brand, Ghillean Prance, C.S.Lewis, C.T. Studd, Wilfred Grenfell, J.S. Bach, James Clerk Maxwell, Samuel Morse, George Washington Carver, John Bunyan.

Ten Girls who used their Talents:
ISBN 978-1-84550-147-1
Helen Roseveare, Maureen McKenna, Anne Lawson, Harriet Beecher Stowe, Sarah Edwards, Selina Countess of Huntingdon, Mildred Cable, Katie Ann MacKinnon, Patricia St. John, Mary Verghese.

Ten Boys who Changed the World:
ISBN 978-1-85792-579-1
David Livingstone, Billy Graham, Brother Andrew, John Newton, William Carey, George Müller, Nicky Cruz, Eric Liddell, Luis Palau, Adoniram Judson.

Ten Girls who Changed the World:
ISBN 978-1-85792-649-1
Corrie Ten Boom, Mary Slessor, Joni Eareckson Tada, Isobel Kuhn, Amy Carmichael, Elizabeth Fry, Evelyn Brand, Gladys Aylward, Catherine Booth, Jackie Pullinger.

Ten Boys who Made a Difference:
ISBN 978-1-85792-775-7
Augustine of Hippo, Jan Hus, Martin Luther, Ulrich Zwingli, William Tyndale, Hugh Latimer, John Calvin, John Knox, Lord Shaftesbury, Thomas Chalmers.

Ten Girls who Made a Difference:
ISBN 978-1-85792-776-4
Monica of Thagaste, Catherine Luther,
Susanna Wesley, Ann Judson, Maria Taylor,
Susannah Spurgeon, Bethan Lloyd-Jones,
Edith Schaeffer, Sabina Wurmbrand,
Ruth Bell Graham.

Ten Boys who Made History:
ISBN 978-1-85792-836-5
Charles Spurgeon, Jonathan Edwards,
Samuel Rutherford, D L Moody,
Martin Lloyd Jones, A W Tozer, John Owen,
Robert Murray McCheyne, Billy Sunday,
George Whitfield.

Ten Girls who Made History:
ISBN 978-1-85792-837-2
Ida Scudder, Betty Green, Jeanette Li,
Mary Jane Kinnaird, Bessie Adams,
Emma Dryer, Lottie Moon, Florence Nightingale,
Henrietta Mears, Elisabeth Elliot.

Ten Boys who Didn't Give In:
ISBN 978-1-84550-035-1
Polycarp, Alban, Sir John Oldcastle
Thomas Cramer, George Wishart,
James Chalmers, Dietrich Bonhoeffer
Nate Saint, Ivan Moiseyev
Graham Staines

Ten Girls who Didn't Give In:
ISBN 978-1-84550-036-8
Blandina, Perpetua, Lady Jane Grey,
Anne Askew, Lysken Dirks, Marion Harvey,
Margaret Wilson, Judith Weinberg,
Betty Stam, Esther John

CHRISTIAN FOCUS PUBLICATIONS

Christian Focus · Christian Heritage · CF4K · Mentor

Christian Focus Publications publishes books for adults and children under its four main imprints: Christian Focus, CF4K, Mentor and Christian Heritage. Our books reflect our conviction that God's Word is reliable and Jesus is the way to know him, and live for ever with him.

Our children's publication list covers pre-school to early teens. We also publish personal and family devotional titles, biographies and inspirational stories that children will love.

From pre-school board books to teenage apologetics, we have it covered!

Christian Focus Publications Ltd,
Geanies House, Fearn, Ross-shire,
IV20 1TW, Scotland,
United Kingdom.
www.christianfocus.com

CF4K

Because you're never too young to know Jesus

TEN GIRLS WHO CHANGED THE WORLD

LIGHT KEEPERS

Irene Howat

CF4•K

This revised edition printed 2001
Reprinted 2002, 2003 twice, 2004, 2005, 2006, 2007,
2008, 2009, 2010, 2011, 2013, 2014, 2015, 2016, 2020, 2022
Paperback ISBN: 978-1-85792-649-1
E-pub ISBN: 978-1-84550-848-7
Mobi ISBN: 978-1-84550-849-4

Published by Christian Focus Publications, Geanies House, Fearn,
Tain, Ross-shire, IV20 1TW, Scotland, Great Britain
www.christianfocus.com
email:info@christianfocus.com
Cover design by Alister MacInnes.
Cover illustration by Elena Temporin,
Milan Illustrations Agency.
Printed and bound in China

All incidents retold in these stories are based on true situations. Where specific information about childhood incidents has been unobtainable the author has written these paragraphs using other information concerning family life, hobbies, homelife, relationships freely available in other biographies as well as appropriate historical source material.

Front cover: As a young girl growing up in The Netherlands, Corrie ten Boom lived with her father, mother and sister, Betsie, in a little watch shop in Haarlem, a fifteen minute train ride west of Amsterdam. Corrie herself went on to be one of the first qualified female watchmakers in The Netherlands. During the second world war her home was used as a refuge for Jewish people on the run from the Nazi authorities. Corrie and her sister were later imprisoned in a concentration camp. Betsie died but Corrie survived to tell their story.

For
Georgia Holly

Contents

Isobel Kuhn

Isobel and her brother sat in the tree-house in their garden, waiting and watching for their parents' visitors to arrive.

'They've come all the way from China,' Isobel said. 'I guess they'll have lots of interesting stories to tell us.'

Both the children loved stories and looked forward to visitors coming from interesting faraway places. As she also loved telling stories, Isabel told her brother a story as they waited for their visitors to arrive.

'A long time ago and a long way away there were two missionaries whose names were Paul and Barnabas. One day they saw a man who had never walked in all of his life. When the man looked up Paul told him to stand on his feet. Guess what the man did?'

'Did he tell Paul that he couldn't do that?' asked the boy.

'No, he didn't,' Isobel told him. 'The man jumped up and began to walk!'

Her brother was wide-eyed.

'That's a miracle,' he announced.

Isabel agreed. 'And as that story is in the Bible we know it's true,' she added.

Just then a little group of people arrived at the gate.

'Shoosh!' Isobel whispered. 'There they are.'

The pair of them clambered down the tree and ran towards the house.

'Do you never get tired of all the missionaries Dad invites home?' the boy asked breathlessly.

Isobel grinned. 'No, and I never get tired of telling stories either!'

Isobel and her brother soon realised that these visitors weren't really that different to them. The brother and sister climbed down the tree to run to meet and greet their visitors from another country.

They were soon running about and playing together just like children the world over.

'They've come all the way from China,' Isobel marvelled. 'I wonder what that must be like?'

When Isobel Miller (that was what she was called before she married) went to university, she decided that she didn't believe in God. That made her father and mother very sad. They prayed for her, asking God to show their daughter how much she needed the Saviour. It took some years, but eventually their prayers were answered. Isobel, who was by then a teacher, discovered for herself that believing in Jesus and trusting in him is not dull and boring and only for old people. It made her happier than she had ever been before.

At a conference Isobel heard a missionary speak about his work with the Lisu people in China. As he was speaking, she longed to go there and to tell these people about the Lord Jesus.

'We need men to work with the Lisu,' the speaker said, as he finished his talk.

'I wonder if they need women too?' Isobel thought to herself.

Someone she met at that conference paid for Isobel to go to Bible College in America and it was there that she met John Kuhn. He was also training to be a missionary, and he too felt God wanted him to go to China.

John, who was a year ahead of Isobel at College, finished his course and left for the mission field. They were by then very much in love. How Isobel missed him.

It wasn't until nearly two years later, in October 1928, that Isobel boarded a ship at Vancouver dock and set sail for China and her husband-to-be. But it was a long time until the Kuhns went from the great plains of China to work with the Lisu people in the faraway mountains and by then they had a little daughter, Kathryn. Isobel could hardly believe it when they eventually arrived in Lisuland!

'Jesus loves me, this I know,
for the Bible tells me so,'

Kathryn sang to her friends in the language of the Lisu. 'Now you sing.' Six smiling dark-eyed children sang along with her.

'Little ones to him belong.
They are weak but he is strong.'

Her mother's voice joined in,

'Yes, Jesus loves me,
the Bible tells me so.'

'Lord,' Isobel prayed. 'Thank you that even Kathryn is a missionary here. Please let these little children really hear what she's saying and learn that you love them.'

When the Kuhns were in Lisuland, China and Japan were at war. Sometimes soldiers came to the village they lived in and made the people very afraid. When the time came for John and Isobel to go home on leave and introduce little Kathryn to her family in Canada and America, they were sorry to go, because it came at a bad time for the Lisu people. But their home leave soon passed and they set out again for China, despite the Second World War making travel hazardous.

'There's a telegram for you,' John was told when their boat called at Hong Kong.

His wife watched as he opened it. 'Was it bad news from home?' she wondered.

'Send Kathryn to Chefoo with Grace Liddell,' John read.

Isobel's face turned white. 'But that means saying goodbye to her here and now!'

The Kuhns had expected Kathryn to go away to school when they arrived back in China but now the mission was instructing them to send her with another missionary who was travelling to a mission school in what is now Malaysia. They weren't even going to be in the same country!

There were very sad farewells but everyone tried to be brave. Thankfully John and Isobel didn't know that Chefoo School would soon be captured by the Japanese and that it would be a very long time before they even received a letter from Kathryn to say that she was safe and well. Isobel broke her heart when Kathryn left and it took a while before she lost her deep sadness.

'I wonder what's the best way to make an impact on these mountain villages?' John thought aloud, as he and Isobel talked in their hut one evening soon after their return to Lisuland.

'Well, one thing's sure,' his wife said, 'we can't be in them all at once.'

There was a silence.

'I've been thinking,' her husband went on. 'The best way forward would be to train the young Christians to be missionaries to their own people.'

'But how do we do that? They can't come here one day a week for classes because some of them live four days' walk away,' Isobel pointed out. 'They can't come in the dry season because they've got to work in the fields. And it's not safe to travel in the rainy season, it's too easy to slip on the mountain paths. Every year that happens and people are killed.'

'I was wondering,' John continued, 'if we could have a Rainy Season Bible School. The young men could come before the rains made walking dangerous, stay here and study until the worst of the rain had passed and it was safe to go home again.'

Isobel's eyes lit up. 'That's a wonderful idea!'

John grinned. 'Thank you, I think so too!'

The Rainy Season Bible School was born, and it was a great success. Young men came from long distances to study the Bible. Each weekend during the Bible School they went to nearby villages where they preached and taught the children.

At the end of their studies they went back to their homes and told the people there about the Lord God.

Having seen the success of the boys' Bible School, Isobel decided to have one for girls too. The men in the church just laughed at the idea. They thought girls didn't have enough brains to learn things from books!

John was working in another part of China when the first Bible School for girls was held. Isobel wrote to tell him about it.

'Twenty-two girls attended,' she wrote. 'We held tests and gave out certificates to those who passed. The results were good. One even got first-class honours.

Can you guess who that was?

It was the blind girl from Mountain Top Village! I asked her how she had learned her Bible passages. She smiled as she told me.

"I could hear the other girls in my hut going over their notes and learning their verses, so I studied by listening to them." '

During the Bible School, some of the girls held a Sunday School in the village the Kuhns lived in.

But every time Isobel heard the children singing 'Jesus loves me' she thought about her own little girlie and prayed that she was safe and that God was caring for the missionary children at Chefoo.

'Ohh ... Ohh ...' Isobel moaned in her sleep. 'My tooth is so sore.'

John didn't hear her. He was hundreds of miles away on mission business.

The tooth was no better in the morning and the pain grew dreadfully as time passed. The nearest dentist was two weeks' journey away but eventually the missionary decided that she had to go.

A young Lisu man went with Isobel to keep her company, and to protect her as soldiers and bandits were making the area unsafe for travel.

'I'll meet up with John and we can come home together,' she told her companion.

But the war between China and Japan caught up with her and it was months before she and her husband were back in the village. Something else caught up with Isobel too, a letter from Kathryn saying that the Japanese were looking after the schoolchildren well and that there was no need to worry.

'I'm so glad that tooth brought me to the town,' she told a missionary friend. 'If I'd still been in the village I probably wouldn't have got Kathryn's letter.'

After that, regular letters got through to Chefoo and one was full of lovely news.

'My dear girlie,' Isobel wrote, 'you're now a big sister! Little Danny was born yesterday and I'm writing right away so that you'll know the news as soon as you possibly can.

Your brother has tiny ears, just like sea shells. His eyes are like deep pools of water.

I've checked his fingers and toes, and he has ten of each of them. He is such a cutie, just like you were when you were born.'

When Kathryn got the letter, she wrote back immediately.

'I can't believe that I really have a baby brother! It's the bestest news I could possibly get. I was working it out, and if everything goes as we've planned, I'll see Danny when he's just a year old. He'll still be a bit of a baby then, won't he? I do want to see him while he's still a baby. Ask someone who's artistic to draw me a picture of Danny. I'd just LOVE to see him.'

For Kathryn that year passed slowly. As she was now in her teens, she travelled to America with some missionaries who were returning home. When she arrived she was looked after by another Christian family who became a sort of foster family to her.

'I can't wait for the family to come,' she told her friends. 'I've never even met my baby brother.'

John, Isobel and Danny were on their way to America. It was a dangerous journey because the Second World War was still raging and ships didn't always arrive at their destinations. Many were torpedoed as they crossed the oceans. But God looked after the little missionary family and they met with each other at last, the first time ever all four of them had been together.

'Allo Kafin,' Danny said, a little shyly at first.

Kathryn held out her arms to her baby brother.

The toddler looked at his mum, then at his dad, and saw they were smiling. So he walked unsteadily to his sister, held up his arms and snuggled into her neck when she lifted him. Kathryn was glad the little boy could not see her face. She was crying, crying tears of joy and delight.

For over a year John and Isobel, Kathryn and Danny lived a normal family life. Because they had been so often separated, that was very special to them.

Kathryn got to know her parents again, for she had grown up in the time they'd been apart. And she got to know Danny, who thought having a big sister was a splendid thing.

But the day came when they had to say 'goodbye' again, and Kathryn waved the family off on their long journey back to China. It was a heartbreaking time for Isobel and John Kuhn and their daughter Kathryn.

Kathryn stayed in America because of her education. But despite all the times that being missionaries had meant that her family were countries apart from each other, when Kathryn Kuhn decided what she would do with her life, she felt that God wanted her to be a missionary too.

The years of separation the Kuhn family had undergone didn't discourage their eldest daughter from a life of missionary service for her God. She knew what to expect and decided that she wanted to give her life to God and to telling people about him and his son, Jesus Christ.

Eventually Isobel Kuhn was forced to leave the mission field and return to life in America. Her health was poor and she could no longer stay with the Lisu people she loved so much. Mission work was now out of the question. Isobel needed urgent surgery that she could only receive in the United States. But it meant being reunited with Kathryn and Danny. Both Isobel's children were by then living in America.

And one day Isobel Kuhn waved goodbye to another young woman who was heading off to the other side of the world as a missionary, just as she had done many years before. As they took their last farewells, Isobel wiped a tear from her eye and breathed a sigh of relief. It was good to realise that all the separation, heartache and suffering hadn't harmed Kathryn too much. Isobel's little girlie had grown up and she too was leaving to become a missionary, a missionary in China!

That evening Isobel thought back to all her years in China. Then her eye caught sight of the books she had written about the Lisu people since her return to America. She picked up her pen. Isobel knew she hadn't long to live, but she still had work to do.

Isobel Kuhn died and went home to Jesus in 1957.

FACT FILE

Posting a letter - mail used to be delivered by hand. You would either employ someone to deliver your letter for you or send it with a travelling friend. It was a very expensive and unreliable system.

The postage stamp was invented in 1840. It is really a receipt to show that you have paid a fee for the letter to be delivered by the Post Office.

When Isobel was in China, mail would take months to arrive. Today, a letter can be sent by airmail to China in a matter of days and an e-mail in a matter of minutes.

Keynote: Isobel and her family were often apart from one another. It was always very difficult to say goodbye, but it was a comfort to know that God was with them all.

Learn from Isobel's experience that as a Christian you are never alone. Jesus promises never to leave you.

Think: Have you ever thought about writing a letter to a missionary? Getting news from home and some encouraging words will mean so much to a missionary who is far away from family and friends.

Prayer: Lord Jesus, thank you for missionaries who leave their homes, families and friends to bring the message of Jesus to people who have never heard about you.

Comfort them when they are lonely and be with those at home who miss them most. Amen.

Elizabeth Fry

The child screwed up her face and looked in the mirror. "Am I beautiful?" she asked herself. So many beautiful ladies came to see her Mama that sometimes Elizabeth's home, Earlham Hall near Norwich, seemed as though it were lived in by butterflies rather than people. The ladies wore long dresses in every colour of silk, dresses that rustled as they moved. And when they brushed against her she loved to feel their cool softness.

'I can't wait to be a lady,' she told her reflection. 'I'll wear the most splendid dresses of all.'

'Have you finished brushing your hair, Miss Elizabeth?' her maid Jane, asked.

The girl jumped. She had forgotten why she was in front of the mirror!

'You help me,' she said. 'My arm gets tired with all the brushing.'

'How many have you done?' asked the woman.

Elizabeth was torn between honesty and her dislike of having her long hair brushed. Honesty won. 'None.'

Taking the brush in one hand and loosening the child's hair with the other, Jane started to count, one for each long stroke. 'One, two, three ...,' till after what seemed a very long time, 'ninety eight, ninety nine, a hundred.'

With a deep sigh the woman laid down the brush. 'Sometimes I wish your hair wasn't quite so long,' she said. 'It hurts my poor back to bend down so far.'

The child swung round, her hair swirling behind her. 'Dance with me,' she said. 'Let's pretend we are at one of Papa and Mama's great parties.'

Elizabeth's maid laughed, bowed to her young partner, then danced one of the formal dances of the day with her.

When she was being tucked up in bed that night, Elizabeth looked thoughtful.

'A penny for your thoughts,' Jane said.

'I was wondering what I'll be doing in the year 1800. That's ten years from now and I'll be twenty years old. I'll have fine silk dresses and I'll go to a party every week and I'll dance with the handsomest of all the young men. Do you think I'll do all that when I'm twenty?'

The maid folded over her linen sheet and tucked in the blankets. 'What I think is this,' she said, 'tomorrow is Sunday and you'd best be thinking about Sunday things not about parties and all.'

Elizabeth Gurney closed her eyes until the door was shut then opened them again. She loved watching the coal fire in the nursery after her candle was blown out.

'Sunday,' she thought. 'Why are there so many Sundays. They are not nearly such fun as other days. The services at the Friends' Meeting House are so long. And the sermons are so boring, boring that I run out of things to think about!'

She turned on to her side, closed her eyes and tired to forget that tomorrow was Sunday.

By the year 1800 Elizabeth felt differently. Three years earlier, when she was seventeen years old she heard an American preacher, William Savery, and learned from him that Jesus died to save her from her sins. She was thrilled by what she heard and trusted her heart to the Lord. And, some months afterwards, when she was told at a Quaker meeting (her family were from a well known and very wealthy Quaker family) that she would be, 'a light to the blind, speech to the dumb and feet to the lame, Elizabeth felt sure that God had special work for her to do. From then on she kept herself busy doing good where she saw any kind of need.

'Will you miss the work you do?' Joseph Fry, Elizabeth's fiancé, asked her just before they were to be married when she was twenty years old.

She nodded. 'I think I may, but I can't take my Sunday School class to London with me, and I don't expect I'll have time to make clothes for the poor. I'll be so busy running our home.'

'I think you will,' Joseph smiled. 'But may I ask you something?'

Elizabeth looked up sharply. 'Is there anything wrong?'

'Not at all. I was just wondering if you'll continue to wear Plain Quaker clothes when you come to the capital.'

The lovely young woman looked down at her simple grey wool dress and put her hand up to touch her grey bonnet. 'Yes,' she said gently. 'Yes, I believe I will. I don't think the Lord means me to be dressed like a showy parrot in all sorts of bright colours. It would just draw attention to myself and that doesn't seem right.'

Elizabeth wore Plain Quaker clothes for the rest of her life. The women of the Quaker group in which she had been brought up had no restriction of what they wore, the more glamorous they were the better and their social diaries were full. Plain Quakers were different, they lived quietly and simply and dressed in the plainest of clothes. When she remembered back to her childhood dreams, the new Mrs Fry smiled and shook her head.

She was busy after she was married, but it wasn't a business that satisfied her. So, when eight years later in 1808 Elizabeth and her husband moved to Plashet in Essex, she was more than ready to find some useful things to do in the community. First she employed a teacher and set up a school. Then she organised a place where poor people could have a bowl of hot soup. And when she heard people in the neighbourhood were sick, she visited them, taking a basketful of good things with her. In those days if men were ill and could not work no money came into the house at all. Families were sometimes in real danger of starving. Elizabeth Fry did all that she could to help when she heard of hardship of any kind.

It was 1813, and Elizabeth Fry was speaking urgently to a group of women, all dressed as simply as she was.

'I've called you together to tell you about Mr Stephen Grellet, the American Quaker.'

The women were interested, a visitor from the other side of the Atlantic Ocean was still unusual.

'He took the opportunity to visit Newgate Prison and was shocked by what he found. There are women and children as well as men locked up in that place. Apparently it is filthy and smells disgusting.'

'What can we do?' one of the company asked.

'We should do something,' another said.

'We must go there,' Elizabeth told them.

'We must go and see for ourselves what can be done.'

'Could we take clothing with us?'

'And blankets?'

'Some nourishing food will be needed, I'm sure.'

What started as Elizabeth telling about Newgate Prison turned into a planning meeting with its sole topic how to change things there. With her group of Quaker ladies, Elizabeth Fry went to the prison carrying bundles and bags and baskets. The conditions shocked them. Even women and children slept on the floor with only a thin layer of rotten straw underneath them. Before leaving, the ladies paid the turnkey (the jailor) to replace the straw regularly. The women in the prison must have wondered if they would ever see their visitors again, or had they just come as a one-off effort at helping. If that's what they thought they were wrong.

Newgate Prison held three hundred women and children in just four rooms. All they did, they did there: cooking, eating, sleeping and everything else as well. Each day the women and men were allowed to mix together and Elizabeth was appalled that their time was spent gambling and drinking, fighting and dancing. It wasn't a pleasant atmosphere and certainly not one for young children, and there were many children there. Not all of the prisoners were guilty of a crime, many were just there awaiting trial. And those who were criminals came out worse than when they went in.

'It's that Quaker lady,' one woman prisoner said to another when Elizabeth next visited. 'It's taken her years to come back. I thought we'd never see her again.'

'Wot kept ye?' she yelled, when Mrs Fry was shown into the dark and smelly room.

Elizabeth explained that for the four years since her last visit she had been unable to give time to much else but her family. But now she intended doing something about their prison conditions.

'Wot are ye gonna do?' a women said from the corner where she was nursing her baby. An older boy and girl cuddled in beside her.

'First of all I hope to start a school for these children,' Mrs Fry explained. 'They shouldn't be here at all and the least we can do is give them schooling.'

'A school!'

'In here!'

A thin woman brought her skinny little girl to the visitor. 'Will you take my Ann for a pupil?'

Elizabeth smiled at the dirty child.

'Yes,' she said. 'She'll be the school's very first pupil.'

It wasn't long until the school was running and mothers were offering help with it. Others wanted to be taught themselves.

'Are you serious?' Elizabeth asked.

Several heads nodded eagerly.

'What do you want to be taught?'

'Sewing,' said one, 'then I'll be able to earn some money when I get out of here.'

'Knitting,' another suggested. 'My little Cathy needs warm clothes for the winter. It's freezing in here come October.'

'And we could sell what we make,' one bright young woman added. 'Then we could buy things the children need. I want my John to have shoes this winter. Last year he cried himself to sleep every night because of his chilblains.'

There was no shortage of suggestions, and Elizabeth was not short of enthusiasm. Soon several classes of twelve women were set up, each doing a different craft. And Mrs Fry opened a shop in the prison where the women could buy things with the little money they earned. A group of her Quaker friends joined with her and at least one of them visited the prison every single day.

At 9am and 6pm each day Elizabeth went to Newgate to take a short service. She didn't only preach to the women, she helped them in all sorts of other ways too. Many prisoners were moved by what she said, especially as she didn't only preach to them she helped them in practical ways too. Her prison work became so well known that committees like her one were set up all over the country to help women in prisons just as bad as Newgate. And the news of what was happening there travelled further still, and so did Elizabeth. She went as far as Russia telling people about the need to do something about prison conditions.

'I can hardly take in what you're saying!' Elizabeth Fry gasped when, in 1818, she heard for the first time about the evils of transportation. 'Tell me exactly what's happening.'

The man took a deep breath and began. 'A convict can be transported to the colonies for life if he steals an apron or a side of bacon. And for taking half a kilo of potatoes or a pair of shoes he can be sent away for fourteen years.'

'They are sent half way round the world! What happens to the women?' she asked.

'They are chained together and carried to the ships in open carts.'

Her eyes opened wide.

'And when they get to the colonies they're treated no better than slaves. They're given nowhere to stay and no decent work to do.'

'I must do something about this,' Elizabeth said. 'Indeed, I really must.'

It didn't take long for Elizabeth to persuade the Governor of Newgate to treat the transports better. By then he knew that his prison visitor meant business. In any case, the women in prison were much less trouble since the school and craft classes started. But Elizabeth didn't just stop at changing things for the Newgate transports. She took her complaint right to the government and made sure the Members of Parliament listened to her too. As a result of her campaign women transports were given proper places to stay and work to do when they reached the colonies.

For the next twenty five years Elizabeth Fry checked when convict ships sailing from London docks were to be carrying women, and she visited them with a Bible and sewing kit for each woman. A total of 126 ships with 12,000 prisoners left London docks over that time. But, thanks mainly to Elizabeth, the number of people transported began to go down and by 1854 no more people were sent to the faraway colonies at all.

'You've done wonders over the years,' a friend told Elizabeth, when they were both quite elderly women.

Mrs Fry shook her head. 'I could have done so much more,' she said.

Her friend spoke a little crossly. 'What else could you have done? As well as all your work for prison reform you've opened a night shelter for the homeless, founded a Nurses' training home, not to mention all the District Charity Societies and the ....'

'Stop!' Elizabeth said. 'Stop! I've done absolutely nothing without help. The Quaker ladies have been right behind me all the time, and my family have supported me, and countless other people too. Take Newgate, for example. Without the Governor's help we could have done nothing at all.'

'But it was all your idea,' her friend insisted.

Elizabeth Fry sighed wearily. 'When I was a young woman I was told that God had a special work for me. He wanted me to be a light to the blind, speech to the dumb and feet to the lame. That's all I've tried to do. And the amazing thing about working for the Lord is that he gives enough of his strength for each day's work. I've failed him often but he has never let me down.'

In 1845, when she was 65 years old, Elizabeth's strength failed and she died peacefully. Although she found it hard to accept praise on earth, when she died the

Lord had something to say to her. 'Well done, good and faithful servant. Welcome home.'

FACT FILE

Transportation: In the 1700s a prisoner could be sentenced to transportation for crimes such as stealing an apron or a side of bacon. Transportation meant being sent on a ship to either the American colonies or Botany Bay in Australia. They could be sentenced to 14 years in prison for stealing potatoes or a pair of shoes. Prior to Elizabeth Fry's involvement in prison reform on arrival at the colonies there was no accommodation or employment for the women.

Keynote: Elizabeth was someone who was anxious to lead a useful life. Opening a school, running a soup kitchen and tending the sick were not easy to do and then she also visited the prisons! We can learn from Elizabeth's life and determination. Elizabeth wanted to make her life useful to God - so should we.

Think: Elizabeth didn't concentrate on what she couldn't do. She saw a need and did her utmost to meet it. She was fearless and in God's strength accomplished much. Elizabeth must have been exhausted some days with all the work she did. She wasn't afraid to make a sacrifice. Jesus has done so much for us we will never be able to thank him enough. He has given his life and has given us salvation.

Prayer: Lord Jesus, I sometimes feel that I'm not able to do much, but show me what I can do and make me willing to do everything I can for you. Amen.

Amy Carmichael

For over a hundred years the flour mill in the seaside village of Millisle in Northern Ireland was where many of the villagers worked. Others farmed and fished, but they too were involved with the flour mill because the farmers took their grain there to be made into flour, and the fishermen's wives bought their bread flour at the mill. For all of that time the mill belonged to the Carmichael family.

1867 was an exciting year for the young Carmichael couple because they were expecting their first child. She was born just nine days before Christmas, and they called the little girl Amy Beatrice.

Amy was not to be the only child of the mill owners; six others were born over the years that followed.

It was a very busy household. There were probably only three times in the day when the house was quiet. One was when the children were all tucked up in bed and asleep and the other two were when the family met round the table to have morning and evening prayers.

Amy had a special time each night. 'After the nursery light was turned low and I was quite alone,' she told a friend once, 'I used to smooth a little place on the sheet and say aloud, but softly, to our Father, "Please come and sit with me".'

But Amy was not talking about her dad when she said that, she was talking about her heavenly Father. From when she was quite a little girl, Amy Carmichael loved God in a special way. He really was her very best friend and the person she most enjoyed spending time with.

'Would you like to come to Belfast with me?' Mrs Carmichael asked Amy one day.

Her face lit up. 'Yes please, I'd love to.'

Amy's younger brothers and sisters were full of questions.

'What are you going to Belfast for?'

'Can you bring back a treat for us?'

'What will you do when you're there?'

Mrs Carmichael laughed.

'We're going to Belfast to visit the shops,' she told one child. 'We will bring you back a treat,' she said to another. 'And one thing we're planning to do is go out for tea at a tea-shop.'

Amy felt so grown up at the thought of going to a tea-shop with her mother!

'Will you tell us all about it?' her youngest sister asked.

'Of course I will,' laughed Amy. 'I'll even tell you what I eat in the tea-shop!'

After a busy and exciting day in town, Amy sat down by the fire to tell the family all about her trip. They were especially interested in the tea-shop and in the pink icing on the biscuit Amy had with her sweet milky tea.

'A little girl came and stood near the door and looked though the window of the tea-shop,' she told the other children. 'Delicious cakes and sweets were set out in the window. As we left we saw the little girl with her face pressed close to the glass. She was looking at all the cakes and sweets. She was a poor little girl in a thin ragged dress. It was raining, and her bare feet on the wet pavement looked very cold.'

When Father called the family to have worship, Amy was not the only one who prayed for that poor little girl. And when her brothers and sisters were tucked up in bed that night, Amy sat on by the nursery fire. She couldn't get that poor girl out of her mind, so much so that she wrote a poem about her.

When I grow up and money have,
I know what I will do,
I'll build a great big lovely place
For little girls like you.

Years later, when Amy was grown-up, she thought about that little girl. Again she was in Belfast but this time she had not come from Millisle, she was going there. As she sat in the pony-pulled trap, warm in her rug, she saw a woman about her own age, ragged and with only sacking tied round her feet for shoes. Beside her were two little children, aged about eight and ten, and they reminded Amy of the tea-shop, of the biscuit with its pink icing, and of the poor little girl with her face pressed up against the glass as she looked at the cakes inside. Amy felt sad, especially because she was ill and exhausted herself.

'It's all so confusing,' she told her parents that evening as they finished their meal. 'I'm absolutely convinced that the Lord wants me to be a missionary overseas, yet first of all China Inland Mission turns me down, then, when I go out to work in Japan I'm so ill that I'm sent all the way home to recover.'

'Perhaps he wants you to serve him here,' her father suggested. 'There's plenty of need.'

Amy thought of the woman and her two little children and knew that was true.

'These are big issues to be discussing when you've just come halfway across the world,' her sensible mother said. 'There will be plenty of time to think it all through. In the meantime, you've to rest and concentrate on getting better.'

As Amy's eyes were already closing, she didn't need persuading to go to bed.

In 1895, when she had recovered her health, Amy was totally convinced that God wanted her in India.

Her family may have wondered about the wisdom of her decision but, as she was persuaded that was what the Lord was telling her to do, they waved their goodbyes and prayed for her daily. It was to the south of India that Amy went, to an area called Tinnevelly.

Much that Amy Carmichael saw in India was very beautiful. She loved the people, especially the dark-eyed children. She delighted in the colourfulness of clothes, in the beauty of the country, in the bustle of the market and in the friendship of the Christians she met there.

But there were other things, horrible things, that she could hardly believe were true. And the worst of these was to do with the Hindu temples.

'I can't take in what you're saying,' she told a converted Hindu woman. 'Tell me again to make sure I'm understanding you properly.'

'Amma,' the woman said, (that's Indian for Mother), 'what I am telling you is true. In this country a girl child is not a happy thing. Before a baby is born many Hindu parents tell the gods that if it is a girl they can have her as an offering. You see,' she went on, 'otherwise they will have to keep her, feed her and clothe her when what they really want to do is get rid of her and have another child, a boy.'

'Do you mean that they are killed as offerings?' the horrified missionary asked.

'No,' was the slow reply, 'they are not killed. But what happens is almost as bad. They are given to women who are prisoners in the temples and they are kept there and become prisoners too. Then, when they are five or six years old, they are given to the priests and are slaves to them until they are no longer young and beautiful.'

Amy gasped. 'What happens then?' she asked.

'They are put out of the temple,' the woman explained, 'and nobody wants to know them. It is as though they have a disease.'

'Where are they all now?'

'They are the devadassis, the little huddles of women you see in the poorest parts of the town.'

'But why are there not more of them?' Amy asked, thinking of all the little girls imprisoned within the temple walls.

Her friend looked sad. 'Many little girls in there,' she nodded towards the temple, 'don't live to get out.'

A shudder went down Amy's spine at the thought of what was happening just a short distance away. 'I must do something for those children,' she thought. 'I MUST do something.'

Soon afterwards, a baby girl was brought to her, tiny, fragile and creamy coloured, like a doll made of wax. Then two other tiny babies arrived. Amma was well named as she became the children's mother.

More babies followed. Toddlers were brought to her too, especially very pretty little girls whose parents thought that the gods would make them rich if they gave their daughters to them. Some temple women, who desperately didn't want girls to go through all they had been through, risked their lives to get new babies and toddlers out of the temple and into Amy's safe hands.

Lala was one of Amy's rescued children. When she was five, she was kidnapped from Dohnavur, which was where Amy's ever increasing family lived, and taken back to a temple in the mountains. Poor little Lala became ill and died. Amy was so sad when she heard that news but along with the news came an interesting story.

'I was there when Lala died,' a woman told her. 'She said things before she died that I remember and can tell you.'

'What did she say?' asked Amy.

'Lala said she was a Jesus child,' the woman said. 'And she did not seem afraid of dying. Then she said she saw three shining ones come into the room where she was lying. Her face was not fearful and when she saw the shining ones, Lala smiled. Then she died.'

For years Amy was mother to unwanted little girls. She gave them a home, she loved them as though they were her own and she taught them about the Lord Jesus. Not all of them survived because of the illnesses for which there were no medicines at that time, but Amy prayed that if any were to die they would, like Lala, die believing in Jesus.

One day Amy had an accident. She fell, breaking her leg and damaging her ankle badly. Nowadays she would probably have had surgery and would have been able to walk again. But things were different then, especially in a poor land like India.

For the twenty years and more that followed, Amy Carmichael was mostly in her bed and rarely out of her bedroom. That didn't stop her loving her rescued children and it gave her time to pray for them. It was as though she was a little girl again, lying on her bed asking Jesus to come and sit by her and let her talk to him about her rescued girls.

Amy also wrote poems and books as she rested in bed, many of which are still read now, many years after her death in 1951.

But one of Amy's poems was written about a time much earlier in her life. As a little brown eyed Irish girl, she prayed that God would make her eyes blue. She longed to have clear blue eyes.

'So she prayed for two blue eyes,
Said 'Goodnight',
Went to sleep in deep content
And delight.
Woke up early, climbed a chair
By a mirror. Where, O where
Could the blue eyes be? Not there;
Jesus hadn't answered.

Hadn't answered her at all;
Never more
Could she pray; her eyes were brown
As before.
Did a little soft wind blow?
Came a whisper soft and low,
'Jesus answered. He said, No;
Isn't No an answer?'

Jesus' answer to Amy's prayer for blue eyes was 'No'. Years later she understood why, for everyone in India has brown eyes, and she would not have fitted in at all if her eyes had been blue. God had work for Amy to do in India and he was preparing her to do it even when he chose the colour of her eyes.

FACT FILE

Eyes - when she was young, Amy spent a lot of time wishing her eyes were blue.

Look at your eyes in a mirror. The front of your eye contains the iris and the pupil - the circle of colour and the black dot in its centre - and it is their job to let light into the eye.

The pupil lets the light in and the iris decides the amount let in by controlling the size of pupil . The iris and the pupil together are just like a camera shutter that opens and closes.

Keynote: Amy had several setbacks before she got to India. First of all, she wasn't accepted by a missionary organisation and then she became ill. Later, Amy was confined to bed for almost twenty years.

But Amy trusted God and nothing stopped her from sharing the message of Jesus and caring for the many homeless children who came her way.

Learn from Amy's absolute trust in God in every situation.

Think: Remember that God has made you just the way you are. Even the minute details were planned by him!

God cares about all the details of your life too. So don't be afraid to share your worries with him.

Prayer: Lord Jesus, thank you for caring so much that you came to die for me. I'm sorry for the times that I complain about what I don't have. Help me to be thankful for everything you have given me. Amen.

Gladys Aylward

'I'm too old to go to Sunday School,' fourteen-year-old Gladys told her mother. 'Sunday School is for babies!'

Mrs Aylward looked sad. Her daughter was going through the terrible teens and she was getting rather tired of it.

'Well I hope you don't forget what you learned there,' her mother said, 'because if you do you'll come to a bad end.'

Gladys hardly heard what was said, she was too busy admiring herself in the mirror. Taking a comb, she redid her centre parting and smoothed out her dark hair on either side of it. 'I'm grown up now and I'm going to enjoy myself,' she decided.

Gladys wheezed as she breathed in cigarette smoke that night. She tried hard not to splutter. What would her friends think of her if she did that.

'Is this your first smoke?' a fair-haired girl asked her.

Still trying not to go into a fit of coughing, Gladys shook her head.

'No,' she lied eventually, 'I've smoked in secret for ages.'

Her friends didn't believe a word she said.

Trying to look as though she did this every day, Gladys put the cigarette to her mouth again. Although by then her stomach was heaving, she smoked her way to the bitter end of her first cigarette and reckoned she'd grown up.

As soon as she stopped Sunday School, Gladys filed everything to do with Christianity away in the back of her mind. She thought it was just for babies and grannies.

She found a job as a housemaid in the centre of London and her free time was spent with her various boyfriends, sometimes gambling, sometimes drinking and always smoking.

For the next twelve years she didn't give God a thought, even though she used his name as a swear word. But God hadn't forgotten Gladys.

'Where are you going tonight?' she asked a group of her friends one afternoon.

They looked embarrassed. 'We're going to a meeting in Kensington.'

'What kind of a meeting?'

'A religious one.'

'Can I come?' Gladys asked.

Her friends looked at each other.

Gladys grinned. 'Anything for a laugh,' she said.

But that night things changed for Gladys Aylward. She heard things she'd forgotten from Sunday School days - that Jesus loved her, that Jesus died for her and that he wanted to forgive all her sins. The past twelve years spun round in her head and Gladys realised she had done many wrong things. Before she left that meeting she asked Jesus to forgive all her sins and to be her Saviour and friend.

Instead of going drinking on her next night off, Gladys went to a Young Life Campaign meeting and she went every week from then on. That was where she picked up a magazine which said that missionaries were needed in China.

Gladys applied to go as a missionary but had to leave college after three months because she'd learned almost nothing at all. Everything she heard and read seemed to go out of her head as soon as it went in. For a while she looked after two retired lady missionaries, then she worked in Swansea as a missionary to needy women there. She walked along the docks looking for them, then took them back to the mission hall.

China was never far from Gladys's mind, though, and she was quite sure that God wanted her to go there. One day, as she read in her Bible that when Nehemiah felt God wanted him in Jerusalem he went there, she suddenly thought to herself, 'If God wants me in China then I'll have to save up and go.' She had just moved to a new job and had been given 15p for her travelling expenses. Looking at the three coins, she thought, 'it's not much but it's a start.'

Because Gladys took every job she could fit into her spare time she had soon saved up £3.

'How much is a ticket to China?' she asked in a travel shop.

'China!' the man said.

Gladys pulled herself up to her full height. 'Yes,' she agreed. 'China.'

'Come back in two days and I'll tell you,' the booking clerk said.

Two days later, Gladys was back.

'If you were to go by train through Europe, Russian and Siberia it would cost £47.50,' she was told.

Putting her £3 on the desk she explained that was all she had, but that she'd come in every time she'd saved £1 and pay it up £1 at a time.

The man scratched his head in wonder as his strangest ever customer closed the door behind her.

Before she had saved all she needed, Gladys heard about Mrs Lawson, an elderly missionary in China, who was looking for a companion. A letter was written right away and, after what seemed like ages, Gladys had a reply. Mrs Lawson wanted her to come to China!

On 15th October 1932, just after she was 30, Gladys Aylward set off by train for China. Her luggage consisted of two suitcases, one of them full of food for the journey, a bedroll, a small stove, a kettle and a saucepan. She looked like a one-woman Girl Guide camp!

The journey to China was full of adventures, not all of them nice. In Russia officials tried to force her to stay because they wanted her to work in a factory. That was because they read 'missionary' on her passport and thought that it said 'machinery'! Later she found herself in the middle of a war and one night Gladys slept outside with the sound of wolves howling in the distance. Her fresh food grew stale and in Siberia it was so cold that her tinned food froze solid. Nearly a month after leaving London, on 10th November, Gladys Aylward took her first steps on Chinese soil. Very soon she met up with Mrs Lawson and discovered what her job would involve.

'I'm going to open an inn for muleteers,' the elderly lady explained. 'And when they stay for the night we'll tell them about Jesus.'

Gladys was startled. 'But I don't speak any Chinese,' she said.

Mrs Lawson laughed. 'Neither do the mules. Your job will be to stand outside the inn and grab the mules by their manes as they pass by. By evening the muleteers will be so tired they won't argue about coming here for the night. For the time being you'll have to let Mr Lu, the evangelist, do the talking. And when he's not here, I'll do it myself.'

Having come from London, Gladys was more than a little worried about the mules.

'Do they bite?' she asked.

Shaking her head, Mrs Lawson said that they were fine if caught in the right way!

Gladys was not reassured.

Before long the new missionary knew exactly which part of the mule to grab and most nights she had hauled so many inside that the inn was full. It became a popular place for muleteers to stay. Not only did they get shelter for the night, they were told stories by a white woman too.

Mrs Lawson fell ill the year after Gladys went out and, when she died, Gladys was left to run the inn with Mr Lu's help. By then she had learned enough Chinese to do some of the speaking and she felt, at last, that she was a real missionary in China.

At that time Japan and China were at war and even the inn was bombed. It became a very dangerous part of the world to be in. Refugees moved from place to place depending on where the fighting was but Gladys stayed where she was. Everybody knew her because she was the only European in that part of China.

'We can't take Dusty Heap with us,' a group of guerrillas said, as they thrust a boy into her home one day. 'You look after him.'

Gladys looked at the lad. 'His name suits him,' she thought, 'he's so ragged and dirty.'

Suddenly it was as if a magnet drew children to her and before long she was running a home for over a hundred homeless children!

The war crept closer. 'What are we to do with the children?' she asked Mr Lu.

It was agreed that she would stay where she was and he would take the children to safety.

'I'll be back in a month,' he said. 'Pray for us as we go.'

Day by day Gladys prayed for Mr Lu and for the children, that they would get out of the war zone to a safe place.

By the time the month had passed, the missionary found herself looking after another hundred children. 'Where are they all coming from?' she often asked herself. And where is Mr Lu?

'You must take these children and leave here,' a Chinese Army officer told her.

Gladys shook her head. 'God called me here and I'll stay here. But please take the children to somewhere safe.'

The officer ordered his men to escort the children to Chong Tsuen, a town a short distance away.

Only when he came back to her door with a Japanese poster saying that she was a wanted person, did Gladys agree to leave and when she did she had to duck bullets and dodge soldiers for the first part of the way. At Chong Tsuen Gladys was reunited with the children. But even there it was not safe so she decided to take them to Shensi. Like the Pied Piper of Hamlyn she set out through the countryside with a hundred children in a long trail behind her. She carried the little ones in turns and the older children did the same. At Shensi the missionary discovered that Mr Lu was in prison. No wonder he hadn't come home.

But even Shensi wasn't a safe place for them. How Gladys must have prayed before taking a hundred children over mountains thousands of feet high to reach the safety of Sian. For twelve days they walked, begging in little villages for food and sleeping in whatever shelter they could find.

'Let's sing a song,' she shouted, when exhausted children thought they could walk not one step more. And when they tired of singing, she played games with them. 'I spy, with my little eye, something that starts with b.' 'Boys!' one child called out. Gladys shook her head. 'Birds!' called another. And when they were bored and tired of that little game, the missionary had to think of something else.

For twelve days they snaked through the mountains, for twelve nights they slept cuddled together for warmth.

'How far is it now?' children pleaded, hundreds of times a day.

'Every step is one step nearer,' Gladys said, to encourage them on.

'What's that down there?' a boy asked, when even the missionary thought she could go no further.

'It's the Yellow River!' someone shouted. We're nearly there!

A cheer went through the crowd of children, and excitement gave them the energy to go on. But, relieved though she was to see the river, Gladys knew that wasn't the end of their journey. There was still a long way to go.

God knew that the weary travellers weren't able to take much more. They crossed the river in boats then, after a further two days' walking, they were able to travel,for most of what was left of the journey, hidden among the coal on a train. When Gladys eventually delivered her children to the safety of an orphanage near Sian, she collapsed, ill and utterly exhausted. The villagers who found her expected her to die. It was a long time until Gladys Aylward was fit to travel and her next journey was home to England for a much needed rest, before going back to her beloved China.

FACT FILE

Aeroplanes - Gladys Aylward travelled all the way to China by train and it took her almost a month. How much easier it would have been for her to fly there, as we can do today!

The story of air travel began just a year after Gladys was born. The first true aeroplane was Flyer 1, piloted by an American engineer called Orville Wright on 17th December 1903.

Within 16 years an aeroplane had flown across the Atlantic Ocean and air travel has gone on developing rapidly ever since.

Keynote: If, when she was young, Gladys had been told that one day she would lead over 100 children on a 12 day trek across a mountain range in China she would probably have thought it was impossible. But she soon learnt that with God, nothing is impossible.

Learn, as Gladys did, that God can make even the impossible happen!

Think: Gladys didn't just say that she trusted God, she proved that God is worth trusting in everything she did.

Think of a challenge or a problem you're facing right now. Remember that God is on your side and you can trust him to help you through it!

Prayer: Lord Jesus, sometimes I worry about things and when I face a problem I panic. Help me to trust in you completely no matter what and to go ahead knowing that you are with me. Amen.

Mary Slessor

Mary crawled under the loom, found the two broken ends of jute, tied them together and then crawled out again. Her hair was tied up in a cloth to prevent it getting caught in the workings of the loom. Some workers in the factory had had great chunks of hair yanked out of their scalps by being careless and Mary didn't want that to happen to her. Mary had lovely, golden red hair and a temper to match it.

Clambering back to her place in front of the loom Mary Slessor watched the machine carefully. If the boss saw her taking her eyes off it there would be a clip on the ear or worse.

The clatter of machinery ripped through Mary Slessor's head. To get away from it she imagined the seashore at Aberdeen on a stormy day, imagined that the noise was the roar of the waves and that she could feel the salt spray on her face. But if she thought too much about Aberdeen the only salt she felt was salt tears.

'I wish we hadn't had to come to Dundee,' the girl said aloud. It didn't matter if she spoke out loud in the factory, as nobody could hear a word that was said. 'I wish Dad hadn't drunk so much that he lost his job.' Mary's life was a difficult one. Her family was poor. Some of Mary's brothers and sisters had died. They didn't have enough money to pay for a doctor. Then Mary's father drank too much and made the whole family's life a misery. Mary often went to bed hungry and right now she was ravenous.

She couldn't hear it but she felt her stomach rumbling. 'I wish I didn't always feel so hungry.' Just then the jute snapped. Mary pulled the cloth over her hair and ducked under the machine again.

They always did it, the Slessor children, they listened at the door before they went in to hear if their dad was raging. What they wanted to hear was him snoring because if he fell into a drunken sleep he wouldn't cause trouble for a few hours. Mary listened, sounds of snoring reassured her and she went inside.

'Well, Mary,' her mother said. 'That's another week over.'

'Thank goodness for that,' the thirteen-year-old sighed. 'I just live for Saturday evenings and the great feeling that I don't need to go back to work till Monday.'

Mrs Slessor put her arm round her daughter's shoulder. 'I'm really sorry you have to work,' she said. 'But you and I need to earn enough to keep the family fed. Since your brother died your dad's not been fit for anything.'

'Is that really what made him like this?' Mary nodded towards her drunk father.

'Yes it is,' her mother said. 'And try to remember that when you feel angry with him.'

'It's Sunday,' Mary's little sister said, shaking her awake. 'And the sun's shining.'

Mary Slessor rubbed her eyes. She didn't want to miss a minute of Sunday or a minute of sunshine. All week she went to the mill in the dark and came home in the dark.

'You get dressed and we'll go for a walk before church.'

The girls pulled on their clothes. On the way through the back court they splashed cold water on their faces. Then, hand in hand, they walked along the road, through the town to the River Tay.

'Look how it sparkles,' the little girl said. 'It's like a treasure chest.'

'It sparkles just like your eyes,' Mary told her sister as she tousled her hair. 'Would you like a piggyback home?'

'I knew you'd be here on time,' Mrs Slessor said, as they went in the door. 'We're just about ready.'

The family, apart from Mr Slessor, walked to church and settled in the pew to enjoy the service. Their home was dark and dingy, but the church was bright and clean. The week was hard work, but in church they could relax. But most of all, and best of all, they wanted to hear about Jesus' love. Mary's mother was in love with the Lord and the warmth of her faith made her children long to be the same.

'Sunday School time!' said the littlest Slessor. 'I love the stories.'

Mary did too, especially the stories about missionaries in Africa.

Back in the mill on Monday, Mary thought about Africa. She thought about all the little African children who had never heard about Jesus and she wished she was with them.

'I'd love to be there with all the little African children round me, playing games with them and telling them Bible stories... but I don't think that will ever happen... I'll probably never go past the edge of Dundee!'

Mary thought that her dreams would never amount to anything and that nothing would ever happen. But when she was twenty-eight years old her dreams came true. She sailed for Calabar in Africa (south eastern Nigeria today) on the SS Ethiopa!

'I think I can see land.' she said, five weeks after leaving Liverpool.

'That's Calabar,' her fellow passenger told her.

Mary's heart raced. She could hardly speak for excitement.

'Look at the children!' she squealed, as they neared the harbour. 'Look at their bright eyes! Look at their shiny white teeth! Look at their beautiful curly hair!'

The missionary who met Mary could hardly get the young woman away from the little group of children who surrounded her as soon as she got off the ship. Eventually she forced herself to wave goodbye to them and go with her new colleague to the mission house.

'Tell me all about Calabar,' Mary pleaded, as she ate a meal with the missionaries she was staying with.

'You begin,' said the wife.

Her husband finished what was on his plate before speaking.

'Most of the people here don't know anything about Jesus. A lot of them believe in evil spirits and are scared stiff of them. The villages are run by chiefs and what the chief says goes. Anyone who goes against the chief doesn't last long.'

'Eat up your meal,' the missionary's wife encouraged.

Mary had been so interested in what she was hearing that she'd forgotten to eat!

'The women have a bad time,' the wife went on. 'They're just slaves to the men and some terrible things happen to them.'

'What kind of things?' Mary asked.

'I think we've talked enough about the sad side of Calabar for now,' her husband said. 'Would you like a short walk?'

No sooner were they outside than a group of children gathered round Mary.

'I think it's your red hair they're interested in,' her companion said.

Mary knelt down, picked up two stones, threw one in the air then hit it with the other. The children watched. She did it again, then a third time. Suddenly there was a scramble of children trying to find two stones. Mary smiled when the missionaries went back into their house in case they were hit by flying stones.

'Despite the awful stories,' she thought, 'I'm going to love it here.'

After a time with the missionary couple, Mary moved a little way into the country. By then she knew some of the language.

'I heard that baby crying in the bush,' an African woman said to two others as they passed Mary Slessor one afternoon.

'It's amazing it's still alive. It's been out there for five days now.'

'What are you talking about?' Mary asked the women.

They shrugged their shoulders.

'Tell me what you were saying,' she insisted.

The story she heard sent a shiver down her spine.

'One of the village women had a baby five days ago,' she was told. 'The mother died, so the baby was put out in the bush to die too.'

Mary could hardly believe her ears.

'It had an evil spirit,' the woman went on. 'That's why its mother died and that's why nobody else wants it. If anyone took the baby they would die too.'

Mary was on her feet.

'Where is it?' she demanded. 'Where did the cries come from?'

Two women shook their heads. The third pointed vaguely into the bush.

'Tell me exactly where you heard it, exactly!'

Mary listened to the directions and ran like the wind. When she thought she'd gone far enough, she stopped and listened. But her breathing was so noisy that she had to wait for a minute before she heard a cry. Then she followed the sound, till she came to a tiny baby girl lying under a dried-up bush.

'My lamb,' she said, lifting the baby into her arms. 'My lamb.'

Nobody went near her when she went back to the village. The Calabar people believed that Mary would be punished by the evil spirits. They were scared and didn't want to go anywhere near her just in case something awful happened to them. They didn't know any better and when they caught sight of her they would say, 'Just you wait and see. The evil spirit will kill her.'

Mary overheard these comments but ignored them all. Holding the little baby girl gently but firmly in her arms, she bathed the tiny body and put the only cream she had on her skin. The little girl had been terribly eaten by white ants.

Mary really didn't think the little girl would live. But then she thought what a strong baby she must have been to survive the first five days of her life in the bush with no milk at all.

But the people were still suspicious. 'The white woman with red hair will die soon,' women said to each other, as Mary cared for the baby. They stayed away from the missionary and the little one. In their opinion she was dangerous.

But Mary Slessor didn't die, and eventually the villagers decided that the baby didn't have an evil spirit at all. Perhaps, after all, they could keep babies whose mothers died.

One day there was a great sadness is Mary's village.

'What's wrong?' she asked the women.

'My sister has had twins,' a sad faced African woman said, 'so the babies will be killed and she'll be chased away into the bush.'

'WHAT!!!' roared Mary, jumping to her feet. 'Take me to her!'

The poor woman hesitated.

'NOW!'

There was a huddle of people around the hut. As long as she was there, Mary knew the babies were safe.

'Explain what's happening,' she pleaded.

'When twin babies are born one of them is the child of an evil spirit. But, as we don't know which one, they're both killed. And because the mother has had a spirit child, she's put out in the bush to be killed by wild animals.'

'NO SHE IS NOT!'

There was no arguing with Mary Slessor.

'I'll look after the twins,' she said. 'Just wait and see what happens. Neither of them is the child of an evil spirit. The Lord God made them both.'

Because of Mary's anger and determination, the woman survived and so did the children. Mary was gathering quite a little family about her. The villagers were impressed that there didn't seem to be evil spirits in the babies. News about that spread and eventually the people of Calabar stopped leaving babies whose mothers died out in the bush and they stopped killing twins.

'Jesus loves children,' Mary told her adopted family. 'He loves them so much that he came down from heaven for them.'

Village women, and even some men, sat where they could hear her speaking.

'Does your Jesus love us too?' the women asked later.

Mary told them the Bible story and some of the people believed it.

When Mary Slessor went to Calabar the people she met believed in evil spirits and that led to much fear and unhappiness. But when they trusted in the Lord Jesus their fear and unhappiness was taken away and she could see the difference in their sparkling eyes.

FACT FILE

Africa - another famous Scot who went to Africa was David Livingstone, who is regarded as the greatest of Africa's explorers. Very little was known about the continent of Africa before Livingstone came along!

On one expedition on the Zambesi river, Livingstone discovered some amazing waterfalls. He called them the 'Victoria Falls' after Queen Victoria, but they were already known as 'the smoke that thundered' by the African people who lived nearby. Why not look up an atlas and try to find them?

Keynote: Mary was never slow to speak up when she saw evil around her but she didn't just point out the sins. She showed people an alternative and better way. She showed them what Jesus wanted them to do. Learn from Mary's eagerness to tell others what Jesus wants us to do.

Think: As a child Mary had a very strong character and a short temper, but God went on to use her determination and strong will in a wonderful way.

You are unique and God can use you in a special way too. Start by doing small things for him and don't be shy to tell others about Jesus. He's worth sharing!

Prayer: Lord Jesus, thank you for making me just the way I am. Please show me what I can do for you and give me the courage to speak up for you whenever I can. Amen.

Catherine Booth

The little girl sat in front of the fire with her picture book. Martha, her doll, was at her side. 'See Martha,' she said, pointing to the words in the book. 'Those letters are c-a-t and the word says cat.' She turned the page. 'Those letters are f-o-x and the word says fox.' She pointed to the x. 'But that sometimes means kiss,' she explained then picked up her doll and kissed her.

'She really is a clever little girl,' smiled Mrs Mumford's visitor. 'What age did you say she is?'

'Catherine is three,' she replied. 'She just seems to pick up letters as I read books to her.'

'You'll have to watch you don't exhaust her brain,' warned the visitor.

Mrs Mumford smiled. She knew that Catherine's brain was not very likely to tire out.

By the time the girl was five, in 1834, she had regular lessons from her mother although she didn't go to school. The book they read most together was the Bible and by Catherine's twelfth birthday she had read it right through eight times! But life was not all work. When her father went on business trips some distance away from their home in Boston in Lincolnshire, he sometimes took her with him.

'Would you like to learn to drive the horse?' Father asked, when she was about nine years old.

Catherine's eyes shone. 'Yes please, Papa.'

Pulling her on to his knee, he handed her the reins, while holding them gently to stop the horse should he bolt. 'Easy now,' he said. 'Just let the horse have his head.' The creature walked along quite steadily. 'Now let's try more difficult things,' suggested Father, at a quiet part of the road. 'Pull the right rein gently and see what happens. The horse turned towards the right and walked on. 'Now do the same with the left rein.' The girl did as she was told and was delighted when the horse immediately obeyed her instruction and turned towards the left.

'Mama!' she called out, when they returned home that afternoon, 'I can drive the horse and carriage! Papa let me drive!'

'Catherine has a way with horses,' her father said.

Mrs Mumford looked at her daughter. 'You love all animals, don't you?'

It was because Catherine loved animals that she was brokenhearted when her dog was put down when she was twelve. She found it difficult to talk about how upset she was, though she did pray about it. Soon after this sad happening, the girl went to school. And how she loved it! But that freedom didn't last for long. Catherine developed a problem with her spine and had to lie in bed for a whole year.

'What would you like to do today?' her mother asked every morning when they had finished their lessons. But she already knew the answer.

'I'm quite happy with my books,' was the girl's daily reply.

For a year Catherine read books that most adults don't even read. At the end of it, when her back was better, she had read very thick and serious books about God. For the next few years she puzzled about the Lord. Did he really love her? Did she need to be forgiven? How could she know she would go to heaven? But, when she was seventeen, the truth dawned on her. Jesus did love her. Yes, she did need to be forgiven. And yes, she knew she was going to heaven because that's what the Bible said happened to those who trusted in Jesus. And she was convinced that the Bible was true. Catherine was happy at last!

Catherine and her mother were at a Christian meeting three years later and it was there that they first met William Booth, an apprentice pawnbroker. However, by the time he and Catherine fell in love, William was on his way to becoming a travelling preacher. For six years the young couple wrote to each other, first once a week, then twice a week, then nearly every day until they were married on July 16th, 1855. They were both 26 years old.

'How are you managing all the travelling?' Mrs Mumford asked Catherine in a letter.

Her daughter answered the next day. 'Dear Mama, William's tours are not as exhausting as you would think. We are usually in each place for about a month and people make us feel very much at home everywhere we go. I've seen some interesting places I'd never visited before. Hull was full of fishwives. They travel round the coast depending on where the herring is being landed. Then we were in Sheffield where cutlery is made. After that we were a month in Halifax. Please don't worry about the travelling, Mama. William looks after me wonderfully well.'

'I've been asked to be Superintendent in Gateshead,' William told his wife some years later.

She thought for a moment. 'It would be nice to stay in one place though I've loved our time of travelling.'

William's preaching still sometimes took him away from home, but Catherine was busy about her own things. By then she had begun to do Christian work herself. This started when she spoke to women on the street about the Lord Jesus and before long she was taking services!

'I'm very surprised at myself.' she told William, when he returned from two weeks away.

He wondered what was coming.

'The Lord seemed to be leading me to speak to some people who where drunk. At first I felt very nervous. But he gave me the words to say and now I find I can approach such people and tell them about the Lord Jesus.'

William was not as surprised as Catherine had been. He had watched her becoming more involved in the work even though she now had their children to look after. 'Where would this lead?' he wondered.

From Gateshead they moved south, eventually to London. More and more invitations came for Catherine to speak and fewer came for William. It was a difficult time for them. One night she was home before him and sitting by the fire when he came in.

'Oh Catherine,' he said, slumping down in his chair, 'when I passed the drinking dens tonight, I seemed to hear a voice in my head asking me where else I could find so many men in need of the good news about Jesus as in places like that. I feel that the Lord is leading me into working here in the East End of London with these men and women.'

Catherine gazed into the fire. 'Where will the money come to support us?' she wondered. 'The men in the drinking dens certainly won't keep seven of us in food and clothes and there's another baby on the way.'

But when she spoke, that was not what she said. 'The Lord has never let us down before. If he wants you to do that, he'll provide for us.'

William wrote to a Christian newspaper, outlining his plans. 'Because most people in areas like this don't go to church we will visit them and hold services where they are, in the open air, in theatres and other places too. We'll go where people are, not wait for them to come to us.' And that was the very beginning of The Salvation Army.

It was 1870 and, after a huge effort to raise money, the People's Mission Hall was opened in one of the poorest parts of London.

'When are your meetings?' a visitor at the opening service, asked Catherine.

'We're open every night,' was the surprising reply. 'There will always be an open door here for people in need. That's why we have a soup kitchen. Have you any idea how many hungry people there are around here?'

The visitor took some pound notes out of his wallet and gave them to Catherine.

'Here,' he said. 'That will buy vegetables for tomorrow's soup.'

The Salvation Army reached out to the poor and needy, taking the good news about Jesus in one hand and soup and warm clothes in the other. Where people were hungry, the Army was there to feed them. Where people were cold, the Army was there to give them clothes. And where people needed Jesus, the Salvation Army was there to tell them that he loved them enough to die for them. William became General Booth, a general in the Lord's army. And Catherine was given a title too, the Army Mother. The Booths never forgot their call to serve the people with a drink problem, treating them with a love that they found nowhere else. Men, women and young people were loved into the Salvation Army, loved by the General and the Army Mother, and loved by the Lord Jesus Christ.

'Tell me about a Salvation Army meeting,' a Scottish friend wrote to Catherine when he sent her money for the work.

'If you were in London,' she wrote back, 'you would know us right away because of our Army uniforms and flags. The men wear hats and the women wear bonnets with crimson bands on which are written The Salvation Army. Our meetings are lively, lots of singing and Hallelujahs. There is nothing dismal and dull about our services at all. People come in off the streets just because of our cheerful music and joyful singing. Most of our people are poor, and many of them would never go into an ordinary church. But everyone is welcome at the Army. Women and children have a special place. Women officers preach in the Army as well as men and we hold special services and missions for children.'

'Will you come and help us on the streets this evening?' Catherine asked a church visitor to their work.

'What would I have to do?' the young woman wanted to know.

'Two of you will patrol the streets you're given, looking out for people in need. You'll find wives whose husbands have thrown them out, sometimes wearing only nightclothes with a coat on top, and often with children too. You'll find young people who have argued with their parents and run away. And you'll find men and women who have mental health problems too.'

The woman looked horrified. 'But I've never met people like that before. I wouldn't know what to say.'

Catherine Booth looked into her eyes.

'How long have you been a Christian?'

'Eight years.'

'And you've never reached out to the people who need you most?' the Army Mother said sadly.

The young woman's expression softened. 'No,' she said. 'I've not. But I will tonight, and I will from now on.'

Later that evening the two women met again in the soup kitchen. The visitor was flushed with excitement.

'Did God use you tonight?' asked Catherine Booth.

Her companion nodded her head. 'He surely did and he taught me a lesson.'

'What was that?' the older woman wanted to know.

Smiling, the visitor put into words what one evening on the streets meant to her. 'I've discovered that being a Christian means being like Jesus, and tonight I've done what he did, I've held out my hand in love to people who aren't loveable but there's one thing I'd like to ask you.'

Catherine wondered what that would be.

'I know you have a big family,' she said. 'How did you manage to bring them up and still be so busy for the Lord. Didn't they feel neglected?'

The Army Mother smiled at the thought of her children. 'I've always made time for my children,' she answered. 'You see, they are the first mission field the Lord gave me. Every one of them is a Christian and all but one is a Salvation Army Officer.'

'Thank you, that answers my question. You're the Army Mother and you're a real mother to your own children too.'

FACT FILE

Railways - Catherine was born just the year before the first passenger carrying railway opened in England in 1830.

For hundreds of years the fastest way of getting from place to place over land was on horseback or horsedrawn carriage. Catherine and her father travelled like that.

Railways brought the biggest ever change in people's way of travelling and by the time Catherine was in her fifties, most of the major countries in the world had railway lines and more were being built every year.

Keynote: Catherine brought God's love to people who were unloved. She cared for the drunk, fed the hungry, clothed the homeless and told them about Jesus.

Learn from how Catherine loved the unloved and be prepared to roll up your sleeves and work hard for God!

Think: Look around you and see what you could do to show God's love in a practical way.

Why not donate some of your toys or clothes to a charity shop or do a sponsored activity to raise money for helping the homeless? You could have fun and help others at the same time!

Prayer: Lord Jesus, open my eyes to see that all around me there are people who need help and who need you. Show me what I can do to make a difference. Help me to say and do the right thing. Amen.

Jackie Pullinger

'This is like a huge xylophone!', Jackie told her twin, as she ran a toy along the radiator. She banged a little harder. A satisfying 'Bong!' went from that radiator along the pipes to the one in the kitchen. Mrs Pullinger ran out to see what was wrong with the central heating. She was met by twin grins.

'I'd rather you stuck to the piano,' she laughed.

Jackie's twin climbed on to the stool and tried to play a tune on the piano, not easy when you are just four years old. But Jackie sat down with her back to the radiator and had a long think. She knew she was always found out when she did something naughty and she tried to work out if it would be better to try to be good. These were complicated thoughts for a very little girl.

At Sunday School a year later, a missionary told the children about the work she did.

'Perhaps God wants you to go to the mission field,' the woman said.

Jackie thought about that. In her mind she saw a big green field, that's what she imagined a mission field would look like. In the middle of the field there was a mud hut and she tried hard to imagine herself sitting outside it. 'That's what it must be like to be on the mission field,' she decided. Then she thought a bit more about what the woman had said and decided that God wanted everyone to be on the mission field. The picture in her mind's eye must have looked a little crowded by then!

'You have a real gift for music,' Jackie's teacher said, when she had started boarding school. 'What was your first instrument?'

The girl thought. 'The radiator, Miss,' she answered truthfully.

Her teacher wondered if she had heard correctly. She had. 'Well, I think you should stick to the piano and oboe. We don't have musical radiators here.'

Jackie looked at the radiator under the window and wondered if what her teacher had said was true. But she did work hard at her piano and oboe, and after leaving school she went to the Royal College of Music in London to continue her studies there.

It was when she was a student that Jackie came to believe in God in a new way. She discovered that he was really interested in her, really loved her and that he really did want her to become a missionary.

'Dear Sir,' she wrote at the top of several identical letters, all going to different missionary societies, 'I'm convinced that God wants me to be a missionary. I have studied music and I'd like to know if I could go abroad with your organisation as a music teacher.'

One by one the answers came back.

'I'm afraid we don't need music teachers at present.'

'We cannot consider your application until you have some experience.'

'We do not take people under twenty-five years of age.'

Jackie placed all the answers on the table and frowned over them. 'So where do I go from here?' she asked herself. And she asked a minister friend the same question.

'If you really believe that's what God wants you to do, then go ahead and do it,' was his advice. 'Buy yourself a ticket for as far away as you can afford and get off where the Lord tells you to.'

That made perfect sense to Jackie Pullinger and that's how she came to be disembarking from a ship in Hong Kong in the mid-1960s.

Having spent nearly all her money on travel, Jackie needed to find a job as soon as she arrived in Hong Kong. Before long she was doing some music teaching, not full time, but enough to feed her and pay for accommodation. 'What do you want me to do here?' she asked her heavenly Father every day in her prayers.

'Will you come and visit my school in Hak Nam?' a Christian lady called Mrs Donnithorne asked her.

Jackie agreed to go. And it was on that visit she discovered the answer to her prayers.

'Hak Nam is the Chinese name for the Walled City,' her guide told her as they walked. 'It's the poorest and most notorious area of Hong Kong. When you're in Hak Nam you need eyes in the back of your head.'

Jackie followed her friend though a tiny gap between two shops into the Walled City. What hit her first was the smell, then the slime under her feet, then darkness because the buildings were crushed together with only a tiny space between them, then it was water. Or was it?

'You need eyes on the top of your head too,' Mrs Donnithorne said, ducking into the shelter of a doorway. 'Rubbish is just thrown out of windows into the alleys where people walk.'

Jackie wiped her hair then looked at her hand. It wasn't water, and from the colour and the smell of it she decided not to try to work out what it was.

A boy of about twelve bumped into Jackie as he made his unsteady way long the alley.

'Poor lad,' the teacher said. 'He came to my school once and now he doesn't even recognise me. He's pumped full of drugs and he always is.'

'And look at her,' the elderly lady pointed to a girl aged no more than eight. 'She does that about eighteen hours a day. If she falls asleep someone kicks her awake again and tells her to get on with it.'

Jackie's eyes took a minute to get used to the darkness in which the little girl sat.

She was pushing bright red plastic flower petals on to green wire stems. On one side of her was a mountain of petals bigger than herself and on the other was a pile of finished flowers. The little girl's fingers moved quickly but her eyes didn't move at all. They looked dull and dead as she stared straight ahead.

'Why isn't she at school?' Jackie asked.

The older lady explained. 'In some Chinese communities, and the Walled City is one of them, Chinese parents reckon that their children should repay all that they've cost their parents. That little girl is working to pay back what's been spent on her food and clothes since she was born.'

Jackie looked at the child and wondered what her parents were charging for the rags she was wearing.

Soon Jackie realised that the Walled City was where God wanted her to work.

When Mrs Donnithorne asked if she would teach in her school, Jackie's immediate answer was 'yes'. And on Sundays the new young missionary peddled at what seemed a hundred miles an hour to keep the harmonium going for the service that was held in the school.

'I think God wants me to start a youth club here,' Jackie told Mrs Donnithorne soon afterwards.

The elderly lady, whose heart was full of love for the people of Hak Nam, was thrilled. 'Is this the person God's sending to make a difference here?' she wondered.

The room was bare apart from an ancient table tennis table, a dart board on the wall, skittles, a few board games and a bookshelf of Christian books.

'What's going on here?' two boys demanded, as they forced their way in.

'I'm starting a youth club,' Jackie told them.

One sneered. 'What's in it for you?'

She shook her head. 'Nothing at all.'

'Whose gang's running it?' the other boy asked.

Everything in the Walled City was run by one or other of the famous Chinese Triad gangs.

'No gang,' Jackie told them.

'That'll be right,' growled the first boy, picking up a table tennis bat as he spoke.

Soon a game was underway and, as if by magnetism, other boys came in to referee the match.

'Thank you, Lord,' Jackie prayed that night. 'The youth club's up and running!'

But the work wasn't easy. Nobody in the Walled City trusted anyone else. Each Triad gang thought one of the other gangs was supporting the youth club. Drug addicts caused trouble, fights broke out, murders happened round about, and the only people there to keep any kind of peace were the Triad gangs. Regular police work wouldn't have lasted quarter-of-an-hour in Hak Nam.

When the police did try to crack down, they just arrested people then found crimes to charge them with. The better they knew someone's face, the more likely they were to arrest him even if they didn't have anything to charge him with. There were always plenty of crimes going spare.

Power ruled and the power changed depending on where in the Walled City you were and which was top gang at the time. But good things happened in that bad place.

A boy, who had more of a skeleton than a body, came to the youth club regularly. He was into gang wars and gambling and he took drugs too.

'Jesus loves you,' Jackie told him one evening.

He wouldn't look at her. 'Oh yeah,' he said, not believing that anyone at all could love him.

'When Jesus was on earth he spent time on the streets with people like you. He didn't sit around in churches waiting for good guys to turn up.'

The boy was interested.

Jackie told him about the Lord, that he loved bad people so much that he died to save them so that one day they could go to heaven.

There was a stifled sound beside her. When Jackie turned round, the boy was praying and crying, asking Jesus to forgive him. When he opened his eyes they were full of tears but they were beautiful. For the first time ever that boy was really happy.

After some years working in the Walled City, Jackie Pullinger wrote a letter to a friend from the Royal College of Music, telling her about the work she was doing.

'It started off as a youth club but it's grown from that. We now have four houses where people can stay. So many of them have just been kicked out of their homes. Some lived in drug dens anyway so they're better out of them.

We have girls who have had babies staying there too. Many of our guests have been drug addicts and have criminal records as long as my arm. A number of them have run away from cruel homes where terrible things were done to them. And we have some older people staying too. I didn't want that at first but it turned out to be a good idea.

Because I can't be in four places at once, I have helpers working with me. And before you write back to nag me, yes, I do still play my oboe! I wouldn't like to be without it.'

Maria was a young teenager when Jackie met her. She had been brought up in a terrible home and, when things became unbearable, she escaped from the Walled City and found work in another part of Hong Kong. Jackie didn't forget the girl and kept praying for her. One day they met again.

'I'm in terrible debt,' Maria confessed. 'I've been working in a ballroom. The man there gave me dresses to wear for my work and now he's making me pay for them. I'm his slave until I pay and I haven't got any money.' She began to cry.

'What about the money you earn?' Jackie asked.

'He won't give me anything till I've paid for the dresses,' she wailed.

Over the months Maria's situation grew worse and worse.

'What can I do for her?' Jackie prayed over and over again.

Then she realised the answer to her prayers. Taking her oboe out of its case, she played it for the last time. It sold for exactly the amount of money Maria needed to repay her debt and to free her from slavery to that evil man.

When Jackie Pullinger was a little girl she thought the mission field was a huge green field with a mud hut in the middle.

Her mission field turned out to be very different. It was a vast lawless slum in the middle of Hong Kong. There was no field, there wasn't any grass there at all. There was slime and smells and gangs and drugs and poverty and crime. But there was love too.

Through Jackie many people in the Walled City came to know the love of Jesus, and were loved for the first time in their lives.

FACT FILE

Outer space - at the same time as Jackie Pullinger was stepping off a ship in Hong Kong, man was in a race to travel much further - all the way to the moon!

A Russian, Yuri Gagarin, was the first man in space, when he orbited the earth in April 1961.

Then, after further daring space flights around the earth, an American astronaut, Neil Armstrong, became the first man to set foot on the dry and dusty surface of the moon on 20 July 1969.

Keynote: Jackie was willing to go anywhere for God, even into the Walled City. She was also willing to give up a prized possession - her oboe - to show God's love to someone in trouble.

Learn from Jackie's willingness to go anywhere, do anything and give up everything for God.

Think: Write down a list of the ten things that you value most. When you look at your list you might think you couldn't imagine life without your ten treasures.

What about Jesus? How much does he mean to you? Start to treasure Jesus. Just think about how much he has done for you!

Prayer: Lord Jesus, thank you for everything. Thank you for all the special things you've given me. Most of all thank you for loving me so much that you died for me. Help me not to love anything more than I love you. Amen.

Evelyn Brand

'You have another beautiful daughter,' the nurse told Mrs Harris. 'What a family! Nine children, imagine that!'

Mrs Harris cuddled her newborn daughter and smiled at her husband.

'Have you chosen a name?' the nurse asked.

Without taking his eyes off his new little daughter, Mr Harris answered. 'She's called Evelyn Constance.'

'Nice name,' said the nurse. 'My sister's called Evelyn though we all call her Evie.'

'And will you be called Evie?' Mrs Harris asked the tiny child. It was 1879. By 1880 everyone called her Evie.

Before Evie was very old, another two children had been born into the Harris home. All of them, nine girls and two boys, had the happiest of childhoods in a most beautiful place.

'Chase you to the greenhouse!' was often heard in the summer. And when they came out of the greenhouse to find another game to play there were often red marks on their lips because there were vines in the greenhouse heavy with grapes.

Each summer the gardener grew marrows, and the children watched in amazement as they got bigger ... and bigger ... and bigger still. Sometimes the littlest children could not hold their arms wide enough apart to show how big the biggest marrows were!

'Count up to twenty then come and find us.' But it wasn't always easy to find all the children scattered among the gooseberry and blackcurrant bushes, hiding behind the tall rhubarb or in the fernery where huge fern fronds made splendid hidey places.

Life, however, was not all play for the Harris children, there was school work, church and Sunday School to attend and things to be done for the poor. Although the family was well off, the children knew a lot about poor people. Their mother and father made sure of that.

'Have you put your pennies in the mission box?' the children were asked on Sundays.

'Why do we put money in the box?' the littlest one sometimes asked.

Mother was always ready to explain. 'The poor people in places like India don't know about Jesus so we collect pennies to send people out to tell them.'

That was a very strange thought to the Harris children. In their wildest dreams they couldn't imagine anyone not knowing about Jesus. Didn't everyone's father read them Bible stories? Didn't everyone's mother teach them how to pray? As they grew old enough to understand, they discovered that even in London, not very far from where they lived, there were people who didn't know Jesus.

One of Evie's older sisters married and went to Australia. Evie missed Florrie very much and was delighted when she had to bring her little daughter home for a time. She was still more delighted when her father suggested that she travel back to Australia with Florrie to keep her company. The journey out seemed wonderful to Evie and her time in Australia was too. But it was the journey back that changed her life, for she met a missionary on that boat and God began to call her to missionary service too.

Very soon after she returned to England, Evie heard a missionary speaking about his work in South India. Jesse Brand, a young man home on leave, told about the poverty of the people there, about the disease and starvation, about the dirt and creepy crawlies too. Evie's heart seemed to beat fast. 'Could she go there?' she asked herself. 'Could that be where God wanted her to go?'

When Mr Brand came back to her home for tea, she was too shy to suggest to him that she might go to India. But she knew that she would one day. And that day came quite soon for when Evie made up her mind she went ahead and did things.

'What a noise!' the new arrival in India said to the missionary couple who met her in Madras.

The wife laughed. 'It's a mixture of clattering cart wheels, pounding drums, crows cawing, beggars begging and men shouting out what they have to sell.'

'And if you're wondering what the smell is,' the husband added, 'it's a mixture too, of sandalwood, sweat, jasmine, cow-dung smoke and food.'

Evie struggled to take it all in. 'Could anything be more different from home?' she wondered. But there was no time to be wasted. There was a language to learn and work to be done. Very soon she was visiting Zenana homes with Bible women and deep in study of the language. To her surprise Jesse Brand was in Madras when she arrived. And to nobody's surprise at all the young couple began to fall in love.

In 1913 Jesse and Evie were married and set up home in the hill country among the Tamil-speaking people.

'I so enjoy travelling in this beautiful place,' Evie told her new husband, as they climbed onto their horses for a three day long journey to visit several villages. While Jesse treated the sick, she gathered the women around her and told them in simple Tamil the good news of the Bible.

Just a year after they were married, their little son Paul was born. That meant some changes to their home. Jesse decided that the thick thatched roof, which was home to rats, snakes and other creatures, had to be removed and replaced with corrugated iron. It was a great improvement apart from in the monsoon rains, when it sounded like a whole orchestra of drums beating!

Jesse became well-known for his medical skills though he had only done a one year course in medicine. Sometimes Evie nearly fainted with horror at the patients who arrived at their home. To her they seemed more dead than alive. Jesse didn't fuss, he just did what he needed to do and prayed that God would give healing.

Paul was delighted when his little sister, Connie, was born. The Brand family was complete. Having two children did not stop Jesse and Evie travelling. Leaving Paul and Connie with Christian helpers, they went from village to village as before, caring for those who were sick, making gallons of watery rice for those who were too ill to eat and telling people everywhere they went about the Lord Jesus Christ.

Evie found she had another job too. By 1920 four other children had joined the family. They were Indian children who needed a home and the Brand home was always open to them. But the children who were on Evie's mind at that time were her own for she knew that when the family went back to England on home leave, Paul and Connie would remain there in the care of her family.

'As I stood watching them wave goodbye,' Evie said later, 'something just died in me.'

For the first part of the journey by sea back to India, Evie kept wishing her children were with her. But in the Mediterranean there was such a fearful storm she was glad they were safely home in England.

'We'll write every day,' Jesse had promised the children. And they did. Every evening both Evie and Jesse wrote part of a letter home and, when it was long enough, they sent it off. Paul and Connie were good letter-writers too.

Sadly, letters were all they were ever to have of their father again. Jesse died of fever in 1929 when he was just forty-four years old. It was a heartbreaking letter that told the children that news.

Evie seemed to do enough work for two after Jesse died. That was her way of trying to fill the space he left behind. She visited the village mission stations and held clinics in each one. She inspected schools, gave talks, held prayer meetings, kept the accounts and looked after the Children's Home. Riding Jesse's horse, a rather wild creature of which she'd sometimes been afraid, she picked her way along the trails to distant villages. But help was coming. Ruth, her niece and a doctor, arrived from England and did what she could to assist Evie with her work. The two women lived and worked well together. Evie was especially grateful for her niece when it came time to go on home leave again. It was so hard to face England, to see Paul and Connie, without Jesse at her side.

The children seemed quite grown up to Evie. They had become teenagers in the time they'd been apart. But, much though they loved their mother, there were some things about which Paul and Connie disagreed with her strongly.

'You CAN'T wear that dress!' Connie wailed. 'It came out of Noah's ark.'

Her mother frowned. 'Rubbish. It was my best dress before I went to India, and it has a lot of wear in it still.'

'But people will just laugh at you,' moaned Connie, near to tears.

Connie's aunt came to her rescue. 'Wear this,' she insisted, handing her sister a more modern dress of her own. And, seeing the determination in two sets of eyes, Evie gave in.

Before she left to go back to India, Evie knew that her children loved Jesus for themselves. That gave her courage to say good-bye. Whatever happened to any of them, she was sure they would meet again in heaven.

On her return to India, Evie was given a job in Madras supervising a group of Bible women.

'Time to go,' she said each afternoon, even when the temperature was over 110 degrees. 'I go by rickshaw to the nearer places,' she wrote to Paul and Connie, 'and by bus when I have further to travel. But the buses are so crowded I feel like pulp when I arrive!' She liked trains too, even if they were full of cockroaches!

As the war moved nearer South India, Evie found herself thinking about the bombs that were falling in London, where both Paul and Connie lived. Paul had nearly finished training as a doctor and, as he hoped to work in India, his mother found out about possible jobs for him. In 1947 Paul arrived in the country of his birth, bringing his wife with him.

'If they think I'm going to retire and get under their feet,' Evie told a friend, 'they should think again. I have plans.'

There was a twinkle in her eye and her friend guessed what her plans were.

'I'm going back to the hills again. I'll live in a tiny native hut made of woven bamboo and covered with mud and whitewashed. It'll have a thatched peaked roof like all the other village huts. And I'll be happy there, being a missionary for as long as I can.'

Evie Brand didn't know what it meant to retire. No sooner was she settled in her village hut than she gathered a family of children about her. Some were ill and she nursed them back to health, others were unwanted by their families but never unwanted by Evie.

In 1952, when she was well over seventy years old, Granny Brand, as she was then called, was being carried down a steep hillside on a dholi (chair) with side poles when one of the bearers fell. She lurched forward and landed head first on a rock.

'We need to go back and get help,' the bearers decided.

'No,' Granny Brand insisted, through the pain that pounded inside her. 'We'll go on.'

Miles of being carried in the dholi followed, then a rickety train journey for over a hundred miles and a hot and bumpy bus ride after that. It was a very pained and ill old lady who arrived in hospital in Vellore. Although it took her a long time to recover, that was not the end of Granny Brand's missionary work. Over the years that followed she saw many people trust in Jesus as she shared his story with them.

'That makes it all worthwhile,' she told Paul. 'The work and the pain are all worthwhile if they believe in Jesus.'

Paul knew what she meant. He felt the same.

In 1959, when Granny Brand was nearly eighty, a dream she had had for a very long time came true. Connie, whose home was in Africa, was able to visit India to see her mother. With both of her children beside her, Granny Brand was happy. The hill people, among whom Connie and Paul had been born, made a great celebration to welcome them home.

Evelyn Brand died in India and went home to Jesus in 1974.

FACT FILE

Smell - when she arrived in India, Evie immediately noticed the different smells.

Our sense of smell is controlled by two small areas with many nerve cells, right at the top of the nose.

Humans have a much poorer sense of smell than animals which hunt for prey or have to be on the lookout for enemies.

The human sense of smell also gets tired easily. Have you ever noticed that if you smell a weak smell for several minutes you become unable to smell it at all?

Keynote: Evie began her life in a well-off family in England and ended up in a hut in India, all because of her deep love for Jesus and her love for the Indian people who needed Jesus so much.

Learn from Evie's love for Jesus and how that inspired her to bring his message of love to others.

Think: Evie took the message of Jesus to the people of India, but have you ever thought that you can be a missionary for Jesus right where you are?

The people in your home town need Jesus too so always be on the lookout for ways in which you can share Jesus with them.

Prayer: Lord Jesus, thank you for the people who first told me about you. Help me to love you so much that I will want to share you with others.

Give me the courage to speak up for you whenever I can. Amen.

Joni Eareckson Tada

Tumbleweed trotted through the long grass, then came to the open meadow.

Joni, eleven years old and a rider since she was old enough to sit on a pony, encouraged her horse into a gallop and covered the ground in no time. A sharp tug on the reins slowed the mare down as they reached the little group on the ridge.

'We thought you were never coming,' one of Joni's sisters called, 'but we decided to give you another couple of minutes.'

The four Eareckson girls set out at a trot for their picnic.

'I think this is the most beautiful place in the whole of America,' Kathy said.

Joni agreed. 'I'd hate to live in the town.'

'Being twenty miles away from the bustle suits me fine,' her oldest sister said, 'though I love it when Mum takes us to the shops.'

The other three laughed. 'That's because you want to look at wedding dresses. Wonder why!' Joni spoke for them all. Weddings had been very much in their older sister's mind since she met a certain nice young man.

After their picnic, the four sisters decided to gallop back to the ranch that was their home. As usual the eldest gave the others a few minutes start so that she could keep an eye on them as she rode.

'Really!' she thought as she looked ahead. 'Joni's the limit! She's got Tumbleweed jumping over fences.' Nudging her own horse to move faster, she caught up with her youngest sister. 'Careful!' she called as she neared her, 'You don't want to take a fall!'

Joni laughed and pulled her horse to a trot. 'Tumbleweed wouldn't do that to me.'

'You don't take anything seriously,' the older girl said.

'That's because I never have accidents,' laughed Joni, kicking Tumbleweed into a gallop again.

Her sister grinned and shook her head.

Four years later, when Joni was fifteen years old, she did some serious thinking. At a Christian camp she thought for herself about what the Lord Jesus had done when he died on the cross. Before that she had believed without thinking. A great flood of joy filled her when she realised that Jesus loved her, Joni Eareckson, so much that he died to save her from her sins. Her parents were thrilled when she told them that she was a Christian, for they had prayed for all their daughters since before they were born.

'It's a glorious day,' Kathy said, stretching in the sand.

Their friend Butch threw a beach ball in her direction.

'Joni'll play with you,' yawned Kathy. 'I'm far too busy relaxing.'

Joni and Butch tossed the ball from one to the other, laughing when it went out of reach and racing after it. But the sun was warm and it wasn't long before they collapsed in a tired heap at Kathy's side.

'Time for a swim,' Butch suggested. He looked at Joni and winked. Then he grabbed one of Kathy's hands, Joni took the other and they dragged the girl to the sea. All three ran through the ever-deepening waves and swam back to the shore.

'Like to see a prize-winning dive?' Joni asked.

The other two nodded and waited. Joni's diving was worth watching.

Poised for the dive, Joni took a long breath and jumped. She slid into the warm silkiness of the water in a graceful curve and ......

Butch and Kathy waited to see the curve turn upwards and Joni rise, dripping diamonds of water in the sunshine.

'Joni!' Kathy yelled, instinct telling her that something was wrong. She ran to where her sister hadn't surfaced. Butch followed in a fury of splashing water.

Panic filled Joni when she didn't rise ... when she couldn't rise. She couldn't move ... she couldn't breathe. Her mind was bursting with fear. Her lungs were desperate for air. And still she couldn't rise. Her body and mind screamed for help ... but there was only stillness and a roaring noise in her head that made no sense.

A wave came in, its swell raising the girl a little from the sea-bed.

'Joni!' she heard the echo of Kathy's scream. Then there were strong arms round her, Kathy's arms. Joni saw her sister's eyes. They were bulging with terror. But a cold fear filled Joni. Kathy's arms were round her, she could see that, but she could feel nothing at all. Was her body there? She didn't know. Somehow they got back to the shore.

'Can you feel that?' Kathy begged, touching her sister's leg.

Joni's 'no' was weak.

'Or that?' Kathy's hand was moving up.

'No.'

Then a rush of relief. Joni felt something, it was her sister's fearful, shaking, fingers touching her neck. She tried to reach out to hold Kathy's hand but nothing happened, nothing at all.

There was the screech of an ambulance's brakes. Joni found herself harnessed into a neck brace, lifted by the emergency team into the ambulance and, with siren wailing, the slow procession left the beach for the hospital. Kathy wept noiselessly, clutching her sister's hand in both of hers. But it gave Joni no comfort because she couldn't feel it. Butch followed in the car. He prayed as he drove. Kathy wept all her tears to God. And Joni, seventeen years old and paralysed from the neck down, said the only words that came to her. 'The Lord is my shepherd ... The Lord is my shepherd.' It was 30th July 1967.

The months that followed were terrible. Joni was strapped into a bed that turned her over like a sausage on a barbecue so that she didn't develop sores. For part of each day she was on her back looking at the ceiling, some of the time she was on one or other side facing the walls and for the rest of the day she was suspended from the bed looking at the floor.

'Hi up there,' said Kathy, who was lying on the floor under her sister in order to see her face. 'You won't fall on me, will you?'

Joni looked down. She tried not to cry, but couldn't stop herself. A tear fell from her face and landed on her sister's forehead. Kathy scrambled up and wiped the others that followed. Then she wiped her sister's nose for her.

'You can't imagine what this is like,' Joni whispered, when the tears has stopped. 'Imagine not being able to wipe your nose, or go to the toilet, or even know when you need to go. Imagine having to be fed, having to be washed, having to have your teeth cleaned for you.'

Kathy tried to imagine it, but her mind just couldn't take in the awfulness of it all.

Joni saw the desperation in her sister's eyes. 'No,' she said. 'Don't try to imagine it. It hurts too much.'

As the months passed Joni became more aware of what was happening around her, of other patients who, like her, had broken their necks. Sometimes that was a comfort but mostly it just made the hurt worse to know that other people were as utterly helpless as she was. Her parents, sisters and friends did everything to help but Joni had to travel through her feelings alone.

'Sometimes I remember what it felt like to gallop on Tumbleweed,' she told a school friend. 'I can almost feel the wind in my hair. But then I remember that I'll never ride my chestnut mare again.'

'Try not to think about it if it hurts that much,' her friend suggested.

Joni snapped. 'But how can I not think about it! That's all I have left of a normal life, just memories. And I've nothing to look forward too, all I can do is look back!'

After her friend left, Joni prayed as she'd never prayed before. 'Nobody understands apart from you,' she told the Lord. 'I can only get through the days if you help me. And I just can't imagine how I'll get through life.'

Many years later Joni did some mental arithmetic.

'I've just worked something out,' she told her husband.

'What's that?' smiled Ken Tada, Joni's husband.

'I'm thirty four years old,' she said. 'My accident happened when I was seventeen. That means that for half my life I've been virtually paralysed from the neck down.'

'How does that make you feel?'

Joni thought for a while.

'I guess I feel grateful. After the accident I didn't think I'd live. When I realised I wasn't going to die, I didn't know how I'd cope with living. I spent hundreds of hours just thinking,' she went on. 'I thought I'd be useless, that I'd spend all my life in hospital, that I'd never get married, never travel, never laugh again.'

'Well you thought wrong. Thank God for that.'

Joni nodded.

'There was a song we sang as children. Let's see if I can sing it to you.'

Joni's beautiful singing voice rang out in the evening stillness.

'Count your blessings,
name them one by one.
Count your blessings,
see what God has done.
Count your blessings,
name them one by one;
and it will surprise you
what the Lord has done.'

I do count my blessings sometimes,' she said. 'I actually count them.'

Joni's husband looked at his wife's face, bathed in evening sunlight. She looked beautiful, sitting there in her wheelchair, eyes sparkling as she spoke.

'Would you like to hear some of them?' she asked, just a little shyly.

'I certainly would.'

'You're the first one,' she grinned cheekily, 'though I can't imagine why!' Number two is this beautiful home. I'm so thankful for that. Three is my family and all the people who help so that I can live at home, writing letters, washing, doing my hair, taking down dictation for my books, fetching and carrying things when I need them.'

'That's a lot for one blessing,' her husband laughed. 'What's number four?'

Joni looked serious. 'When I was in hospital I thought I'd never be able to work. Now I have more work than I can keep up with. I never dreamed I'd be a world -wide author. It's such a blessing to write about what God has done in my life and to help others who are going through tough times.'

'And number five?'

'That's my painting,' she nodded in the direction of her easel and palette. 'I wouldn't have believed it was possible to paint holding the brush in my mouth. And to think people actually buy my paintings! Wow! That still amazes me.'

'Any more blessings you want to share?' Joni's husband asked.

'The other thing that really surprises me is the amount of travelling I'm able to do. Just look at my diary for this month. I've got several speaking engagements all over the state, plus one is Washington.

Next month I go to England for a series of meetings there. That's exciting. And the amazing thing is that nobody would ever have heard of me if I hadn't broken my neck. God has brought so many good things out of that terrible accident.'

'Could you bring over my easel, please,' Joni asked. 'That sunset is just begging to be painted.'

Minutes later she was lost in her art. Holding the long handle of the brush in her mouth, Joni mixed the colours of the evening sky on her palette and with swift skilful movements put them on paper. Dark tree branches seemed to reach out of the picture, and her husband, watching her work, could almost feel the warm glow of the bright setting sun on the paper.

'And if you hadn't had your accident, we might not have met,' he thought as he stood behind her stroking her neck so that she could feel his touch.

FACT FILE

Painting - Stone Age artists did the earliest paintings we know of. These paintings were done on the walls of caves.

Joni draws and paints beautifully by holding the brush in her mouth.

Stone Age painters also used their mouths when painting. They blew colour on to the walls through bone tubes. To make the colours stay on they put a kind of glue on the wall.

Right up until A.D. 1400, murals (wall paintings) continued to be one of the main kinds of art.

Keynote: Looking back, it would have been easy for Joni to concentrate on what could have been. Instead she counted her blessings and that made her heart sing.

Learn from Joni's thankful spirit even when things don't

go as you expected. Start by counting your blessings too!

Think: Each time you are tempted to wish for something you don't have, write out a list of the blessings that God has already given you.

Look over the list and you'll find 'it will surprise you what the Lord has done!'

Prayer: Lord Jesus, thank you for everything you have given me. I'm sorry for the times when I am disgruntled and jealous of what others have. Help me to be content.

Thank you especially for your gift of salvation. Amen.

Corrie ten Boom

Corrie's father put on his magnifying eyeglass and looked at the inside workings of the watch. Taking a tiny screwdriver he adjusted a screw the size of a pinhead. Corrie watched him work. He was concentrating so hard he forgot she was there. Although she was only six, Corrie had learned to be very quiet when her father was working on watches and clocks.

Sometimes Corrie wondered what would happen if she let out a great big sneeze. "Atishoo!"

But even when she felt a sneeze twitching inside her nose she always managed to stop herself.

'Would you like to see this through my glass?' Papa ten Boom asked.

Corrie grinned. 'Yes please!' she said, although it was very hard for her to keep his eyeglass in place on her little face. She had to screw her eyes up hard to do it.

'Those are diamonds,' her father told her. 'Can you count how many there are?'

'One, two, three ... four ....five! Who's watch is it, Papa? The lady must be very rich.'

Mr ten Boom smiled. 'Yes, she is very rich.'

'You must be the best watchmaker in Holland,' Corrie said delightedly, 'when rich ladies bring their watches to you. I love being here in the shop with you.'

'I like you being here too,' Father ten Boom said, 'you are quiet as a mouse.'

By the time Corrie had grown up, the Second World War was going on all around her. English and Nazi planes often fought overhead. One night, when the planes were so noisy that Corrie and her sister Betsie couldn't sleep, they went down the twisting stair of their quaint Dutch house and had a cup of tea together. When Corrie went back to bed a long piece of shrapnel lay on her pillow.

'If I'd been asleep it would have killed me,' she told her sister.

Betsie nodded. 'God must have saved you for a reason,' she said.

Corrie, who loved the Lord Jesus very much, agreed. 'But what can the reason be?' she asked. 'I wish I knew.'

It was not long before she found out.

A few months later the ten Boom family discussed the war as they ate their rye bread and Gouda cheese.

'The Nazis are insisting that all Jewish people wear a yellow star, a Star of David,' Betsie said. 'But I don't understand why.'

Papa ten Boom looked very serious. 'Nor do I, but it makes me afraid for them. You don't mark people out for nothing.'

And he was right. The following week Corrie heard Nazi soldiers saying terrible things to young Jewish boys just because they were wearing yellow stars. Then there was word that Jewish men were being taken away to prison camps. But worse was to come. One day Corrie saw Jewish families being pushed on to a lorry and driven away. She knew in her heart that they would never come home again.

'Precious Jesus,' she prayed that night, 'isn't there anything I can do for these poor people?' As Corrie lay in bed that night, she remembered that Jesus was a Jew, and that made her want to help them even more.

'I've an idea,' Mama ten Boom told her daughters after they had seen another lorryload of Jews driven away. 'Our house is such a funny place, with twisting stairs and tiny rooms, attics and underfloor spaces...'

Nollie, Corrie's other sister, interrupted. 'I was thinking the same. We could hide Jews here!'

Corrie and Betsie looked at each other.

'It's like a rabbit warren,' Betsie said. 'We used to play hide and seek when we were girls and sometimes it took ages even for us to find each other!'

Corrie's heart beat fast. 'Was this what God wanted her to do?' she wondered.

The ten Booms made plans. They fixed an alarm bell upstairs so that if any Nazis came into the shop intending going upstairs to search the house, whoever was in the shop could warn the family and any Jews who were there. They would have just two minutes to disappear into one of the many hidey-holes.

'I'm worried about one thing,' Nollie said, when the preparations were nearly done.

'Will children be able to be quiet if they're hidden under the floorboards or in one of the attics? The dust might make them sneeze.'

Every face in the room took on a worried expression apart from Corrie's. 'Yes,' she said firmly. 'They'll be quiet, and they won't sneeze.'

'What makes you so sure?' Betsie asked.

'When we were girls,' Corrie reminded her sisters, 'we were quiet as mice when Papa was working on watches. When we needed to sneeze we stopped ourselves. And our lives didn't depend on it.'

Many Jews were saved because of the ten Boom family but there were hairy moments. One day the whole family and several 'guests' were sitting round the kitchen table when a window cleaner climbed up his ladder and started to clean the outside of the window! One of the Jews thought quickly. 'Start singing Happy Birthday,' he whispered, 'then they'll think we're having a party.' And that's what they did. They all sang Happy Birthday to Papa ten Boom and they never did find out if the window cleaner had just come to the wrong house or if he was a German spy!

But the Nazis eventually discovered the 'safe house' and the ten Booms were arrested, separated and put in prison. It seemed ages before they heard news of each other. One day Corrie got a coded message that all the watches in the cupboard were safe. She knew that meant that the Jews who were hidden in her home when it was raided had got away safely. Corrie was thrilled and she poured out her thanks to God. But the next news she heard broke her heart. Papa ten Boom had died.

'Get dressed and pack your things!' yelled the guards early one morning. The prisoners looked at each other with a mixture of hope and terror. Corrie prayed while she struggled into her clothes.

Guards herded the prisoners into buses and vans outside the prison. But it was not long before they knew they were not being released and sent back home. The buses and vans drew up outside the railway station and the prisoners were dragged off like animals.

That was when it happened. Corrie saw Betsie! She edged her way to her sister without attracting the guards' attention and they clung together. Betsie could just hear Corrie above the noise of the rest of the prisoners. 'Praise the Lord!' she was saying. 'Praise the Lord!'

When an engine pulling cattle trucks stopped at the platform, men, women and children were shoved aboard until they were pressed against each other like sardines in a tin. Corrie and Betsie linked arms so they weren't pushed apart. They talked and talked about what had happened to them during their time apart. And they cried too, especially when they thought about Papa ten Boom.

'We're going to Germany,' a man shouted above the noise. 'We're passing near my home and it's on the way to Germany.'

A woman's voice wailed. 'What'll they do to us there? What'll they do to our children?'

'Nobody ever comes back from Germany,' someone said darkly.

And everyone thought he was speaking the truth.

'I need the toilet,' a child's voice cried.

There was a sudden silence in the carriage.

It was a tearful mother's voice that answered her child, 'You'll just have to do it where you are.'

And everyone in the carriage hoped they would arrive in Germany before they too needed the toilet and had to do it just where they were.

Corrie and Betsie were taken to Ravensbruck, one of Hitler's notorious concentration camps. There they were treated like animals. Each day they had to parade naked in front of the guards, even in the very coldest weather. There was no mercy in the Ravensbruck guards.

'I can't begin to work out how many people are here,' Corrie said one day to her sister.

Betsie couldn't either. 'But I do know something,' she said. 'There must be ten rats for every person.'

'And a hundred fleas,' her sister added.

'I thank God for the fleas,' Betsie said. 'I thank him every single day for the fleas.'

Corrie knew what she meant. The Nazi guards didn't like fleas so when the fleas were especially bad in a hut they didn't go in as often.

'Why didn't God let us go on helping the Jews?' Corrie wondered aloud one day.

Betsie knew the answer to that question. 'Because he had work for us to do here and we'll not do it by being sorry for ourselves.'

Her sister knew that was true. There was so little they could do in the concentration camp but in a place like that little things meant such a lot. Corrie and Betsie looked for ways of helping their fellow prisoners. It's hard to imagine but they even tried to hold birthday celebrations, especially for the young girls there. They cared for sickly children to let mothers rest, and they did what they could for those who were ill and dying. There was love even in Ravensbruck.

'You're so thin,' Corrie told her sister as winter came round, 'and you're shivering with cold.'

'There's nobody here overweight,' Betsie said. Then she smiled. 'And you'd better call out the engineer for the heating seems to have broken down!'

'How like Betsie to try to joke,' Corrie thought. 'Even here. Even now. Even though she's terribly ill.'

Betsie went into a spasm of coughing. But nobody, apart from Corrie, noticed for coughing was the normal background noise in the hut.

As long as she was able, Betsie held Bible studies and little prayer groups. 'That's the best help we can be here,' she often told her sister. 'We don't know how long any of us will live so it's important that we're ready to die.'

Sometimes Corrie prayed that Betsie would get better but other times she prayed that her sister would die and go from the horrors of Ravensbruck into the wonder and beauty of heaven. And that is what happened. Betsie didn't get better. Jesus took her home to himself.

Not long after Betsie died, Corrie was released from the concentration camp. Before she left, she had to sign a form saying that she had been well-treated there and that she had kept in good health. But Corrie was so ill that she was taken straight to hospital. When she was there, she looked in a mirror and didn't recognise herself. Time passed and she recovered enough to go home.

'Do you still have work for me to do?' she asked God often in her prayers. And he did. Corrie opened a home in Holland where other victims of the war came for help and for peace.

One day, a long time later, a man spoke to Corrie after a church service. He had been a guard at Ravensbruck. 'Isn't it wonderful that Jesus has washed my sins away,' he said, holding out his hand to shake hers. So many things went though Corrie's mind. Had he forced her to parade naked? Had he laughed at poor dear Betsie when she coughed herself sick? For a minute her arm seemed glued to her side. Then she prayed a quick silent prayer and God filled her heart with forgiveness. Corrie ten Boom took the man's hand in hers and shook it warmly. And that was a miracle.

FACT FILE

World War II - the Second World War lasted from 1939 to 1945. The Netherlands, where Corrie lived, was attacked by the Nazi army in May 1940 and the country was overrun in four days.

The Dutch underground movement bravely resisted Nazi rule. But more than 100,000 Dutch Jews died in concentration camps and nearly 500,000 Dutch people were sent to work in Germany.

After a terrible winter of famine and cold in the west and heavy fighting in the east, the Nazi forces in the Netherlands surrendered in May 1945.

Keynote: Corrie and her family suffered so much that it would have been easy for Corrie to become bitter and angry. But God gave her real peace in her heart and the ability to forgive those who had been her enemies.

Remember the even greater miracle that Jesus can forgive your sins.

Think: Maybe you feel you have the right to hate some people because of what they've done. But hatred will make your heart cold and bitter.

It won't be easy but ask God to help you to forgive them and start praying for them too.

Prayer: Lord Jesus, thank you for being willing to forgive me when I have sinned against you so many times. Help me to forgive others and even to learn to love my enemies as you tell me to do. Amen.

Author Information: Irene Howat

Irene Howat is an award-winning author and poet who lives in Scotland. She has published many biographical books for all ages and is particularly well-known for her biographical material. She has written many books about the lives of different Christians from around the world. She has also written an autobiographical work entitled: *Pain My Companion*.

Quiz

How much can you remember about these ten girls who changed the world?

Try answering these questions to find out ...

ISOBEL KUHN

1. Isobel went to China, but what was the name of the people she worked with>?
2. What was the name of the special school that John and Isobel ran in the wet season?
3. What were the names of Isobel's children?

ELIZABETH FRY

4. Who was the American gospel preacher that Elizabeth listened to one day?
5. What did Elizabeth give the prisoners before they were transported?
6. How many women were crammed into four rooms at Newgate prison?

AMY CARMICHAEL

7. Which country was Amy from?
8. What colour were Amy's eyes?
9. Where did Amy go as a missionary?

GLADYS AYLWARD

10. How did Gladys travel to China?
11. Where did Gladys work when she came to China?
12. How long did it take Gladys and the children to trek across the mountains to safety?

MARY SLESSOR

13. Where did Mary work as a child?
14. What area of Africa did Mary go to?
15. Before Mary came along, what had the African people done when twins were born?

CATHERINE BOOTH

16. Why did Catherine have to stay in bed for a year?
17. What was the name of the organisation founded by Catherine and William Booth?
18. What was the name of the hall that they opened in one of the poorest parts of London?

JACKIE PULLINGER

19. What was the first musical instrument that Jackie played as a child?
20. What was the name of the area of Hong Kong that Jackie went to work in?
21 Which treasured possession did Jackie sell to pay off a young girl's debts?

EVELYN BRAND

22. What was Evelyn's nickname as a child?
23. Which part of India did Evelyn and her husband work in?
24. Which of Evelyn's children trained as a doctor and returned to work in India?

JONI EARECKSON TADA

25. What was the name of Joni's horse?
26. What had Joni been doing when she became paralysed from the neck down?
27. How does Joni draw and paint?

CORRIE TEN BOOM

28. What job did Corrie's father do?
29. During the war, what did the Nazis insist that all Jewish people wore?
30. What was the name of the concentration camp that Corrie was sent to?

How well did you do?

Turn over to find out ...

ANSWERS

1. The Lisu people.
2. Rainy Season Bible School.
3. Kathryn and Danny.

4. William Savery.
5. A Bible and a sewing kit.
6. 300.

7. Northern Ireland.
8. Brown.
9. India.

10. By train.
11. At an inn for muleteers.
12. Twelve days.

13. In a jute mill in Dundee.
14. Calabar.
15. They killed the babies and sent the mother away.

16. She had a problem with her spine.
17. The Salvation Army.
18. The People's Mission Hall.

ANSWERS

19. A radiator.
20. Hok Nam - the Walled City.
21. Her oboe.

22. Evie.
23. The south of India.
24. Her son, Paul.

25. Tumbleweed.
26. Diving into the sea.
27. By holding the brush or pencil in her mouth.

28. He was a watchmaker.
29. A Yellow Star - the Star of David.
30. Ravensbruck.

Start collecting this series now!

Ten Boys who used their Talents:
ISBN 978-1-84550-146-4
Paul Brand, Ghillean Prance, C.S.Lewis, C.T. Studd, Wilfred Grenfell, J.S. Bach, James Clerk Maxwell, Samuel Morse, George Washington Carver, John Bunyan.

Ten Girls who used their Talents:
ISBN 978-1-84550-147-1
Helen Roseveare, Maureen McKenna, Anne Lawson, Harriet Beecher Stowe, Sarah Edwards, Selina Countess of Huntingdon, Mildred Cable, Katie Ann MacKinnon, Patricia St. John, Mary Verghese.

Ten Boys who Changed the World:
ISBN 978-1-85792-579-1
David Livingstone, Billy Graham, Brother Andrew, John Newton, William Carey, George Müller, Nicky Cruz, Eric Liddell, Luis Palau, Adoniram Judson.

Ten Girls who Changed the World:
ISBN 978-1-85792-649-1
Corrie Ten Boom, Mary Slessor, Joni Eareckson Tada, Isobel Kuhn, Amy Carmichael, Elizabeth Fry, Evelyn Brand, Gladys Aylward, Catherine Booth, Jackie Pullinger.

Ten Boys who Made a Difference:
ISBN 978-1-85792-775-7
Augustine of Hippo, Jan Hus, Martin Luther, Ulrich Zwingli, William Tyndale, Hugh Latimer, John Calvin, John Knox, Lord Shaftesbury, Thomas Chalmers.

Ten Girls who Made a Difference:
ISBN 978-1-85792-776-4
Monica of Thagaste, Catherine Luther,
Susanna Wesley, Ann Judson, Maria Taylor,
Susannah Spurgeon, Bethan Lloyd-Jones,
Edith Schaeffer, Sabina Wurmbrand,
Ruth Bell Graham.

Ten Boys who Made History:
ISBN 978-1-85792-836-5
Charles Spurgeon, Jonathan Edwards,
Samuel Rutherford, D L Moody,
Martin Lloyd Jones, A W Tozer, John Owen,
Robert Murray McCheyne, Billy Sunday,
George Whitfield.

Ten Girls who Made History:
ISBN 978-1-85792-837-2
Ida Scudder, Betty Green, Jeanette Li,
Mary Jane Kinnaird, Bessie Adams,
Emma Dryer, Lottie Moon, Florence Nightingale,
Henrietta Mears, Elisabeth Elliot.

Ten Boys who Didn't Give In:
ISBN 978-1-84550-035-1
Polycarp, Alban, Sir John Oldcastle
Thomas Cramer, George Wishart,
James Chalmers, Dietrich Bonhoeffer
Nate Saint, Ivan Moiseyev
Graham Staines

Ten Girls who Didn't Give In:
ISBN 978-1-84550-036-8
Blandina, Perpetua, Lady Jane Grey,
Anne Askew, Lysken Dirks, Marion Harvey,
Margaret Wilson, Judith Weinberg,
Betty Stam, Esther John

CHRISTIAN FOCUS PUBLICATIONS

Christian Focus · Christian Heritage · CF4K · Mentor

Christian Focus Publications publishes books for adults and children under its four main imprints: Christian Focus, CF4K, Mentor and Christian Heritage. Our books reflect our conviction that God's Word is reliable and Jesus is the way to know him, and live for ever with him.

Our children's publication list covers pre-school to early teens. We also publish personal and family devotional titles, biographies and inspirational stories that children will love.

From pre-school board books to teenage apologetics, we have it covered!

Christian Focus Publications Ltd,
Geanies House, Fearn, Ross-shire,
IV20 1TW, Scotland,
United Kingdom.
www.christianfocus.com

CF4•K

Because you're never too young to know Jesus

TEN GIRLS WHO MADE HISTORY

TEN GIRLS WHO MADE HISTORY

LIGHT KEEPERS

Irene Howat

CF4·K

For Muriel and Matthew

Reprinted 2004, 2005, 2006, 2007, 2009, 2011,
2012, 2015, 2016, 2017, 2019, 2020, 2022
Paperback ISBN: 978-1-85792-837-2
epub ISBN: 978-1-84550-854-8
mobi ISBN: 978-1-84550-855-5
Published by Christian Focus Publications,
Geanies House, Fearn, Tain, Ross-shire
IV20 1TW, Scotland, U.K.
www.christianfocus.com
e-mail:info@christianfocus.com
Cover Design by Alister MacInnes
Cover Illustration by Elena Temporin
Printed and bound in China

All incidents retold in these stories are based on true situations. Where specific information about childhood incidents has been unobtainable the author has written these paragraphs using other information concerning family life, hobbies, home life and relationships freely available in other biographies.

Cover illustration: Henrietta Mears suffered from muscular rheumatism as a young girl and often had to sit and watch her friends enjoying fresh air and exercise outside. But after she was healed she said to her sister, 'I learned a lot in those two years. I've especially learned to trust my future to God.'

Contents

Mary Jane Kinnaird

The little girl looked round the circle of her brothers and sisters. Their faces all reflected the flickering of the coal fire, and their eyes seemed to dance with the light from it. There were six in the family, and she was the youngest of them all by several years. It was Christmas time, and they had gathered at their grandparents' house where they could spend some time together. Sir Gerard Noel and Lady Barham loved their grandchildren dearly.

'It's very sad,' Mary Jane said. 'You can all remember Papa and Mama, and I can't remember them at all.'

Her oldest sister turned in her direction.

'I was very upset when they died,' she said. 'And I remember feeling especially sad for you because I knew you wouldn't have any memories of them.'

'Tell me about them,' the child pleaded. 'Then I can imagine that I knew them.'

Mary Jane's oldest sister took charge.

'Let's go round the circle and tell something that we remember about our parents. You start,' she said to her brother.

'Papa was a banker,' the lad said.

'And he always wore very smart clothes,' said the next along.

'Mama was gentle and kind,' Mary Jane's sister added.

'And she was quite a serious person,' commented her brother.

'Mama was very kind,' the oldest sister said. 'In fact, Mary Jane, although you don't remember her, you are really very like Mama. You are gentle and kind and serious. So despite not knowing her at all, there is something of Mama in you.'

That night, Mary Jane went to bed happier than she had felt for some time because, over the weeks that had gone before, she had thought a lot about not knowing her parents.

'The holiday's over now, I'm afraid,' said Miss Holloway. 'And I think we should start today with your piano lesson.'

Mary Jane smiled at her governess. She had played the piano for her brothers and sisters many times over the holiday and had learned a new tune. Sitting down at the piano, she began to play. Miss Holloway's eyes opened wide, then a smile played on her face.

'Who taught you that tune?' she asked.

'My brother William,' the child said. 'He said it would be a nice surprise for you.'

'He was quite right,' laughed Miss Holloway. 'And I would really enjoy hearing it over again.'

Happy that she had pleased her governess, Mary Jane settled back at the piano and began to play. Mary Jane's brother, who had taught her the tune, came into the room as his little sister played.

'Well done, Twinkle,' he said, clapping at her performance.

The little girl's face broke into a wide smile. Her older brothers and sisters may have had homes and families of their own, but there was something special about their times together at Grandma and Grandpa's. It was Mary Jane's home, and she loved it, but she loved it even more when all the family was there ... and she adored William, even if he did call her that awful pet name!

'I suggest you write your thank-you letters this afternoon,' Miss Holloway said, as they finished the morning's school work. 'You have one to write to your godmother and one to your uncle.'

Although Mary was a clever child, she neither read nor wrote quickly. So the writing of two thank-you letters took some time. After she had finished telling her godmother how much she liked the gift she had sent her, there was still a lot of empty paper on the page. As she thought what else she could say, an idea came to her mind, and she wrote it down before it escaped.

'I hope that whenever you call, I shall be able to say my catechism (Bible questions and answers) perfectly.'

Then, signing her name, she folded the paper, glad that the job was done.

'She really does like learning her catechism,' Miss Holloway thought, as she checked the letter for spelling mistakes. 'Young though Mary Jane is, I think she is a Christian.'

By the time Mary Jane was fifteen years old, she had begun to keep a diary. And her diary shows that she thought a lot about what it meant to be a Christian.

'3rd December, 1831 - This week I've not prayed nearly enough for other people! One night I was very unkind and I've let little things annoy me. Every day when we've had family prayers, my mind has wandered all over the place. And I've wasted a lot of time too.'

'10th December, 1831 - I think that pride is my biggest sin, and it shows itself in so many ways. Sometimes I feel so unthankful and discontented. And often I forget about God.'

'17th December, 1831 - The Bible says we should copy Jesus, and I hardly do that at all. He was so kind, and I'm only kind to people I really like.'

But if anyone else had read Mary Jane's diary, they might have thought she was being very hard on herself, for the teenager was kind and gentle, and really did seem to try to live the kind of life a young Christian person should live.

'I think it is time we bought you some new dresses,' Lady Barham told her youngest granddaughter.

Mary Jane looked at herself in the mirror.

'This dress is fine,' she said. 'And my other dresses will do another year too. I've not grown quickly this last while.'

Lady Barham sat down and looked at the girl.

'I still think you need new dresses. These ones may still fit you, but they don't fit the fashion. You don't want to look old-fashioned at your age surely!'

Although she didn't care at all about fashion, Mary Jane agreed to go to her grandmother's dressmaker. But she found it difficult to endure an afternoon of looking at cloth that didn't interest her, deciding on styles she couldn't care less about, and being pinned and tucked into boredom. It was with the greatest relief that the fitting was done, and she could put on her old, blue dress and go home. By the time her new dresses were delivered, she had forgotten all about them.

'I don't know what we'll do with Mary Jane,' Lady Barham commented to her husband. 'She just doesn't care about the things most girls her age are interested in. I often wonder what she will do with her life.'

When Mary Jane was twenty-one years old, she went to live with her uncle, Rev Baptist Noel. She loved sitting at the table and listening to him talk. Fancy dresses didn't matter in his home; there were much more interesting things for a girl to be thinking about.

'I visited a rookery in St Giles today,' Uncle Noel told her one day.

'Tell me about it,' Mary Jane said. 'I want to know how poor people really live.'

Uncle Noel looked at his niece and knew she was telling the truth. He sat down beside her on the window seat and told her what he had seen.

'I suppose rookeries get their name because they are very tall and narrow buildings, although it's hard to imagine anything less like a tree covered with rooks' nests. The one I visited today had over 300 people living in it, and every one of them desperately poor. Sometimes several families live in one room. I heard of one small room where five families lived, one family in each corner and another in the middle of the room. When someone asked how they managed, the husband of one of the corner families said that it had been fine until the family in the middle of the room took in a lodger. The poverty is terrible,' he concluded, 'but what is worse is that hardly any person, in the rookery I visited, knows that Jesus can save their souls.'

'Is that why you helped to start the London City Mission two years ago?' Mary Jane asked.

Uncle Noel looked at the serious girl at his side. 'Yes,' he said. 'That's why I hope that the London City Mission will be a great success. They will employ ordinary people rather than ministers to go out to the ordinary people of London.'

'I'll pray for the missionaries,' promised Mary Jane.

And Uncle Noel knew that she would.

In 1841, just four years after she had moved to her uncle's home, Mary Jane founded an organization of her own. It was the St John's Training School for Domestic Servants. As each girl came for training, Mary Jane took down her details and kept a record of the work she did. And she continued to do that for many years, until over 1,000 young women had passed through her training school.

Not only that, she used a lot of her own money to fund the training as well as raising funds from her friends. Even when she married the Honourable Arthur Kinnaird, when she was twenty-six years old, her interest in helping people continued.

Over the years that followed, Mary Jane tried to interest her friends in the things that interested her and not fashions that she could never be bothered with. She sent out invitations for tea and discussion, and the discussions were on serious topics.

Her invitation for one Wednesday in May 1848 listed that afternoon's topics as:

1. Christian education - especially for ragged and poor children.
2. The problems of British colonies.
3. How to improve conditions for the people of London.
4. How to spread the good news of Jesus in Europe.

The following Wednesday her friends were invited to discuss:

1. Education.
2. Emigration.
3. Young men in towns.
4. Problems of people living in the countryside.

Having tea with Mary Jane Kinnaird could be hard work!

Because she could not remember her mother, when Mary Jane's children were born, she worked hard at being a good mother.

'I know the fashion is only to see your children for a short time before they go to bed,' she told her husband, 'but I won't have that in our home. They can come into my room anytime without knocking.'

Sir Arthur looked rather shocked.

'You'll never have any peace,' he said. 'They'll run in and out all day.'

Mary Jane smiled. 'I hope they do.'

Lady Kinnaird was the kind of mother she would have wished to have had herself. Whatever she was doing, her children were welcome. Every night she prayed with them as they went to bed, whatever was going on in the house and no matter what important people were staying. Even as her children grew older, they were constantly in her thoughts and prayers. Amazingly, when her son went off to boarding school, she wrote a letter to him every single day!

During the Crimean War, in 1854-55, Lady Kinnaird became aware of a problem and set out to do something about it.

'I hear that soldiers injured in the Crimea are not receiving the care they need, and many are dying unnecessarily,' she told her friends.

'I know,' one agreed. 'What they need are trained nurses to go out there and help.'

'But where would we find trained nurses?' asked the other.

'We wouldn't find them anywhere,' said Lady Kinnaird. 'We'd train them here in London, then send them out when they know what they are doing.'

A building was found and a home opened where young women in training would live. That was when Florence Nightingale became involved, and the two women worked together from then on.

'It's all very well training nurses for the Crimea,' Mary Jane said to her husband. 'But what will happen when the war is over?'

'I suppose they'll go home to their families,' he suggested, though he was sure that was not what his wife had in mind.

'Young women will still need to come to London to train as nurses or to work,' Lady Kinnaird thought aloud, 'and we could provide a home where they could live simply and safely, like the nurses' home.'

'Talk it over with your friends,' said Sir Arthur. 'See what they think.'

Lady Kinnaird wrote to several friends the following day - as she still read and wrote slowly it took most of the afternoon - and invited them for tea and discussion. The topic was to be 'providing a home for young women who come to London for training or employment.'

A small organisation was founded which soon joined with another and became the Young Women's Christian Association. Lady Kinnaird was president. The YWCA (as it was soon called) was not an instant success. Those who believed in it, had to work hard to make it work. But it did work, and over the years, homes were opened in other cities as well as London. Mary Jane Kinnaird didn't live to see it, but eventually the YWCA spread to many different countries and provided homes for hundreds of thousands of young women who had to move to cities to study or work.

'I've just heard the most awful news,' Lady Kinnaird told her daughter. 'There have been some terrible murders in Whitechapel in London. I know I'm dying and can't do anything to help keep the girls of Whitechapel safe, but you could open a home for them.'

Mary Jane was right, she was dying. Even in the last few days of her life, she encouraged her daughter to take over from where she left off. So when Lady Mary Jane Kinnaird died and went home to Jesus, her work on earth went on. A place of safety was opened in Whitechapel. It was called the Kinnaird Rooms.

FACT FILE

The Crimean War: This war was fought on the Crimean peninsula, which is in the Black Sea between Turkey and Russia. The war is well known for the unnecessary loss of life caused by lack of organisation. The troops were sent out without adequate food, equipment or medical supplies. When the nurses arrived in the Crimea, they found that the hospital had no medicine, bandages or cleaning materials. The work of the nurses who went out made a huge difference to how injured soldiers were cared for.

Keynote: Mary Jane was well off and could have spent her time thinking about things like dresses and parties. However, she was very concerned for the welfare of the poor. She didn't stop helping when the crisis of the Crimean War was over: she was willing to carry on the work afterwards. It is important to try to help people and to do it all the time, even when it is hard and there is no one to praise us for doing it.

Think: Although Mary Jane was very busy trying to help all sorts of people, she did not forget her own family. She was always willing to see her children, no matter what she was doing, and she wrote to her son at boarding school every day. Do you think that he always wrote back? She would have been very pleased if he had. Think about ways in which you can show kindness and affection to those who try to help you, and make sure that you don't take them for granted.

Prayer: Lord Jesus, thank you for being willing to make sacrifices and to suffer so that you can save people from their sins. Thank you for helping those whom important people usually ignored. Please teach me not to be selfish and help me to do all that I can to help others. Amen.

Emma Dryer

Emma stood at the window while her mother brushed her long hair.

'One, two, three, four ...,' she counted, as the brush tugged.

'Five, six, seven, seventy-seven, seventy-eight ...,' the girl continued.

'I don't think so,' Mrs Dryer said. 'Your hair needs brushed a hundred times every day to make it shine. And you don't get to a hundred by missing out all the numbers between seven and seventy-seven!'

Emma grinned. Sometimes her mother's mind was so far away when she brushed her hair, that the girl got off with her trick of missing out numbers.

'I'll not skip so many tomorrow,' decided Emma. 'If I miss out just a few here and there, she'll not notice.'

'Are you ready for church?' Mr Dryer called from the bottom of the stair.

Pulling her hat down on her newly brushed hair, Emma dashed out of her room and down to her father.

'Ready!' she said, snapping her feet to attention in front of him.

'And so you are ... not,' her father smiled. 'Your hair is brushed, your hat and coat are on, but they look really funny with your pink slippers!'

Emma glanced down, and where her polished, brown boots should have been, there was a pair of pink, knitted slippers.

'Quick as you can!' her father said, pushing her gently in the direction of the stairs.

'One, two, three, four ...,' Emma counted, as she ran up, and 'eleven, twelve, thirteen,' as she landed at the bottom again.

'Let's go,' said Mr Dryer, taking his daughter by the hand.

Mrs Dryer, who was not feeling very well, stayed at home that day.

'Let's play the number game,' Emma suggested, as they set out on their walk to church. 'You be "it".'

This was the girl's favourite game because she had invented it herself. The person who was 'it' had to give a number, and the other person had to guess which story the number came from and then tell the story.'

Mr Dryer thought for a minute. 'What story does ninety-nine come from?' he asked.

'That's easy,' laughed Emma. 'It's the story Jesus told about the shepherd who had a hundred sheep. One went missing, and that left only ninety-nine. The shepherd searched for the missing sheep until he found it. Then he carried it all the way home.'

'Your turn now,' her father said.

Emma screwed up her face as she tried to think of a hard one. Then she grinned. 'What story does twelve come from?' she asked.

'Is it about the disciples?' queried her father.

The girl shook her head.

'Is it about Jacob's sons?'

'That's right,' laughed Emma. 'Now you've got to tell me the story.'

By the time Mr Dryer had finished the long story of Jacob and his twelve sons, the pair of them were nearly at church.

'Will you tell me about the service?' Mrs Dryer asked her husband, when they arrived back home.

Emma had gone upstairs to take off her coat, hat and boots.

Mr Dryer told his wife about the hymns, the Bible readings and the sermon.

'And what was Emma chatting about as you walked?' she asked.

'We played her number game on the way there, and on the way back we talked about the people who were at the service.'

'I've never known a child so fascinated by numbers,' Mrs Dryer said. 'She counts everything, even the peas in their pods when she's shelling them! And it's all your fault,' she concluded, smiling.

'My fault?' puzzled her husband.

'Yes, indeed. Don't you remember the first thing you taught her when she was just a few months old?'

He shook his head.

'You cuddled her on your knee, and taking every one of her tiny toes in turn, you counted up to ten and down again, tickling her each time you finished! Before she was a year old, she was counting them with you.'

Mr Dryer laughed. 'I had no idea I was launching her on a career in mathematics!'

But Emma's happy home life was not to last for many years. While she was still a girl, both of her parents died, and Emma was sent to live with her aunt in New York State. Although her aunt was kind to her, sometimes the girl felt very sad. Often she went for long walks on her own, and as she walked, she remembered walks with her parents and the word and number games they had played together. Sometimes the memories made her feel warm inside, and other times they made her want to cry.

'Be sure you're home before dark,' Emma was often told, as she left on her walks.

'Aunt,' the girl said early one evening. 'I always come home before dark because you tell me to, but I'd really like to stay out later this evening.'

'Why's that?' she was asked.

Realising that her aunt was worried, the teenager smiled broadly.

'I won't get up to mischief,' she giggled. 'It's just that I love being out in the starlight. Often I sit for hours with my room window open just watching the stars, and tonight I'd like to walk for a while in the starlight.'

Her aunt laughed. 'I don't think you'll come to any harm doing that,' she agreed.

As Emma grew older, two things fascinated her: mathematics and the stars. She made up number puzzles for her classmates, and some of them were so hard their teacher had to work them out. And, in the late evenings, when the stars shone, Emma drew plans of the constellations and sky maps of the different times of year.

'What do you want to do with your life?' her aunt asked, when Emma was nearly grown up. 'I expect you want a handsome and rich husband and a houseful of happy children.'

The girl smiled.

'I suppose I might want that one day,' she agreed. 'But right now I'd like to go to college to study mathematics and astronomy.'

Emma's aunt nodded. 'I thought that's what you would say. And there's no reason why in this modern age you should not do just that. When I was a girl in the 1810s, things were different. Not many girls went on to study after they left school, in those far-off days.'

From school, Emma went to a women's college, and from there she went to university. She was such a brilliant student that she became a university teacher and eventually she was appointed Head of the Women's Faculty of Illinois State Normal University.

'I wish my parents had lived to know how well I've done,' she found herself thinking, when she heard the news that she had got the job. 'They would have been so pleased to see me settled for life in such a secure position.'

In 1870, when Emma was thirty-five years old, something happened that changed things. In fact, she almost lost her life to typhoid fever. Emma was already a Christian by then, but the seriousness of her illness made her do some very hard thinking.

'How are you feeling today?' Martha asked, when she came to visit.

Still too weak to raise her head from the pillow, Emma smiled in her friend's direction.

'I'm feeling a bit better,' she said. 'And I think I'm going to live after all.'

'Of course you're going to live,' scolded Martha.

Emma's face grew serious. 'There's no of course about it,' she stated simply. 'I know I nearly died. And of this I'm sure; someone who has come so close to death can't just pick up the pieces and go on as they were going before.'

Martha looked concerned. 'Is she still a little delirious?' she wondered.

Some months later Martha and Emma were deep in conversation.

'You're looking wonderfully well despite your brush with death,' Martha announced. 'In fact, you're absolutely back to normal.'

'I thank God for healing me,' smiled Emma. 'And for showing me the direction in which I should go.'

'Direction?' queried her friend. 'What do you mean?'

Emma took a deep breath before breaking her news.

'I believe that God is leading me to give up my job and work full-time for him.'

'Give up your job!' gasped her astonished friend. 'But you've got a wonderful, well-paid, important position. You can't just give it all up like that!'

'I can,' Emma assured her. 'And I have. My notice has already been given.'

'Are you sure you're feeling all right?' Martha asked sincerely. She wondered if her friend's illness had returned and caused her to be confused.

'I'm feeling very well indeed,' Emma announced. 'In fact, I've never felt better or more content in all of my life.'

Later that year, Emma Dryer moved to Chicago and took up an unpaid job there.

'Dear Martha,' she wrote at the head of a sheet of paper. 'You've been so good to me you deserve a letter, now that I've settled down in my new position. Let me tell you what life is like here. I'm lodging with a family, which is a new experience for me, and I'm enjoying it. However, I must admit that after the academic life I've led over the last few years, the hustle and bustle of a family home took a little getting used to! My job is befriending young women who are in trouble, and there is no end of them here in Chicago. Many are poor girls who have never had a chance in life. Others have got themselves into trouble of their own making.

But whatever the reason, they are in need of help and support. Of course, what they most need is a Saviour, and as often as I can I tell them about the Lord Jesus. Recently, one young woman was very cross with me. She said that it was all right for me, coming from a happy and wealthy home, and that I couldn't possibly understand what life was like for 'ordinary' girls. When I explained to her that my parents died when I was very young and that I was brought up by an aunt, she settled down, and we were able to have a really good talk. One last bit of news before I finish; I'm attending Illinois Street Church which was founded by Dwight L. Moody, and I love it.'

'Dwight L. Moody,' thought Martha, when she read the letter. 'He's the most famous preacher in America. I wonder if Emma will ever meet him.'

Emma did meet Mr and Mrs Moody, and they became very good friends.

In 1871, a terrible fire blazed its way through the heart of Chicago, leaving whole streets just heaps of ash and charred timber.

'We've got to do everything we can to help,' Dwight Moody told a group who met to pray for the city. 'Let's raise as much money as we can to provide food, clothing and shelter for those who have been burned out of their homes.'

The prayer meeting turned into a planning meeting, as people got their heads together to work out how best to help.

'I've a job specially for you,' Dwight told Emma. 'The Bible study class here is huge, and your experience is needed to make it a really worthwhile training ground.'

'That won't help with fire damage,' she pointed out.

Moody agreed, then added that it would do more lasting good than building new houses.

Because she knew that Martha would have heard about the great fire, Emma wrote to assure her friend that she had not been injured.

'Although I was unaffected by the fire, it has changed the work I do,' she wrote. 'I'm now very involved in Bible teaching (though our church was burned down) and I also hold mothers' meetings and sewing classes for girls. Now, Martha, don't you be smiling at that! How my old university students would laugh if they could see me now! But I am where I believe God wants me to be, and I'm happy.'

Moody recognised in Emma a very clever woman and a splendid teacher. He persuaded her to open a school where young women, who felt called to home or foreign mission, would be trained.

'Tell me about the training you do?' a visitor asked Emma.

'It is a one year course,' she explained. 'The students do a mixture of lectures and practical work here in Chicago. They do house-to-house visits, take meetings in homes and churches, help with Sunday Schools and mothers' meetings as well as doing what they can for the homeless, poor people of the city.'

By 1878, seventeen of Emma's former students were doing Bible work in the city, and many others were missionaries abroad. Moody's dream was becoming reality. But his dream was bigger than Emma knew. He dreamed of a college for men and women, somewhere young people could be trained for two or three years, a college that would send missionaries to the furthest parts of the world to tell people about the Lord Jesus. It took a long time, and it was not always easy going, but the Bible school that Emma Dryer founded became the place that Dwight L. Moody dreamed of. Today The Moody Bible Institute in Chicago is one of the most famous missionary training colleges in the whole world.

FACT FILE

Women in education: Emma Dryer was a pioneer in education. For a long time people thought that university education was only for men. America, however, admitted women to university before the United Kingdom did. Emma was able to attend Illinois State Normal University, but Oxford University did not admit women until 1878 (when Emma was forty-three) while men and boys had been going to Oxford University since the twelfth century! Women like Emma have helped to overcome prejudice, and now more women go to university than men.

Keynote: Emma was very successful, and most people would have agreed with her friend, Martha, that she should settle down in her important job. She felt that God wanted her to do special work for him instead. It might have been very scary to give up everything that she had worked towards and move to the busy city of Chicago, but Emma did it, and God helped her. Doing what God wants can be daunting. However, he will give us the strength to do what we should.

Think: Although Emma had moved away from the university, her special skills came in useful later on when she helped to train young women who were called to work as missionaries abroad and in America. She could not see how God would tie everything together when she decided to go to Chicago, but God could. We don't always know what God will want us to do, but he does want us to use the skills that we have to serve him and to help others. Think about some of the skills that you have. How might God use these for his glory?

Prayer: Lord Jesus, thank you for the chance to learn about mathematics and science. Thank you for giving me the opportunity to learn about you. Please help me to use all of the experiences that I have to serve you. Give me the courage to do what you tell me, even when it is hard or scary to do so. Amen.

Florence Nightingale

Florence and her sister were not sorry to be parted. They were so very different. Parthe (whose full name was Parthenope) loved parties and frilly dresses. Flo, as Florence was known, liked books and studying. Both thought the other was boring.

'I love staying with you,' Flo told her cousin Hilary. 'We do such exciting things!'

Hilary smiled cheekily.

'Would you like to come visiting today?'

Thinking that meant dressing up and sitting in parlours, Flo screwed up her face.

'No thanks,' she said. 'I get that at home.'

Her cousin giggled. 'Not that kind of visiting,' Hilary explained. 'My governess is visiting the poor today, and I sometimes go with her. Do you want to come too?'

Flo, who was eight years old, knew about visiting the poor. Sometimes she went with her mother delivering food to the hungry.

'Yes, I'll come,' she said. 'I think I'd like that.'

'What a wonderful afternoon I've had,' Flo wrote in her diary before going to bed.

'Miss Johnson took us to a number of cottages where very poor people live. She actually goes INSIDE the cottages. They were so dark! Miss Johnson was very nice to the people, treating them like friends. And when we went into one cottage where there was a sick baby, she picked up the child and hugged him. Then she examined the poor little thing and said she'd bring medicine to help his chesty cough. I stroked the baby, and he stopped crying. It felt wonderful to be really helping someone.'

Closing her diary carefully, Flo lay back on her pillows and thought over the day. She imagined herself as a grown-up, going from cottage to cottage with a basket of fruit and helping the sick people she visited. Before she knew it, she had fallen asleep and begun dreaming, then it was morning and time to get up!

A few months later, in early 1829, dreadful news came to the Nightingale home. One of their little cousins had died. Both girls had been very fond of him. After the period of mourning was over, Parthe and Flo's governess, Miss Christie, decided that they needed something new to focus their energies on, something practical, fulfilling and creative.

'I have a new project for you,' their governess said. 'I want you to do something to help the poor village people.'

'Cook will give us food to take to them,' announced Parthe. 'And the gardener can dig up some vegetables.'

'No,' Miss Christie said, 'I want you to think of ways of earning money so that you can do something for them yourselves.'

'Earning money?' quizzed Parthe, who knew she would never have to earn money in all her life. Her family was quite rich enough to keep her comfortably.

'I think that's a good idea,' Flo said. 'I'll embroider handkerchiefs and I could tidy Mum's threads for her. You could do some drawings to sell to our relatives,' she told her sister. 'You're brilliant at drawing.'

Over the weeks that followed, Parthe and Flo did all sorts of things and raised enough money to give the village children a party, complete with food and gifts to take home.

'I LOVE helping people,' Flo wrote in her diary. 'And I love keeping notes of everything I do and see. Perhaps one day I'll write a book.'

In 1831, when Flo was eleven years old, Miss Christie spoke to her very quietly. By the time Miss Christie had finished speaking, tears were rolling down Flo's cheeks.

'You're leaving?' she said softly. 'You're leaving us to get married?'

'Yes,' the young woman said. 'But we will write and we will pray for each other.'

Flo believed both these things would happen, but she knew that when Miss Christie left, her life would change. Nothing would ever be the same again. If a tear smudged the ink in her diary that night, it was only one of the many that fell. But many more tears were shed the following year when her governess died in childbirth.

Praying was as much part of Flo's life as writing her diary, but in the weeks that followed her dear friend's death, many of Flo's prayers were in the form of questions.

'Why did she die, Lord? Why could she and the baby not both have lived?'

Flo's grandmother came to stay some weeks later, and helping to look after the old lady helped the girl to get over her grief. In fact, helping people always helped Flo too. It gave her a good feeling.

'What will I do with my life?' Flo often asked herself. 'I can't just spend my time going to dinner parties and balls. And I'm not going to prance about in fancy gowns every day, that's for sure!' Night after night she prayed that God would make her useful. Then, on 7th February 1837, the Lord answered her prayers. The seventeen-year-old knew without a shadow of a doubt that he had called her into his service. She didn't know what God would ask her to do, but she knew that something useful would come out of her life.

'You'll enjoy seeing where you were born,' Flo's father told her. 'In our grand trip round Europe we'll visit Florence, the city that gave you your name.'

Flo didn't particularly want to spend ages touring Europe, but that's what the family did. They took so much with them that her father's coach needed six horses to pull it! The Nightingales, servants and all, left home in September that year and didn't return for nineteen months! The most important event in the family diary after that was the day that Parthenope and Florence met the new, young Queen Victoria.

Although Florence continued to live in high society, her interests lay elsewhere. 'Oliver Twist' had just been published, and this opened her eyes to the poverty in London. Her aunt was very involved in campaigning against slavery. Florence even started reading government reports on health, the employment of children and housing the poor! In fact, she was developing what is called a social conscience. That means that she was becoming aware of problems that really existed, and felt she wanted to help.

When she was twenty-four, an American doctor and his wife visited the Nightingale home. He worked with deaf and blind people, but he also talked about work he wanted to do with those who were sick in body or mind. Florence could hardly wait to talk to him.

'Do you think a young English woman like me could work in a hospital?' she asked at the first opportunity.

The doctor looked at Florence.

'It would certainly be most unusual for someone from your kind of family to do work like that,' he said. 'But if you think that's what you should be doing, go for it. And God will go with you.'

The young woman's heart pounded with excitement. From then on, her mind was made up. God had called her into his service, and she would find a way of serving him.

It was not until 1853 that Florence found what she was wanting. That was when she became manager of the Institute for the Care of Sick Gentlewomen, and she only got the job because she had spent much of the previous few years nursing one or other aged or ill relative as well as spending a short time in a hospital in Germany.

'This is what I was made to do,' Flo told her cousin. 'This is my service to God.'

'What does the job involve?' her cousin asked.

Florence thought back over her first few months with the Institute.

'It has involved travelling to Paris to research nursing there. And here in London I've assisted in operations and cared for patients after their surgery. I've nursed women with tuberculosis and I've tried my best to comfort those suffering from stress.'

'Is that all?' her cousin laughed jokingly.

Florence thought she was being serious. 'No,' she said, 'that's not quite all. I've also ordered the furniture for the Institute, put up shelves to hold things, kept the accounts and looked after the stores.'

Having looked for something useful to do, Florence Nightingale was now incredibly busy ... and loving it.

In March 1854, Britain and France declared war on Russia. The Crimean War had begun. Six months later, a worrying report was published.

'Insufficient plans have been made for the care of the wounded. Not only are there not enough surgeons ... not only are there no dressers and nurses ... there are not even linens to make bandages.'

Just five days later, Florence Nightingale wrote to her cousin, 'A small private expedition of nurses has been organised for Scutari, and I have been asked to command it. I believe we may be of use.'

Florence and her thirty-seven nurses arrived just after a battle and they could hardly believe what met them. As usual, she took very detailed notes.

'I've been given five damp rooms for my nurses. The dead body of a Russian general is in one of them, and rats are in all five. The men are fed with half-cooked meat soup and no vegetables at all. There are so many of them that the bath rota means each is bathed once every eighty days! Not only that, the same sponge is used to wash everyone.'

Utterly shocked, Florence set out to organise her nurses into some kind of useful order. Although the doctors were not too keen to have nurses helping them, Florence made sure they got down to work.

'Go to the market and buy as many vegetables as you can carry,' she told some of them.

'Set up the portable stoves we brought with us,' she instructed others, 'and get ready to cook some decent food for these poor men.'

'Wash these bandages and rip more linen into strips,' she said to some who were still looking for jobs. 'Then wash anything in sight. Everything here is disgusting!'

The new nurses were hardly settled in when news came of terrible losses at the Battle of Balaclava. Soon the number of injured doubled from 2,000 to 4,000 men.

Florence wrote to a friend in London, describing the scene.

'We now have four miles of beds, and not eighteen inches apart. ... As I did my night rounds among the wounded, there was not one murmur, not one groan. These poor fellows bear pain with superhuman heroism.' Then, on the subject of cleanliness, she added, 'We have no basins, not a bit of soap, not a broom. I have ordered 300 scrubbing brushes!'

Florence Nightingale was far from timid. When she saw something needed done, she went all out to make sure it was done.

'Every patient should have his own bed,' she demanded, 'and they should all have exactly the right food for their condition.'

When objections were raised about how to do that, she had her answer ready.

'Ward masters will have to be appointed. They will see to the running of their own wards and make sure they are kept clean.'

'But... but...' the official tried to argue. However, he didn't stand a chance. Florence continued, 'The hospital needs a governor with four men under him. One will organise the day-to-day running of the hospital, the second will arrange the food, the third will look after the furniture and clothing, and the fourth will be in charge of the doctors.'

The official was lost for words. Nurse Nightingale knew how to get things done!

Despite all that Florence and her nurses did, 3,000 soldiers died in battle, and a further 20,000 died of their injuries. That gave her much to think about, and Nurse Nightingale thought hard. Because of the detailed notes she always kept, she was full of ideas for improving army medical services. One of them was to open an Army Medical School, and she pushed and nagged until that happened. It took its first batch of students in 1860.

Soon after returning from the war, Florence became an invalid herself and spent most of her time in bed. That didn't stop her planning a better nursing service. Nor did it prevent her writing things down in one of her hundreds of notebooks.

'The first thing a nurse should think about is her patients,' she wrote. 'And the second is their need of fresh air. They should be able to see out the window, to hear friendly voices, to have peace from unfamiliar noises.'

'What else would you suggest?' a colleague who was visiting her asked, after reading her notes.

Florence pulled herself up in bed.

'Patients should have flowers round about them, food when they are able to take it, comfortable pillows supporting them. Hospitals should be kept as clean as humanly possible ... and patients' skin should be washed and dried carefully to prevent sores.'

'I think you should have a rest,' the visitor said.

Florence's eyes were closed, but she continued speaking.

'Nurses should wash their hands often. They should learn to watch every little detail...'

'She never stops,' the visitor said, as she left Florence's room.

'We should thank God for that,' the woman with her commented. 'Florence Nightingale's non-stop work has changed nursing amazingly, especially the nursing of soldiers.

FACT FILE

Nursing: Before Florence's efforts, nurses were not well-trained or highly regarded. Healthcare in Britain at that time was not very advanced, and hospitals were dirty and often dangerous places. Florence helped to change this situation after her return from the Crimea. Other nursing schools were modelled on the one that she founded, and the Royal College of Nursing was founded in 1916. Registration of nurses was introduced in 1921. This meant that nurses received a standard training. Now many nurses train in universities and qualify with a degree in nursing.

Keynote: Florence encountered a good deal of disapproval and resistance to her attempts to reform nursing. Even some of the army officials did not approve of her efforts, but she pressed on. Florence believed that God had called her to be useful and to try and help others. She was able to press on because she realised that serving God and helping people was more important than making sure that important people liked her.

Think: Florence found that she actually enjoyed helping people. When she was sad after the death of her cousin, she threw herself into trying to help people rather than brooding. It is easy to think that we only enjoy ourselves when we aren't thinking about anyone else, but that is not really the case. Think about some of the times that you have been able to help people. You will probably find that you actually enjoyed what you had to do for others.

Prayer: Lord Jesus, thank you for your example in working to help people and not being lazy. Thank you for the satisfaction that I can get from trying to do good for other people. Please help me to see the needs of others and to develop a social conscience just as Florence did. Please help those who aren't as well off as I am. Amen.

Lottie Moon

Lottie sat on the back step of her lovely home in Virginia, her cousin Sarah at her side.

'I just can't imagine living anywhere else but here,' said ten-year-old Lottie. 'It's the most beautiful place in the whole wide world.'

Sarah, looking around, agreed. 'I'm going to miss the plantation when we go to Jerusalem. There won't be servants there to do everything for us, and there won't be slaves to do the outside work either.'

In the distance, Lottie could see two slaves working. She wondered why her uncle was giving all this up to be a missionary.

'Do you really want to go?' she asked her cousin.

'I really do,' said Sarah. 'All of us do.'

Grabbing a handful of pea pods crossly, Lottie tried not to cry.

'Well, I don't know why,' she complained. 'The Bible is just a storybook, and it's a long way from Virginia to Jerusalem just to tell people fairy stories.'

Sarah looked sad. 'It's silly to say that.'

'It is not,' spat Lottie. 'It's missionaries that are silly, not me!'

When Sarah left for home that day, Lottie went to look for her older sister. She knew Orie would understand, for she didn't believe in God either.

'I hate when people go away,' Lottie told her father, three years later. 'Do you really have to go?'

Mr Moon smiled at his daughter. 'I'm afraid I do,' he said. 'But New Orleans is not on the other side of the world, and I'll be back before you have time to miss me.'

Lottie knew that wasn't true, because she loved her father very much and missed him even if he was only away overnight.

Just six days later, an envelope was delivered to her home. It was edged in black, and Mrs Moon's hand shook as she slit it open. And in the minute it took her mother to read the letter, Lottie's life changed forever. Her father had been aboard a steamboat that went on fire. Although he jumped to safety, Mr Moon died soon afterwards of a heart attack. Lottie's mother wept and prayed, but the girl had nobody to pray to because she didn't believe in God.

In 1855, when she was fourteen years old, Lottie went with her younger sister to Virginia Female Seminary to study.

Sometimes Lottie could be very serious, but there was a mischievous side to her too.

'It's April Fools' Day tomorrow,' she remembered in her bed, when nearly everyone else was asleep. 'What could I do for that?'

She thought, and thought, and thought. Then she nearly laughed aloud. It seemed to her that the days were full of bells tolling. One chime told them it was time to get up, another that lessons were beginning, and another that dinner was ready. Lottie and her friends felt bells tolling ruled their lives.

'I know what I'll do,' she decided, slipping silently out of bed. Taking her rolled-up blankets with her, she left the room and went to the bottom of the bell tower. Then she climbed the belfry ladder, crossed the rafters and climbed up a second ladder to the big brass bell.

'Shh,' she said to both herself and the bell, as she wrapped her blankets round the clapper so that, when the bell was rung to wake them at 6 am, there would be just the dullest of thuds. And that's what happened.

'Who was responsible for that little trick?' the girls were asked.

There was no point in denying it, for Lottie was the only one who had no blankets on her bed!

When she moved on to college in 1857, Lottie enjoyed much more freedom.

'Do you need help?' she would ask her friends, as they struggled with their languages. She had no trouble learning languages and, at the end of Lottie's first year, she was top of the class in Greek, French, Spanish and Italian!

'What does the D stand for in Lottie D. Moon?' one of her friends asked, as they walked to their French class.

'It stands for Devil,' Lottie laughed.

Her friend's eyes opened wide. 'Does it really?'

Lottie hooted with laughter. 'It would suit me,' she giggled. 'The only reason I ever go to church is to see the good-looking boys and to pick holes in the minister's sermons.'

Although she knew that was true, her friend was still not convinced that D stood for Devil. It didn't.

'What are you two talking about?' Lottie asked Kate and Laura.

The girls looked uncomfortable.

'We were discussing whether to go to the special services at the Baptist Church,' Kate admitted.

'I suppose I could give myself an 18th birthday treat and go along too,' teased Lottie. 'That could be quite a laugh.'

Her friends looked embarrassed and changed the subject. They were even more embarrassed when Lottie appeared at the first service and took a seat right at the front of the church! And their faces were plum-coloured by the time their friend had looked round the church for them and winked.

'I must be losing my touch,' Lottie thought, as the service went on. 'I've not wanted to burst out laughing once so far. What a waste of time!'

That night she tossed and turned, and turned and tossed.

'This pillow's too hard,' she thought, punching it into a new shape.

'I wish that dog would stop barking! It's keeping me awake.'

At last, deciding that she just wasn't going to get to sleep, she turned on her back and thought.

'I wonder if there is anything in Christianity. I stopped believing because I saw Christians arguing with each other when I was a little girl, but maybe that was a bit rash,' she reasoned. 'That's not really a logical reason for giving something up, I suppose. People might argue over a game, but that doesn't mean they should stop playing it for ever.'

By the following morning, Lottie had decided that she would become a Christian. As she knew there was an early-morning prayer meeting, she got up in time to go to it.

'What does she want?' asked Kate, who was there before her. 'I bet she's looking for trouble.'

But Lottie was not. She was looking for a Saviour, the Lord Jesus Christ. And by the end of the day she had found him. Lottie D (not for Devil) became a Christian.

After training to be teachers, Lottie and her friend Anna opened a school for girls in Cartersville, Georgia. And while they were working there, God called them both to be missionaries in China. One of Lottie's sisters was already there.

'Getting to San Francisco is just about as big an adventure as the sea voyage,' Lottie thought as her train crossed America. 'I just can't believe we're travelling so fast. Someone told me the train is going at twenty-two miles per hour!'

But the next part of the journey was not so pleasant, as the new young missionary wasn't a good sailor. Her hand was very shaky as she wrote a description of a hurricane in her diary. What was written under that was steadier. 'I can see the coast of China at last. Tomorrow, 7th October, 1873, I will set foot on China for the very first time. I can hardly wait!'

Before she had been in China very long, Lottie was helping her sister run a school there. But something was bothering Lottie.

'I can't bear to look at the women's tiny feet,' she told her sister, Eddie. 'How do they make them so small?'

'Girls have their toes bent and tied under their feet until the bones break, when they are four or five years old. After that has happened, their toes can be turned back towards their ankles. They are then bound tightly to stop them from growing any bigger.'

Looking at a girl who was staggering along the road, it was obvious to Lottie that she was in great pain.

Eddie shook her head. 'Some girls can't walk for months when their feet are first bound. And none can run or skip ever again. But that's not the worst of it.'

Lottie wondered what could be worse than that.

'Some girls develop infections and eventually lose their legs. None recover from that. They all die.'

The smell of the market they were walking in, had been making Lottie feel squeamish, but the thought of what Chinese girls went through made her feel thoroughly sick.

'What are they saying?' the new missionary asked her sister.

Eddie translated. 'They want to know if you are married, how many children you have, and why your mother-in-law lets you go out.'

'I don't have a mother-in-law!' Lottie protested. 'It's not their business anyway. And can you tell those girls to stop pawing me.'

A teenager was running her hand through Lottie's ringlets, and two smaller girls stroked her silk dress with their very grubby fingers.

'You are going to have to learn to put up with that,' Eddie warned. 'And worse too.'

'Worse?' queried her sister.

'You'll have to get used to being called Foreign Devil and other such nasty names.'

Lottie had a sudden flashback to her college days. 'Is Lottie, D for Devil, Moon coming back to plague me?' she wondered.

Eddie became unwell, and Lottie took her back to America. When Lottie returned to China, her dream was to open a school for girls.

'Why girls?' she was asked. 'They don't need to be educated to get married and have children.'

That kind of thinking really upset the missionary.

'Education will help free the girls,' she argued. 'At the moment they're not allowed to make any choices; everything is decided for them. They can't decide not to have their feet bound, but if they are educated they'll be able to choose to let their daughters run and jump and skip with normal comfortable feet. Girls who are educated will educate their daughters and things will be different for them.'

'You want to open a school here in Tengtchow?' she was asked.

Lottie said that was right.

'Well,' commented her companion. 'I don't think any girls will come.'

She could not have been more wrong. By the end of the school's first year, Lottie had thirteen pupils. Because nobody would pay to have a girl educated, the missionary had to pay all the expenses for the girls: food, medicine and accommodation. But she knew it was worth it.

In the winter of 1878, Lottie and another missionary went on a trip deep into the Chinese countryside to visit remote villages. They got such a welcome that they were able to tell many people about the Lord Jesus. She had prayed a lot about her disgust at dirt and smells, and about people touching her and asking personal questions. And on this trip, Lottie discovered that God had taken away her disgust. She just loved being with the villagers. In the years that followed, she had many trips to village communities and saw a number of people become Christians.

'I go south to P'ingtu next week,' Lottie told a new missionary. 'No white woman has been there before.'

'How will you get the people to accept you?' she was asked.

'I have my secret weapon,' smiled Lottie. 'Sugar cookies!'

As soon as she set up home in P'ingtu, the missionary baked some sugar cookies. Little boys who came to the door were first to try them. They liked them so much that they told the villagers about the strange, sweet food. Others came to her door, adults as well as children, and before long, Lottie's sugar cookies had won her many friends. When the weather in P'ingtu grew so cold she couldn't stop shivering despite wearing all her clothes at once, Lottie Moon had some Chinese clothes made for her. The villagers liked her even more for that, and because they liked her, they listened to her stories of Jesus.

'We have come on behalf of Dan Ho-bang,' said one of three men who came to her house. 'He wants you to go to our village and tell us about Jesus.'

Lottie went with the men and discovered that many people really wanted to know God's good news. Crowds came to Dan Ho-bang's house to hear what she had to say. To Lottie's delight, that was the beginning of a new and lively church.

It became difficult for Christians in China at the end of the 19th Century, and many thousands were killed. Dan Ho-bang was treated terribly. When Lottie heard that a crowd was beating him, she yelled above the noise.

'If you try to destroy the church here and the Christians who worship in it, you will have to kill me first. Our Master, Jesus, gave his life for us Christians, and now I am ready to die for him.'

'Then you will die, Foreign Devil,' a young man screamed, lifting a huge sword to strike Lottie down.

Suddenly his arm dropped, and the sword clanged to the ground. God had stopped him from killing the missionary. The crowd, confused by what they had seen, melted away.

'Let me help you,' Lottie said, lifting Dan Ho-bang to his feet and taking him back to his home.

'The white woman does the things that her Jesus did,' people said, who listened to Lottie and watched how she lived. And they were able to watch her as she grew old too, because she remained in China until 1912 and died on the ship as she travelled home to America.

FACT FILE

The Boxer Uprising. Much of the persecution of Christians in China at the end of the 19th century was due to a movement known as the Boxer Uprising. Big defeats in the European wars led to a lot of resentment of foreigners in China. The dowager empress of China allowed the growth of a secret, anti-foreign society known as the Boxers (or Righteous Fists). In 1899 they began to attack foreigners and Chinese Christians, whom they felt had adopted the religion of foreigners. In 1900 they besieged the Chinese capital, but this siege was eventually broken. Many Christians, both Chinese and foreign, were killed during the Boxer Uprising.

Keynote: Lottie was willing to go deep into China, even to places where no white woman had gone before, to tell people about Jesus. She was even willing to bake sugar cookies for them so that they would listen to her! The trip was dangerous, and she was in an unknown country where she didn't know anybody. Lottie was willing to do all of this because she realised that Jesus had come to save Chinese people just as much as white people.

Think: When Lottie was young, she didn't take Christianity very seriously at all, and she was annoyed when her uncle decided to go off to Jerusalem to be a missionary. She had written off Christianity because she had seen Christians arguing. She later realised that this did not really disprove the faith. Can you think of any other things that are true but people still argue about?

Prayer: Lord Jesus, thank you for the good news about what you did to save people from their sins. Thank you that we can believe it and know that it is true. Thank you for people who travel all over the world to tell people about you and for those who tell their next-door neighbours too. Please help everyone who tries to tell someone else about you today. Amen.

Ida Scudder

The eight girls in Dorm 3 raced to their beds, jumped in, pulled their blankets up to their chins and smiled sweetly when their teacher came in.

'Everyone tucked up and ready to sleep?' Miss Tomkins asked.

'Yes, Miss,' eight voices replied in unison.

'Goodnight, girls,' their teacher said.

'Goodnight, Miss Tomkins,' answered the girls sleepily.

But when the door clicked behind Miss Tomkins, all eight sat up in bed, as wide awake as could be.

'What are we going to discuss tonight?' Florence asked.

'Let's talk about being grown up,' suggested Mary. 'That always gives me something nice to dream about.'

Ida laughed quietly. 'We'll have to watch what we say or we'll give Mary nightmares!'

'What do you want to be, Ida?' Mary asked. 'And make it something nice.'

Ida lay back on her pillow. 'I'd like to marry a rich and handsome man; then I wouldn't have to work. I'd stay in bed until lunchtime each day reading and drinking coffee. Some afternoons I'd play tennis, and others I'd go driving. And there would be a party to go to every single evening. Most nights we'd not get home till about 3am, which is why I'd stay in bed till lunchtime.'

Florence giggled. 'I'm quite sure that dream won't come true.'

'Why not?' Ida demanded.

'Because you'll be a missionary like your parents, and that means you'll be poor and up early every morning. The only parties you'll get to are babies' birthday parties!'

Ida sat up crossly. 'I won't be a missionary!' she raged. 'I won't!'

Florence was sorry she'd upset her friend, so she tried to change the subject.

'What will you do when you grow up?' she asked the girl in the next bed.

Mary sighed dreamily. 'I think I might like to be a missionary,' she said. 'African and Indian children are so cute, and it would be warm in these faraway places. The food is exotic, and the clothes are so elegant. I can just see myself in a shimmering, gold sari.'

Ida sat up in bed. She'd heard quite enough nonsense and felt it was time to tell her friends what it was really like in India.

'It's not exotic at all,' she began. 'And the weather is much better here in America. In India it is either so hot that absolutely everything is covered in dust, or so wet that everything is drowned in mud.'

'Ugh!' said Mary. 'Maybe I'll stay right here.'

'And as for babies' birthday parties,' Ida went on, 'when I was just six years old, I had to feed children that were dying of starvation. They were so weak I had to break the bread into crumbs and put it into their mouths.' She shuddered at the memory. 'I've even seen dead bodies lying in the streets.'

'That decides it,' Mary announced. 'Whatever I do, I'll not be a missionary.'

'And nor will I,' said Ida. 'I definitely won't!'

Florence shushed her friends. 'Be quiet!' she whispered. 'I think I can hear Miss Tomkins!'

When the time came for the girls to leave school, Ida's mother was ill and needed her help.

'I've got to go back to India to help Mum,' she told Florence. 'But as soon as she's better, I'll be heading right home to America.'

'I'll write to you,' her friend promised. 'And I'll tell you all the fun things we're doing.'

So Ida found herself back in South India. She nursed her mother well, mostly because she wanted her to get better, but also because she wanted to leave India as quickly as she possibly could.

'Is that another letter from Florence?' Mrs Scudder asked Ida one day.

Her daughter nodded and took the letter to her room to read it in peace.

Ida felt so homesick for America as she read her friend's news of parties and picnics and boyfriends. And she was feeling sorry for herself when she heard footsteps outside on the veranda. When Ida went out, she found a tall Brahmin man there.

'Amma,' he said, bowing his head and holding his hands together, 'please come and help my wife.'

'What's wrong with her?' Ida asked.

'She is having a baby, and things are not well with her.'

'I'll get my father,' Ida told the man. 'He'll be able to help because he's a doctor.'

The Brahmin shook his head. 'It needs to be a woman,' he said. 'My religion won't allow a male doctor to see a female patient.'

Ida explained that she knew nothing about medicine and couldn't help.

That same night two other men came to ask her to help their young wives. In the morning, Ida heard that these three young women had all died because there wasn't a woman doctor to help them have their babies. Ida did some very hard thinking that sad morning, and she realised that God had to come first in her life, above friends and parties and everything else. And she knew what she had to do with her life. Ida went looking for her parents.

'I have something to tell you,' she announced, when she found them. 'I want to go back to America to study medicine, then I'll come and help the poor women who are not allowed to see a male doctor.'

On 1st January, 1900, Dr Ida Scudder arrived back in India. She was so excited at the prospect of seeing her parents again. But sad news was waiting for her.

'Your father's very ill,' she was told, 'and nothing seems to be helping him.'

Although the new, young doctor did all she could, her father's condition grew worse.

'I can't work on my own,' she worried. 'I thought Dad would be here to help me.'

'Even if I do recover,' her father told Ida, 'it will be a long time before I'm fit to work again. So I think you should make a start with the women.'

Ida felt that things were working out very badly. She prayed about what she should do and felt that God was showing her that her father was right. Doctor Ida set up a tiny clinic in the mission house that had been her childhood home, and within an amazingly short time poor women heard that she was willing to treat them and came to the clinic. Wealthier women also wanted her help, but they expected her to visit them in their homes.

Just five months after Ida arrived back in India, her father died.

'How am I going to cope with doing operations without Dad's advice?' she asked herself, over and over again.

But the day came when she had no choice but to perform a big operation on a very ill woman. When she had finished the surgery, Ida paced the veranda, not knowing if the woman would get better or die. But within two days her patient was sitting up in bed and doing very well. Ida thanked God from the bottom of her heart and did a further two operations almost immediately. Young Doctor Scudder very quickly became well known, and before long her work outgrew the mission bungalow, and a hospital was built. She had taken money from America to build a hospital at Vellore, but an outbreak of plague meant that it wasn't completed until 1902.

Doctor-Amma (that's what Ida was known as) worked hard to make the hospital as good as it could possibly be, and the nurses and other staff did too. Patients came from many miles away, almost all of them women who would not otherwise have got medical help at all, as the only other doctors were men. Many, many women who would have died had the hospital not been there, recovered from their illnesses and told all their friends about Doctor-Amma.

'We can't take on any more work,' the nursing sister told Ida one day. 'Between the hospital and your roadside clinics the staff are worked off their feet.'

Dr Scudder nodded in agreement. 'We need more staff,' she said, 'and not only nurses. We need more doctors too.'

'Would some come from America, or perhaps Britain, to help?' Sister asked.

'I don't think there's any chance of that,' Doctor-Amma said slowly ... something was buzzing round in her mind. 'Was this the time to tell Sister what she'd been thinking about for a long time?' Ida wondered. She decided it was.

'We've been training our own nurses for several years. Could we not train our own doctors?' she asked.

The Sister, who had been folding a sheet, stopped what she was doing and looked at her friend. 'You're not serious, are you?'

But Ida Scudder had never been more serious in her life.

For the following five years Ida discussed the possibility with people who knew about medical training, and with the Surgeon General in Madras. Eventually, in 1918, she got his permission to open a Christian medical school for girls, even though he made it quite clear he thought she wouldn't get any students, and even if she did, they wouldn't make it to be doctors. Ida advertised the course, and out of those who applied, she chose her first class of students. Before they arrived to begin their studies, Doctor-Amma arranged the building of a shed for dissections, hired a hall for lectures, and bought books, a microscope and a skeleton.

'Doctor-Amma is like a hen with chickens,' Sister told her friend Ruth, sometime after the medical school was up and running. 'Everywhere she goes she has this trail of students behind her. She does most of the lecturing herself, though the other doctors help, and they go on all her ward rounds with her. She takes hardly any time off.'

Ruth looked surprised. 'Does she teach them in the evenings too?' she asked.

'No,' Sister smiled. 'She plays tennis and basketball with them or takes them out in that car of hers.'

'She sounds more of a friend than a college principal,' Ruth suggested.

Sister laughed. 'Because she relaxes with them doesn't mean they get off lightly in their work. Let me tell you a story Ida told me just the other day.'

Sipping her tea, Ruth listened.

'It happened on a day when the locals were on holiday. When Doctor-Amma went into the lecture hall, one of the students asked if they might have a holiday too. Ida demanded to know why they should have a holiday when she'd been up till two in the morning preparing a lecture for them. She was so cross that she walked out of the lecture hall, banging the door behind her. A few hours later, the student who had asked for the holiday arrived at the hospital with flowers for Ida and to explain they had wanted the day off to revise for an exam!'

'What did Doctor-Amma say to that?' Ruth asked.

Sister grinned. 'She was so ashamed at having given them a row, she let them have the afternoon off to study and prepared a tea party to celebrate the holiday!'

The two women walked along the road towards the hospital.

'With all the girls being Christians, they'll no doubt forgive Doctor-Amma for her impatience,' said Ruth.

Sister looked at her. 'What makes you think they are all Christians?' she asked.

'I assumed they were because it's a Christian medical college.'

'Not at all,' her friend explained. 'Ida chose the cleverest students, not just the Christian ones. We have Hindu and Muslim girls as well. Of course, Ida prays for them and tells them about the Lord Jesus as well as about infectious diseases.'

It took several years to teach the girls all they needed to know to be doctors, but eventually the great day came when they took their final examinations. They sat the exam, not at the hospital, but at the university with all the other medical students. It was an anxious wait for the results. And when they came, the male students heard first.

'Only one in every five of them passed,' a university official told Ida.

The students overheard. 'That would mean only two out of the fourteen of us would pass,' she said to her friend.

Doctor-Amma looked sympathetic as the thought passed through her mind that none of them might pass at all. Eventually she was called into the office to be told the results.

'Here she comes,' one of her students whispered, as the office door opened.

'You've passed!' Ida told the girls. 'You've passed! Every one of you! Not only that, but four of you got First Class degrees, and another two won gold medals!'

The fourteen new, young doctors hugged and kissed each other in their excitement, and in the midst of the huddle was Ida Scudder, who was every bit as delighted as they were.

Ida Scudder retired in 1946, aged seventy-five, though she continued advising on difficult patients and teaching a weekly Bible Class for ten years after that. When she retired, one of her own students took over her work. Ida's first clinic had just one bed, but she lived to see the building of the Vellore Christian Medical School and College, with nearly 500 beds, 100 doctors, its own nursing school and a college taking 200 new medical students each year.

FACT FILE

India: Ida's parents were medical missionaries in India. India is a subcontinent south-west of China. When they were there, India was part of the British Empire. Parts of India were very poor indeed and were troubled by lack of food and proper medical care. When India became independent from Britain in 1947, the northern (and mainly Muslim) part was separated to form Pakistan. There are still problems with diseases such as leprosy and cholera in parts of India, and several aid agencies carry out a good deal of their work there.

Keynote: Ida knew what it meant to be a missionary in India because she had seen what her parents did. She did not have any of the romantic notions that some of her friends had. When she was a little girl, Ida knew that it would not be easy and did not want to be a missionary. But she went there all the same when she saw the need and felt God's call. Although the things that we are asked to do are not always pleasant at first, we will usually find, as Ida did, that they are worthwhile in the long run.

Think: There was a world of difference between the life that Ida led when she was in America with her friends, and that which she led in India, but God watched over her in both places. God knows us and can see us wherever we are in the world. He is able to care for us even when he asks us to go to faraway places that are different from anything that we know. When were you furthest from your home? What did it feel like?

Prayer: Lord Jesus, thank you for the way you helped sick people when you lived on earth, and the way you care for us today. Please bless missionary doctors who are willing to go and help the sick and suffering in faraway lands. Help me to be willing to do what you want me to do in my life. Amen.

Jeanette Li

When Mooi Nga[1] was five years old, she saw a big boy hurt a girl much younger than himself. Mooi Nga was furious! She punched the boy and, when he swore at her, she swore back. Mooi Nga's father passed along the road just as the fight took place.

'Mooi Nga, come here!' he called.

The child ran to his side, expecting her usual hug. Instead he marched her home and told his wife to punish her!

'That kind of behaviour is a disgrace to the family, and in public too!' he said crossly. 'Don't you ever do anything like that again!'

When her father thought she had been punished enough, he took the child out into the garden.

'Your name, Mooi Nga, means Jasmine Bud,' he told her. 'And that's a beautiful thing. When you were born, your mother thought that might tempt evil spirits to

1. At home Jeanette was called Mooi Nga. Her English name is Jeanette Li.

harm you; that's why she calls you Ch'ao Nga which means ugly crybaby.'

'Tell me about when I was born,' the girl asked.

Her father sighed deeply. 'When the midwife saw you were a girl, she wanted me to put you in an orphanage. But your mother and I couldn't do that. Even though you weren't a boy, you were precious to us, you were still a gift from the Buddha.'

Mooi Nga often thought back to that conversation, especially the following year, when life seemed to crash about her.

'What does it mean to be dead?' she asked her mother.

The poor woman's husband had just died, and she couldn't explain to her two little daughters that they would never see their father again.

'He's gone to be with the ancestors,' she said.

Even when Mooi Nga saw her father in his coffin, she could not take in that he had gone forever. Not only did the girl lose her father, very soon she lost her sister too. Her mother was tricked into giving her sister away in order to repay her father's debts.

Two years later, when Mooi Nga was eight years old, she suddenly became seriously ill.

'Take her to the Mission Hospital,' a relative said to her mother.

But her mother was too scared to do that.

'I've heard that they take children's eyeballs out,' she said fearfully. 'And I won't let them do that to my daughter.'

But Mooi Nga grew worse and eventually she was taken to the hospital where she was treated very well.

'Father! Where are you?' she called out all night in her fever.

'Your Heavenly Father is with you,' the missionaries told her. 'He won't leave you.'

But the little girl did not want a Heavenly Father; she wanted her dad back again. However, as the kind missionaries told her about God, she discovered that she did want a Heavenly Father after all, and that she wanted the Lord Jesus to be her Saviour. By the time she was well, Mooi Nga was a Christian. Both she and her mother were baptised not long afterwards, and then she became a pupil in the mission school.

It was 1915, and Mooi Nga was about to be married.

'I want to study,' she told her mother, 'not cook and clean for my husband and mother-in-law.'

'You have been promised to Lei Wing Kan since you were nine years old,' she was told. 'It is now time you were married.'

Although the girl argued her case loudly and strongly, the marriage still went ahead. She and her husband were both the same age; they were just fifteen. In the next few years they had a son and a daughter. Sadly, their little girl died. Eventually Lei Wing Kan went off to study and left his wife behind. They never lived together again, and Mooi Nga brought up her son, called Min Ch'iu, as a single mother. Her job as a teacher gave them enough money to live on.

When Min Ch'iu was twelve years old, his mother became a student at Bible School.

'God has put it in my heart to be a missionary right here at home to my own Chinese people,' Mooi Nga explained to him.

So in 1931 they moved to Changsha, and to Bible School. Three years later, newly qualified as a Bible woman, Mooi Nga prepared to go to the Black Dragon Province of Manchuria, and her son went into boarding school to finish his education. She sent him a letter shortly after she arrived.

'I boarded the train at Nanking on 24th August,' she wrote, 'and travelled the thousand miles to my new home. A missionary was on the platform waiting for me when I arrived. There are two lady missionaries here, and I will be working with them. We soon found a suitable house. But when we moved in, we discovered we were not the only residents. On the first night, I woke up with something crawling over my face. I turned on a light and saw cockroaches everywhere! The walls were thick with them. The next day we cemented all the cracks we could find and hoped that would stop them coming in. But we were woken by the tapping of hundreds of tiny cockroach feet! Eventually we got rid of the cockroaches ... only to be overrun with mice and rats. Now that we've trapped the last of them, we'll get on with our work for the Lord.'

Three months later, Mooi Nga wrote to her son again, this time with news of her first trip into the country.

'When we arrived in Mengshui, we made a procession around the town carrying a big poster announcing our meetings. One person carried the poster, another gave out leaflets about the Lord Jesus, and I rang a bell to attract people's attention. By the time we held our open-air service, quite a crowd had gathered around us. And at the end an old Christian man introduced himself and invited us to his home.'

But when she wrote at Christmas time, her letter painted quite a different picture.

'In Mengshui we rented a building large enough for over a hundred people. Because it had been empty for two years, draughts came in everywhere. Although there was a fire, it was impossible to keep warm. It was so cold that the tea we had left in the teapot froze and cracked the teapot! We are to be here till February next year, so please pray that your poor mother doesn't freeze to death.'

'What's the name of the man who comes round the doors selling things?' Mooi Nga asked her neighbour.

'He is Mr Wang,' she was told, 'and he sells jewellery, toys, kitchen idols and images of Buddha.'

The missionaries took every opportunity to tell Mr Wang about Jesus, and eventually he became a Christian.

'I don't know what to do,' he told Mooi Nga soon afterwards. 'I have a stock of idols and Buddhas still to sell, and I can't afford just to destroy them.'

'A Christian can't sell idols,' he was told. 'God would not like that.'

Over the next week or two Mr Wang's sales went right down until he wasn't earning enough to keep his family. One night he heard a sermon that showed him what the problem was. He hadn't destroyed the idols, and God was not pleased with him.

'I'm going right home to destroy them all,' he told his friends at church. He did just that, and the following day people started buying things from him again.

In the spring of 1940, Mooi Nga moved to Taikang. She was unsure of how to begin her work there, but God showed her she should first work with children. 'But how can I interest them?' she wondered.

Just then a cart of grass was driven along the road, and she noticed children darting out and stealing grass off the cart.

'Excuse me!' she called to the man whose cart it was. 'If I pay for the grass the children have stolen, will you promise not to get them into trouble?'

The man agreed, and told her to take the boys and girls away and teach them not to steal. Very soon she had a lively children's club. Not only did the children stop stealing, but they also learned about Jesus.

During the Second World War there was also a war between China and Japan. The

Japanese occupied Manchuria, the area in which Mooi Nga worked.

'The Emperor of Japan has passed a law saying that every home must have a shrine, a god-shelf, at which they are to worship the Emperor idols.'

'Every home!' declared Mooi Nga. 'There won't be idols in my home! And I most certainly won't be worshipping the Emperor of Japan!'

One day an official came to see if the missionary was keeping the law.

'I will only worship the Lord God,' she told him, showing him where in the Bible it said idols should not be worshipped.

'Do you worship your ancestors?' the man asked.

'No,' Mooi Nga explained. 'I only worship the one true God.'

From then on she was watched very closely and with great suspicion. Friends of hers were arrested as prisoners of war. Although things became very difficult and dangerous, Mooi Nga continued her missionary work and did good even to those who were determined to harm her.

By 1948 most countries were beginning to recover after the Second World War, but China was going from bad to worse. The Communists had taken over the country, and people were terribly oppressed. Mooi Nga went back to her home area of Tak Hing, where she was asked to take over the running of an orphanage.

'Why should I do that?' she asked. 'My job is to tell people about Jesus.'

'We believe you are the right person,' she was told.

And after she had prayed about it, the missionary decided they were right. Her work changed completely, as she found herself in charge of an orphanage full of needy children.

'What age of children do you have to care for?' Mooi Nga's son asked in a letter.

'We have both boys and girls,' she replied, 'and they are from a few months old to fourteen or fifteen. One of the first things I did when I came here was get some good cats to catch the rats. But they were so good the Communists stole them!'

Rats were not Mooi Nga's only problem. The orphanage had been run badly, and she set out to improve it.

'We have sixty-four children here,' she told her helper, 'so we need to divide them into groups, each group with an older person in charge. And we need to encourage the children to work and study. If they are busy, they'll be less aware of the troubled time we are living in, and of the dangers all around us.'

But Mooi Nga could not protect the children from the Communists, because they were all around. Nor could she protect herself.

'There are some people looking for you,' the water-carrier told her, one morning.

'What do they want?' she asked.

The old man did not know.

Mooi Nga didn't go to look for the visitors as it was Sunday, and the service was just about to begin. They found her afterwards and told her she was under arrest.

How glad the orphanage staff were to see her back late that night. But Mooi Nga knew that she would be arrested again and that she would not get out in a day next time.

The People's Government of Communist China declared that there was no God. Those who were 'foolish' enough to think that God did exist were required to register with their local authorities. A law passed in 1950 limited what Christians could do and made mission work illegal. The Red Army ruled the country and everyone from the richest to the poorest, was closely controlled. Christians were constantly spied on and always in danger.

The following year, while Mooi Nga was working in the church garden, more than sixty men entered the church and the orphanage.

'Give us the keys to all the rooms, chests, drawers and desks,' they demanded.

She gave them what they wanted.

'What are you doing?' Mooi Nga asked, as the men sealed each door with an official seal.

A soldier stared her in the eye. 'The People's Government of China is taking over the orphanage and church,' he said in his bossiest voice.

The missionary continued to work at the orphanage under a Communist overseer. It saddened her terribly when the older children were sent out to beg or to spy.

Over the years that followed, Mooi Nga was imprisoned several times; she was even brainwashed. Following her release in 1953, she moved to Canton, then later made her home in Hong Kong, where she continued in mission work. By then her son and his family had made their home in the United States, and in 1962 she joined them there. Mooi Nga's heart was always with her beloved people in China, to many of whom she had given a hope and a future when life was unspeakably difficult.

FACT FILE
The Cultural Revolution: The Communists took control of China in 1948 in a revolution which sought to overturn many of the traditional Chinese practices and make it impossible ever to return to capitalism. People from universities were forced to work in the fields, and many private businesses and organisations like the orphanage were seized. Children in schools were forced to read the writings of the Communist leader. China is one of the few countries in the world that still maintains a Communist system of government although it has been trying to engage more and more with the outside world in recent years.

Keynote: Mooi Nga wanted her dad when she was ill and feverish in the Mission Hospital, and the thought of a heavenly Father did not cheer her up much. Before she left the hospital, however, she had discovered her need of her heavenly Father and she went on to tell lots of other people about God so that they could know their heavenly Father too. The missionaries had said that he would never leave her, and he didn't, even in the dark days of the Japanese invasion and the Cultural Revolution.

Think: Mooi Nga's mother was scared to take her to the Mission Hospital because she thought that they would gouge her eyes out. Of course, the missionaries were there to help the people not to hurt them. It might seem as if our parents and teachers are doing things just to take away all our fun but they do it for our good. We may even discover, as Mooi Nga did, that we learn things from them about Jesus that are far more amazing than anything that we could have imagined.

Prayer: Lord Jesus, thank you for being in control even in the dark and difficult times. Please help me to trust you even when things do not go as I would like them to. Thank you for the people who continued to trust in you even through the Cultural Revolution. Please be with all those who are suffering because they trust in you today. Amen.

Henrietta Mears

Elizabeth pulled the long, red gown over her head and thrust her arms down its sleeves.

'You'll have to roll up the sleeves,' Henrietta told her, 'or you'll not be able to eat your cookies.'

The two girls giggled. Henrietta had on a black, velvet dress that went down to the ground then wrapped itself round her feet. Over that she wore a lacy stole. And on top of the miniature fashion statement was a hat, and what a hat!

'Did your mum ever wear that hat?' Elizabeth asked, trying hard not to laugh.

Henrietta managed to get to the full-length mirror without tripping over the crumpled velvet at her feet. Standing in front of it, she gave a report on herself of the kind that was sometimes in the Minnesota newspapers.

'Miss Henrietta Mears from Duluth was present at the function,' she said, in her most grown-up and official voice. 'She wore a shimmering dress of rich, black velvet, topped with a handmade, lace stole. Her hat, created by the designer Blah-di-Blah, was a confection of delicate lace flowers and bird feathers. An ostrich feather, dyed a delightful shade of powder blue, wrapped itself round the brim and reached out to tickle the neck of her escort. Miss Mears' gold-rimmed spectacles glinted from underneath her splendid hat.'

Laughter tears streamed down Elizabeth's face as Henrietta turned round from the mirror, and they both dissolved in giggles when she tripped over the tail of her dress and landed on the bed beside her friend. The confection of delicate lace flowers and bird feathers sailed off her head and landed on her doll's house.

As they packed the dressing-up clothes away, the two girls worked carefully. The dresses were folded into a trunk, with camphor balls in between them to keep away the moths. Scarves, stoles and gloves were wrapped in tissue paper and placed in a drawer. They had just tidied things away when there was a knock at the door.

'Time for cookies,' Henrietta's sister Margaret said, smiling broadly, her head peering round the door frame at the two youngsters.

'Have you been dressing up again?' she asked.

Henrietta said that they had.

'I don't know anyone else who has so many dressing-up clothes,' Elizabeth commented.

'That's because you don't know anyone else who has six brothers and sisters, and whose next sister up is eleven years older than her. Lots of these clothes were mine, but they are way out of fashion nowadays.'

Elizabeth looked puzzled. 'I didn't know you have six brothers and sisters,' she said to her friend.

'Two of them died and are in heaven with Jesus,' Henrietta explained.

'I love Easter!' Henrietta announced. 'It's one of my favourite times of the year.'

'Mine too,' said her mother. 'The day that reminds us about Jesus rising from the dead is very special indeed.'

The seven-year-old looked serious. 'That's because he died to save us from our sins,' she agreed, 'so that we can be forgiven and go to heaven, like my brother and sister.'

Mrs Mears was brushing Henrietta's long hair when the girl turned round and looked at her mother seriously.

'I'm ready to become a Christian and join the church,' she said.

Her mother stopped brushing. 'I'm afraid you're so young that some people might think you don't really understand.'

'But I do understand,' insisted the girl. 'I know I'm a sinner and I know Jesus is my Saviour. That means I'm ready to join the church.'

Wrapping her daughter's ringlets round her fingers, Mrs Mears suggested that they speak to their minister. A few weeks later Henrietta and her cousin, who was just the same age, stood at the front of the congregation and answered questions about their faith in the Lord Jesus. A week or two later, the girls were baptised and became members of the church.

'Why do we have to get up early even on Saturdays and holidays?' Henrietta asked her sister at the end of the next school term.

'Mum doesn't like us wasting time,' Margaret said. 'Have you ever seen her waste a minute?'

Henrietta sat up in bed and thought.

'No,' she decided. 'If she has five minutes between doing things, she plays the piano or reads a little bit of a book.' The girl giggled at something that came into her mind. 'Sometimes when I'm reading,' she said, 'Mum snaps my book shut and asks me what I've read, just to make sure I'm taking it in.'

'I know,' laughed Margaret. 'She used to do the same to me!'

That evening, before settling down to sleep, Henrietta thought about her mother's life and wrote down some things her mother did that she wanted to do too.

'I will never waste time,' she wrote. 'I will always read good books. I will help people in need. I will talk to others about Jesus. I will pray for others as well as for myself.'

'I'm not feeling very well,' Henrietta told her mother one day.

'What's the matter with you?' she was asked.

'I ache all over and I have a headache,' the twelve-year-old explained.

'That sounds like flu,' Mrs Mears decided. 'Go to bed and you may feel better after a sleep.'

Henrietta went to bed and slept, but she felt worse when she woke up. In the days that followed, her muscles grew stiff and sore, and her joints ached terribly. She had a raging fever and was very unwell. Mr and Mrs Mears sent for the doctor. After he had examined the girl, he looked most serious.

'I'm afraid the news is not good,' he told Mrs Mears. 'Henrietta has muscular rheumatism. Recovery is a long and slow process, and not everyone recovers.'

'You mean it can be fatal?'

'Your daughter's a strong girl,' the doctor said gently. 'But, yes, it can be.'

Mrs Mears put her head in her hands. For a second the doctor thought she was crying, but she was praying for the daughter she loved so much.

Henrietta's condition grew worse over the weeks and months that followed, until she was hardly able to move at all.

'Some other children in the area have the same thing,' the doctor told Mrs Mears, when he visited. 'One of them is critically ill.'

'Who is that?' the woman asked.

When the doctor told her the girl's name, Mrs Mears recognised it as Henrietta's good friend. She died shortly afterwards.

As well as suffering from muscular rheumatism, Henrietta began having very serious nosebleeds. An elder from her church came and prayed for her, and they stopped right away, though her rheumatism remained the same. Henrietta could not walk more than a few steps for nearly two years. It was as though she was stuck in one position, and she wondered if she would be like that for the rest of her life. When friends came to visit her, Henrietta was laid on a little bed near the garden where she could talk to them and watch them playing their games.

'My legs can't run and jump now,' she told them. 'But my heart can still dance.'

Eventually, when the girl was fourteen years old, the elder came back and prayed with her again. God answered their prayers, and Henrietta immediately began to recover.

'I've learned a lot in these two years,' she told her sister. 'I've especially learned to trust my future to God and not to fret about it. But that doesn't stop me wondering what he has in store for me.'

Margaret looked at the frail teenager and wondered the same thing.

A further challenge faced Henrietta when she started studying at the University of Minnesota. She had always worn spectacles, but she noticed that her eyesight was getting worse.

'You have a choice,' the eye specialist told her. 'You can give up reading and keep your eyesight, or you can continue reading and studying and be blind by the time you are thirty.'

Henrietta thought long and hard about that, and prayed over it too.

'If I'm going to be blind by the time I'm thirty,' she decided, 'then blind I shall be! But I'll want something in my head to think about, so I'm going to study as hard as I can for as long as I can.'

And that's what she did. After doing very well at university, she became a school teacher and Sunday schoolteacher too.

'I really need your help,' Margaret Mears said. 'The girls in my Sunday school class call themselves The Snobs. They won't let anyone else join the class, and they won't listen to me either!'

Henrietta took over the class, and the girls changed a lot. Two of them even went round the neighbourhood inviting other girls in! One week later, fifty-five girls turned up, and within ten years Henrietta's class numbered over 500! A special hall had to be built for them.

'What hat will Teacher have on today?' the girls used to ask. 'Will it have ostrich feathers or wax grapes on it?'

Henrietta was popular, and her amazing collection of hats became famous!

Henrietta Mears' 30th birthday came and went, and much to her delight her eyesight did not fail. It seemed that she was not becoming blind after all.

In 1928, when Henrietta was thirty-eight years old, she and her sister Margaret moved to Hollywood. She had accepted a job as Director of Christian Education at the First Presbyterian

Church of Hollywood. When she arrived, there were 450 students; two-and-a-half years later the number had grown to 4,200.

'How does she do it?' people asked.

One man who knew her well answered the question. 'She trusts in God and expects him to do great things. When Henrietta prays, she really expects answers. As soon as she opens her eyes, she looks around to see what the answer is.'

'You want us to write our own Sunday school books!' one of her teachers said. 'What's wrong with the ones we use at present?'

Henrietta explained that she had been unable to find teaching books that really taught what the Bible said.

'Most of them seem to be written by people who don't believe the Bible, and what's the use of teaching children that what the God of truth says is not always true? Do you know what a boy said to me the other day?' she asked the teacher. 'He told me he didn't want to go to Sunday school any more because he was told the same story over and over again, and each time it just got dumber! We've got to make sure that doesn't happen here!'

That was the beginning of Henrietta writing Sunday school lessons, and it ended up as a publishing company that supplied books by the thousand! At the end of 1933, just five years after she went to Hollywood, she had 6,500 pupils in her Sunday school, and over 13,000 copies of her workbooks had been sold in twenty-five states of the USA. Gospel Light Press, as the company was called, grew to be very famous.

'It's grand having young people on Sundays,' Henrietta told her fellow teachers, 'but we want to take them off to camps too, so that we can have longer spells of time with them.'

'You mean conferences for the university students?' one asked.

'I mean good fun Bible holidays for anyone, clever or not!'

One campsite was found, then another, then a third, and many young people became Christians at them.

'I have a dream for a much bigger campsite,' Henrietta said to her sister Margaret.

'That's your motto, "Dream Big",' Margaret laughed.

'So it is!' agreed Henrietta, as she straightened her hat in the mirror. 'I like this one,' she added. 'The feathers along the side look really pretty.'

'I've heard about a place called Forest Home,' a friend told the Mears sisters. 'And I'm taking you to see it.'

They drove to view the beautiful house and estate.

'This is the most elegant place I've ever seen,' said Henrietta, 'but you can drive right past, because we can't possibly afford it.'

'The place is worth $350,000,' their friend Bill explained. 'Let's try offering $50,000 and see what happens.'

The offer was put in, and people were asked to pray about it. Months passed, then one day there was a tremendous thunderstorm near Forest Home. Trees crashed down, some cabins were destroyed. Hillsides were washed away, but Forest Home and the campsite round about it escaped serious damage. In the calm after the storm, Henrietta's telephone rang.

'It's Bill,' a voice said at the end of the line. 'The son of the owner of Forest Home has offered to sell it to us for $30,000!'

A day or two later, when the announcement was made in church, Henrietta's hat was the most amazing celebration of colour. But it was nothing to the joy in her heart. She was dreaming big, and in her big dreams she saw many hundreds of young people becoming Christians at Forest Home. And because Henrietta's dreams were also her prayers, she saw them come true.

FACT FILE

Hats: Henrietta was well known for her collection of spectacular hats. In the 19th and early 20th centuries it was much more common for ladies to wear hats when they went out (and especially when they went to church) than it is today. Hats are still worn at certain social occasions like weddings. One of the best known in Britain is Royal Ascot, which is a series of horse races. Many women attend, often in very fancy and expensive hats.

Keynote: Henrietta saw her mother's good example and wanted to follow it. The good things Mrs Mears did, she had learned from the Bible. Later on, Henrietta became a good example to those who saw her successes in Sunday school teaching. The Bible tells us that it is important that we encourage one another in faith by words and example. Trying to read good books, help people in need, tell others about Jesus and pray for others as well as ourselves, are good ways to start doing this.

Think: After Henrietta went to the First Presbyterian Church of Hollywood, she decided that she needed to write her own material because the materials that they were using did not really teach what the Bible said. She realised how important it was to teach what the Bible actually said. The Bible tells us that God hears and answers the prayers of people who trust in him. Henrietta didn't just believe that, she acted on it. She was ambitious in what she tried to achieve for God, and she was successful because she did it prayerfully.

Prayer: Lord Jesus, thank you for living a life that was such a good example for all of us. Help me to follow your example and that of those around me who obey you. Thank you for the Bible and for all the amazing promises that it has for us. Please help me to really believe and trust when I pray to you. Amen.

Bessie Adams

An easterly wind blew along the English Channel, and it seemed to blow its way through Bessie. She ran to heat herself up and arrived home puffed but reasonably warm.

'My,' said her mother, 'you're in a right hurry today.'

'I ran because I was shivering with cold,' the girl explained.

Mrs Miners took a long, hard look at her daughter.

'That coat's too short and too tight,' she decided. 'The buttons hardly close on you. No wonder you're feeling the cold.' 'Do I need a new coat?' the eleven-year-old asked, knowing that coats cost money, and that with so many brothers and sisters there was not much of that to go round. Smiling at her daughter, Mrs Miners explained what she would do. 'You remember your sister's coat from two years ago?' she asked.

Bessie nodded.

'Well, there's plenty of material in it to make you a coat that will look quite different. I'll unpick all the seams and cut one to a new design. And I'll turn the material inside out so that it looks like new. Would you like navy trimming round the collar and pocket flaps?'

Thrilled at the idea, Bessie nodded her head eagerly.

That very night, Mrs Miners looked out the old coat and started unpicking its seams. Bessie could see that it was a lot of work, but she knew that her mother was enjoying making her something new. Even though they had a big family - Bessie was the eighth of twelve children - somehow their parents made each one feel special.

Although Bessie's new coat was ready the following Friday, she decided that she wouldn't wear it until Sunday, so that it would get its very first showing at church. 'We must look like a snake winding its way along the road,' one of her brothers teased, as they walked to the morning service. 'There is such a long string of us!' Bessie laughed. This was her favourite day of the week. The family was all together. There was no school, and the house was full of joy. When Bessie was a grown-up thinking back to her childhood home, she often remembered the joy she had known there.

'Do you really like going to church so often?' a friend asked Bessie the following Monday. The girl looked surprised at the question. 'Yes,' she said. 'I love it! Don't you?'

Her friend scowled. 'I don't,' she grumbled. 'Sunday's a horrible day. We're not allowed to do anything interesting and the church services are so boring.'

Bessie was shocked at the idea. 'I've never even been bored on a weekday!' she laughed. 'And Sundays in our home are really special. Usually we all gather round the old pump organ and sing together.' 'Ugh!' her friend said. 'You mean you have another service at home!'

'Will you come to the shop with me,' her friend asked some time later. Bessie was happy to do that, but what happened in the shop troubled her for months until she could sort it out. Having bought what she went for, her friend was about to leave the shop counter when she noticed a shilling lying on it. Quick as a flash she picked it up and put it in her pocket.

'Look what I've got!' the girl told Bessie when they were a safe distance away. Bessie's eyes nearly popped out of her head at the sight of the shilling! 'Let's go and buy sweets,' her friend suggested. 'Then we'll find a den and eat them.'

Because Bessie came from such a big family, there was rarely any money for sweets. She went along with her friend and watched as she chose chocolate and candy bars. Then the pair of them headed for their den to eat them. But even as the chocolate melted in her mouth, Bessie's enjoyment of it melted away. Although she hadn't stolen the money, she knew that what she was doing was wrong. It took her a long time to do it, but she saved up a shilling and returned it to the lady who ran the shop.

By the time Bessie was twelve years old, she knew a lot about money. She knew that you didn't have to have much to be happy, and that although her parents had no extra money at all, God had always given the whole family all that they needed. From the escapade with the shilling, she learned that money you should not have brings no enjoyment at all.

When Bessie was sixteen years old, she was sitting one day in church when her life changed completely.

'God really spoke to my heart,' she explained to her friend the following morning. 'I got up and walked to the front of the church because I wanted to ask the Lord Jesus to forgive my sins and to save me.'

Her friend looked puzzled. 'But you're not a sinner!' she said. 'You've never been brave enough to do anything wrong!' Bessie explained that she **was** a sinner - that she had done, said and thought many wrong things - and that she needed to be forgiven before she could go to heaven. 'You'll be wanting to be a missionary before long!' her friend teased.

Something in Bessie's heart thrilled at the very thought.

'Good afternoon,' a warm, Irish voice said. Bessie looked up from the counter of the little restaurant in which she worked. 'Good afternoon,' she replied. 'What can I get you?'

After serving the young man, the two got into conversation. He was a preacher, and they found themselves talking about their faith. What he said made a great impression on the girl.

'Lord,' Bessie prayed, after her customer had paid his bill and left, 'I'll do anything you want me to do. I'll be anything you want me to be. I'll go anywhere you want me to go.'

And having prayed that prayer, Bessie wondered what God would do with her life. From the rugged coastline of her home village of Porthleven, Bessie could look out to the English Channel. Most often what caught her eye was her father's fishing boat, but from time to time she saw a ship voyaging west.

'I wonder where that's going,' she would find herself thinking. 'Maybe it's making its way to Africa or India or the South Sea Islands. Perhaps one day God will call me to go abroad as a missionary for him, and the family will watch my ship heading out past the Isles of Scilly to the Atlantic Ocean.'

Bessie smiled at that memory when God did show her what he wanted her to do. And he used another customer at the restaurant to point her in the right direction. He was with a group called the Friends Evangelistic Band, that toured rural villages telling people about Jesus. When she thought about the work they did, she knew in her heart that she should join them.

'But I'd need to leave home,' she worried. 'And my family mean so much to me. I just can't imagine not being with them. Can God really be calling me to do that?'

Bessie thought about it, prayed about it and eventually talked to her minister, before coming to a final decision.

'I believe that God's calling me to join the Friends Evangelistic Band,' she told her parents. 'But the minister doesn't agree,' she added honestly.

Bessie's father smiled gently. 'He told me so. I'm afraid he doesn't think a young woman should be touring the country in a horse-drawn gypsy caravan, even if she has another young woman with her. Nor does he think you should work for a group that doesn't pay its workers.'

'God will supply all I need,' Bessie said confidently.

Her parents smiled. 'We agree with you,' her mother said. 'He's supplied all we've ever needed. If that's what you feel God wants you to do, then do it with our blessing.'

The horse-drawn caravan became a well-known sight in Cornish villages, and Bessie and her fellow missionaries were welcomed as they travelled round the country lanes. 'Look what I found!' she exclaimed when they arrived back from visiting a village. 'This was under the caravan step.' Opening the basket, they discovered it was full of good things: six eggs, a newly-baked loaf, a tin of corned beef, some milk and a little money wrapped in a twist of brown paper. Sitting on the grass beside the basket, the two young women thanked God for giving them just what they needed.

In 1938, a young man appeared on the scene, one who was doing the same kind of work. His name was Kenneth Adams, and just three months later Bessie became his wife. After their wedding they went off on a touring honeymoon, eventually arriving at

Campbeltown in the west of Scotland, where Kenneth had held missionary meetings the previous year. As they sat on the slopes of Beinn Ghuilean overlooking Campbeltown Loch, they talked about their hopes and plans for the future. They didn't know where God would lead them, or exactly the kind of work he wanted them to do, but they felt it right to make an important decision about their future.

Within a few days of being married, they committed themselves to doing God's work without receiving any payment ... because they believed that God would provide everything they needed. And he did, as they discovered while they toured the villages Bessie had grown to love. Their home was another gypsy caravan, and their equipment was a tent that could seat 150 people, and a big box of Christian books. What they didn't know was that the books held the key to an amazing future together.

The young missionaries were just coming to the conclusion that God could really use a Christian literature team when a letter arrived. It had 'Confidential' written on the envelope.

'I think I know what this is about,' Kenneth said.

Bessie smiled. 'So do I.'

They opened the letter to find they were both correct. The Friends Evangelistic Band had written asking them to establish a literature ministry to service its travelling workers. Kenneth and Bessie gladly agreed to give up their village meetings for a year to start the new work, if they would be allowed to go back to their gypsy life thereafter. But God had other plans.

The literature work grew, and the young couple knew that God wanted them to continue in it. Eventually, when they took over the work and founded Christian Literature Crusade (CLC) in 1941, they could never have guessed what the outcome would be. Two years later, someone wrote an article suggesting that they should aim to have 200 Christian bookshops and become a kind of 'spiritual Woolworths'! Kenneth and Bessie swallowed hard because they were wise enough to recognise the danger of things growing too quickly.

Within twenty years CLC had grown and spread to many countries of the world, and Kenneth and Bessie had made their home in Fort Washington, near Philadelphia, U.S.A. By then they had two daughters, Margaret and Janet, who became very used to waving their father goodbye as he set off on his travels to visit the ever-expanding shops and workers of CLC.

'Do you mind Kenneth being away so often?' someone asked Bessie one day. She smiled before answering. 'Of course I miss him a lot,' she said. 'But he was the Lord's before he was mine, so I can hardly complain about him doing the Lord's work.' The friend had another question she wanted to ask. 'Do you not mind that he's able to do missionary work while you're left here at home?'

Bessie looked seriously at the person who had asked the question, then her face broke into a smile. 'My dear,' she said kindly. 'I don't know what my husband has done this morning, but I've already spoken to two people about the Lord.'

Her friend looked shamefaced. 'That was a really stupid question,' she admitted. 'Of all the people I've ever met, you are the one who speaks to most people about Jesus.' When Margaret and Janet were old enough, Bessie began to join Kenneth on his travels. But she never felt any more a missionary when she was abroad than she did when she was at home.

CLC spread throughout the world, with all of its workers relying on God to supply their needs. Bibles and challenging Christian books were not only sold from shops, but also from market stalls and barrows. Kenneth and Bessie visited as many of the workers as they possibly could. Their passports were full of interesting stamps from which you could almost make an alphabet of places. Among other countries God built up the work of CLC in Africa, Brazil, Chile, Dominica, Europe, Finland, Guyana, Hong Kong, Indonesia, Japan, Korea, Liberia, Mozambique, New Zealand, Panama, Romania, Scotland, Thailand, Uruguay, Venezuela and Wales. Perhaps one day CLC will also work in countries beginning with O, Q, X, Y and Z!

'You could have been a wealthy woman with a worldwide chain of shops,' someone commented to Kenneth and his wife, when they were old enough to retire but still working.

'I am,' Bessie replied. 'I may have no money except what we need today, but I have all the love of a worldwide family and the riches of heaven to look forward to one day. You can't be richer than that!'

Bessie died in 1986, and she is now enjoying all of heaven's riches in the presence of Jesus whom she loved and served.

FACT FILE

Passports: Bessie's husband, Kenneth, travelled all over the world because of his work with CLC. If you want to travel from one country to another, you need a passport. This is a small book with your photo and some information about you. It is important because it gives proof of identity, which means that people can't enter or leave countries illegally. When you enter a foreign country, they will often put a stamp in your passport to show that you have visited that country.

Keynote: Bessie never had much money. Even when she was a little girl, her family was large and they did not have a lot of money. She learned, after her friend stole the shilling, that money itself does not make us happy, especially if the money is not really ours. She never had a job with a settled wage although she worked hard for all of her adult life. Bessie never lacked anything that she needed.

God always provided for her and those around her. God will always provide for those who trust in him.

Think: Bessie's friend thought that she might be frustrated because her husband was travelling all over the world doing missionary work while she had to stay at home. Bessie was able to show her that she could talk to people about Jesus in everyday situations too. God can use us wherever we are, even when the situation doesn't seem very fancy or glamorous. Think about ways in which you can try to serve God where you are just now.

Prayer: Lord Jesus, thank you for providing all that we need to live. Please help me to remember to thank you for my food and all the other practical things that you give me. Thank you for the gospel and for the hope that it gives us. Help me to believe it with all of my heart and mind. Amen.

Betty Greene

Betty lay on her back on the grass looking up into the air. High above her, two birds swooped and circled above the trees. She turned on her side and looked at her twin brother. Bill, who had closed his eyes against the glare of the sun, had fallen asleep. Seven-year-old Betty took a long piece of grass and tickled his ear with it. Bill jerked in his sleep, then settled down again. His sister waited for a minute then tickled him once again. The boy sat up abruptly. Thinking that an insect had crawled into his ear, he asked his sister to check. It was only when she burst out laughing that he realised the tickling had not been an insect at all, but his twin sister up to her usual tricks.

'Serves you right for falling asleep when there are things to see and do,' she told him.

'It's too warm to do anything,' Bill retorted, 'and there's nothing to see.'

'Yes, there is,' Betty argued, pointing high in the sky. 'There are two birds up there, and I've been watching them for ages. They must see something on the ground because they keep circling over the same place.'

Bill shaded his eyes with his hand then lay back to watch the birds with his sister.

'I wonder what it's like being a bird,' he said. 'You'd think they would have to flap their wings really hard to keep up in the air, but their wings hardly seem to be moving.'

'I was reading a book about condors,' commented Betty. 'They are huge, but when they fly, the air thermals help to support them so they can go for long distances without flapping their wings at all.'

Bill grinned. 'That sounds like fun. Imagine flying high in the air above here. We could spy on Joe and Albert and then keep them guessing how we knew what they'd been doing.'

Betty wasn't sure that their older brothers would be all that interesting to watch from the air!

That evening Betty stretched out on her bed to read more about condors. She discovered that they lived in South America, and that they were most common in the mountains of the High Andes. The book had some good pictures in it, and her imagination took over when she closed it and tried to get to sleep. That night she dreamed about South America. In her dream she was high in the air looking down on the River Amazon as it snaked through the jungle far below. From her great height she could see tiny clearings in the rainforest where villages nestled, each a long way from its neighbour. She dreamed that she swooped down above the villages and saw the people who lived in them. Betty was just about to perch on a tree to take a closer look, when her mother called to tell her it was morning. Taking a quick glance at her condor book before climbing out of bed, she discovered that her dream was exactly like a picture in the book!

'Do you know anything about the people who live in the Andes?' she asked her father at breakfast. She was glad it was Saturday and that she didn't have to rush off to school.

Mr Greene thought for a moment. 'I'll tell you what I know,' he said. 'From about the 1200s to the 1530s, a very advanced civilization called the Incas lived in parts of South America. They built wonderful cities, some of which can still be seen today. Because of the direction their buildings face, it's thought that they were sun worshippers. But, in the 1530s, the Spaniards invaded their lands. That was called the Spanish Conquest. Sadly the invaders brought diseases like measles with them, and many of the Incas who were not killed in the fighting died of diseases the Europeans carried.'

'Do people there still worship the sun?' Bill asked, fascinated by the story he had just heard.

'There may be some who still do,' Mr Greene said, 'for there are many parts of South America where nobody has yet gone to tell the people about the Lord Jesus.'

'But why don't missionaries go there?' puzzled the boy.

Mr Greene sipped his coffee before answering. 'I'll have to give you a short geography lesson if you are to understand the answer to your questions,' he said. 'Much of South America is covered in rainforest, and many thousands of little villages are dotted around the deepest parts of the forest. There are no roads to most of them. Those that are on rivers sometimes have visits from missionaries who reach them by canoe, but getting to the villages in the dense jungle is much harder. No one has yet worked out how to reach them.'

'But how do you know the villages exist if nobody has ever gone to them?' asked Bill.

His father smiled.

'It's amazing what we've discovered about remote parts of the country since aeroplanes were invented,' he said.

Betty listened carefully to what her father was saying. 'I know another way of reaching these villages,' she thought, as she helped her mother clear the breakfast things. 'You could travel by condor!'

Just a few months later, the Greene family piled into their car and headed to the University of Washington to see a man who had made history.

'Do you think he'll get here?' Bill asked.

Mr Greene smiled. 'I sure do,' he said. 'After all, Charles Lindbergh flew nonstop across the Atlantic Ocean from Roosevelt Field, Long Island, New York to Paris, France in just 33.5 hours. Just imagine that! And he's only twenty-five years old!'

'I guess if he flew that far, he'll get to Seattle alright,' Betty laughed.

'Charles Lindbergh must be very famous,' commented Bill.

'He certainly is,' Mr Greene agreed. 'And the year 1927 will be remembered for him taking that huge step forward in the progress of flight.

'Where did he start from?' Betty wanted to know.

Her twin was able to answer that. 'He's flown from Paris. And if he arrives on time, the flight will have taken 33 or 34 hours. Imagine crossing the Atlantic in that time!'

Betty smiled. 'I can't wait to see his aeroplane. The Spirit of St Louis is such a lovely name.'

Soon they joined the thousands of others who had gathered to watch Lindbergh arrive.

'There he is!' yelled Bill. 'Look!'

Everyone followed his finger, and one by one people saw the tiny dot in the distance. All eyes were fixed on the silver monoplane as it circled in the air before landing at Sand Point. Cheers rose from the crowd. But they were nothing to the cheer that greeted Lindbergh when he was driven back to the stadium for the recognition ceremony.

That night Betty didn't dream of condors. Instead, she saw herself climbing into the cockpit of a silver monoplane and flying off into the far blue yonder. Over the years that followed, Betty dreamed about flying even when she was wide awake, which may be why their parents gave Bill and Betty a flight in an aeroplane for their sixteenth birthday present.

At the beginning of the Second World War, Betty Greene joined the Women

Airforce Service Pilots. Flying training could be dangerous in those days, as one of her friends found out. Betty wrote home about it. 'Today I saw a PT-19 taxi up to the line with the instructor in the rear cockpit and no one in the front - only earphones hanging over the side blowing in the wind. One of my classmates, as she levelled from a spin, had floated out of the cockpit when her safety belt failed! Thankfully she managed to pull the ripcord on her parachute and land safely.' Betty did so well in her basic training that she became a test pilot and engaged in high-altitude flying.

'God saved my life,' she told her friend Ann, when she landed one afternoon.

Ann looked concerned.

'We flew up into the stratosphere to conduct tests on oxygen masks and electric flying suits,' explained Betty. 'All the windows and doors were open, and a bitterly cold wind whisked through the plane. All sorts of tests were going on with various bits of equipment. Suddenly I noticed that the needle on my oxygen bottle registered zero! I wasn't getting any oxygen at all.'

'That could have been fatal,' Ann said in a shocked voice.

Betty nodded. 'I signalled to the lieutenant in charge, and he came immediately. I held my breath, and he helped me crush the ice that had formed in the intake tube and shake it out. I was desperate for breath by the time I was connected up again.'

That night, as Betty lay in her bed, she thought over what had happened. Her heart just overflowed with love for God who had saved her life as well as saving her soul. 'What,' wondered Betty, 'does my Heavenly Father want me to do with my life? Whatever it is, I'll do it with all my heart.' And as she lay in the darkness, she remembered what the Lord Jesus had done for her.

When the Women Airforce Service Pilots were disbanded in December 1944, Betty knew what God wanted her to do. She became the first woman pilot to join Christian Airmen's Missionary Fellowship. (CAMF later changed its name to Mission Aviation Fellowship, as that was the name used by the sister organisation in the United Kingdom.) As Betty was increasing her flying hours high in the air, missionary translators worked on the ground in many parts of Central and South America, creating written languages from those that, till then, had only been spoken. CAMF was asked to help transport these people, and as Betty was the only free pilot, she was delegated to make the organisation's first flight into Mexico.

'February 23, 1946,' she wrote in her diary. 'Today I started out for Mexico in a beautiful red four-seater Waco biplane. Both my passengers were as excited as I was. Maximum speed - just over 100 miles per hour. Arrived safety at Phoenix.'

Every day she added details of the flight to her diary. After many stops for refuelling, the biplane reached Mexico City. Betty Greene had made history! But she was not allowed a holiday just because of that; the following day she was in the air again, taking a missionary to the south of Mexico.

'It's solid jungle down there,' Mr Townsend said.

Betty looked down at the beauty of it. Suddenly the biplane's engine died. Time seemed to freeze, and the silence was deafening. Betty scanned the ground for a possible landing site, but there was none. Then she switched fuel tanks and pressed the starter. The engine fired up immediately. She looked over at her passenger only to find him as calm as he had been before, and still enjoying the view!

A few months later, Betty was asked to fly in Peru, and on December 19th she tackled her toughest assignment so far - a flight over the Andes mountains.

'It was an amazing experience,' she told her friends later. 'From Lima we climbed through a 10,000 feet cloud blanket before reaching clear skies. But that was just the beginning of our climb. At 12,000 feet I put on my oxygen mask, and we were still climbing. It was so clear at 16,000 feet I felt I could have touched the trees below us. Suddenly we hit a cloudbank, and visibility was non-existent. I brought the plane down below cloud level and flew along the broad back of the mountain. Then, as I looked down on the forest with its tiny village clearings, I suddenly remembered my childhood dream. I saw what condors see on their flights over the high Andes! I could see tiny villages to which missionaries could be taken with the help of a plane, villages that were virtually inaccessible otherwise.'

Although she didn't know it at the time, Betty Greene had made history once again. She was the first woman pilot to cross the Andes and to fly over the rainforest.

Betty Greene's service with Mission Aviation Fellowship was not limited to Central and South America. In February 1951, she moved to Nigeria where she flew as an MAF pilot on loan to a missionary society. Her next assignment took her to the Sudan. Then, in 1958, she travelled south to work in Irian Jaya (Now called West Papua, that's the west side of the huge island of New

Guinea, which is north and east of Australia. Papua New Guinea is the east side of the island). As well as transporting missionaries and local Christian workers, she was involved in airlifting seriously ill patients to hospital, taking food to remote villages where there was famine or drought, and ferrying medical teams, equipment and supplies to hospitals and clinics in rural areas.

Betty's influence continued long after her flying career ended. George Boggs, a former MAF pilot, said, 'Betty Greene had a dream of reaching the remotest places on earth for the Lord through the use of airplanes ... It was she who gave me that first missionary pilot inspiration.' And George was not the only MAF pilot to have taken to the air after being inspired by the story of Betty Greene. Another former MAF pilot, Chuck Bennett, commented, 'Betty Greene was the first to fly across the Andes, and the first missionary pilot to fly in Mexico, Peru and Nigeria. Without a doubt she was the most amazing woman I've ever known.'

Today Mission Aviation Fellowship has over 150 aircraft flying in thirty of the poorest countries. Every three minutes an MAF plane takes off or lands somewhere in the world, and each in its own way brings help and hope to the people it serves.

FACT FILE

The Andes: Betty Greene was the first woman to fly across the Andes, the longest mountain range in the world. It stretches all the way from near the Caribbean Sea to Cape Horn at the very south of South America. For much of their length they are over 12,000 feet high - nearly three times as high as Ben Nevis, the highest mountain in Britain. The height of the Andes means that some of the weather conditions there are very extreme. Towns such as Arica in Chile may only have rain once every hundred years!

Keynote: Betty had seen Charles Lindbergh make history when he crossed the Atlantic in The Spirit of St Louis but she made history herself a few times in the course of her work with MAF. She didn't set out to break records or make history; it just happened as she tried to serve God. We don't need to try to make ourselves important. What really matters is serving

God, but we might find that we end up doing some important things as we try to serve him.

Think: Betty nearly died when her oxygen pipe became blocked with ice during the test flight. She realised that she had only survived because God had saved her life, and that she should live her whole life for him. Betty was keen to do whatever God wanted her to do with all her heart. It is important to be enthusiastic about doing what God asks us to do. It would be very ungrateful to grudge obeying someone who has done so much for us. Think about things that you can thank God for.

Prayer: Lord Jesus, thank you for all that you have done for me. Please help me to do all that I can to serve you. Show me all of the ways that you have blessed me so that I can be thankful for them. Please help those who are working with MAF planes today. Amen.

Elisabeth Elliot

As the sun poured through the window, Elisabeth could see tiny specs of dust floating in the air. She blew gently, and those close to her danced before settling down to float once again. Raising her hand to catch one, she noticed that the movement sent them spinning upwards as though they were trying to get away from her.

'Look Mum,' she said, as the room door opened, 'aren't they beautiful?'

Mrs Howard smiled. 'They are indeed,' she agreed. 'But if I came over to see them from where you are, I'd knock them in all directions, and you would lose their beauty.'

'Why do lovely things have to change and go away?' the six-year-old asked. 'Why can't they always be there for us?'

Sitting down on a seat near the window, Mrs Howard smiled kindly at her daughter. 'I think you know the reason for that,' she suggested.

Puzzled, Elisabeth turned in her direction. Then she puzzled even more.

'I suppose everything was always beautiful when Adam and Eve were in the Garden of Eden,' she said.

Her mother nodded. 'And in a way that we don't understand, every single thing was changed when they disobeyed God. Everything became less beautiful.'

'But there are still nice things in the world,' the child insisted.

Mrs Howard agreed. 'There certainly are, and each one of them is a gift from God for us to treasure.'

When Elisabeth went to bed that night, her heart was heavy. The next day she was going to a new school, and that felt very scary. As she lay in bed, she remembered back to an awful day not long after she went to Miss Dietz's kindergarten, which was just round the corner from her home.

'I loved playing with the little china cat in the toy box there,' she remembered. 'I played all kinds of pretend games with it. Often I used the building bricks to make a home for it. Then one day another girl got the white china cat first. I tried to snatch it from her, but she ran away with the cat.'

Even in the dark Elisabeth blushed at the memory of what happened next.

'I chased after her, shouting that the china cat was mine. Miss Dietz soon put a stop to both our nonsense and told me very firmly that the cat was not mine at all. It was for all of the children in the kindergarten to play with.'

There was a lump in her throat that made Elisabeth feel she might cry.

'It was horrible,' she remembered. 'Although I'd had rows from Dad and Mum for being naughty, it was much worse to get a row from someone else ... and in front of all my friends.'

Before the girl went to sleep that night, she made up her mind that she would try to be very, very good at her new school. Everything might be less beautiful than it was in the Garden of Eden, but she was determined to make her tiny part of the world beautiful.

The following morning Elisabeth wakened with a funny feeling in her tummy and a hundred thoughts in her mind.

'I won't know where to go in Henry School. I'll get lost there. I'll not understand the arithmetic. I don't know anybody. Nobody will want to be my friend.'

Mrs Howard prayed with her anxious little daughter before she went off to school that day. And God answered her prayers in the gift of Miss Scott.

'My teacher's lovely!' Elisabeth told her parents, when she arrived home. 'She has a soft voice and snow-white hair. And she can make rainbows!'

'How does she do that?' asked her father.

Elisabeth smiled at the memory.

'When the sun shone through the high sashed windows, Miss Scott turned a crystal prism that hung on one of the shade pulls, and suddenly the room was filled with lots of rainbows. She even let us try to catch them!'

Her parents looked at each other and smiled.

'And do you know what?' Elisabeth added excitedly. 'Miss Scott says that sometimes, when we've been very, very good, she might make more rainbows for us to catch!'

Henry School was a dismal building, and the road between home and school was no better. But Elisabeth knew that even there God had given her something beautiful. And although she, like all the others in her class, sometimes found schoolwork difficult, Miss Scott was there to help. She didn't have to cope all on her own. As she grew older and trusted in the Lord Jesus for herself, she discovered again and again that although life was sometimes difficult, he was always there to help her.

'Have you always lived in Philadelphia?' a friend asked one day, when they were thirteen years old.

'No,' Elisabeth said. 'I was born in Brussels.'

'Where's that?' the other girl queried, not being too good at geography.

'Brussels is in Belgium,' Elisabeth explained.

'Isn't that dangerously near Germany?' enquired her friend. 'My dad says that Hitler will soon invade all the countries round about Germany because he wants to conquer the whole of Europe.'

Thinking back to her parents' concern for their Belgian friends, Elisabeth agreed that Philadelphia was a safer place than Brussels in 1939.

'Why were your parents in Belgium when you were born?' the other girl asked.

'They were missionaries there,' Elisabeth explained.

'That must be hard work,' her friend commented. 'Imagine having to speak in a different language all the time.'

Elisabeth was fascinated by different languages, and the ones that especially interested her were those that were still unwritten.

'How do people make a written language from one that's only spoken?' she asked her father.

Mr Howard tried his best to answer his daughter's question.

'They have to live with the people and listen hard to everything that's said. Spending time with mothers and children is often a great help to them. Tiny bit by tiny bit they pick up words and phrases, trying out each one over and over to make sure they really do understand its meaning. People are often pleased that a stranger from another country is interested in their language, and then they do their best to help.'

'How do they decide how the words should be written?' queried the girl.

'I don't think there's a problem with sounds that are also in our language, but they have to use symbols other than the English alphabet for sounds we don't have.'

'Give me an example,' said Elisabeth, who was really interested in what she was hearing.

Mr Howard scratched his head as he thought of an example. Then he smiled.

'Some languages have clicks in them,' he told his daughter, 'so they have to use other symbols to represent those.'

The writing down of unwritten languages became Elisabeth's chief interest, and when grown-ups asked her what she wanted to do with her life, she always told them she wanted to do that more than anything else. When she went to Wheaton to study, she majored in Greek because she knew that would help her. Another student was studying Greek for the same reason. His name was Jim Elliot. When she was twenty-two, in 1948, Elisabeth spent the summer at an Institute of Linguistics before moving to Canada to attend missionary training college. In 1952, Jim Elliot and Elisabeth Howard left separately for Ecuador as mission workers. Elisabeth went to the western jungle to work among the Colorado Indians, and Jim went to the eastern jungle and the Quichua people. Although the young couple were deeply attracted to each other, they wanted to know for sure that God's will was for them to marry. Doing what God wanted them to do was more important to them than their love for each other.

'Some of the trees are wonders for size and majesty,' Jim wrote in one of his many letters to Elisabeth. 'One that we can see on the other side of the airstrip from the house has roots which run away from the trunk like walls, bracing the height like structural triangles. I have seen one of these uchu putus with holes five feet across in the roots, where the Indians have hacked out a piece of wood for their huge trays, which they use for mashing chonta fruit, or as a butcher's block.'

The airstrip Jim mentioned was his lifeline, because the area in which he and a small group of other missionaries worked was very remote indeed.

'I was sitting as usual at a little table in a thatched-roofed house in the western jungle, working over my Colorado language notes,' Elisabeth wrote later, 'when suddenly the sound of horse's hoofs broke through the clicking, singing, rattling and buzzing of the night noises. I took the lantern outside and was greeted by a friend from a village about eight miles away. He handed me a telegram. Jim was waiting for me in Quito!'

Jim's next letter home explained the reason for his visit.

'I gave Betty an engagement ring last night,' he told his parents.

They were married in 1953, and God gave them a daughter, Valerie, two years later.

'Do you think it would be possible to reach the Auca Indians?' Jim asked his young wife. 'They have a terrible reputation for violence, but they need to hear about the Lord Jesus just as much as anyone else. We can't just shy away from them because of their reputation ... or,' he added, 'because of our fears.'

Elisabeth prayed about the Auca people and waited to see what would happen. Jim's desire to reach them grew as time passed, until he was absolutely sure that was what God wanted done.

'Nate Saint, from Mission Aviation Fellowship, is prepared to help us,' Jim told his wife. 'But we need to make our plans most carefully.'

Knowing the dangers involved, but remembering what she had learned as a child - that Jesus is right with his people when things are difficult - Elisabeth backed up all the plans with her prayers. Four other missionaries' wives did the same.

Nate flew the MAF light aircraft low over the Auca settlement many, many times to accustom the people to their visitors. Then gifts were lowered in a bucket to show that they were friendly. The message seemed to get through, because eventually some little gifts were put in the bucket for the missionaries. How thrilled they were when that happened! The day that Jim, Nate and their fellow missionaries had looked forward to for so long came eventually in January 1956. They had agreed on a riverside landing site and they went off to meet the Auca Indians face to face.

What happened when the missionaries and the Auca people came in contact is hard to write about. Elisabeth described it later.

'About 11 o'clock on Friday, 6th January, Nate and Pete sat in the small cooking shelter they had built on the sand. Ed was at the upper end of the beach, Rog in the centre, Jim at the lower end. They were calling out Auca words in case anyone was within hearing range. At 11.15 their hearts jumped when a man's voice boomed out from across the river. Immediately three Aucas stepped into the open. They were a young man, and two women. Amazed, the missionaries managed to shout, in Auca, "Puinani!", which means "welcome". Before long the three had joined the missionaries and many "punanis" and smiles were exchanged. Things looked hopeful.'

With a final radio message back to their wives, the five men set out on the greatest adventure of their lives. They did meet some of the Auca people. But while Jim and his friends took with them the good news that Jesus saves, the Indians brought wooden spears with which they killed God's messengers. Jim Elliot, Nate Saint, Ed McCully, Rog Youderian and Pete Fleming one minute saw the faces of their killers, and the next their lovely Lord Jesus. They were martyred for him here on earth, but they were immediately taken home to heaven.

'To the world at large this was a sad waste of five young lives,' Elisabeth wrote later. 'But God has his plan and purpose in all things.'

After spending a short time at home in America, Elisabeth went back to Equador to continue working on the Quetchua language. With little Valerie she made her home there. Later, with Rachel Saint (Nate's sister), they moved back to live and work with the Auca people for a time. Elisabeth rediscovered what she had learned as a child, that there is beauty even in deepest darkness. They grew to love the people and had the thrill of seeing many trust in the Lord Jesus, even some of those who had been involved in their husbands' murders.

In 2000, the Auca (now called the Waorani) people watched MAF light aircraft carry loads of building materials into their region of Ecuador. On the ground, men and boys were already beginning to build what was to become a Bible college. There God's good news would be taught to the Waorani people, so that they can tell others that whatever horrible things their past lives hold, Jesus is able to forgive them and save them from their sins. Out of the awful experience through which Elisabeth Elliot and the other four young widows came, something very wonderful was born. From the horrible darkness of terrible sin, God can make beautiful things happen.

FACT FILE

Bible translators: One of the main reasons that Elisabeth and her friends worked on writing down the languages of the peoples of South America was to enable them to have the Bible in their own languages. Many Christians have spent a lot of time translating the Bible into various languages. There are still some languages that do not have a Bible translation, but organizations like Wycliffe Bible Translators are working hard to make sure that there will be a translation for every language by 2025.

Keynote: When Elisabeth was little she wondered why beautiful things are so fragile. She later saw that, even in the darkest places that sin can create, God is able to make something beautiful. She found that, because Jesus was always there to help her, she was never alone. His love and grace can make anyone beautiful. The place where Jim was murdered must have seemed very dark and dangerous to her, but she still had the love and faith to go there and to teach the people about Jesus.

Think: Elisabeth loved Jim very much. It must have been hard as well as scary for her to go back to the place where he and his friends had been killed. In doing so she was a real example of someone who forgave others for the bad things they had done to her. Jesus tells us to do that. Forgiving people isn't always easy, but that doesn't mean that we shouldn't do it. Try to think of someone whom you can forgive today.

Pray: Lord Jesus, thank you for dying so that people can be forgiven for their sins. Help me to remember how great your love and forgiveness is. Please teach me to forgive those who do bad things to me, just as you would want me to. Amen.

Quiz

How much can you remember about these ten girls who made history? Try answering these questions to find out.

Mary Jane Kinnaird

1. What was the special name for the overcrowded building that Mary Jane's uncle visited?
2. Which war did Mary Jane help to train nurses for?
3. What was the name of the organisation that she was involved in setting up to provide a home for young women coming to London for training and employment?

Emma Dryer

4. Why did Emma want to go walking late at night?
5. What happened to Emma just before she decided to go to Chicago to work for God?
6. What is the name of the Bible college that grew out of Emma's efforts with D.L. Moody to train young people for mission?

Florence Nightingale

7. Which queen did Florence and her sister go to see?
8. What jobs did Florence give to the nurses who went with her to the Crimea when they arrived?
9. What did Florence do after the war to improve army medical services?

Lottie Moon

10. Where was Lottie's uncle going to be a missionary?
11. What kind of subject was Lottie very good at?
12. What happened when the man tried to kill Lottie with a sword?

Ida Scudder

13. Why couldn't Ida's father attend to the Brahmin's wife?
14. What did the Indians call Ida?
15. How many of Ida's first class of students passed the medical exam?

Jeannette Li

16. How old was Mooi Nga when she got married?
17. What was the name of the travelling salesman who became a Christian?
18 Which country occupied China during the Second World War?

Henrietta Mears

19. What illness did Henrietta have when she was a child?
20. What did the girls in Margaret's Sunday school class call themselves?
21. How much did they pay for the campsite that was supposed to be worth $350,000?

Bessie Adams

22. What did Bessie and Kenneth travel in when they were touring the villages?
23. Which Scottish town did they visit at the end of their honeymoon?
24. What does CLC stand for?

Betty Greene

25. What kind of birds did Betty dream about when she was young?
26. What did Bill and Betty get for their 16th birthday present?
27. Which organization did Bessie join after the Second World War?

Elisabeth Elliot

28. What kind of sounds do some languages in South America and Africa have that English doesn't?
29. What language did Elisabeth study to help her with writing down unwritten languages?
30. What were the Indians called who murdered Jim and his friends?

Answers

1. A rookery.
2. The Crimean War.
3. The Young Women's Christian Association.
4. So that she could look at the stars.
5. She was very ill with typhoid fever.
6. The Moody Bible Institute.
7. Queen Victoria
8. Buying vegetables, setting up stoves and cooking food, making bandages and washing the whole hospital.
9. She pushed for the creation of the Army Medical School, which opened in 1860.
10. Jerusalem
11. Languages
12. God stopped him and made him drop his sword.
13. The Brahmin's religion said that

female patients could only be attended by female doctors.

14. Doctor Amma.
15. All of them.
16. 15
17. Mr Wang.
18. Japan.
19. Muscular Rheumatism.
20. The Snobs.
21. $30,000
22. A gypsy caravan.
23. Campbeltown
24. Christian Literature Crusade.
25. Condors
26. A flight in an aeroplane.
27. Christian Airmen's Missionary Fellowship.
28. Clicks
29. Greek
30. Auca indians.

This is what one man said about

Henrietta Mears

"I doubt if any other woman outside my wife and mother has had such a marked influence on my life. She is certainly one of the greatest Christians I have ever known!" *Billy Graham*

Author Information: Irene Howat

Irene Howat is an award-winning author who lives in Scotland. She has published many biographical books for all ages and is particularly well-known for her biographical material. She has written many books about the lives of different Christians from around the world. She has also written a biographical work about her own life entitled: *Pain My Companion.* Irene has many other interests including painting, dog walking and editing her Church's young people's magazine called *The Instructor.*

Start collecting this series now!

Ten Boys who used their Talents:
ISBN 978-1-84550-146-4
Paul Brand, Ghillean Prance, C.S.Lewis,
C.T. Studd, Wilfred Grenfell, J.S. Bach,
James Clerk Maxwell, Samuel Morse,
George Washington Carver, John Bunyan.

Ten Girls who used their Talents:
ISBN 978-1-84550-147-1
Helen Roseveare, Maureen McKenna,
Anne Lawson, Harriet Beecher Stowe,
Sarah Edwards, Selina Countess of Huntingdon, Mildred Cable,
Katie Ann MacKinnon,
Patricia St. John, Mary Verghese.

Ten Boys who Changed the World:
ISBN 978-1-85792-579-1
David Livingstone, Billy Graham, Brother Andrew,
John Newton, William Carey, George Müller,
Nicky Cruz, Eric Liddell, Luis Palau,
Adoniram Judson.

Ten Girls who Changed the World:
ISBN 978-1-85792-649-1
Corrie Ten Boom, Mary Slessor,
Joni Eareckson Tada, Isobel Kuhn,
Amy Carmichael, Elizabeth Fry, Evelyn Brand, Gladys Aylward,
Catherine Booth, Jackie Pullinger.

Ten Boys who Made a Difference:
ISBN 978-1-85792-775-7
Augustine of Hippo, Jan Hus, Martin Luther,
Ulrich Zwingli, William Tyndale, Hugh Latimer,
John Calvin, John Knox, Lord Shaftesbury,
Thomas Chalmers.

Ten Girls who Made a Difference:
ISBN 978-1-85792-776-4
Monica of Thagaste, Catherine Luther,
Susanna Wesley, Ann Judson, Maria Taylor,
Susannah Spurgeon, Bethan Lloyd-Jones,
Edith Schaeffer, Sabina Wurmbrand,
Ruth Bell Graham.

Ten Boys who Made History:
ISBN 978-1-85792-836-5
Charles Spurgeon, Jonathan Edwards,
Samuel Rutherford, D L Moody,
Martin Lloyd Jones, A W Tozer, John Owen, Robert Murray
McCheyne, Billy Sunday,
George Whitfield.

Ten Girls who Made History:
ISBN 978-1-85792-837-2
Ida Scudder, Betty Green, Jeanette Li,
Mary Jane Kinnaird, Bessie Adams,
Emma Dryer, Lottie Moon, Florence Nightingale, Henrietta
Mears, Elisabeth Elliot.

Ten Boys who Didn't Give In:
ISBN 978-1-84550-035-1
Polycarp, Alban, Sir John Oldcastle
Thomas Cramer, George Wishart,
James Chalmers, Dietrich Bonhoeffer
Nate Saint, Ivan Moiseyev, Graham Staines

Ten Girls who Didn't Give In:
ISBN 978-1-84550-036-8
Blandina, Perpetua, Lady Jane Grey,
Anne Askew, Lysken Dirks, Marion Harvey,
Margaret Wilson, Judith Weinberg,
Betty Stam, Esther John

CHRISTIAN FOCUS PUBLICATIONS

Christian Focus · Christian Heritage · CF4K · Mentor

Christian Focus Publications publishes books for adults and children under its four main imprints: Christian Focus, CF4K, Mentor and Christian Heritage. Our books reflect our conviction that God's Word is reliable and Jesus is the way to know him, and live for ever with him.

Our children's publication list covers pre-school to early teens. We also publish personal and family devotional titles, biographies and inspirational stories that children will love.

From pre-school board books to teenage apologetics, we have it covered!

Christian Focus Publications Ltd,
Geanies House, Fearn, Ross-shire,
IV20 1TW, Scotland,
United Kingdom.
www.christianfocus.com

CF4•K
Because you're never too young to know Jesus